PELICAN B[...]

A 284

THE LEGACY OF THE [...]

VOLUME [...]

W. G. DE BURGH

THE LEGACY OF THE ANCIENT WORLD

BY

W. G. DE BURGH, M.A.

LATE PROFESSOR EMERITUS OF PHILOSOPHY IN
THE UNIVERSITY OF READING
FELLOW OF THE BRITISH ACADEMY

*

VOLUME ONE

*

PENGUIN BOOKS
MELBOURNE · LONDON · BALTIMORE

Penguin Books Ltd, Harmondsworth, Middlesex

U.S.A. : Penguin Books Inc., 3300 Clipper Mill Road, Baltimore 11, Md
(*Educational Representative:*
D. C. Heath & Co., 285 Columbus Avenue, Boston 16, Mass)

AUSTRALIA : Penguin Books Pty Ltd, 200 Normanby Road,
Melbourne, S.C.5, Victoria

AGENT IN CANADA : Riverside Books Ltd, 47 Green Street,
Saint Lambert, Montreal, P.Q.

—

Made and printed in Great Britain by
The Whitefriars Press Ltd, Tonbridge

—

First published 1923
New and revised edition 1947
First published in Pelican Books 1953

To

ARTHUR R. NICHOLS, M.C., B.A.

(First Class Honours in Philosophy, 1913);
Captain, King's Liverpool Regiment;
who fell near Le Cateau, October 23, 1918;

and

ALEXANDER SEGGIE, B.A.

(First Class Honours in Philosophy, 1913);
2nd Lieut., Royal Irish Fusiliers;
who fell on the Somme, July 1, 1916

*

ἐμνήσθην δ' ὁσσάκις . . . ἥλιον ἐν λέσχῃ κατεδύσαμεν

CALLIMACHUS

CONTENTS OF VOLUME ONE

*

CHAPTER THREE

CHAPTER FOUR

CHAPTER FIVE

CHAPTER SIX

PREFACE

*

THIS book is designed as an introduction to the study of ancient civilization for those unacquainted with its history. There is a growing desire, among men and women of all classes and callings in life, for whom Israel, Greece, and Rome are little more than names, to learn something of the nature of their achievements. This demand cannot be satisfied by elementary manuals. Those who have minds, and wish to use them, need no bare summary of facts, but a guide to the best thought of antiquity on man and his relations to the world and to God. It is an error to suppose that the public is indifferent to, or unable to understand, the problems of religion and philosophy. There are many, not only in universities and schools, but in the larger world outside, and especially among the workers in industrial towns, who are keenly alive to such questions and determined to think them out for themselves. They are turning towards the legacy of the past, in the belief that here they will gain enlightenment for the solution of their own difficulties. It is primarily for such as these that this book has been written.

There are many, again, who have received a classical education, yet have never formed a coherent view of ancient civilization as a whole. They have studied portions of the Old Testament, selected books of certain Greek and Latin authors, and the outlines of Greek history to Alexander and of Roman history to Augustus. But they possess the vaguest notions of the connexions and relationships that gave structure to the life of antiquity, or of the manner in which its several civilizations combined to influence the medieval and the modern world. How few there are, even among those who have graduated in Arts in our universities, who could tell within a century the dates of Constantine, Augustine, Justinian, Mohammed, and Charles the Great; or could give an intelligent account of their historical significance! How few have even a shadowy conception of the results of Alexander's empire on the early life of Christianity, or of the place of Constantinople in world-history! How few, again, have ever learnt that Amos and Hosea played as memorable a part in the religious development of humanity, as Copernicus and Galileo in that of modern science! The study of antiquity is still overmuch confined within water-tight compartments. Courses in universal history should surely form part of the ordinary curriculum in our colleges and schools.[1]

The fact that the present is an age of historical specialism is a further reason why a book of this kind should prove of service. Historical knowledge is advanced, mainly, by work in two directions: by minute research in highly specialized fields, embodied in learned periodicals; and by publications, based directly on these researches, which cover a wider ground and treat of the several periods and aspects of history. These tasks fall to trained experts, whose writings are addressed to professed students rather than to the general reader. But there is a real danger, at the present time, not only in history but in all branches of knowledge, of a divorce between the learning of the specialist and the mind of the non-academic public. History itself can teach us that, if the breach remains unbridged, the issue will prove disastrous. Such, for instance, was the outcome of the clerical monopoly of theological learning in the age preceding the Reformation. In this country, at all events, scientific and philosophical thinking has always striven to keep in contact with that of the larger world. As knowledge grows more specialized and the reading public more democratic, this honourable tradition must not be suffered to fall into abeyance.

Bearing these needs in mind, I have tried to convey an impression of the living continuity of ancient civilization. I felt that there was an advantage in presenting the whole sequence of development, however imperfectly, in a single view. The history of antiquity is no mere aggregate of periods and peoples, but a whole of parts, linked together in internal cohesion. When the parts are studied in isolation, the unity is apt to elude the grasp.

> Dann hat er die Teile in seiner Hand,
> Fehlt leider nur das geistige Band.

I have taken the term 'history' with something of the broad meaning that it bore to its first authors, the Greeks, i.e. as the whole record of man's life in relation to the world surrounding him, and as including interpretation as well as narrative description.[2] The attempt to cover so wide a field has necessitated both compression and elimina-

1. Such courses should prove invaluable to university students in Science and in Faculties other than that of Arts.
2. See the striking fragment of Euripides (*fr.* 902, Dindorf); 'Happy is he who has laid hold of the lore of history (*historia*) . . . seeking to behold the ageless order (*kosmos*) of deathless nature (*physis*), the manner of its structure, and whence it arose, and how.' On the meaning of *physis* for the Greeks, see below, pp. 122 ff.

tion. General views had often to be stated without the evidence supporting them. A multitude of details would only confuse the reader's mind. If illustrations have been drawn from leading personalities rather than from the average level of achievement, it is because the aim has been, not to sketch the life of ancient peoples in its whole compass, but to indicate their legacy to the modern world. In no part of the book has any previous knowledge of the facts been presupposed. It is designed to leave the reader unsatisfied, and to inspire him with the desire to study more thoroughly, with the aid of the original sources, the civilizations of Israel, Greece, and Rome.

Two omissions require brief explanation.

(i) In treating of the Hellenic legacy, I have touched but lightly on art and poetry, though these are the aspects of Hellenism which appeal most directly to the reading public. But I confess to a deep mistrust of talk *about* art and poetry addressed to those who are unacquainted with the originals. The masterpieces of Greek literature are accessible to all in English translations. Let the beginner begin with these. As regards Greek art, let him visit the Elgin room and the galleries of our national museum. I have, therefore, given only so much introductory explanation as will indicate the historical and intellectual context amid which the Greek poets and artists produced their work.

(ii) In the ninth chapter, on Christianity, it may seem that undue emphasis has been laid on the institutional history of the Church and on the development of theological dogma. I have expressly stated that these were but the external embodiments of the inward spiritual life which inspired the Christian community. But I have said little or nothing about the nature of that inward principle, or its source in the personality and teaching of Jesus of Nazareth. The task demands qualifications, not only of scholarship but of religious insight, which I cannot claim to possess. While affirming my conviction that the history of Christianity can only be accounted for by the unique personality of its founder, I have confined attention to its basis in Judaism and its contacts with Rome and Hellenism.

The notes are intended, partly, to give references to such sources as are easily available in translations, e.g. to the Old and New Testaments and the best known Greek and Latin authors; partly, to qualify statements which require to be taken with reservations; partly, to suggest, more discursively, analogies to modern developments and problems. The appended bibliography makes no claim to be exhaustive; it is merely a provisional selection of good English works, as a guide to further study.

I wish to express my thanks to all who have helped me in the preparation of this book. I am specially indebted to my colleague, Professor P. N. Ure, who read and commented on the whole work in proof; to Mr Vernon Rendall, who not only rendered me a like service, but placed freely at my disposal his wide knowledge of classical and modern literature; and to my wife, whose help and criticism have been from first to last my chief encouragement.

W. G. DE B.

ASHMORE, *August 1923*

NOTE

THE preparation of this new edition of *The Legacy of the Ancient World* was completed by my husband shortly before his death in August 1943. He left on record that he wished to thank the Editor of the Aristotelian Society's Proceedings and the Editor of the *Hibbert Journal* for permission to print matter that has appeared in their publications; also he wished to say that in revising the earlier chapters he had received much help from Sir John Myres, and, in Chapter III, from Dr Wheeler Robinson. While for what is printed he is solely responsible, he felt that he owed very much to their kind interest and aid. He desired also to acknowledge his appreciation of the suggestions of Sir Richard Livingstone, President of Corpus; of Professor Fordyce of Glasgow, and Professor Knox of St Andrews, and to express his indebtedness to reviewers of the first edition, and to correspondents thereupon, more particularly to the late Professor A. E. Taylor, and the late Rev. P. H. Wicksteed. He felt encouraged in the work of preparation for the reissue of this book by the knowledge that it had been appreciated and recommended by men whose judgement cannot lightly be passed over: especially John Burnet, Samuel Alexander, and Professor Taylor.

It will be noticed that in addition to sundry small changes in the text and the insertion here and there of new matter, there are three appendices at the end of this new edition designed to amplify the argument and conclusions of the book.

E. DE B.

READING, *January 1947*

THE LEGACY OF THE
ANCIENT WORLD

*

CHAPTER ONE

INTRODUCTION

*

§ 1. AMONG the peoples of the ancient world there are three who bequeathed a legacy that is a living power at the present day. These three peoples are the Hebrew, the Greek, and the Roman. The creations of their genius, Hebrew prophecy, the philosophy, poetry, and sculpture of Greece, the law and political organization of Rome, constitute a heritage of lasting inspiration to mankind. They have borne a memorable part in shaping the civilization of after-time. *Civilization*, like many words in common speech, is hard to define, and suggests now a wider, and now a more restricted, meaning. A formal definition, such as is appropriate at the outset of a mathematical or scientific treatise, if it is to be of service in a work like this, must come not at the beginning but at the close; when the reader has become familiarized with varied types of civilization in their chequered course of growth, maturity, and decay, and has learnt that a cultured achievement never perishes, but even in its apparent disintegration bears what is often its richest fruit in fostering the life of its successor. 'That which thou thyself sowest is not quickened, except it die'; these words are true of peoples and cultured epochs as well as of individuals. So the Roman Empire declined but did not fall; like Hellenism and medieval Christianity, it persists with ever-renewed vitality in the civilization of the modern world. In these pages we mean by civilization the character of the life exhibited by the higher races at different periods of their history. It embraces at once a world of ideals and a world of accomplished facts. It covers the entire body of social custom and enacted law, of religious, moral, and political institutions, of industry and commerce, arts and sciences, literature and philosophy, which represents the cumulative achievement of a people. But it covers more than this. Man is an ideal-forming animal, stirred at every stage of his development by aspirations which transcend the level of his actual attainment; and his civilization, at any given epoch, comprises also the world of his religious, moral, and economic values, his intellectual outlook upon life, his personal beliefs as to his function and destiny, his standards of moral goodness and social welfare. It is in the light of such ideals, determining our conception of human progress, that we distinguish civilization from barbarism.[1] Applying this distinction to the history of antiquity, we find that long before our Celtic, Germanic, and Scandinavian forefathers had emerged from barbarism, the three races above mentioned had attained to a high plane of civilization. Thus they were enabled, when the hour of contact arrived, to influence profoundly the less-cultured peoples who have grown into the leading nations of to-day. When, for instance, the rude barbarians accepted Christianity, they accepted therewith the legacy of Jewish religious and moral traditions, of Greek philosophy, and of the Roman legal and political system. The purpose of this book is to trace the story of that inheritance. We shall begin with a brief indication of the special service rendered by each of these three peoples to the civilization of the modern world.

§ 2. *The Hebrews*. – The debt which modern civilization owes to the Hebrews lies almost wholly in the field of religion. Their poetry, the surest guide to the thought and feeling of a people, is essentially religious poetry. Its value lies not so much in literary form or in speculative argument as in the deep spiritual insight to which it gives expression. The Hebrew race was but little distinguished in war or politics; save for a brief period of empire under King David, its secular achievements would pass almost unnoticed in world-history. It was the

1. See Vol. II, Appendix I.

spiritual genius of prophets, such as Amos and Hosea in Israel and Isaiah in Judah in the eighth century B.C., which first transformed an exclusive tribal faith into a religion of universal meaning for the world. Jehovah was revealed no longer as a jealous tribal God leading his people to victory over equally real tribal gods of their enemies, but as the divine ruler of the universe, who punished Israel through their enemies for sin, desired mercy and not sacrifice, and claimed the worship, not of personal gift, but of righteous dealing between man and man. This transformation of Hebrew religion contributed, it is true, to break up the political unity of the Hebrew state. But the seed sown by the early prophets ripened, during the bitter experience of national humiliation and captivity, into a purified religion, which in due season gave birth to the faith that conquered the civilized world. The Hebrews were the first of historic peoples to attain to the belief in one God, the creator and ruler of the universe, and the Father of all mankind. Christ, born of a Jewish mother and bred in the strict observance of the Jewish law, came not to destroy that law but to fulfil. The influence of Greece and Rome on the growth of Christianity, of which we shall speak later in this book, has obscured but has never obliterated the hall-mark of its Hebrew origin. We have only to think of the Puritans of the seventeenth century to realize how deeply modern Christianity has been permeated by the Hebraic spirit.

§ 3. *The Greeks*. – It is more difficult to indicate in a few words the work of the Greeks, or *Hellenes*, as they styled themselves, in history. They influenced modern religion not so much through their religion as through their philosophy. The Olympian deities were fashioned in the likeness of men, with human passions and interests. Though stronger, more beautiful, more jealous, and more amorous, though immortal and enjoying a richer life than mortals, in all essentials they felt and acted as Greek men and women felt and acted. We shall see how philosophers strove to spiritualize the popular faiths and how the effort resulted in a breach between the reasoned conclusions of the few and the religious beliefs of the many. Greek religion has afforded in all times a rich field for art and poetry, and its tales are still a delight to the imagination; but it could not satisfy the intellectual or the moral aspirations of a more reflective age. On the other hand, our debt to the Greeks embraces the whole domain of secular culture. In philosophy and science, in art and literature, the Greek genius achieved results which for their range and value are without comparison in the history of mankind. 'The period which intervened between the birth of Pericles and the death of Aristotle', i.e. the fifth and fourth centuries B.C. in Greek history, 'is undoubtedly, whether considered by itself or with reference to the effects which it produced upon the subsequent destinies of civilized man, the most memorable in the history of the world'. So wrote Shelley; and all thinkers and poets are witnesses to the truth of his words. Freedom and individuality are present everywhere in the life of the ancient Greeks. What strikes us most is their wonderful energy. Their whole history is a record of bold experiment in thought and practice. They were at once eager and courageous in intellectual inquiry and full of delight in life and action. Their intellectual genius was the fountain-head of philosophy and science; their practical genius found expression alike in political activity, in war and commerce, in literary and artistic creation. Almost every type of poetry and speculation was initiated by the Greeks and carried far on the path towards perfection. Their ideal was that of a gifted and harmonious personality, controlled by inward principle and reason; of energy, not wild and ungoverned, but ruled by self-knowledge and clear judgement. No race has been so free from other-worldliness or has striven to embody aims and values so entirely in the actual conditions of human experience. Resisting every craving after the impossible, they set themselves resolutely to understand the nature of man and the world in which he lives, and, with a clear grasp of the truth of things, to use that world as a field for the realization of their ideals of life. The characteristic gifts of the race bore with them their curse. The individuality and freedom that made the Greeks supreme in art and science proved the ruin of their political independence. It is true, as we shall see later on, that Greek culture found its stimulus and its scope in the atmosphere of free discussion which prevailed in the city-state, and that the Greek genius was manifested alike in their political theory and in their political practice. But there is another side to the picture. The political life of the Greek cities presents a dark scene of restless ambition, personal jealousy and party faction, aversion from federal solidarity, continual revolution and civil strife. It was this lack of national unity that left Greece so easy a prey to the armies, first of the Macedonian kings, and afterwards of the Roman republic. But the Greek spirit had its revenge; as under Alexander it leavened the culture of the East, so, later, it permeated the Roman conquerors and through Rome moulded the thought and culture of the modern world.

§ 4. *The Romans.* — Rome was the imperial state of antiquity, and the Roman people were the great empire-builders of world-history. Their religion was strictly subordinate to the political authority. An instance may serve to bring this home. Caesar, a frank sceptic, whose private life was certainly not above suspicion, staked all at a critical moment of his career on his election as supreme pontiff: it was merely a step on the ladder of political ambition. The influence of Rome on Christianity is most evident in the field of ecclesiastical organization. By nature the Roman had little appreciation either of art or science; in early days he regarded a poet as a vagabond and philosophy as a danger to morality. Far otherwise was it with the Greeks in Homer; for them the blind poet had been bereft by the gods of sight, but in its stead had received the gift of godlike song. The impulse to poetry and art came to Rome from Greece; though, when once they had learnt their lesson, the Romans expressed their national spirit with no servile imitation in imperishable verse. Their poets knew and recognized wherein lay the true genius of the race. 'Others may mould in softer lines the breathing bronze — ay, and cause living features to start from the marble; they may plead their lawsuits better, and trace the motions of the heavens and the rising of the stars; be it thine, O son of Rome, to rule the nations: these shall be thy arts, to impose the habit of peace, to spare the vanquished, and to crush the haughty by the sword.' [1] Like all empire-builders whose work has stood the stress of time, the Romans had no wild thirst for conquest. They were a race not so much of warriors as of lawgivers and administrators. 'To lay down the law of peace,' the *pax Romana*, to repress anarchy and disorder around their ever-expanding dominion was their peculiar mission. Children beside the Greeks in culture, with a marked vein of inhumanity and coarseness in their nature, the Romans were strong precisely where the Greeks were weak, in racial solidarity, in political union, in subjection of individuality to the service of the state. To 'do at Rome as Rome does' was the virtue of the Roman citizen. Greek history is the history of cities and individuals: Roman history is the history of a people. Governed by no deliberate policy of conquest, but by the logic of hard fact, the fortune of the Roman people led them to incorporate in their empire the whole civilized world, as it stood at the time of Christ's birth. To gather up in one vast organization the peoples and civilizations of antiquity, to police the Mediterranean and ordain peace over a disordered world, to hand on to the barbarians of the north and west of Europe the culture of the past, tempered by their own genius for law and government; these were the functions and the destiny of Rome. Thus 'all roads lead to Rome'. As the great military highways of the Romans radiated from Rome over the empire, so the currents of ancient and modern history alike find their meeting-point in Rome. The nations of to-day owe a great part of their law, their language, and their institutions to the genius of Imperial Rome.

§ 5. These three peoples had all of them their home by the shores of the Mediterranean; the Mediterranean and its coastlands formed their world. Trained as we are from childhood to think in terms of two hemispheres with their continents and oceans, it is hard to appreciate a time when the world meant merely a narrow ring of countries converging upon an inland sea. Behind these coastlands in all directions lay a mysterious and illimitable waste, in the west the impenetrable Atlantic, to north and south the abodes of wild barbarians, who brought

1. Virgil, *Aeneid*, vi, 847–53.

down their wares for barter to the dwellers on the Mediterranean shore. Only towards the east was the veil lifted, as far as the line where the plateau of Iran (Persia) rose high above the Mesopotamian and Babylonian plains. Within these limits there was civilization. Hence, to the peoples of antiquity, the distinction of three continents, Europe, Africa, and Asia, seemed artificial and irrelevant.[1] Long before the Hebrews, Greeks, and Romans began to play their part in history, the Mediterranean had been the meeting-place of the world's trade. Through all ages commerce and civilization have developed hand in hand; commercial highways, the links of international intercourse, aid the distribution not merely of material products, but of ideas and habits of life. Thus from earliest recorded time the history of civilization has been the history of the Mediterranean area, and such it remained, until the discoveries of great navigators at the close of the fifteenth century bore fruit in the Oceanic civilization amidst which we live to-day.[2] The voyages of Diaz, da Gama, and Columbus did more than disclose new markets and fields for empire in the Indies and the New World. They changed the centre of gravity of human culture. The Oceanic civilization that has arisen upon their foundations is even yet scarcely ripe for history. If what Lancashire thinks to-day, England will think to-morrow; if our island is no longer an outwork on the north-western frontier of civilization, but holds a central position in the economic and intellectual intercourse of the nations; if the life of the world pulses in lands unknown to the ancients, in America, in the British Dominions beyond the seas; this is due to changes initiated only four or five centuries ago, the issues of which, enlarging from hour to hour before our eyes, form material for the journalist rather than for the historian. The

1. Herodotus, iv. 45. 'I am unable to understand why it is that to the earth, which is one, three different names have been given, all derived from women . . .; nor can I find out who they were who fixed the boundaries, or from whom they gave the names.'

2. 'The grand object of travelling,' said Dr Johnson, 'is to see the shores of the Mediterranean. On those shores were the four great empires of the world, the Assyrian, the Persian, the Grecian and the Roman. All our religion, almost all our law, almost all our arts, almost all that sets us above savages, has come to us from the shores of the Mediterranean' (Boswell).

days when Rome's empire over the Mediterranean area brought the whole civilized world under her sway seem indeed remote. Yet such is the solidarity of history through the successive epochs of its development, that even this momentous revolution received its stimulus from the inheritance of Graeco-Roman culture. There is no impassable breach of continuity between the Oceanic civilization of the present and that moulded more than twenty centuries ago by the peoples of the Mediterranean world.

§ 6. The Hebrews, Greeks, and Romans, though sharing in a common Mediterranean habitation, were sundered by a difference of origin, which goes far to account for the distinctive character of their civilizations. The Hebrews were a branch of the Semitic stock, whose home was Arabia, one of the great nurseries of the human race. In the next chapter we shall meet with other nations, Babylonians and Assyrians, and the dwellers in Phoenicia and Syria, who were members of the same Semitic family. The Greeks and the Romans, on the contrary, belonged, at all events in the main, to the Indo-European family, whose home was probably in the steppe-lands north of the Caucasus. Already in remote antiquity this family had parted into two great branches. One of these passed westwards into Europe; from it sprang not only the Greeks and Italians, but also our Celtic, Germanic, and Scandinavian ancestors. The other branch struck south-east; part settled on the table land of Iran, and gave birth to the Medes and Persians of ancient history, while part passed the mountains into the valleys of the Indus and the Ganges, and colonized northern India. All these migrations took place in remote ages; the historic peoples of antiquity were rarely, if ever, free from racial intermixture.

§ 7. The divergence in the life and character of the three peoples was not such as to preclude an ultimate fusion. The truth is rather the reverse; each created and bequeathed to after-ages one of the essentials in the idea of a complete civilization. The Greeks were the first to realize, in their practice as in their theory, the worth of individual liberty, as the soil wherein alone man's imagination and intellect can flourish and bear fruit. In the domains of art and philosophy the human spirit is its own law. But man is called upon also to act, and the effective realization of his practical purposes demands their accommodation to the hard facts of human nature and of the world of circumstance. The adjustment can be accomplished only by aid of external authority and government. This disciplinary function in the history of civilization was fulfilled by Rome. But, alike in the field of thought and in that of action, the spirit of man is doomed to waste in anarchy or bondage, unless inspired by the knowledge of its ideal goal. 'Where there is no vision, the people perish.' [1] The Hebrews had seen the vision; and they transmitted it, through a faith that had its roots in the spiritual life of Israel, to the Aryan peoples of the West. Freedom, law, and the kingdom of God; these form the threefold legacy of antiquity to the modern world.

§ 8. The historian, looking back upon the past from a distance of twenty centuries, is bound to throw into relief the outstanding and distinctive features of these civilizations. But we must not think of them as cast in rigid moulds or exaggerate the clearness of their outlines. The sequel will show how the life of the Hebrew, Greek, and Roman peoples, like that of the individuals composing them, was ever on the move, shaping itself as it grew, and changing from moment to moment in relation to its physical and social context. It is a far cry from the Israel that gathered round Elijah on mount Carmel to the Israel which nine centuries later clamoured before a Roman governor for the release of Barabbas. The Pharisee of Jerusalem at the time of Christ moved in a different world from the Hellenized Jew of Alexandria. The gulf between the Greek merchant-princes of the sixth century and St Paul's auditors at Corinth or Athens was as wide as that which parted the former from the wild sea-rovers, who, forsaking the tombs of their forefathers and their ancestral gods, sought new homes in the Aegean at the close of the second millennium B.C. Hellenic culture meant one thing at Syracuse, another at Miletus; the Rome which tamed the Spaniard in the days of Cato would have scarcely been recognized as Rome

1. Prov. xxix. 18 (R.V. 'cast off restraint').

by the Slav and the Bulgar who knew only the Christian and Byzantine empire of the early Middle Ages. We can best appreciate this constant variability of civilization if we think of the world as it is to-day. All the resources of modern ingenuity for facilitating swift communication and the diffusion of ideas, such as the printing press, steam, electricity, the aeroplane, and radio, have not availed to break down the barriers which sever even contemporaries of a common stock. The Dorset peasant and the Northumbrian miner live in alien worlds. The Oxford scholar's outlook upon life has little in common with that of his fellow-countryman in Manitoba or New Zealand. Wider still is the chasm that parts any one of these twentieth-century Englishmen from his ancestor in the thirteenth. If we think of the difference between the England that we know and the England of the Plantagenets, we can form some measure of the difficulty of gathering into a single view the ever-changing phases of the civilization of antiquity. Further, we shall see as we go forward how the legacy was modified in the course of transmission to the modern world. The fruits of the Hebrew, Greek, and Roman genius have been fused with one another and with elements derived from Teutonic and Scandinavian sources. Their significance has been altered by their entry into new forms of combination. The present, in assimilating the past, clothes it with a meaning, richer it may be or poorer than it once bore, but always new. The clearest illustration of this is furnished by language. A man need not be an expert in philology to recognize the origin of many of our English words. Some, e.g. *law*, *order*, *state*, *colony*, *responsibility*, *person*, are obviously derived from the Latin; others, e.g. *dogma*, *atom*, *history*, *biology*, *logic*, from the Greek; others again, e.g. *friend*, *body*, *king*, *God*, betray a Norse or Germanic ancestry. The forms of these words have been modified in the process of reception; *lex* has become *law*, *atomon*, atom; in some cases the change is more radical, and it requires some experience to detect the Latin *metipsimum* beneath its modern French derivative *même*. What is true of the verbal forms is true also of their meanings. Our examples show how words signifying legal and political ideas have often been inherited from the Romans, who were the world's masters in those fields, while scientific terminology tends to preserve the speech of the creators of science, the ancient Greeks. Yet, despite this unimpeachable lineage, such terms as *responsibility* and *law* are fraught to us with a meaning drawn not merely or mainly from the experience of Roman jurists, but from that of the generations which have inherited and enriched their legacy during some 2000 years. The historian and the physicist of the twentieth century conceive of *history* and of the *atom* very differently from Herodotus and Democritus. What we have said of language applies to every aspect of civilization; the past, in passing into the present, changes its character as past, and dies phoenix-like to be reborn in a new form.

§ 9. This process of continuity amid ceaseless change is hard to unravel. The task may be approached in two different ways. We may take present-day civilization as our starting-point and work backwards, step by step, to its sources in the past. Or we may begin at the beginning, with the races of antiquity, and trace the effects on subsequent generations till we reach the confines of modern history. The latter is the course we propose to follow. Its treatment will, however, be subject to two restrictions. In the first place, we must select, from the wealth of available material, those features in the life of the Hebrews, Greeks, and Romans which impressed themselves most markedly on after-times. There is always the danger that we may fail to see the wood for the trees. Thus we shall concentrate attention on the religion of Israel, on the science and philosophy of Greece, and on the mission of Rome in mediating the transition from ancient to medieval civilization; touching but lightly on other aspects of their history, however great their intrinsic interest. The second restriction has reference to the other races which peopled the ancient world. Among these we may draw a three-fold distinction. There are (i) races, such as the primitive inhabitants of a large part of Africa, who never succeeded in emerging from a state of barbarism. Full of interest for the anthropologist and the student of primeval religious and social

custom, they left no distinctive trace on the higher civilizations of antiquity, and therefore call for no mention in this
book. The same is true of (ii) the civilized peoples of the
Farther East, in India, China, and Japan. These were almost
wholly precluded by geographical barriers from active intercourse with the culture of the Mediterranean area.[1] Now,
when contact has been established through the opening of
Oceanic highways and facilitated by the aeroplane and wire-
less, the art of China and Japan and the religious thought of the
higher Indian peoples evoke an increasing interest among
Europeans. The historian of five centuries hence may have
much to say on the issues of this intercourse alike in East and
West; but as yet they lie hidden from our view. The grant of
autonomy, in conjunction with the growth of commerce and
industrialization, are bound to prove disintegrating influences
on the traditional outlook upon life among the peoples of
India, and this not merely in the domains of economics and
politics. Whether a closer familiarity with their religious and
metaphysical inheritance will affect our Western civilization
to a like extent is more disputable. The cleavage between the
mind of the West and that of the East cuts very deep; the West
takes for granted much that is alien and even antagonistic to
Indian thought, which finds itself faced by almost insuperable
obstacles to a reciprocal understanding. For one thing, Indian
thinkers have never taken time seriously. The temporal process that forms the material of history has seemed to them to
be little more than an illusion (*maya*), veiling the changeless
reality of the Absolute. That is why India, which has given
birth to great philosophers and religious mystics, has produced
no historians.[2] So, again, Indian political leaders seem to find

1. The obvious exception to this very general statement is furnished by
Alexander the Great's conquest of the Punjâb. The contact thus established
between the West and India was of brief duration, and memorable rather for
Greek influence upon India than for Indian influence upon Greece. Trade by
overland caravan routes from the Far East persisted throughout antiquity, but
the effects on Western civilization were secondary and indirect. Nor have the
Tartar invasions of the West in post-Christian times, from the Huns of the
fifth century onwards, contributed anything positive to Western culture.

2. In our own day, she produced in Ramanujan a mathematician of genius;
but mathematics, like metaphysics, is unconcerned with the course of tem-

difficulty in realizing what to the Western mind is a matter of
course, that self-government can only prove of lasting benefit if
achieved as the fruit of a gradual process of political education.
If, as is admitted on all sides, it is good, and therefore desirable, what ground is there in reason for delaying its fulfilment?
Why not complete the good work, here and now, by a stroke
of the pen? The mind of the West, on the contrary, for all its
faith in an eternal other-worldly reality, has rarely, if ever,
denied a measure of genuine actuality to the temporal process.[1] There is a further cleavage to be noted. A conviction of
the indefeasible worth of human personality is deeply rooted in
the Western mind, which has hardly been touched by the
desire for absorption in the Absolute, which has won possession of the hearts of Indian sages. Here lies the radical difference between Christian and Hindu mysticism.[2] These reflec-
tions lead to the suggestion that if the spiritual barriers
parting Western from Indian cultures are ever to be broken
down, it will be through the spread in India of historical
studies and of Christianity. However this may be, the future
of the Indian, as of other Oriental peoples, lies beyond the
scope of this volume. It is otherwise with a third group (iii),
the civilizations that arose in very early times on the banks of
two great rivers, the Nile and the Euphrates, and in Crete.
These arrest our attention, not only by the intrinsic value of
their culture, but as furnishing the historical antecedents to the
story of Israel, Greece, and Rome. They form part of the life
of the Mediterranean world. This is obvious in the case of
Crete; but the civilization of Egypt also gravitated northwards

poral events. Even modern historians of Indian philosophy, like Radhakrishnan
and Dasgupta, while successful in exposition of the several systems, fail to display their historical sequence as arising one from the other in a natural order of
development.

1. Spinoza, for instance, who held time to be a product of low-grade thinking (*auxilium imaginationis*) never questioned the actuality of temporal occur-
rences. He simply denied that, as temporal, they were fully real. Christian
thought has always attached a high significance to the spatio-temporal world as
the scene of man's probation. His vocation is 'so to pass through things temporal as not to lose finally the things eternal'. This implies that the 'things
temporal' are anything but illusory.

2. Christian mystics aspire after direct communion, not after fusion of
being, with God.

to the shores of the Delta, while that of the Babylonian plain expanded ever westwards towards the Aegean and the Levant. It is true that their influence on later ages was indirect, and mediated by the three peoples who form the chief subject of our study. But they left their mark on the life-work of Israel, Greece, and Rome; and they formed the historical context amid which these nations arose and played their part. We shall therefore attempt a brief survey of these earlier civilizations in the ensuing chapter. This will help us to realize the essential solidarity of the ancient world, and to think of its several peoples, not as isolated atoms which can be studied piecemeal, but as members of a community of nations, with mutual relationships of hostility or of co-operation which conditioned their distinctive contributions to the march of human history.

CHAPTER TWO

THE EARLY CIVILIZATIONS OF THE EAST

*

I. INTRODUCTORY

§ 1. THE early civilizations which claim our notice as a preparation for the study of Israel, Greece, and Rome, are those
(i) of Egypt, (ii) of the nations who successively dominated the
Euphrates–Tigris valley – the Babylonians and Assyrians, (iii) of
the peoples who inhabited the lands between the last-mentioned and the Mediterranean sea-board, Syria, Canaan, and
eastern Asia Minor, (iv) of Crete, which permeated the
Aegean and a large portion of the Mediterranean area. We
shall carry our brief survey of these civilizations forward to the
time when they were, for the most part, absorbed in the
mighty world-empire of Persia (sixth century B.C.). Finally
(v) we shall indicate the character of the Persian empire and
its civilization, up to the Graeco-Macedonian conquest by
Alexander the Great (334–323). The subsequent history of
Egypt and the Middle East, under Graeco-Macedonian and
Roman sovereignty, belongs naturally to the later chapters,
dealing with Greece and Rome.

II. EGYPT [1]

§ 2. 'Egypt,' wrote the Greek historian Herodotus, who
visited the land in the fifth century B.C., 'is the gift of the
Nile.' [2] Soil, products, vegetation, animals and human life are

1. In the matter of early Egyptian chronology, as in much else in this section, I have followed Breasted's conclusions, as given in his *History of Egypt* (2nd
edition, 1919). While the majority of Egyptologists are in substantial agreement with Breasted's chronology of the earlier dynasties, it must be borne in
mind that the dates are still a subject of controversy prior to the eighteenth
dynasty (1580 B.C.). The reader should consult the synchronistic tables in the
earlier volumes of the *Cambridge Ancient History* on all questions of chronology
that arise in connexion with this chapter.
2. Her., ii. 5.

alike determined by the great river, which, long before man's advent, widened a limestone fracture into a gorge, filled the gorge with debris from the southern highlands, and encroaching upon the Mediterranean formed the Delta. The country is a long narrow oasis stretching for 750 miles from the First Cataract, the ancient southern boundary, to the Delta; the valley, ten to thirty miles in breadth, is imprisoned by desert-barriers to east and west. Its prosperity depends, now as seventy centuries ago, on one great natural phenomenon, the annual inundation of the Nile, caused by the spring rains and the melting of the snows in the far highlands of the south. The uniformity of these simple physical conditions is paralleled by a like uniformity in the life and habits of the people. The fellaheen under Mehemet Ali in the nineteenth century of our era plied the same monotonous tasks of tilling the soil and forced labour as the nameless serfs who built the pyramids in the third millennium B.C. The economic wealth of Egypt has always been agricultural. The Egyptians called their country 'the Black land', contrasting the 'Red' desert on either side, and the black alluvial soil of the Nile valley, which, under an efficient system of irrigation, proved of extraordinary fertility. The river was the highway down which the corn-trade passed to the Delta ports, and the link of communication between Egypt and the outside world. The irregularity of the Nile's overflow early evoked human effort to ward off the periodic danger of famine. Nowhere has man's cunning fought so persistently with nature. The land was permeated by canals, dykes, and reservoirs, in the construction of which the engineers of ancient Egypt displayed a mastery of mechanical art. The vast reservoir of lake Moeris, the work of Theban Pharaohs of the twelfth dynasty (early second millennium), bears witness to the same energy of purpose as the Assouan dam completed by British engineers under the direction of Lord Cromer.

§ 3. Our knowledge of the early history of Egypt originated during the invasion by Napoleon (1798). In 1799 a French officer discovered near Rosetta a stone, now in the British Museum, bearing an inscription in three scripts, hieroglyphic, demotic or popular, and Greek. The proper names, which

were the same in the Greek as in the hieroglyphics, gave after
long study the key to the hieroglyphic writing on Egyptian
monuments. The last century has witnessed the gradual un-
veiling of the shroud that hid the remote past. Imagination is
dazzled as scholars have revealed cycle upon cycle of past history, stretching back at least into the fourth millennium B.C.;
a history not merely of the wars and conquests of kings, but of
beliefs and customs, art and culture, comprising a series of
rich civilizations hitherto unsuspected by mankind.

§ 4. The story of Egypt from its first union under a single
government in the fourth millennium to the Persian conquest
in 525 B.C. presents a succession of cycles of civilization, each
with its periods of rise and fall, and parted one from the other
by intervals of stagnation and decadence. Recent archaeo-
logical research has carried the record yet farther back, to a
time when tribes of African origin, but modified by Semitic
immigrations, dwelt in local centres under separate chieftains.
These pre-dynastic Egyptians had already mastered the arts of
workmanship in clay and stone, and framed the calendar
year of 365 days, adopted more than 3000 years later by
Julius Caesar, and in current use at the present day.[1] Early in
the fourth millennium we find two kingdoms, one in the
Delta, the other in Upper Egypt, which were consolidated
into a single state by Menes, the first king of the first dynasty
(c. 3400). From this point onwards Egyptian history may be
gathered round the rise and fall of three great cycles of
development: the Old Kingdom, the Middle Kingdom, and
the New Empire.[2]

1. The calendar was introduced in 4241 B.C., the earliest fixed date in history. Breasted, *Ancient Records, Egypt*, i. 25 ff., argued that the calendar began
with the commencement of the inundation of the Nile, which from time to
time coincided approximately with the feast of the rising of Sirius (*Sothis*) at
sunrise on the eastern horizon on July 19. But the Sothic year (i.e. the interval
between the two successive risings of Sirius) was a quarter of a day longer than
the calendar year of 365 days. The Sothic and calendar years began on the same
day in 4241, 2780, 1320 B.C., and 140–41 to 143–44 A.D. It has, however,
been questioned whether the cycle was observed as early as 4241 B.C. More
likely there was a subsequent back-reckoning.

2. Egypt has never known any form of government save despotism. The
foundations of political liberty are being laid, for the first time, in our own
day.

(I) *The Old Kingdom* (Dynasties I–VI).[1] – This epoch, lasting a thousand years, reached its climax under the kings of the fourth dynasty at Memphis (from 2900 B.C.), who extended their sovereignty westwards over Libya and southwards over Nubia, worked the mines of Sinai, and traded with their fleets over the Red Sea and the Levant. They were great administrators and great builders, who organized an elaborate fiscal system and ruled Egypt with an army of officials, brought the irrigation of the country to a high state of perfection, and erected as their tombs the mighty pyramids of Gizeh. The mastery of mechanical contrivance and the vast resources of labour necessary for these constructions may be gathered from the fact that the pyramid of Khufu was built of more than two million blocks of masonry, each of an average weight of $2\frac{1}{2}$ tons. The art of the same period, especially in portrait-sculpture and reliefs on tombs and temples, was of a beauty unequalled in any subsequent epoch of Egyptian culture.

(II) *The Middle Kingdom* (Dynasties XI–XII). – The Old Kingdom fell, in the middle of the third millennium, at the hands of the landed nobility, which it had fostered at its peril. There followed some three centuries of disintegration, power resting, as in the pre-dynastic age, with the local chieftains, until a second centralized monarchy, known as the Middle Kingdom, arose at Thebes in Upper Egypt, under the powerful Pharaohs [2] of the eleventh and twelfth dynasties (2150–1780). Commerce was restored on an extended scale with Punt (Somaliland) to the south by the Red Sea, with the Semites of Syria and Canaan, and with the maritime peoples of the eastern Mediterranean. Minoan pottery of the epoch is found in Egypt, and Minoan art shows signs of Egyptian influence.[3] Under the Middle Kingdom, the industrial arts reached their highest development; literature flourished; the sculptures, if more

1. Manetho, an Egyptian priest who wrote under the first Ptolemies (third century B.C.), grouped the kings of Egypt in thirty-one dynasties. His grouping is frequently inaccurate, but is still in general use for purposes of historical reference.

2. *Pharaoh* (*Per-O*), meaning literally 'the great house', was a title originally applied to the seat of government, and afterwards to the person of the monarch.

3. See below, § 16.

conventional, rival those of the fourth and fifth dynasties.

(III) *The New Empire* (Dynasties XVIII–XIX). — The close of the twelfth dynasty was followed by an obscure period, in which a divided Egypt lay at the mercy of foreign invaders. Semitic nomads (the *Hyksos* or so-called shepherd-kings), among them possibly an Israelite tribe,[1] ruled in the land. Unity was again restored by Theban princes, and the most brilliant epoch, if not of Egyptian culture at least of Egyptian political power, opens with the eighteenth dynasty (1580 B.C.). The Egyptians were by nature an unwarlike people; but internal disorder had led to the formation of an organized professional army, and the Pharaohs of the New Empire were the military rulers of a military state. They conquered Syria and Phoenicia, fought the Mitanni (a tribe with Aryan chiefs) and the Hittites on the upper Euphrates, and reigned supreme from that river to the Libyan desert and the confines of Ethiopia. They received tribute from beyond the Mediterranean; Egypt was open to the merchants of the Aegean (Keftiu), her products were in use at Cnossus, and her own decorative art influenced that of the Mycenaean craftsmen.[2] The Empire was administered by a huge body of state-officials and the state-religion by an organized priestly class. This was the greatest age of Egyptian architecture; the temple of the god Ammon at Karnak was one of the most splendid religious monuments of antiquity. A commemorative obelisk, erected by the most brilliant conqueror of the eighteenth dynasty, Thothmes (Thutmose) III, stands to-day on the Thames Embankment. After two centuries of imperial grandeur the inevitable signs of dissolution began to appear; the strange effort of the religious reformer, Ikhnaton (Amenhotep IV, 1375–1358), to establish a spiritual monotheism outraged priestly and popular feeling;[3]

1. Scarabs of a king of this period bear the name of *Jacob-her* or *Jacob-et* (Breasted, p. 220).

2. For the Hittites, see below, § 12; for Cnossus and Mycenae, §§ 15–16.

3. The Tell-el-Amarna letters, the archives of Ikhnaton's foreign correspondence, discovered in 1885, throw much light on the diplomacy of the New Empire. Tell-el-Amarna is the site of the capital, Akhetaton, which Ikhnaton founded as the centre of the monotheistic worship of Aton. For this monotheistic religion, see Ikhnaton's hymn to Aton, translated in Breasted, pp. 371 ff.

the nineteenth dynasty failed to maintain the prestige of Egypt abroad, and well before the close of the second millennium Syria and Canaan had passed from Egyptian hands and the sea-peoples of the Aegean were harrying the Delta.[1] It was during this period of incipient decline that the children of Israel sojourned in the land of Goshen; the exodus to the Sinaitic desert took place at latest under one of the Pharaohs of the nineteenth dynasty (c. 1320–1200).

In the centuries of disintegration that followed the fall of the New Empire, we find Libyan mercenary-chiefs ruling in the Delta and Ethiopian princes in upper Egypt.[2] Late in the seventh century (670) the Assyrians, who had for some time menaced Egyptian independence, conquered the Delta under Esarhaddon and made Egypt a vassal-state.[3] The age of foreign domination had begun. As the power of Assyria waned before that of Babylon, there came one more chance of independence; under the kings of the twenty-sixth dynasty (at Sais in the Delta, 663–525) we witness a brief and somewhat artificial revival of culture, and an abortive reassertion of imperial aspirations. Egypt was allied with Lydia and the Asiatic Greeks; Greek mercenaries were enlisted in the royal service; a settlement was allotted to Greek traders at Naucratis (= 'Sea-power') in the Delta. Necho (609–593) conquered Canaan, and fought Nebuchadrezzar of Babylon on the Euphrates. His offering of the cloak that he wore when he defeated Josiah at Megiddo to the temple of the Milesian Apollo at Branchidae is a significant illustration of historical contact between Egypt, Judah, Babylon, and Greece.[4] But the restoration of inde-

1. The Keftiu (Minoans) vanish from Egyptian monuments about 1350; a century and a half later the Akaiuasha (Achaeans) make their appearance. See below, § 15.

2. Sheshonk I (the *Shishak* of the Old Testament) was one of the former; he had been Solomon's ally, gave shelter to Jeroboam the founder of the northern (Ephraimite) kingdom, and attacked Rehoboam, the ruler of the southern kingdom (Judah), c. 926 (1 Kings ix. 15–17; xi. 40; xiv. 25).

3. The Assyrian armies had reached the frontier of Egypt twice in the eighth century; Sennacherib's abortive invasion occurred in 701. The weakness of Egypt is clearly realized by Isaiah, who denounced the policy of alliance between Judah and Egypt against Assyria (Is. xxx. 1–7; xxxi. 1–3).

4. Necho was defeated at Carchemish in 604: the Babylonian conquest of Judah followed quickly on this victory. See 2 Kings xxiii. 29 and Herodotus, ii.

pendence was short-lived; when Babylon fell before the
Persians, the doom of Egypt was already imminent. In 525
Cambyses conquered Egypt, and the land remained subject to
the Persian empire, save for fitful and transitory revolts, till the
advent of Alexander of Macedon (332–330).

§ 5. It remains to ask, how far the civilization of the ancient
Egyptians affected that which developed during the last millennium B.C. in the Mediterranean world. Looking first (a) to
religion, which in Egypt, as among all early races, was the
focus of culture, we find a multitude of local faiths and worships unified by the Pharaohs of the early dynasties in a state-
religion with certain central deities, whose tales and ritual
were moulded, as time went on, into systematic and stereotyped form by priestly scribes. They contain little of speculative or spiritual value, with the solitary exception of Ikhnaton's attempt, referred to above, to replace the established
cults by the monotheistic worship of the sun-god Aton. His
revolution seems to have been provoked by a genuine speculative idealism; but it proved abortive and without influence
even in his own land. The religious writings, such as *The
Book of the Dead*, concerning the fortunes of the soul in a future
life, a collection originating under the Middle Kingdom and
shaped into definite form at the time of the eighteenth
dynasty, were dominated by magic and reveal a thoroughly
materialist conception of the soul. The belief in a moral
judgement after death, associated with the cult of Osiris, had
a certain ethical value. In the early 'pyramid texts' the conception of a moral order in the world may be seen arising out
of popular judgements on conduct 'according to rule' in
family and village. But there is no evidence that Egyptian
religion seriously influenced the outside world. The worship
of Jehovah had its home in the desert of Sinai, not in Egypt.
At a later epoch, when East and West met under Macedonian
princes at Alexandria, native Egyptian worships, such as those

159. Megiddo was in the plain of Jezreel or Esdraelon, the scene of the battle
between the Israelites and Sisera (Judges iv, v) and the Armageddon (R.V.
Harmagedon = mountains of Megiddo) of Rev. xvi. 16. The text of the latter
passage is, however, open to doubt.

of Isis and Sarapis, togther with the beliefs in immortality and faith-healing associated with those deities, and the practice of moral allegorism that marked Egyptian priestly teaching, spread widely over the Graeco-Roman world. But before this date the religions of Israel, Greece, and Rome had already developed to their maturity.

(b) The so-called 'wisdom' of the Egyptians, again, was a thing of little scientific value. Their intellectual interests were utilitarian, and they displayed slight aptitude for pure science or philosophy. They devised ingenious rules for measuring fields and buildings, but geometry meant for them land-surveying and nothing more. Neither here nor in their astrology did they evidence any grasp of scientific method. When awkward remainders appeared in their calculations, they simply left them out. Plato was entirely justified when he criticized Egyptian mathematics as restricted to purely practical ends.[1] Their medicine, again, was a medley of rule-of-thumb recipes and magical incantations. Early medical writings show close observation of the human body, common-sense treatment of injuries and speculations on the physiological functions that may have reached the Greeks and served as a stimulus to the first Hellenic men of science. But, until illuminated by the search for causes and reasons, they remained little more than collections of pre-scientific data.[2] When the Greeks visited the land under the twenty-sixth dynasty, their imagination was naturally impressed by its antiquity. 'You Greeks are always children: there is not an old man among you'; so the Egyptian priest is said to have told Solon; reverence for the age-long monuments, strengthened by the dignified reserve of the priestly interpreters, led the northern travellers to idealize, in terms of their own intellec-

1. *Laws*, 747. See the account of the Rhind papyrus in Burnet's *Early Greek Philosophy*, 3rd edition, pp. 18 ff., and his remarks on the alleged scientific attainments of the Egyptians. On Egyptian medicine, contrasted with that of the Greeks, see Brett: *History of Psychology*, pp. 219 ff.

2. See the Edwin Smith *Surgical Papyrus* (ed. Breasted). Treatment is prescribed according to rule ('Thou shalt say, etc.'). A study of this interesting document leaves the reader with the impression that the modern medical practitioner, though fortified by a vastly extended groundwork of facts, has preserved not a little of the mentality of his primitive forerunners.

tual achievement, the learning of a people with so remote a
past.[1] On the other hand, in the mechanical arts, the influence
of Egypt was considerable in after-times.[2]

(c) Egyptian culture was artistic rather than literary, though
popular tales and a religious drama arose under the Middle
Kingdom, and the papyrus, a gift of the Nile marshes, made
correspondence and written record portable and easy. But it
was the art of Egypt which impressed its influence on the outside world, as is evident from the traces discernible in the
pottery and reliefs of Minoan and Mycenaean workmanship.
This was prior to the dawn of Hellenic culture; when that day
came, the art of Egypt had degenerated. A single exception lay
in architecture. The Egyptians built immense temples and
tombs, and used columns and colonnades to admit light to
interiors, while limiting themselves to the simplest constructions and relying for decoration on low relief and colour.
Their later sculpture influenced that of the Greeks in its early
stages, but its rigid conventions were soon outgrown. The
Macedonian rulers of Egypt fostered a revival of native art, but
Greek copies were tasteless and inaccurate. To-day, thanks to
the archaeologists, it is otherwise. The great works of the
sculptors of the early dynasties have been revealed in their
beauty, to serve as a fresh source of inspiration to the artists of
the modern world.

III. BABYLONIA AND ASSYRIA[3]

§ 6. The second great fluvial civilization of antiquity was that
of Babylon. The alluvial plain of Chaldaea, between the lower
waters of the Euphrates and the Tigris, was, like Egypt, capable under proper irrigation of great fertility, and supported in
ancient times a vast population. To-day, after centuries of mis-

1. Plato, *Timaeus*, 22.
2. They could move heavy objects and pile them together, but not more.
The fact that they never attempted a barrage of the Nile shows how limited was
their proficiency as engineers.
3. Here again the early chronology is unsettled. Where there is division of
opinion among scholars, lower dates rather than higher have been preferred,
e.g. for Sargon of Akkad and the first Babylonian dynasty. See the tables in the
Cambridge Ancient History.

rule have blighted its prosperity, it requires an effort of imagination to realize that Babylonia was once, like Egypt, one of the chief granaries of the world, where the crops bore fruit two and even three hundred-fold, and the land, even after the second reaping, furnished abundant pasture.[1] The capital city that arose on the banks of the Euphrates and became from the dawn of the second millennium a great seat of empire, was from its huge size a marvel to antiquity; the inner wall was nearly forty miles in circuit. Babylon, says Aristotle, is more like a nation than a city.[2] To its agricultural resources was added the wealth derived from textile industries and a great trade.[3] From the second millennium Babylon was the market of the East, a cosmopolitan centre, which drew to its bazaars and wharves the produce of India and Iran, and formed the terminus of the traffic along the desert-routes to the Euphrates from the Mediterranean countries in the west. The natural course of Babylonian expansion lay up-stream, for the Chaldaean plain was enclosed to the south and west by the desert, and to the east by the plateau of Iran; already in the third millennium we find that Sargon of Akkad, the founder of the first Semitic kingdom, had overrun Assyria and Mesopotamia and penetrated round the north of the desert as far as Syria and Canaan.[4] Thus early did the Babylonians develop beyond the limits of a fluvial into a Mediterranean civilization, though when they reached the sea, they made little use of it. For 2000 years the rulers of the Euphrates–Tigris valley looked west-

1. Mesopotamian civilization was wrecked by the Mongols, and the Turks failed to effect a restoration. Theophrastus, the most celebrated of Aristotle's pupils, wrote in his *History of Plants*: 'In Babylon the wheat fields are regularly mown twice, and then fed off with beasts to keep down the luxuriance of the leaf; otherwise the plant does not run to ear. When this is done the return in lands that are badly cultivated is fiftyfold; while in those that are well farmed it is a hundredfold' (quoted by Rogers, i. 419); compare Herodotus's yet more generous estimate, i. 193.

2. Arist., *Pol.*, iii. 3, 1276a. Herodotus's description (i. 178–87) should be read; but his estimate of the circuit has been criticized by Rogers (i. 438) in the light of recent excavations.

3. Hence it was not necessary to limit the population by infanticide. But the climate of the Chaldaean plain ensured a high death rate.

4. Rogers dates Sargon c. 3000 B.C., but this date errs by being too high. See the tables in *Cambridge Ancient History*. It may be noted that Babylonia was more accessible to invasion, even from the mountainous side, than Egypt.

wards to the Mediterranean waters as the goal of their ambition.

§ 7. The historic culture of Babylonia and Assyria was Semitic, though, prior to the descent of Semites from Arabia, native tribes had developed a civilization known as Sumerian (*Sumer* – S. Chaldaea), laying the foundations of religion, language, law, irrigation, and urban life, which persisted long after the Semites had established their supremacy. Gem-cutting, an art in which the Babylonians excelled, had in Sumerian times been carried to high perfection; inscriptions were engraved in pictographic and later in cuneiform (arrow-headed) characters; we read already of astronomical observations, the composition of grammars and dictionaries and the formation of a royal library. Late in the third or early in the second millennium we find a dynasty, known as the first Babylonian dynasty, with its seat at Babylon, henceforward the capital of western Asia. Religion is all-important in Babylonian history; the priesthood possessed immense wealth and power; the kings were frequently dependent on their favour, and, even in the days of Assyrian overlordship, the conqueror could secure his authority in Babylon only by doing homage to Marduk. It was Khammurabi, the greatest sovereign of this dynasty, who centralized the local cults of Chaldaea in the worship of Marduk, the patron-deity of Babylon. Khammurabi organized the administrative system of the empire, subdued Elam to the east and Assyria to the north, and extended his sovereignty to the coasts of the Mediterranean.[1] The culture of his age is evidenced by numerous literary remains, including contract-tablets and royal correspondence. But the chief monument of his reign is the code of laws, discovered in the first years of this century by French archaeologists at Susa.[2] This code – 'the judgements of righteousness, which Khammurabi, the great king, set up' – regulated with precision the

1. Khammurabi (Hammurabi, Hemmurapi) is *possibly* the Amraphel of Gen. xiv. 1. Rogers dates the first Babylonian dynasty from 2232 to 1932, and Khammurabi from 2130 to 2087.

2. Fragments have also been discovered in the library of Assur-bani-pal at Nineveh. The code is translated by the Rev. C. H. W. Johns, *The Oldest Code in the World*.

civil law of Babylon, including property and contracts, agriculture, trade and banking, marriage, adoption and bequest,
as well as the machinery of judicial administration, and testifies to the central position which Babylon had already attained
in the commerce of the nations. It forms an elaborate system
of state law; though traces survive of earlier custom, e.g.
ordeal and the *lex talionis*, it represents an enormous advance
on the customary law of early societies. Blood-revenge is prohibited; the *lex talionis* can only be applied through the
established courts; all classes, the stranger as well as the home-
born, are under the protection of the law. It is extraordinarily
interesting to read how such modern problems as exemption
from military service, fixity of tenure, compensation for
agricultural improvements, control of the liquor traffic, banking deposits, liability for a wife's debts, and the legal rights of
women and children, were regulated by this Babylonian
sovereign at the close of the third millennium B.C. As Babylonian civilization spread over Syria and Palestine, the code of
Khammurabi and the later law which rested on it set their
mark on the legislation of the western Semites.[1] The code
itself remained in force well on into the Christian era, and
influenced subsequently the laws of the Mohammedan conquerors of the East. The Babylonians already stand forth as a
civilizing force in western Asia; their language, currency, and
measures of weight prevailed over all the East; their women
enjoyed a legalized status of dignity, and a man could ride in
safety from the Persian Gulf to the Mediterranean under the
protection of the laws of Khammurabi.

§ 8. As the second millennium wore on, the Babylonian
kingdom grew weak; and to the north a new race rose to
greatness on the banks of the river Tigris round Nineveh. This
people, the children of Asshur, or Assyrians, Semitic colonists
from Babylonia and at first subject to its rulers, became its
conquerors about 1300 B.C. The Babylonians were a nation of

1. On the interesting question of the relation between the Mosaic law and
the Babylonian code, see S. A. Cook, *The Laws of Moses and the Code of Hammurabi*. Analogies are due rather to common Semitic origin than to direct
influence: Babylonian influence on Hebrew law probably dates from the
exile (sixth century B.C.).

agriculturists and traders: religion counted for more in their public economy than the art of war. The Assyrians, on the contrary, were from first to last a warrior race; their kings were generals who commanded a military nobility; ferocious and cruel beyond all other eastern peoples, their history is a record of war and conquest. Such culture as they acquired was borrowed from Babylonia: their sole advance was to build in stone as well as brick. The huge winged bulls and the inscribed slabs in the British Museum record a continuous tale of savage warfare. 'I filled with their corpses the ravines and summits of the mountains,' wrote one of the earlier Assyrian princes of his enemies, 'I cut off their heads and crowned with them the walls of their cities; I brought away slaves, booty, treasure, innumerable.' The Assyrians were fanatically devout; and all their victories were in the name and to the glory of their god Asshur; but the priesthood had little influence in their councils. Their princes were the first to replace annual conscription by a standing army; and their military triumphs were largely due to the introduction of cavalry to supplement chariots. Their capacity for organizing empire is evidenced by an elaborate hierarchy of officials, and the imposition of fixed annual tribute upon the provinces. Their power was at its height at three periods of their history, in the twelfth, and again during the ninth and in the later eighth and early seventh centuries.[1] It was in the ninth century that the scourge of the Assyrian armies descended upon Syria and Canaan, overthrew the kingdom of Israel, and reached the shores of the Mediterranean. Samaria, the capital of the northern (Ephraimite) monarchy, besieged by Shalmaneser IV, fell before Sargon in 721. We have seen how, twenty years later, Sargon's son, Sennacherib, overran Judah and threatened Egypt with invasion; and how the conquest was achieved a generation later by his

1. The third and latest period of Assyrian greatness was inaugurated by Tiglath-Pileser III (746–727), the conqueror of Babylonia and Damascus, and continued by Shalmaneser IV (727–722), Sargon (721–705), Sennacherib (704–682), and Esarhaddon (680–668), the last great monarch. Under Esarhaddon's son, Assur-bani-pal (668–626), who cast a thin veil of culture over the savagery of Assyrian rule, the power of the state rapidly declined. Assur-bani-pal's great library is a main source of our knowledge of Babylonian and Assyrian history.

successor, Esarhaddon, whose empire extended from the plateau of Iran to the Libyan desert and the Levant, including also
the highlands of Media and the island of Cyprus. His death
(668) was followed by the decay of Assyrian power; before the
close of the century it succumbed to a coalition between the
Medes and the Babylonians, who had regained their independence under Nabopolassar.[1] With the fall of Nineveh (612) the
empire of Assyria vanished from history; her records were
soon buried beneath the Mesopotamian sand,

> Her glory mouldered and did cease
> From immemorial Nineveh;

till, in the nineteenth century of our era, Botta and Layard
unearthed the stones that tell the story of her ferocity and her
conquests.[2]

§ 9. The victors apportioned the spoils between them, with
the exception of Egypt, who recovered her independence,
after four years of subjection, in 664; but their triumph was
short-lived. The power of Media decayed swiftly after the
death of its founder, Cyaxares. That of Babylon reached its
climax under Nebuchadrezzar (605–562), who conquered
Syria and Jerusalem and bore away the inhabitants of Judah to
captivity in Babylonia (586).[3] His buildings, temples and
palaces and terraced gardens, made Babylon one of the marvels
of the world. But ere long his dynasty suffered the fate that
sooner or later befell every oriental empire. Hardy warriors
descend from the neighbouring highlands upon the fertile

1. The Scythian (Cimmerian) invasions assisted this decline; see § 17
below.
2. Rossetti: *The Burden of Nineveh*. Her fall was hailed with exultation by the
surrounding peoples. 'All that hear the bruit of thee' (i.e. of thy fall), we
read in Nahum iii. 19, 'clap the hands over thee; for upon whom hath not
thy wickedness passed continually?' The city fell before the Medes, who took
possession of Assyria proper; Mesopotamia and the Syro-Phoenician lands
went to the Babylonians.
3. The dynasty in question was, strictly, Chaldaean. The Chaldaeans were
more warlike than the Babylonians, yet equally capable of a high plane of
culture. Greek writers applied the name Chaldaea to Babylonia generally; it
properly means the land of the Kaldi, Semites who dwelt round the mouths of
the Euphrates and the Tigris, between Babylonia and the Persian Gulf.

plains, win and consolidate a new dominion, to yield in its turn, when luxury has sapped the strength of rulers and people, to a fresh race of conquerors. So now (553) the Persians, a vigorous and martial peasantry of Indo-European stock, dwelling in the mountainous region to the east of the Persian Gulf, rose against their Median overlords under their chieftain, Cyrus (*Kourush*). Fourteen years later (539) they conquered Babylon. After 2000 years of sovereignty the Semitic empires had fallen, and a new type of civilization, of Aryan origin, bore sway over the East.[1]

§ 10. The wide sweep of Babylonian empire and her commercial supremacy in western Asia led to the diffusion of her culture over a larger area than in the case of Egypt. That culture was literary rather than artistic; though gem-cutting, copper-work, embroidery, and kindred arts flourished at Babylon, and 'Babylonian garments' were proverbial throughout the ancient world. The native architecture was of brick and comparatively formless; the temples, their chief buildings, stood on rectangular platforms, rising in successive stories to a considerable height. Later, the Assyrians worked their native stone, and adorned their palaces with the colossal figures and bas-reliefs familiar to every visitor to the British Museum. Three questions arise in regard to the influence of Babylonian culture upon the chief civilizations of antiquity. First, there is a close resemblance between the religious traditions of the Babylonians and those of the Hebrews, as recorded in the early chapters of Genesis. In both we read of the garden of Eden, of the deluge and the ark, of the tower of Babel and the confusion of tongues. The Hebrews told how their forefathers in a nomadic stage had sojourned in Chaldaea. It is hard to determine how far this affinity of tradition was due to direct intercourse with Babylonia in remote times, how far to later association with the peoples of Canaan, who had certainly assimi-

---

1. Cyrus, king of Anshan in Elam, belonged to the Persian clan of the Achaemenids; in 553, after his conquest of Media, he called himself King of the Persians. In 546 Croesus of Lydia, who had attacked him, was crushed, and all Asia Minor lay in Cyrus's hands. Rogers dates the fall of Babylon in 539.

lated Babylonian religion, how far, again, to direct contact
during the captivity.[1] However this may be with details of
Hebrew religious tradition and observances, the fact remains
that the development of the religion of Israel, in the hands of
the prophets, into a spiritual monotheism was as original and
distinctive a creation of the Hebrew religious genius as the
philosophies of Plato and Aristotle were of the intellectual
genius of Greece. Secondly, there is the question of the influence of Chaldaean astronomy upon Greek scientific thought.
The Chaldaeans recorded minute observations of the positions
of the heavenly bodies for a period of more than 2000 years,
distinguished and named the planets, determined empirically
the cyclical recurrence of eclipses, and invented a sexagesimal
system of numeration.[2] They constructed the gnomon, an
instrument indicating by its shadow the solstices and equi-
noxes. These data became known to the Greeks, and, like the
empirical geometry of the Egyptians, stimulated them to
scientific investigation. But here again, mere observation is not
science. This is clear when we inquire as to the use which the
Babylonian astonomers made of their records. Whereas the
Greeks in a single century discovered the true cause of
eclipses, the Babylonians never even attempted to find a
rational explanation. They employed their data for purely astro-
logical purposes. If an eclipse had once been followed by a war
with Elam, a war with Elam was foretold from its recurrence.
Observations, however accurate, which are utilized solely as a
basis for fantastic inferences do not constitute scientific know-

1. Scholars are divided in opinion on this question. The stories in question
are contained in the portion of the book of Genesis compiled in Judaea probably in the ninth century, and known as the Jehovistic narrative (J). They are
certainly pre-exilic, and must be accounted for on one of the two first alternatives mentioned in the text. During the exile Babylon again influenced
Hebrew culture, both in religion and law. At a yet later date, the fusion of
East and West under Macedonian rule led to a further influence of Babylonian
religious thought on that of the Jews, traceable, e.g. in Jewish apocalyptic
literature of the last two centuries B.C., and also in Gnostic ideas in the early
days of Christianity.

2. See Burnet, *Early Greek Philosophy*, pp. 21 ff. and notes. The researches of
Father Kugler have established the limits of their astronomical knowledge.
Both in Babylonia and in Egypt, the so-called 'science' was a monopoly of the
priestly caste.

ledge.[1] Finally, Babylonian civilization exerted a real influence on the industrial and commercial life of the western world. The highway that led round the north of the Syrian desert through Asia Minor to Sardis and the coast of the Aegean was the channel of communication between the East and Greece. In particular, Babylonian currency and measures obtained in the first millennium a wide circulation over Asia and the Mediterranean world; Indians and Greeks alike employed the Babylonian *manah* (Greek *mna*) as the standard of weight. Thus early, in eastern Babylon as in western Carthage, did the Semite enter upon his historic role in the economic history of mankind.

IV. THE HITTITES AND THE WESTERN SEMITES

§ 11. We have seen how Semitic culture set its mark upon the civilization of Egypt, and absorbed that of the earlier Sumerians in the Euphrates–Tigris valley. It was the same in the intervening lands between Mesopotamia and the Mediterranean. The language, religion, and culture of Syria and Canaan were Semitic from very early times. We can distinguish various branches of the stock, the southern Semites of Arabia and Ethiopia, the middle Semites of Canaan, the northern (Aramaic) of Syria, the eastern of Babylonia and Assyria; but all alike were children of one Arabian home, and their mutual affinities are as clearly marked as those of the several Teutonic groups in medieval and modern Europe. It is of the northern and middle branches that we have now to speak; the former comprising the peoples of Syria, the latter the Phoenicians and dwellers in Canaan, and among them the Hebrews. These all, because of their geographical position between two great empires, play the role of buffer states; intermediaries in trade and pawns in the political game for their more powerful neighbours, their history is determined, for welfare or for ruin, by their relationship to Assyria and Egypt.

1. We must draw a distinction between the unscientific astrology of the early Chaldaeans and (1) the later influence of that astrology on popular Greek religion, and (2) the scientific development of astronomy *under Greek influence* in Babylonia, both subsequent to the Macedonian conquest.

§ 12. Among these intermediaries was a nation, almost certainly non-Semitic, which ranked for many centuries as a leading power in western Asia. The records of the second millennium show the Egyptians (under the eighteenth dynasty) and, somewhat later, the Assyrians contending on the upper Euphrates against a people known as the Kheta or Hittites.[1] Their origin is obscure, the pictográphic script of their inscriptions still undeciphered, and their history full of problems that await solution. It seems probable that some, if not all, spoke an Indo–European language, entered Asia Minor from the lower Danube and brought with them a culture and language of their own, modified subsequently by the Semitic influences which were dominant throughout the Middle East.[2] The first centre of their dominion was the tableland of Cappadocia, where many Hittite monuments have been discovered; thence it extended over Cilicia and northern Syria, and over the peoples of western Asia Minor (Phrygia and Lydia).[3] This was between 1700 and 1200; towards the latter date they appear to have lost their sovereignty over Asia Minor and the avenues to Mediterranean and Aegean commerce, events probably connected with the northern incursions into the Aegean area and the fall of the maritime ascendancy of Crete. From this time forward the Syrian Hittites and the new masters of Asia Minor (probably Phrygian) turned their energy to the east and south-east, attracted by the rich Mesopotamian resources. From their new headquarters at Carchemish on the upper waters of the Euphrates they commanded the overland highways between east and west. They treated on equal terms with both Egypt and Assyria, and for several generations

1. They appear as *Kheta* in Egyptian records, as *Khatti* in Assyrian, in the book of Genesis as 'sons of Heth' (Gen. xxiii), and elsewhere in the O.T. as *Hittites*.

2. Some of the cuneiform inscriptions from Boghaz-Keui (their Cappadocian capital) are Semitic, others not so. Semitic was the current tongue of international intercourse in the East. The hieroglyphic inscriptions have been found both in Asia Minor and in North Syria and seem to be later than the cuneiform. The serious study of Hittite remains has made great advances in the last half-century: the pioneers were Wright (1872) and Sayce. See Cowley, *The Hittites* (Schweich Lectures, 1918).

3. Hittite remains have been found from Eyuk in N. Asia Minor to Hamath in Syria, from the Euphrates in the east to the Aegean coast lands in the west.

headed a coalition which blocked the westward expansion of the Mesopotamian Semites.[1] In the ninth and eighth centuries their power succumbed to the Assyrian armies, and received a final blow from Croesus of Lydia in the west, shortly before the advent of the Persians.

§ 13. Passing over the Syrian states, indisputably Semitic, which lay on the caravan routes from Assyria to the Mediterranean and received their culture partly from Egypt but in the main from the Babylonians, we come to the coast lands of northern Canaan, where dwelt, at least from the third millennium, the Phoenician Semites. Their whole life centred in maritime trade. Possessed of a small stretch of territory at home, they planted forts and commercial stations along the inland highways, especially around the shores of the Mediterranean. Sidon was in early times the chief Phoenician city; about the twelfth century she yielded place to Tyre. We read in the Old Testament of the alliance, in the tenth century, between David and Solomon and the Tyrian prince Hiram. The Phoenicians dwelt in city-states, under monarchical government, anticipating thus, though to very different issues, the city-states of Hellenism. The great age of Phoenician sea-power and commercial enterprise was between 1200 and 800, subsequent to the fall of Minoan sea-power in the Mediterranean, and prior to the rise of Greece. The argosies of Phoenicia sailed westwards beyond the pillars of Melkarth (the straits of Gibraltar) into the open Atlantic, settled Tarshish (Tartessus, near Cadiz), navigated the Morocco coast, and penetrated also northwards on the Euxine (Black Sea). Wherever they sailed, they planted colonies, in Sicily, Spain, and Africa; the oldest on record was Utica in northern Africa (c. 1100), the most famous was Carthage. In course of time Carthage threw off her dependence on the mother-city of Tyre, made herself suzerain of the surrounding lands in Africa, planted colonies of her own, and established a monopoly of

1. Carchemish is first mentioned in Egyptian records, c. 1480; it was the centre of Hittite power between the twelfth and ninth centuries. We should think of the Hittites primarily as a barrier between Babylonia and Assyria on the one side, and Asia Minor and the Aegean on the other.

trade in western Mediterranean waters. A Greek version of the fifth-century voyage of the Carthaginian Hanno to the west coast of Africa is still extant. From the seventh century onwards Carthage was engaged in ceaseless commercial conflict with the Greek cities of Sicily and the West, which lasted till the third century, when she was called on to face the rising power of Rome. We shall return to the story of this struggle in a later chapter. The silver mines of Spain proved a source of immense wealth to the Phoenicians. One result of their discovery was the depreciation of silver against gold, which had hitherto been hardly obtainable in Asia and Africa, as the metal of highest value. The Phoenicians also had for a while a monopoly of the purple dye, extracted from sea-molluscs. After the eighth century Phoenicia lost her independence. At a later date she furnished the navy of her new Persian overlords. We would gladly know more of the internal economy of these great cities, where the clash of interests was a constant source of unrest. With all their skill in mining and metal work and their daring on the sea, the Phoenicians were not originators. They were the great middle-men of their time; their work was simply to diffuse the products of other lands among the peoples of the Mediterranean world.

§ 14. The Semitic inhabitants of Canaan, to the south of Phoenicia, owe their historical importance to a close connexion with the children of Israel. After their sojourn on the borders of Egypt, and deliverance by Moses, under the nineteenth dynasty, the Israelites roved the desert of Sinai, until we find them settled at Kadesh in southern Canaan. We shall see later how Moses had already brought into being a Hebrew nation, by his establishment of the worship of Jehovah as the exclusive religion of the Israelite tribes. When, some generations afterwards, the Israelites entered Canaan, they absorbed the culture of the earlier inhabitants and, under Canaanite influence, exchanged the habits of the nomad for a settled agricultural life. At the close of the second millennium, the struggle with the Philistines, a non-Semitic people, probably immigrants from Crete, brought about the institution of kingship under Saul the Benjamite, and ushered in a brief epoch of secular prosperity. David subdued the kindred nations of Moab, Edom, and Ammon, and the Syrian kingdoms to the north. Under his successor, Solomon, commerce was developed, and the Hebrews came into closer contact with Egyptian and Babylonian culture; life became more luxurious, and the old simplicity of manners was overshadowed by the urban civilization of the court. On Solomon's death (c. 933), the northern Israelites, led by the tribe of Ephraim, declared their independence of the south (Judah). The divided monarchy persisted with varying fortunes for more than 200 years; the northern kingdom, the more powerful of the two, played a considerable part in international politics under the house of Omri, of which we have record in Assyrian tablets; but it was manifestly only a question of time before they succumbed to the armies of the east. In 721 Samaria fell to the Assyrian Sargon, and the Ephraimite kingdom ceased to exist. Judah was saved for a season by the timely homage of her sovereigns, and by the failure of Sennacherib in Egypt (701), till Babylonia had replaced Assyria as the dominant power in the East. Then, at the hand of Nebuchadrezzar, the hour of her doom struck (586), and the Jewish people lingered in exile by the waters of Babylon, till Cyrus, the founder of the Persian empire, suffered them to recolonize their old home (538). It was at this epoch that, with a religious faith purified by suffering and a law renovated under the influence of the prophetic teachers, Israel, though of little moment in the secular comity of nations, entered upon her spiritual mission to mankind. Of the Hebrew genius in religion, and of its influence on world-civilization, we shall speak in the next chapter.

V. CRETE

§ 15. We have carried our survey of Egypt, Babylonia and Assyria, Canaan and Syria to the latter half of the sixth century B.C., when they were absorbed in the mighty empire of Persia. But we have yet to speak of another series of civilizations, which arose in Crete, and the islands and shores of the Aegean sea. We have already alluded to the inroads made by sea rovers into Egypt in the time of the nineteenth and twentieth dynasties. Who were these sea-peoples, who bear on Egyptian monuments names (Dardenui, Akaiuasha) akin to the Dardanians (= Trojans) and Achaeans of Homer? There is a special interest in these early Aegean races, over and above that of the wonderful discoveries revealed by archaeologists in recent years, in that they were the forerunners of the Greeks. Some seventy years ago little or nothing was known for certain of their life and history. The pioneer of Aegean archaeology was Heinrich Schliemann. As an errand-boy in a tradesman's shop in Germany his imagination was stirred by the stories in the poems of Homer; he taught himself Greek, won success in business, and amassed wealth, with the single aim of verifying by researches on the site of the Homeric Troy the truth of the narrative in the *Iliad*. At Hissarlik in the Troad (northwest of Asia Minor), the reputed site of Troy, at Mycenae and Tiryns in the Peloponnesus, he unearthed traces of a great civilization dating from the second millennium B.C. [1] Scholars of all nations followed in his steps, and every year is adding to the rich stores of knowledge thus revealed about the early life and culture of the Aegean area. We can only outline here some of the chief results that have been disclosed.

§ 16. In the course of the third millennium there arose in the island of Crete a rich and varied civilization, which spread in the event over the islands of the Aegean, Rhodes and Cyprus, the Greek peninsula, and the Ionian islands, with later off-shoots in North Syria, Sicily, and the western Mediterranean, and led to intercourse with Palestine and Egypt. It has been called 'Minoan', after Minos, the lawgiver and friend of Zeus, of Greek tradition, the memory of whose sovereignty of the seas has been preserved in the pages of Thucydides.[2] The race

1. Schliemann identified the Homeric Troy with the second (from the bottom) in the series of cities discovered at Hissarlik. In fact, this city proved to be of much earlier date (c. 2000), and the Homeric Troy was the sixth city, or perhaps the earlier seventh, in the series (c. 1450–1200).

2. Thuc., i. 4; cf. Herod., i. 171, 173. The ancient Greeks ascribed much of their law (e.g. Lycurgus' legislation at Sparta), art (the legend of the crafts-man Daedalus, the first aeronaut, who made the Labyrinth for Minos, and statues that moved of themselves), and religion (Zeus was born in the cave of Dicte) to Cretan origin.

that inhabited Crete in pre-Hellenic times was not Asiatic, but Mediterranean, belonging, in all probability, to the dark, long-headed, short, and slender stock that had its original home in northern Africa. Crete is a natural link between Europe, Asia, and Africa, and became in time the centre of a powerful commercial and maritime empire. Her civilization was distinct in type from those of Egypt and of Babylonia, and reached its height, first, at the opening of the second millennium (second Middle Minoan period), when the twelfth dynasty ruled in Egypt, and again, a few centuries later (second Late Minoan period), contemporary with the eighteenth Egyptian dynasty. Thus it flourished continuously for some 600 years. Recent excavations have brought to light, at Cnossus, Phaestus and elsewhere, splendid royal palaces adorned with sculptured reliefs and paintings, containing treasures of metal work in gold, bronze, and copper, figures of ivory, porcelain, engraved gems and pottery of rare excellence, that furnish ample evidence of a high plane of culture and refinement. The palace at Cnossus, with its storied maze of chambers, passages, and courts, is a town in itself, the veritable labyrinth through which, as in the legend, now shown to record the truth of history, captives were led to the bull-ring, as offerings to the sacred beast of Cretan worship. The drainage-system and sanitary arrangements were worthy of the twentieth century A.D. When a French scholar was shown the costumes of the women in the wall-paintings, he exclaimed, '*Mais ce sont des Parisiennes!*' They are portrayed in close-fitting attire, with zouave jackets and bishops' sleeves, bodices cut low in front, small-waisted, flounced or bell-shaped skirts, and high collars like those of the court-ladies of Elizabethan England. They were curled and *frisées*, tight-laced, and wore shady hats ornamented with ribbons and rosettes. The men were close-shaven, with their long hair coiled in twists, and with curls over their shoulders, clad in kilts and strong top-boots, belted at the waist, and, like the women, adorned with necklaces and armlets. The Cretan architects and stonemasons rivalled those of Memphis and of Thebes. The Cretans were the first-known of European peoples to use writing; inscriptions, both in hieroglyphic and in linear characters, have been found in abundance; when the efforts to decipher them have proved successful, we shall know more of the detailed history of the early Mediterranean world. This much, however, is already certain: that, by the middle of the second millennium, a uniform culture had been diffused far beyond the limits of the Aegean area. To its later phases belong the discoveries of Schliemann at Tiryns and Mycenae; and it is possible that, as Crete declined from her greatness, Mycenae, the home of the Homeric Agamemnon, inherited a portion of her sea-power. However this may be, there is clear evidence that, at a date somewhere about 1400, the Minoan civilization in Crete suffered a catastrophic overthrow. The charred ruins of the palace at Cnossus tell their own tale. Earthquakes account for much; but barbarian invaders from the north were pressing in successive hordes over the Aegean world; rude fighters with superior weapons and eventually knowledge of iron, who recked little of the brilliant culture that they overthrew. These men, speaking an Indo-European language, were very possibly ancestors of the Greeks of history. An epoch of darkness ensued, which lasted until the relics of the old civilization, in fusion with the temper and genius of new masters, gave birth to the culture of historic Greece.[1]

§ 17. The Aegean shores of Asia Minor, as we shall see presently, were Greek from very early times. When rich commercial cities arose in the eighth and seventh centuries B.C., they were a natural object of envy to the princes of the interior. Asia Minor is a table-land from which valleys descend to the west coast, isolated by mountain ridges. The relief of the land has determined its history. The maritime cities, cut off one from the other by mountains, were an easy prey to conquerors from the inland plateau. In the second millennium the Hittites

1. See below, c. iv. § 1. Some authorities hold that the Greeks inherited their culture, and even their language, from the Minoans (see Burnet, *Early Greek Philosophy*, pp. 2 ff). The revival of popular religion (as distinct from the Olympian cults) in the seventh and sixth centuries points to the survival of the old Minoan religious tradition, which centred in the worship of a goddess of the underworld. The discoveries in Crete during the present century will always be associated with the name of Sir Arthur Evans.

and those who followed them on the plateau had extended their power to the coasts of the Aegean. In the eighth century the roving Cimmerians [1] from the steppes north of the Black Sea swept over Asia Minor, and devastated the Greek cities by the sea. They ruined the ancient monarchy of Phrygia, and dealt a rude blow to the younger power of Lydia. Lydia was at this time (eighth to sixth century B.C.) the buffer state between the Greek world and the great empires of the East. A new Lydian dynasty arose, whose princes assimilated Greek culture and in return gave the Greeks what is usually assigned as the one original invention of the Lydians, a stamped coinage, which replaced the unstamped weighed metal of the Babylonian and other early cultures. [2] About 560 B.C. Croesus became king of Lydia. While he subjugated the Greeks on the Aegean coasts of Asia, he ruled them liberally and was a patron of Greek religion and culture. When Cyrus the Persian had conquered Media (549), Croesus, without waiting for the support of Egypt and other allies, attacked Cyrus, and his defeat cost him his kingdom (546). The fall of Lydia carried with it the submission of the Asiatic Greeks and the empire of Persia stretched from the Hindu-Kush to the Aegean.

VI. THE PERSIAN EMPIRE

§ 18. In prehistoric times a branch of the Indo-European family had left their primeval home in the steppe-lands north of the Caspian, and migrated in a south-easterly direction, some passing through the Khyber pass into the Punjab, while others settled in the east of the great Iranian plateau. Early in the second millennium, these Iranian tribes (they called themselves Aryans, whence the local names Aria and Iran are

1. These Cimmerians were probably nomads from north of the Black Sea. It was a period of incursions from the north; in the seventh century the Scythians, who expelled the Cimmerians, also overran Syria and Canaan (see Herod., i. 103 f., and the prophecies of Jeremiah and Zephaniah referred to in the next chapter, § 9).

2. It is possible that stamped coinage is of even earlier date. It may have arisen in Phrygia; in any case, its origin is connected with the great caravan route which came down from the interior plateau of Asia Minor to the Aegean coast and, in tradition, with the gold-field of Sardis.

derived) moved westwards to the highlands that fringed the
Mesopotamian and Chaldaean plains. A thousand years later we
find Medes to the south of the Caspian, Parthians in Khorassan,
Bactrians on the northern slopes of the Hindu-Kush, and Persians in the mountains that overhang the Persian gulf on the
north-east. The Hindu-Kush and Soliman ranges formed their
barrier towards India. These Aryans brought with them the
horse, a product of the steppe, unknown to the Babylonians of
the days of Khammurabi, but utilized by the Assyrians as an
instrument of war.[1] They brought with them also a distinctive
religion, which contrasts strikingly with that of their Semitic
neighbours on the plain. It differed also, despite a common
groundwork that has maintained itself with astonishing persistence among the Persians to the present day, from that of
their Aryan kinsmen in India.[2] While the Indian faith subordinated all other divinities to a single supreme God, Iranian
religion presented dualistic features; [3] their pantheon grouped
itself round two sovereign powers: one of good, a positive
creative force, the source of light and life, the other of evil,
the negative force of darkness and death, who were called respectively Ahuramazda (Ormuzd) and Ahriman. The supernatural conflict of these two divine forces was reflected in the
course of human history. Between the two stood man, endowed with moral freedom, on the use of which depended his
fate in the world beyond the grave. Iranian religion was
strongly ethical; its deities were not, like those of the Indian
Aryans, speculative abstractions, but moral persons; the goal
of human striving was no mystic absorption in a pantheistic
Absolute, but eternal felicity in the heaven where Ahuramazda
reigned. Human life, its social obligations, its joys and its
sorrows, were no illusion, but the field for energetic action

1. As is evidenced by the Babylonian name for the horse, 'the ass of the
East'.
2. Among the common elements are the cult of Mithra, the sun-god and
dragon-slayer (the Indian Indra), fire-worship, and the belief in a law of
destiny superior to gods and man. See F. Cumont, Les Mystères de Mithra,
pp. 1–3. Varuna, the most ethical deity in the Vedic pantheon, was a parallel
development to Ahuramazda from a common Aryan original.
3. But the supreme Brahma of Hindu monotheism was inaccessible and men
were driven to propitiate lower deities (Siva, Vishnu).

and the fulfilment of moral duty. In its recognition of the worth of secular culture, and in its direction to the end of individual rather than national salvation, the religion of Iran differed from that of Israel, to which its lofty ethical teaching presents a certain resemblance. The Persians tolerated local religions when not hostile to their own, yet their faith spread westwards with the expansion of their empire. In its purity, as developed by the prophet Zoroaster, it was doubtless the faith of a few rather than of the many; it tended in the hands of the Magi (the priestly caste) to degenerate into formal observances, while the masses interpreted its teaching in terms of the old pre-Zoroastrian religion.[1] Its real strength lay in insistence on moral responsibility. The Persians of history present a noble type of character; they were born rulers of men, proud and stately in demeanour, lovers of the banquet and the chase, humane in war, magnanimous to their subject-peoples, ready to tolerate and even to absorb foreign ideas. When in the fourth century Alexander's Macedonians conquered their empire, they could recognize in the Persian nobles, what in fact was the truth, their ancient kinsmen. In art and architecture the Persians showed little originality, and copied from Babylonian models. Commerce they scorned as unworthy of a free man; arms, agriculture, and husbandry were their traditional tasks. The most heinous of crimes was falsehood; and the training of their youth is thus summed up by Herodotus, 'to ride, to shoot with the bow, and to speak the truth'.[2]

§ 19. The drama of the Persian empire took the course that

---

1. Zoroaster (*Zarathustra*) lived probably about 650 B.C. The Persian sacred books, collectively entitled the *Avesta*, contain the Gathas, hymns probably written by the prophet himself. Zoroastrianism is almost monotheistic. Fire-worship was strongly emphasized; fire being the purest manifestation of Ahuramazda. The early Magi seem to have been anti-Zoroastrian. Herodotus' informant had little use for them. Like those of Egypt and Babylonia, Persian cults influenced western religion first in the age succeeding Alexander's conquests. In the Roman period, as we shall see later, Mithra worship was very popular in the Mediterranean world, and Persian dualism influenced eastern Christianity. It is the source of the belief in a personal Satan. See Cumont, *Les Mystères de Mithra*, Intr., pp. vi–viii, and the article 'God (*Iranian*)' in Hastings' *Dictionary of the Bible*.

2. Her., i. 136. Compare the prayer in i. 132. The Persian prayed for the King and all the Persians, never for himself alone.

has become familiar in Oriental history. Conquest, organization, stationary maintenance of power, decadence and fall, follow in logical sequence. Cyrus, the founder, and one of the great empire-builders of history, represents the period of conquest. At his death in 528, his dominions stretched from the Aegean in the west to the Hindu-Kush in the east, from the Caspian in the north to the desert of Arabia in the south. The Persian monarch styled himself 'King of Kings'; nor was the claim to world-empire, thus asserted, without foundation. It was Cyrus's son, Cambyses, who conquered Egypt (525) and the Greek colony of Cyrene. Never before had the civilizations of the Nile and the Euphrates been gathered into a single state. The second epoch, of organization, centres in the person of Darius, son of Hystaspes (521–486). Darius is the type for all time of the Oriental administrator. His vast empire, a medley of all peoples, nations, and languages, with no unity of race, religion, or common interest, was divided into twenty satrapies or vice-royalties. To guard against the ever-present danger of revolt, the civil and military powers in each satrapy were entrusted to different hands; and a high personage at Susa, the official capital, who bore the title of 'the King's Eye', had for his special function the supervision of the satraps. A magnificent system of roads and posts aided to centralize control.[1] As was the general practice in Oriental empires, subject peoples preserved their local religions, customs, and institutions in entire freedom from interference by the central government; the two marks of subjection were the payment of a fixed annual tribute, and the levy for service in the field. The Persian nobility lived in close personal relations with the sovereign; Persians settled through the provinces formed, together with representatives of the native inhabitants, the council of the satrap. The satrap was thus controlled at once

---

1. The royal road from Susa to Sardis (in Lydia) secured for the first time in history the control of Asia Minor by a Mesopotamian power. An army could advance along it at the rate of twenty miles a day, a fact that goes far to explain the successes of Alexander. There were also Persian roads across Asia Minor from N. to S., from Babylon by Ecbatana to Bactria and from Mesopotamia through Phoenicia to Egypt. The highlands of the peninsula, however, were virtually unpoliced till Rome appeared upon the scene.

by his council, by the general of the army, and by the central government. The system thus established by Darius became the model for succeeding Oriental monarchies.[1] Darius also added the Punjab and Arabia to the empire, passed the Hellespont into Europe and received the homage of Thrace and Macedonia. At the close of his long reign he was gathering a great host to effect the subjugation of free Greece. Like other Oriental powers, Persia strove to expand westwards; it was from the West that she met her doom. But the story of the Greek conflict with Persia belongs to a later chapter of this book.

§ 20. The successors of Darius, throughout the next century and a half (486–338), were chiefly concerned to maintain the empire which he had consolidated. Enervation in the ruling house, constant revolts in outlying provinces and especially in Egypt, and the long struggle with Greece, combined to foster its degeneration. The centre of gravity in world-politics had shifted to the shores of the Aegean. By the middle of the fourth century, Persian prestige rested on the support of Greek mercenaries and their captains. The death of the last capable ruler, Artaxerxes III (Ochus), in 338 was followed by an interval of anarchy, which furnished a unique opportunity to the enemy. King Philip of Macedon had already planned a war of revenge for the Persian invasion of Greece in the preceding century, and in 334 his son Alexander crossed the Hellespont and made himself master of Asia Minor. In 331 he won his crowning victory at Gaugamela, and a year later, on the death of the last successor of Darius, both the title and the empire passed to the Macedonian conqueror. Henceforward the history of the Middle East becomes part of that of Hellenic civilization.

VII. CONCLUSION

§ 21. The various civilizations that have passed before us in this chapter, though rich in intrinsic interest, were, with one

---

1. Darius was a great builder, and sought to conciliate his subjects by lavish honours paid to their religions. He employed the same policy beyond the borders of the empire; e.g. in gifts to the oracle at Delphi, which favoured at the outset the Persian attack on Greece.

notable exception, of secondary importance for the future of
the western world. Viewed from this angle, it might be said
that nothing became them better than their eventual absorption into Hellenism. We shall see presently how, when the
fusion of East and West became a living reality under the successors of Alexander, the religious ideas of Egypt, Babylonia,
and Persia evoked a response from within the sphere of Graeco-
Roman culture. But that culture had arisen and developed on
its own lines, in contrast to, rather than by the aid of, the
thought and customs of the East. The solitary exception, referred to above, is, of course, the religion of Israel. In this
field, and in that of morals, the debt of after ages to the Semitic
race is incalculable. A Jew of Tarsus, trained in the strictest
school of Pharisaic orthodoxy, became the apostle of the Gentiles. The following chapter, therefore, will be devoted to a
study of the chief constructive epoch in Hebrew religious
history. We shall then turn westwards to Greece and Rome.
Even the religion of Israel did not seriously influence the West
until Greece and Rome had fashioned the structure of their
civilization. Hellenism had reached its zenith long before the
first missionaries of the gospel set themselves to accommodate
Jewish tradition to the temper and habits of the Graeco-
Roman world. In all its highest expressions, in art, philosophy,
and civil life, Hellenism was the original creation of the Greek
genius. Other races contributed materials to its economic sub-
structure, and a stimulus to its intellectual curiosity; here and
there, as in architecture, they left their traces upon some detail
of its achievement. But the Greeks knew what they meant,
when they contrasted their own culture with the welter of
barbarism that surged around their small communities on
every side.[1] That culture arose, as if by magic, amid an alien
world, as the goddess Athene in the legend sprang from the
head of Zeus; the history of the surrounding peoples serves

1. Bury (*Hellenistic Age*, pp. 24 ff.) suggests that the doctrine of barbarian
inferiority was the product of the Persian Wars. Later it was questioned by
philosophers; Plato conjectured that a philosopher-king might be found
among barbarians, and the Stoics went so far as to conceive one brotherhood of
all mankind. See below, p. 221.

merely to point the contrast, and to furnish the framework for its expression.[1]

1. Grote, in the preface to his *History of Greece* (1846), spoke of 'the spontaneous movement of Grecian intellect, sometimes aided but never borrowed from without, and lighting up a small portion of the world otherwise clouded and stationary'. Much has been discovered since Grote's day, but his assertion of the originality of Greek science remains unshaken.

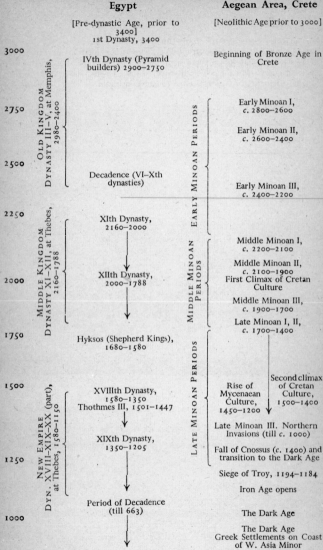

	Egypt	**Aegean Area, Crete**
	[Pre-dynastic Age, prior to 3400] 1st Dynasty, 3400	[Neolithic Age prior to 3000]
3000	IVth Dynasty (Pyramid builders) 2900–2750	Beginning of Bronze Age in Crete
2750		Early Minoan I, c. 2800–2600
		Early Minoan II, c. 2600–2400
2500	Decadence (VI–Xth dynasties)	
		Early Minoan III, c. 2400–2200
2250	XIth Dynasty, 2160–2000	
		Middle Minoan I, c. 2200–2100
2000	XIIth Dynasty, 2000–1788	Middle Minoan II, c. 2100–1900 First Climax of Cretan Culture
		Middle Minoan III, c. 1900–1700
1750	Hyksos (Shepherd Kings), 1680–1580	Late Minoan I, II, c. 1700–1400
1500	XVIIIth Dynasty, 1580–1350 Thothmes III, 1501–1447	Rise of Mycenaean Culture, 1450–1200 — Second climax of Cretan Culture, 1500–1400
	XIXth Dynasty, 1350–1205	Late Minoan III. Northern Invasions (till c. 1000)
1250		Fall of Cnossus (c. 1400) and transition to the Dark Age
		Siege of Troy, 1194–1184
	Period of Decadence (till 663)	Iron Age opens
1000		The Dark Age
		The Dark Age Greek Settlements on Coast of W. Asia Minor

Egypt vertical labels:
OLD KINGDOM DYNASTY III–V, at Memphis, 2980–2400
MIDDLE KINGDOM DYNASTY XI–XII, at Thebes, 2160–1788
NEW EMPIRE DYN. XVIII–XIX–XX (part), at Thebes, 1580–1150

Aegean vertical labels:
EARLY MINOAN PERIODS
MIDDLE MINOAN PERIODS
LATE MINOAN PERIODS

Western Asia	Babylonia and Assyria	
	Sumerians (prior to 3000)	
		3000
	Sargon (a little later)	2750
	Sumerian revival	2500
	Assyrian Kings at Asshur, from c. 2400	
		2250
FIRST BABYLONIAN DYNASTY 2232–1932 — Khammurabi, 2130–2087		
	Aryans to Persia, c. 2000–1600	2000
	Series of Babylonian Dynasties	
The Exodus of Israel (?)		
		1750
	Aryans to India, c. 1600	
Hittite power in Asia Minor, 1700–1200		1500
	Rise of Assyrian power, from 1380	
Exodus of Israel from Egypt, c. 1230 (?) Phoenician Sea-power: Tyre replaces Sidon : first African colonies (12th century) Hittites and their successors at Carchemish, c. 1200	Babylon under Assyrian rule	Shalmaneser I (1276)	1250
	Tiglath-Pileser I, c. 1120	
Kingship in Israel { Saul, c. 1025 { David, c. 1010		1000
	Decline of Assyrian power (to c. 900)	

	Egypt	Aegean Area and

The Dark Age, to *c.* 800

1000 — Period of Decadence (till 663)

Libyan and Ethiopian rulers — Sheshonk (Shishak), 945–924, invades Palestine

Growth of the Greek Epic (vertical)

Phoenician Colonies in Africa and the West (vertical)

900

800

Decline of Phoenician Commercial Power
Epoch of Greek commercial expansion and colonization (to *c.* 600)

700

670. Esarhaddon conquers Egypt
663. Egypt independent, under XXVIth Dynasty at Sais, to 525

Rise of Tyranny

600 — Greek Settlements in Egypt — Necho (609–593)

Solon : Thales and the birth of science

Pisistratus

525. Cambyses' conquest of Egypt.
Egypt under Persian rule to 332

Clisthenes

500

The Persian Wars (490 : 480)

Pericles and the Athenian Empire

Peloponnesian War

400

Rise of Macedon

332–330. Alexander's conquest of Egypt

Battle of Chaeronea (338)

Greece under Macedonian rule

300

Western Asia	Israel	Babylonia and Assyria	
	David, c. 1010–970 Solomon, c. 970–933 Division of N. (Ephraimite) Kingdom from S. (Judah) (933)	Decline of Assyrian power to c. 900	1000
		Recovery of Assyria	900
Decline of the post-Hittite power	Ahab (d. 854) : Elijah		
Cimmerian Invasion			800
	Amos ; Hosea ; JE	746. Assyrian Empire at its height	
	721. Fall of Samaria (N. Kingdom) before Assyria Isaiah	Sennacherib invades Judah	700
		668. Death of Esarhaddon ; decline of Assyria	
	621. Deuteronomic code Jeremiah 597. Babylonian conquest of Judah, first deportation 586. Final captivity of Judah ; Ezekiel	612. Fall of Nineveh. Chaldaean empire at Babylon Nebuchadrezzar (605–562)	600
	The Second Isaiah 538. Restoration under Cyrus	553. Cyrus conquers Media 539. Cyrus conquers Babylon 529. Cambyses King of Persia 522. Darius I King of Persia	
546. Cyrus conquers Lydia. Western Asia under Persian rule to 334		485. Xerxes 465. Artaxerxes I 423. Darius II 404. Artaxerxes II	500
	397. Ezra's Restoration		400
Alexander conquers Western Asia (334)	332. The Jews under Macedonian rule	359. Artaxerxes III (Ochus), to 338 333. Alexander conquers Persia	
			300

Lydian power in Western Asia

CHAPTER THREE

THE RELIGION OF ISRAEL [1]

*

I. INTRODUCTORY

§ 1. THE three great religions of the Mediterranean world, Judaism, Islam, and Christianity, are all of Semitic origin. That they are still of living power among men testifies to the enduring value of the religious genius of the Semites. The appeal of the two former has been almost wholly confined to the Semitic stock. The third, Christianity, early broke the barriers of race, and claimed as a world-religion the allegiance of the Gentile as of the Jew. But its gospel was preached to the Jew first; it arose among the Jews as the historical fulfilment of Hebrew law and Hebrew prophecy. The question confronts us: how did it come about that the tribal faith of an insignificant Semitic people furnished, in the course of its historical development, the basis of a spiritual message for mankind? Where, amid the particularism of the faith and worship of ancient Israel, lay the seeds of universality? In its early phases, the religion of Israel had little to distinguish it from that of the surrounding peoples of Canaan. How was it that, while their gods vanished with the political ruin of the states that worshipped them, the God of Israel survived the captivity and dispersion of his people, and is still reverenced by millions of all races at the present day? The answer to this question is to be found in the study of the Hebrew prophets. As the intellectual genius of Greece, working on methods of universal validity for human thought, transformed the crude data of experience into

1. The Hebrews of Old Testament days called themselves 'the sons of Israel' (*B'ne Isra'el*). The name *Israel* is of obscure origin and has been interpreted 'God (*El*) strives' or 'persists'. The name *Hebrew* is of later application, and, on the traditional view, means 'the people from the other side of' (Heb. *'ibhrim*) the river Euphrates (or the Jordan?). The name *Jew* (*Yehudi*) means 'man of Judah', and applies strictly to the dweller in southern Palestine. Possibly *Israel* and *Hebrew* were originally clan-names.

a structure of reasoned knowledge; as the political genius of
Rome moulded the laws of an Italian city into principles of
jurisprudence for a world-state: so the religious genius of
Israel, manifested through the vision of her prophets, purified
the cult of a tribal deity, whose office was to fight his people's
battles against the rival gods of other lands, into that of the one
God, the creator of the universe, who displayed his spiritual
fatherhood in the righteous government of all nations of the earth.

§ 2. When Moses, in the latter half of the second millennium before Christ, united a group of Semitic clans into a single
community, he founded not merely a nation but a national
religion.[1] It was as the bearer of a religious revelation that, like
Mohammed 2000 years later, he was enabled to initiate a far-
reaching transformation in the otherwise so persistent tribal
customs of Semitic nomads. He fixed the worship of Jehovah
(*Yahweh*) as that of a people, and thereby called a nation into
being.[2] Henceforward Yahweh was the God of Israel, who had
freed their fathers from bondage and led them through the
perils of the wilderness into the promised land. To Moses also
can be assigned the institution of a ritual and a priesthood;
and his oral judgements formed the nucleus for the development of a Law (*Torah*).[3] This religion of Yahweh, as brought
by the Israelites into Canaan, was assuredly primitive and

1. The date of the Exodus is uncertain. Some authorities regard it as coincid-
ing with the expulsion of the *Hyksos* or Semitic shepherd-kings (early sixteenth century); others date it under the eighteenth dynasty (Amenhotep II,
c. 1445); others under Merneptah (nineteenth dynasty), c. 1220 or a generation later.

2. The Jews, from fear of abusing the sacred name *Yahweh*, wrote it with
the vowels of the words *Adonai* (= my lord) or *Elohim* (= my God), as an
indication that these words were to be read aloud in its place. This practice
dates from the introduction of vowel signs, some centuries after the Christian
era. Hebrew writing was originally consonantal. Hence arose the quite misleading form *Jehovah*, referred to early in the sixteenth century A.D. by a
certain Petrus Galatinus (*de arcanis Catholicae veritatis*, 1518). The meaning of
the name *Yahweh* is uncertain. Some scholars hold that Yahweh was worshipped by Israel before the time of Moses; the O.T. is ambiguous on this point,
the Jehovist writer (J, see next note) stating that his worship was pre-Mosaic
(Gen. iv. 26), the Elohist (E) and Priestly (P) writers that it was introduced by
Moses (Exod. iii. 11–14, vi. 2–3), perhaps from Midian. The pre-Mosaic
history is very uncertain and obscure.

3. The Pentateuch (i.e. Gen., Exod., Lev., Num., Deut.) and Joshua represent a compilation of early history and law, which reached its present form

anthropomorphic. Yahweh was conceived as possessing bodily form and a local habitation, and as moved by human passions of jealousy and anger. He was a warrior deity, 'a man of war', who fought ruthlessly for his own people against their enemies, and, like an Oriental potentate, required in return homage and gifts. His concern was not with the individual but with the nation, and with the nation especially in times of war. Yet already in this primitive form of national faith can be detected the germs of an ethical religion. It was, if not monotheistic, avowedly monolatrous; the command had gone forth to Israel, 'Thou shalt have none other gods but me.' [1] Yahweh had no mythology, no pantheon of associated deities, no goddess-consort, such as marked the Canaanite worships.[2] He was the source of right and justice, and his sanctuary the recognized depository of law. 'The great merit of Moses,'

after the Exile. The compilation can be traced to three main sources, designated respectively JE, D, and P.

(a) Two narratives of early history, written, one in the northern (Ephraimite) kingdom, the other in the southern (Judah), probably between 850 and 750, and combined in a single historical work *c*. 750. The former is called E, from the use of the name *Elohim* for God; the latter is called J, from the use of the name *Jahweh* (*Yahweh*). The combined work is called JE.

(b) The Deuteronomic law, called D, dating from the middle of the seventh century (see below, § 8).

(c) The Priestly history and code, called P, probably composed at the time of the captivity (see below, §§ 10, 11).

Gen., Exod., Num. represent the fusion of JE and P; Lev. belongs to P; Deut. to D; Joshua to JE, a Deuteronomic editor, and P.

The reader must understand that the successive editors were compilers rather than original authors, and incorporated in their work pre-existing documents, adding only what was necessary to fit the extracts together. Thus many of the laws and narratives in these books were based on customs, traditions, and songs of much earlier date, and some of them on written records (e.g. Num. xxi. 14 f.; Joshua x. 12 f.). The ancient nucleus of law, called the *Book of the Covenant* (Exod. xx. 22–xxiii. 33), and the *Older Decalogue* (Exod. xxxiv. 17–26), existed in writing before E was compiled. So, too, the latest compilation (P) contains some very ancient law in the *Book of Holiness* (Lev. xvii–xxvi), referred to as H, and probably pre-exilic. While the Law *as we have it* is later than the older prophecy, much of its contents dates back to pre-prophetic times.

On the whole subject, see Driver, *Introduction to the Literature of the O.T.*, pp. 82 ff., 116 ff.

1. Monolatry means that, though many gods may exist, only one is to be worshipped; monotheism that there is only one god.

2. The Elephantine papyri indicate a goddess-consort. But they present the religion of Israel in a debased form. See Cowley, *Aramaic Papyri* (Introduction).

writes an eminent modern scholar, 'lies in the fact of his connexion of the religious idea with the moral life'.[1] Yahweh
stood to his people in the personal relationship of a father to
his children, a relationship that rested not on the natural tie of
blood-kinship, but on choice and will. Yahweh had chosen
Israel, and Israel had accepted Yahweh; we have here the germ
of the later doctrine of the Covenant. It was this moral conviction, exemplified for the Hebrews of that age in Yahweh's
championship of Israel against her foes, that preserved the new-
born nation from being absorbed by the older civilization of
the Canaanites. The settlement in Canaan was a slow process of
fusion, which incidentally left traces on Israel's religion. As
the nomadic immigrants learnt from their neighbours the
habits of agricultural life, they appropriated therewith the cults
of the Canaanite deities (*Baalim* = lords of the land). These
Baalim were not, as was Yahweh, warrior gods, but peaceful
nature-divinities, impersonations of the productive powers of
fertility and life, associated in pairs of male (*Baal*) and female
(*Ashtoreth*), with varying local cults, which were accompanied
by gross sensuality.[2] Had the process of fusion been wholly
pacific, the religion of Israel might easily have sunk to the
Canaanitish level, Yahweh been merged in the Baalim, and
Israel have left no impress on the spiritual history of mankind.
But the invaders had to fight for their inheritance; and the fact
of constant war preserved their national and religious individuality. Yahweh remained, amid all assimilation of Canaanite
worships, such as high places, groves or sacred pillars, the God
of his chosen people. The Song of Deborah, one of the oldest
fragments of Hebrew poetic literature, survives to show how
the faith of Yahweh inspired the clans of Israel in these early
struggles with the surrounding peoples.[3] The consciousness of

1. Kuenen, *Religion of Israel*.
2. That the sensuality referred to was the outcome of ritual requirement
only makes the difference more remarkable. The *Ras Shamra* tablets (fifteenth
to thirteenth century B.C.), discovered in 1929, illustrate the full Canaanite
mythology (see Jack, *The Ras Shamra Tablets*), and furnish evidence of literary
activity in Palestine some centuries prior to the establishment of the Israelite
monarchy.
3. Judges v., cf. the ancient invocation in Num. x. 35, 36, 'Let Jehovah
arise and let his enemies be scattered ', etc.

a distinctive nationality was intensified by the wars with the
Philistines in the eleventh and tenth centuries, which brought
about the institution of the kingship in the person of Saul the
Benjamite. The king was the embodiment at once of national
and of religious independence. Henceforward the worship of
Yahweh, despite a multitude of Canaanite accretions, became
the avowed symbol of Israel's distinctive destiny.

§ 3. Leaving on the one side the obscure problems of the
origin of the cult of Yahweh, and on the other deferring consideration of the development of the religion of Israel under
prophetic influence to pure ethical monotheism, we note the
following persistent characteristics of that religion from the
times of its inauguration by Moses until Judaism attained its
final form as a world-religion in the first two centuries of the
Christian era. They will indicate to the reader the wide gulf
that separates the Hebraic religious tradition, both before
and after its appropriation by Christianity, and that which has
its source in Hellenic speculation, whether on metaphysics or
on theology. In the first place (a), it rested on the unquestioned
conviction of God's existence rather than on any inferential
conclusions as to his existence or his nature and essence. The
only answer vouchsafed to Moses' inquiry as to his name was the
affirmation of his self-existence: 'I am that I am.' [1] As self-
existent, he is the cause as creator of the existence of all that
is: 'In the beginning God created the heavens and the earth.' [2]
These opening words of the Pentateuch express no philosophical hypothesis but a primary datum of the Hebrew religious consciousness. From the first, Yahweh proclaimed himself a living God, to be accepted by faith, transcending the
utmost reach of speculative inquiry. [3] Unlike the God of Plato
and Aristotle, the God of Abraham, Isaac, and Jacob is for the
human intellect a hidden God (*Deus absconditus*). Secondly (b),
Hebrew religion is revelational, deriving its authority and its
claim on man's obedience, not from reason, but solely from its
divine authorship. The revelation is one, as God is one; the

---

1. Ex. iii. 14.   2. Gen. i.1.
3. As Dr Whitehead has put it (*Adventures of Ideas*), the question 'Canst
thou by searching find out God?' is good Hebrew but it is bad Greek.

conception of an anti-God, by means of which Persian religion escaped the problem of the origin of evil, was wholly alien to the Hebrew mind. Moreover, it was final and complete as God himself is perfect and immutable. 'The whole of religion was revealed and the whole content of revelation was religion.' [1] It constituted the *Torah* or Law of God, comprising both the written Law (the Pentateuch) and, as time went on, its oral interpretation as eventually formulated and systematized in the Jewish schools. So it is also with the prophets, who speak not their own words, uttered in their own authority, but the words revealed to them by Yahweh. Thirdly (c), the religion of Israel is pragmatic, being the expression of the divine will, addressed to man as a volitional and active being. It is a body of commands regulative of human conduct, and enforced by sanctions of weal or woe, consequential on man's acceptance or rejection. 'The fear of the Lord, that is wisdom'; [2] in so far as God makes his nature known to Israel in his self-revelation, it is as energy of operation. The universe is brought into being by his free act of power; and the whole record of his dealings with Israel is the embodiment of his initial purpose. Though ineffably transcendent of all processes of time and change, his presence is immanent and his will made manifest in every detail of nature and human history. Not the chosen people only, but the whole universe and all the nations who inhabit it form the scene for his activity. 'Have I not brought up Israel out of the land of Egypt, and the Philistines from Caphtor, and the Syrians from Kir?' [3] Hence the consummation of God's purpose, though, like its inauguration, an act of supernatural intervention into the course of history, is conceived as a catastrophic event in the historical future. The thought of eternal life, congenial to Greek philosophers, was foreign to the Hebrew religious outlook. Yahweh transcended time, not by his timelessness, but by his unending duration: he was 'from everlasting to everlasting'. [4] Finally, it is obvious (a) that a religion inspired by these convictions was pregnant with rich potency of ethical development. Yahweh was a God of

1. G. F. Moore, *Judaism*, i. 112.　　2. Job xxviii. 28.
3. Amos ix. 7.　　4. Ps. xc. 2.

righteousness and mercy, who enjoined acts of righteousness and mercy on his servants. The former of these attributes was exemplified in his rigorous exaction of retributive punishment for sin, i.e. in Johannine phrase, for 'transgression of the Law'; [1] the latter in his never-failing readiness to forgive sin, on the sole condition of repentance in the sinner. There is here no consciousness of the distinction between ethical and religious obligation; every act, whether of the individual or of the community, falls within the field of moral responsibility, and also implies obedience or disobedience to the divine command. For the community, the 'house of Israel', too, stood in a personal relationship to Yahweh, as a real 'corporate person', to be distinguished as ethical from the pre-moral and instinctive herd-consciousness, and as a real entity from the artificial society which is the product of contract on the part of the individuals who are its members.

II. PRE-EXILIC PROPHECY

§ 4. It is at this moment that we first hear of prophets (*nebi'im*) in Israel. King Saul himself on one occasion figured among their number. [2] But these prophets were scarcely distinguishable from the prophets of Baal found among other Canaanite peoples, companies of ecstatic dervishes, who under stimulus of music and dancing experienced possession by their deity. They were men of a type very different from the great teachers who came forward a few generations later as the champions of a purified faith. These latter appear first at the time of the dismemberment of Solomon's monarchy, in the northern or Ephraimite kingdom, in opposition to the spread of alien religious cults and secular civilization. [3] Solomon had already opened the door to foreign trade and fostered dynastic alliances with foreign courts, a policy which led to innovations in time-honoured social custom and to the introduction of foreign worships. Wealth and luxury brought in their train class dis-

---

1. 1 John iii. 4; cf St Paul in Rom. c.iv.   2. 1 Sam. xix. 20–24.
3. The revolt of Jeroboam I and the establishment of a separate Ephraimite kingdom (933) were probably due to dislike of forced labour, and were supported by the prophet Ahijah. See 1 Kings xi. 28 ff.

tinctions and a growing cleavage between rich and poor; forced labour, after the Egyptian model, was required for the building of kings' palaces, fortified towns, and religious sanctuaries; a court, a harem, and a swarm of military and priestly officials became part of the new order of life. These and similar features of Solomon's monarchy were reproduced in the northern kingdom under the dynasty of Omri (from c. 887). When Ahab, Omri's son, legitimized the worship of the Tyrian Baal and stretched the royal prerogative at the expense of traditional custom, Elijah, clad in nomad's garb and voicing the spirit of primitive nomadic simplicity, denounced both the religious and the secular policy of the court.[1] His successor, Elisha, in close association with the prophetic gilds, compassed the overthrow of the dynasty, and guided, as acknowledged adviser, the counsels of Jehu and his son.[2] Prophecy had triumphed in the northern kingdom and established itself as a moral force in the community. It was no mere political victory. Elijah and Elisha stood for the exclusive claim of Yahweh to the allegiance of Israel, and for his law as a law of righteousness, requiring moral service from his chosen children. To worship any other god was sin: to worship Yahweh meant to realize his moral prescripts in the life of the community. This recognition of Yahweh's ethical personality, anticipating the voice of written prophecy, is witnessed to not only by the recorded narratives, but by the older portions of the Pentateuch, composed probably under the influence of Elijah's prophetic mission.

§ 5. The earliest written prophecy, that of Amos, dates from the reign of Jeroboam II in northern Israel (783–745).[3] The Ephraimite kingdom presented a scene of apparent prosperity. But beneath the surface the nation was sick unto death. Court, nobles, and priesthood were alike corrupt;

1. Ahab's infringement of social custom in the matter of Naboth's vineyard stirred popular feeling more than any other feature in his policy. Ahab's reign may be dated after 853.

2. 'The chariot of Israel and the horsemen thereof': so he is styled by the king (2 Kings xiii. 14).

3. Amos' prophecy falls between 765 and 750; Hosea's, also in northern Israel, between 750 and 734. Next in order come Micah and Isaiah, both in Judah, during the last third of the century.

luxury and sensuality, injustice and oppression of the poor abounded; the worship at the great sanctuaries, such as Bethel, furnished occasion not only for sumptuous revelry and splendid ceremonial, but for acts of violence and wrong.[1] The old brotherly-kindliness was vanishing with the spread of wealth and self-indulgence. The free peasantry, hitherto the strength of the nation in peace and war, were falling into decay. Beyond the border, the decline of the buffer-state of Damascus had brought the terrible Assyrian menace to the very doors of Israel.[2] King and people alike were blind to the impending doom; yet to a clear vision ruin was as imminent and certain as it would have been to Belgium in 1914, had she been confronted, without an ally, by the onset of the German armies. It was at such a crisis that Amos, a keeper of flocks and dresser of sycamores from Tekoa in the southern highlands bordering on the Dead Sea, appeared among the careless revellers at Bethel to utter the word of judgement which Yahweh had revealed to his servant. Amos's message, like that of all the earlier prophets, was one of unrelieved gloom. Israel had sinned, and Yahweh's righteous judgement would be manifested in the utter ruin of the nation. Men looked for the 'day of Yahweh', by which they meant the day when by Yahweh's aid Israel would triumph in battle over her enemies. Amos, heralding the Assyrian conqueror as Yahweh's instrument, invested the old catchword with a new and terrible significance. 'Woe unto you that desire the day of Yahweh! wherefore would ye have the day of Yahweh? It is darkness and not light.'[3] For Amos, Yahweh is never 'the God of Israel'; he is 'Yahweh of hosts' (*seba'oth*), Lord, not of the national armies, but of the hosts of heaven and earth. The popular religion saw in defeat a sign that Yahweh had forsaken his people; to Amos the impending downfall was the clearest

1. See Amos and Hosea generally: on injustice and decay of old social bonds, Amos ii. 6–8, iii. 10, v. 11, viii. 4–6; Hos. iv. 1, 2: on licentious worship and idolatry, Amos ii. 7, 8; Hos. iv. 13, 14: on corruption of prophets and priests, Hos. iv. 5, 6; vi. 9.

2. Jeroboam II had recovered all eastern Palestine up to the north of Lebanon, 2 Kings xiv. 25. The Assyrians conquered Damascus in 803; Jeroboam probably paid allegiance to Assyria.

3. Amos v. 18.

vindication of Yahweh's justice upon his people who had forsaken him. It was because he had chosen them to be the recipients of his knowledge that their moral disobedience had provoked his righteous punishment. 'You only have I known of all the families of the earth: therefore will I visit upon you all your iniquities.' 'For three transgressions of Israel, yea, for four, I will not turn away the punishment thereof; because they have sold the righteous for silver and the needy for a pair of shoes.' 'The virgin of Israel is fallen; she shall no more rise: she is cast down upon her land; there is none to raise her up.' [1]

§ 6. The prophecies of Amos and Hosea claim attention not merely as representing the dawn of a new epoch in the spiritual history of Israel but also as embodying the essential characteristics, both in manner and substance, of pre-exilic prophetic teaching. The mission of the prophet was to declare Yahweh's 'word' to his people. The prophecy was the communication of a personal revelation. Its essence does not lie in prediction of future happenings. The prophet is 'one who speaks on behalf of' Yahweh, in conscious opposition to the world of secular rulers, the official priesthood, popular opinion, and even the prophetic gilds. 'I was no prophet,' says Amos, 'neither was I a prophet's son.' [2] His voice is that of one crying in the wilderness, in passionate denunciation of public immortality and the injustice of the social order. The word which he declares is not his own, but Yahweh's. The prophetic office is none of his choosing; he has felt the compelling mastery of Yahweh's hand and utters only what Yahweh has put into his mouth. 'The lion hath roared, who will not fear? The Lord God hath spoken, who can but prophesy?' [3] Hence the intensity of his personal conviction, his absolute certainty of the truth of the message. But his utterance was no mere ecstatic rhapsody, nor was it dependent on artificial stimulation; few traces of physical or mental derangement can be detected in

---

1. Amos iii. 2; ii. 6; v. 2.
2. Amos vii. 14; cf. Hos. ix. 7. The narrative passage, Amos vii. 10–17, brings out clearly this opposition to the policy of the rulers and priesthood.
3. Amos iii. 8; cf. Amos vii. 14 f., Is. vi. Jer. i and xxiii. 9, Ezek. i. 3.

the prophetic writings. The abnormal vision and conditions
that accompany the prophetic experience (most frequently in
Ezekiel, least frequently in Jeremiah) are accepted as objective
and referred to direct inspiration by Yahweh.[1] Yahweh's word
approves itself to his understanding and his conscience. The
revelation may be by vision, or, more frequently, by spoken
word; it may be sanctioned by sign and enforced by analogy
and symbolism; but it is invariably lucid and incisive.[2] Further,
the message is addressed to the nation, rarely to an individual.
The individual counted as yet but lightly in the religion of
Israel. Moral retribution, for weal or woe, was dispensed to
the community in the course of its earthly history. We shall
see in the sequel, how at a later day the claim of the individual
Israelite on the divine justice, and the hope of felicity after
death, won expression in Hebrew religion. But the theme of
the early prophets is the obligation to national righteousness
and Yahweh's judgements on national sin. Once more, the
message, as the revelation of Yahweh's purpose, is its own
warrant and needs no support of argument. If proof be sought,
it is furnished not by abstract inference, but by a sign, that is,
by a concrete sensible indication of its divine origin. We find
no trace of speculative reasoning in Hebrew prophecy. The
prophet's teaching was concerned with practice, not with
theory, and his appeal is not to the intellect, but to the will.[3]
It was stimulated, at each stage, by a practical crisis in the
fortunes of the nation. The Assyrian menace evoked the
messages of Amos, Hosea, and Isaiah, the Babylonian that of
Jeremiah. Herein Hebrew prophecy furnishes a striking
contrast to Greek philosophy. Whereas the Greek thinker required rational explanation for every fact and rational grounds
for every judgement, the Hebrew prophet found full assurance
in the immediate intuition of Yahweh's will, and prefaced his

1. See Wheeler Robinson in *The People and the Book*, pp. 371 ff. 'The
prophet is conscious of the import of the inspiration; like the poet, he "half
creates and half perceives".'

2. Only one vision is recorded by Isaiah during forty years of prophetic
mission. The prophecies are throughout free from any touch of rhapsody.

3. The implication of the term *leb*, usually translated 'heart', is volitional
rather than emotional. See below, p. 85 (1).

utterance with the simple declaration, 'thus spake Yahweh'. The one was the flower of secular culture, the other its uncompromising foe. Both claimed to know the truth, the one by knowledge of reasoned science, the other by that of moral faith.

§ 7. The guarantee of truth lay not only in the manner, but in the substance of the prophetic revelation. The temper of the pre-exilic prophets is one of austere reprobation of Israel's sin, and tragic despair of Israel's repentance. The way of salvation is open, 'Seek good and not evil, that ye may live;' [1] but the prophet has little hope of its adoption. It is the false prophet that cries peace when there is no peace, and, to please men, proclaims an illusory security.[2] When the blow had fallen and Israel was carried away into captivity, the tone changes and Yahweh's message is a promise of blessing and restoration.[3] Already in Isaiah we read of a just remnant of the people who shall be saved in the hour of desolation to form the nucleus of a renovated Israel. But despair of Israel's repentance never clouds for an instant the prophet's faith in Yahweh's righteous government. Let Israel perish, if thereby Yahweh's justice be made manifest. The Assyrian conqueror was but the instrument of his omnipotent and holy will. Yahweh, for Amos and Hosea, is the God of all nations and of the whole earth. His power extends over nature, over the hosts of heaven, even over the realm of the departed (*Sheol* = Hades).[4] He was a moral person, whose unique and universal sovereignty left no place for any divine power but himself. It was his living presence, in

1. Amos v. 14.
2. 1 Kings xxii, Is. xxx. 9–11, Jer. xxviii, and (esp.) Ezek. xiii. Deut. xviii. 21, 22 places the criterion of truth in fulfilment; but cf. Deut. xiii. 1–4. False prophecy may be fulfilled; true prophecy may not. See Charles, *Eschatology*, p. 185 n.
3. Such passages as Amos ix. 8–15 and Hos. xiv, predicting a future restoration, are possibly of later date though the latter is probably genuine. They are accepted by Robertson Smith and by Driver (*Introduction*, pp. 306, 307), who urges that the prophets, guided rather by feeling than by logic, may well have expressed the hope of an ideal restoration at the close of their denunciatory warnings.
4. Amos ix. 2; Is. vii. 11. Yet the primitive conception of Sheol as outside Yahweh's sway persisted for centuries, alongside of monotheism; the speculative inconsistency was not felt as such (see Is. xxxviii. 18; Ps. lxxxviii. 5).

active operation, not his essence, that filled the minds of the
prophets; and they interpreted his activity of will in terms
that precluded the recognition of any other deity. His moral
government was manifested in his dealings with all peoples,
and primarily with his chosen people. Heathen nations, like
Israel, were to be punished for their sins.[1] In the phrase of a
great modern scholar, the prophets conceive a divine drama,
with the earth as the stage, the nations the *dramatis personae*,
Israel the hero of the plot, and Yahweh the author of the
tragedy.[2] The advent of the Assyrian opened their eyes to a
larger world; this enlargement of their imaginative horizon
furthered an advance of spiritual insight. The faith in Yahweh's
moral government sufficed for the greater world as for the less.
Once more, this conception of Yahweh's moral personality
carried with it the requirement of moral service from his
worshippers. Formal observances and empty ceremonial
counted for nothing in his sight. 'I desired mercy [Hesed =
love] and not sacrifice; and the knowledge of God more than
burnt-offerings.' 'I hate, I despise your feast-days, and I will
take no delight [I will not smell − A.V.] in your solemn
assemblies: though ye offer me burnt-offerings and meat-
offerings, I will not accept them. . . . But let judgement run
down as waters and righteousness as a mighty stream.'[3] It is
under the form of knowledge that the prophets express the
moral relationship between Yahweh and his people. Yahweh
knew Israel, and Israel has refused to know Yahweh. 'There is
no truth, nor mercy (love), nor knowledge of God in the
land. . . . My people are destroyed for lack of knowledge; because thou hast rejected knowledge, I will also reject thee.'[4]

1. Amos i, ii and ix. 7. It is for wrongs committed against *Israel* that five
of the six nations referred to in cc. i and ii are to be punished. The later
universalism is still far off. In Is. x. 5–15, Assyria is within the domain of
Yahweh's sovereignty.
2. Wellhausen, who points out further how the prophets absorbed into
their religion the new conception of world-power (i.e. Assyria), which was
destroying other nations and their religions.
3. Hos. vi. 6, Amos. v. 21–4; cf. Is. i. 11–17, xxii. 12–13.
4. Hos. iv. 1, 6; cf. Amos iii. 2, 10, and Hos. ii. 19–20, v. 3, viii. 2. Amos
insists on Yahweh's knowledge of Israel, Hosea on Israel's failure to know
Yahweh.

For Amos, this knowledge lies in the practical recognition of social justice, in the observance of humanity and fair dealing between man and man. For Hosea, its essential note is love, the love of the child for its father, of the bride for her husband. His own bitter experience of the unfaithfulness of the wife he loved lends a unique pathos to Hosea's picture of Yahweh's unfailing tenderness to Israel, and of Israel's desertion of Yahweh to gratify a carnal desire for the Canaanitish Baalim. She has broken the bond of her betrothal; and in anguish of heart Yahweh is driven to pronounce her doom. 'And now will I discover her lewdness in the sight of her lovers, and none shall deliver her out of mine hand.' [1]

§ 8. We have dwelt in some detail on the prophetic message of Amos and Hosea, because it initiated a new era of incalculable significance in the development of the religion of Israel. The essential features of their teaching were unfolded with varied application to the changing course of Hebrew history by the prophets of the succeeding age. With the fall of the northern kingdom (721), the centre of interest shifts southwards to Judah. Here, under kings of the lineage of David, government was centralized and stable. Social life, save in the court at Jerusalem, was simpler and less luxurious. Hitherto the Assyrian menace had been more remote. But now the conquest of Samaria brought the enemy to the very gate. The national crisis provided, as always, the occasion for prophetic revelation, in the persons of Micah, a peasant from the Philistine border, and Isaiah of Jerusalem, the grandest figure in Hebrew prophecy. The work of Isaiah was spread over the last forty years of the eighth century and culminated under king Hezekiah in 701, when Sennacherib's Assyrians invaded Judah and appeared before the walls of the capital. His prophecies are contained in the first thirty-nine chapters of the book which bears his name. [2] In substance they strike the note

1. Hos. ii. 10; cf. i, iii, xi. 1–8, and the final denunciation in xiii.
2. Esp. in cc. i–xii, xiv. 24–xxiii, xxviii–xxxii. The present form of the book of Isaiah is post-exilic. Any discussion of the problems raised by modern criticism lies beyond our province. The reader should consult Robertson Smith, *Prophets of Israel*, lecture v. (esp. *note* 7, p. 422), and Driver's *Introduction to the Literature of the O.T.* For more drastic views see Cheyne's *Introduc-*

already sounded by Amos and Hosea, of stern denunciation of national sin and of Yahweh's impending judgement at the hand of Assyria. Isaiah's governing conception is that of holiness, a term current in the popular religion, to which he gives a new spiritual meaning; Yahweh is not only the 'Lord of hosts' but 'the Holy One of Israel', and Israel a holy people consecrated to his service. It was Yahweh's holiness, in contrast with his own uncleanness and that of Israel, which smote the prophet with shame and terror in the magnificent vision that called him to the prophetic ministry.[1] The law of holiness is exemplified, as in Amos, by the requirement of social justice, as in Hosea, by that of personal devotion. 'The Lord of hosts shall be exalted in judgement, and God that is holy shall be sanctified in righteousness.' The sin of the people is that 'they have cast away the law of the Lord of hosts and despised the word of the Holy One of Israel'.[2] Isaiah is distinguished from his predecessors by the long stretch of his prophetic activity, and by his position as a recognized political adviser of the king.[3] Within the state he preached justice towards the peasantry who formed, as in northern Israel, the backbone of the nation, and the need of realizing religious obligations as an integral part of ordinary life.[4] In foreign policy, he urged that

tion to Isaiah and his article (Isaiah) in the *Encyclopaedia Biblica*. For the Second Isaiah, see § 15, below.

1. Is. vi: the vision should be carefully studied. In the traditional religion, the 'holy' thing was *taboo*, i.e. prohibited to human use, as 'charged' with supernatural properties; see Robertson Smith, *Religion of the Semites*, lecture iv (and *note* B) and Joshua vii (story of Achan), 1 Sam. xv (Saul and Agag), 2 Sam. vi (Uzzah and the ark). In Isaiah, the word has a purely inward and spiritual reference, to consecration and purification of the heart. The fact that the same word is used as the title of the temple-prostitutes, set apart for the sensual rites of the sanctuary, which were not suppressed till the Deuteronomic reformation, will serve as a measure of the gulf between the higher prophecy and the popular religion of the day.

2. Is. v. 24.

3. Cf. his relations with Ahaz at the time of the Syro-Ephraimitish invasion (735–4), Is. vii. 1–16, and with Hezekiah at the time of Sennacherib's invasion (701), 2 Kings xviii. 13–xx (from which source Is. xxxvi–xxxix is mainly derived).

4. Condemnation of injustice and luxury, Is. i. 21–3, iii. 16–23, v. 8–23, x. 1–3; cf. Mic. ii. 2, iii. 2–3, 11.

Condemnation of sorcery and witchcraft, Is. ii. 6, viii. 19.

Condemnation of idolatry, Is. i. 29–30, ii. 8, 18, 20; cf. Mic. i. 7.

Judah should steer clear of international entanglements, especially of alliance with Egypt and other powers against Assyria.[1] 'Take heed and be quiet' was his early counsel to Ahaz, repeated years afterwards to Hezekiah in face of Sennacherib's onset, 'in quietness and confidence shall be your strength'.[2] The ruin of the Assyrian army established Isaiah's authority in the eyes of the king and of the people. It did more than this, for it gave Judah a breathing-space to absorb the lesson of the prophetic teaching. In the northern kingdom, disaster had followed swiftly on the warnings of Amos and Hosea. Neither among the captives in Assyria nor among the relics in Palestine did any trace of the religion of Yahweh survive. Had Judah suffered a like fate at the hand of Sennacherib, before the religious life of her people had won new power from Isaiah's message, the faith in a purely national God would have perished with the nation's downfall. But Isaiah's confidence was justified by the event; the danger passed, and the rapid decline of the Assyrian power staved off the fall of Judah for a century. When that fall came at the hands of Babylon, Isaiah's message had taken root. Already in his lifetime a faithful remnant gathered round him and formed the nucleus of a religious community within, and distinct from, the nation. In this band of disciples [3] the prophet saw the promise of an eventual restoration, after Yahweh had visited his judgement upon the existing state; of a purified Zion, under a prince of the old Davidic line and with a sovereignty over the surrounding peoples; of an Israel made holy by suffering and living its national life in perfect accordance with Yahweh's law. 'Therefore, saith the Lord, the Lord of hosts, the Mighty One of Israel, Ah, I will ease me of mine adversaries and avenge me of mine enemies; and I will turn my hand upon thee, and purely purge away thy dross, and take away all thy

---

Condemnation of priests and prophets, Is. xxviii. 7 f., xxx. 8 f.; Mic. ii. 11, iii. 5–7, 11.

1. The Egyptian alliance is denounced in Is. xxx–xxxi.

2. Is. vii. 4, xxx. 15.

3. Is. viii. 16, which means probably 'I will tie up the testimony and seal the teaching in the heart of my disciples'; cf. Jer. xxxi. 33. The Jewish papyriat Assouan (fifth century B.C.) were found tied up and sealed.

tin; and I will restore thy judges as at the first, and thy coun-
sellors as at the beginning; afterward thou shalt be called the
city of righteousness; the faithful city.' [1] The note of hope had
been sounded, and henceforward the faith in a restoration of
Israel persisted, with ever-growing intensity, as an essential
feature in Hebrew prophecy.

§ 9. Isaiah's influence bore fruit, possibly in his own lifetime, and certainly, after a period of reaction under Manasseh,
in the religious reformation under king Josiah (639–608). The
Deuteronomic code, officially promulgated in 621, was the
work of his school and is pervaded throughout by the spirit of
his teaching.[2] Its aim was intensely practical, to bring the
actual daily life of the Hebrews into conformity with the prophetic ideal. All idolatry and image-worship were forbidden,
together with other survivals of Canaanitish cults; social relations and religious observances alike were regulated in the
spirit of the prophets.[3] Above all, the local sanctuaries were
ruthlessly abolished, and the purified religious worship centralized in the temple at Jerusalem. Had the mass of the nation
proved capable of following in the path thus marked out for
them, the Deuteronomic legislation might have furnished an

---

1 Is. i. 24–6; cf. vii. 3, xxviii. 16 f. Isaiah, the native of Jerusalem and royal
adviser, has none of the prejudice against the city, and in favour of a reversion
to nomadic life, that is characteristic of his prophetic predecessors. If c. ix.
1–7 and c. xi are Isaianic, as many authorities hold them to be, they afford the
most striking expressions of the hope of restoration. The passage in c. xi has had
a memorable history. The fourth Eclogue of the Roman poet Virgil contains
lines that are closely analogous; cf. Ecl. iv. 21 f., v. 60 and Is. xi. 6–8. This
resemblance in Virgil to a prophecy which was interpreted as referring to
Christ goes far to account for the peculiar reverence felt towards Virgil in
early Christian and in mediaeval times. Cheyne notes (Religious Life, p. 103
note) that in the cathedral of Zamora in Spain Virgil is represented among the
Hebrew prophets. Probably both Virgil and the Hebrew prophet gave independent expression to a common oriental idea.

2. It is contained in Deut. v–xxvi, and is a republication of older law,
modified by the prophetic teaching. For the story of the reformation, see
2 Kings xxii–xxiii.

3. Isaiah had condemned the worship of images and of spirits in trees
(i. 29 f., xvii. 10). Image-worship had already been condemned by Hosea (viii.
4–6, x. 5, xiii. 2) whose influence on Deuteronomy was greater than that of
any other of the eighth-century prophets. Deuteronomy enjoins humanity and
justice towards the widow and the orphan, the slave, the foreign settler, and
even dumb animals.

efficient instrument of reformation. But this was not to be;
the prophetic ideal remained an ideal, impotent to change
the hearts, save of a small minority. The contrast between
precept and practice is as evident on the eve of the ruin of
Jerusalem as it had been on the eve of the ruin of Samaria.

§ 10. It was this obstinate rejection of Yahweh's declared
will that branded itself upon the soul of Jeremiah.[1] Once
again, the enemy was at the gates; not the Assyrians, whose day
of empire had passed, but Nebuchadrezzar of Babylon. The
hour of captivity was at hand, and the death-throes of Judah
found utterance in the prophet's cry of despairing anguish.
Jeremiah, the priest from Anathoth, had in his youth championed the Deuteronomic reformation; but now it seemed a
hollow mockery, and its watchword 'the temple of Yahweh' a
shibboleth of lying priests and prophets. The temple of Zion,
the sanctuary of the renovated ritual, would share the doom of
that of Shiloh. 'How do ye say, we are wise and the law of the
Lord with us? Lo, certainly in vain made he it; the pen of the
scribes is in vain.' 'A wonderful and horrible thing is come to
pass in the land; the prophets prophesy falsely, and the priests
bear rule by their means; and my people love to have it so:
and what will ye do in the end thereof?'[2] Jeremiah's call was

1. Jeremiah first came forward as a prophet in 626, at the time of the
Scythian invasion, described by Herodotus (i. 103 f.), which called forth the
prophecies in Jer. iv–vi. Zephaniah, possibly a prince of the blood royal, pro-
phesied at the same crisis (see Zeph. ii. 3 f.). The Scythians helped to weaken
the declining power of Assyria; they annihilated the Philistines and reached
the borders of Egypt, but Judah seems to have been spared. Zephaniah saw in
their coming the 'day of Yahweh', see Zeph. i. 14 f., a passage which inspired
the Christian hymn *Dies irae, dies illa*. Jeremiah survived the final capture of
Jerusalem by Nebuchadrezzar in 586. The chief of his prophecies are contained
in cc. i–xxiv; the restoration-prophecies in cc. xxx–xxxiii have been questioned by some recent critics, but are accepted by Wellhausen, Driver and
Cornill, as substantially the work of Jeremiah (except xxxiii. 14–26). We are
told (c. xxxvi) that the earlier prophecies were republished *with additions* by
Baruch at Jeremiah's command many years after their delivery. The prophecies of Nahum (c. 612, the date of the fall of Nineveh) and Habakkuk
(shortly before 600) belong to the same epoch. Habakkuk gives a new turn to
the conception of 'the day'; as in the popular view, it is a day of Israel's
triumph over Assyria, but interpreted ethically is a triumph of the *righteous*
nation over the *wicked*.

2. Jer. viii. 8, v. 30, 31. On Jeremiah's early preaching of the Deuteronomic law, see c. xi. 1–8; on the temple worship, see c. vii; on the false

to a worship resting not on the formalities of the temple-service, but on inward purity of heart. He appealed from external ordinance and book-religion to a spiritual temple and spiritual sacrifices. In clearer tones than any preceding prophet, he gave utterance to the claims of personal religion. Those of a later age who pleaded against legalism in the name of inward piety looked back with good reason to Jeremiah as a source of inspiration.[1] This tragedy of a sensitive and retiring nature, compelled by an imperious call to denounce the disobedience of rulers and people, and to foretell their impending ruin, appealed with compelling force to the imagination of after-times. Fearless, amid continual risk to life, in the discharge of his vocation, 'like a lamb or an ox that is brought to the slaughter', a hero, as a sympathetic writer has said, not by nature but by grace, Jeremiah was keenly conscious of his isolation. There was not one that doeth justly, that seeketh truth, in all Jerusalem.[2] He longed in vain to be freed from the agony of his mission: 'Oh, that I had in the wilderness a lodging-place of wayfaring men; that I might leave my people and go from them! for they be all adulterers, an assembly of treacherous men.'[3] Jeremiah is the pioneer of the religious lyric and the inspirer of many of the Psalms; some have even seen in him the model for Isaiah liii. Despairing of national repentance, 'Can the Ethiopian change his skin, or the leopard his spots? then may ye also do good, that are accustomed to do evil,'[4] he found refuge in the thought of a new covenant, not as of old between Yahweh and the nation, but between Yahweh and the individual Israelite. 'In those days they shall say no more, the fathers have eaten a sour grape and

prophets, c. xiv. 13–16, xxiii. 9 ff., and c. xxviii, where Hananiah, Jeremiah's adversary, stands for the political faith that inspired Josiah's reformation.

1. Cf. Jeremiah's spiritual conception of the new covenant, xxxi. 31–4, quoted below in the text, with, e.g. Ps. xl. 6–8. It is noteworthy that Jeremiah is the forerunner of a religion that is both inward personal communion of the individual with God and universal in its appeal not only to the Jew but to all mankind. In both respects he heralded the spirit of Christianity, as Ezekiel heralded that of later Judaism.

2. Jer. xi. 19: the writer quoted is Cheyne; Jer. v.1. On the attempts to take his life, see xi. 18 ff. (the men of his native Anathoth), xviii. 18, xxvi. 8 ff., xxxviii. 4.

3. Jer. ix. 2; cf. Ps. lv. 5–8.   4. Jer. xiii. 23.

the children's teeth are set on edge. But every one shall die for his own iniquity: every man that eateth the sour grape, his teeth shall be set on edge. . . . This shall be the covenant that I will make with the house of Israel after those days, saith the Lord; I will put my law in their inward parts, and write it in their hearts; and will be their God and they shall be my people: and they shall teach no more every man his neighbour, and every man his brother, saying, know the Lord: for they shall all know me, from the least of them unto the greatest of them, saith the Lord: for I will forgive their iniquity and I will remember their sin no more.' [1] This utterance strikes a new note in the spiritual education of Israel. The vision of earlier prophets had been dimmed by the absorption of the individual in the life and destiny of the nation. It was not till Jeremiah realized that the true Israel was narrowed to himself that this prejudice could be overcome. Henceforward a consciousness of the worth of personal religion in Yahweh's sight was an abiding possession of Hebrew prophecy. Judah indeed passed into captivity before Jeremiah's eyes, and the gulf that severed the ideal from the actual seemed more impassable than at any previous moment of history. The chief of the people were deported to Babylon in 597; eleven years later Jerusalem was laid in ruins and the Jewish state ceased to exist (586). But Jeremiah's faith in Yahweh as the living God of Israel was unshaken by the political dissolution of the nation. Nebuchadrezzar was Yahweh's servant, and Yahweh had delivered Israel into his hand.[2] The prophet's mission was destined to a richer fulfilment than he dreamed of. If, to all appearance, his words had failed to save the nation's soul, the reverse was literally the truth. Borne away by the captives into exile, they were pregnant with vitalizing energy for the coming time. The hour of secular downfall furnished the occasion for Israel to enter upon her spiritual mission to mankind.

III. THE EXILE AND AFTER

§ 11. The captivity in Babylonia made a profound impression on the original history of the exiles. The temple at Jerusalem,

1. Jer. xxxi. 29–34.   2. Jer. xxvii.

where religious worship had been centralized under the Deuteronomic reformation, lay in ruins.[1] The chosen people lay,
as it were, under an interdict. The hope of the old popular
religion, that Yahweh would save Israel from her enemies,
had been rudely shattered; the 'day', as Amos and Isaiah had
predicted, had proved a day of darkness and not of light. Had
it not been for the seed of a higher faith implanted by the
teaching of the prophets, the exiles might well have been
absorbed, in accordance with the intention of their conquerors,
in the religious and national life of Babylonia. But in fact it was
otherwise; the very circumstance of their isolation gave fresh
vitality to what was highest and most distinctive in their faith.
It proved, first, a powerful stimulus to the religion of personal
piety, which had found expression in the prophecies of Jeremiah. The individual soul sought consolation and refuge in
personal communion with Yahweh. Secondly, in sharp contrast to this devotion of the heart, the exiles recalled with
loyal attachment the traditions of the old temple-worship;
and they gathered, in close and loving study, the inheritance
of ceremonial lore. Priestly scribes interpreted and developed
the law; sabbath-meetings were held for prayer and the reading
of the prophets; fasting and corporate humiliation became the
practice; and the congregation began to take the place of the
vanished nation. The age of the exile was that of the foundation of the Jewish church. Priestly authority and ecclesiastical
institutions acquired a new value. The conviction grew that the
religion of Yahweh could be preserved only by strict fulfilment
of legal precept. The same symptoms were repeated in later
times, both after the restoration in the fifth century, and again
in the legalism of Rabbinic teaching, after the destruction of
the second temple by the Romans and the final dispersion of
the Jewish people. In the third place, the exiles turned for
comfort and hope to the vision of a restored Zion, when
Israel should once more dwell in his own land, and princes
of the lineage of David rule in righteousness as ministers of

---

1. The site was, however, not inaccessible (see Jer. xli. 5) and a continuous
life seems to have gone on among those left in Judaea, though they lacked
sufficient energy to effect any restoration.

Yahweh's will. This is the predominant note of exilic and post-exilic prophecy. The word of Yahweh was no longer one of anger and impending doom. Now that the judgement had fallen on Israel's sin, Yahweh revealed himself in loving-kindness, as the gracious deliverer and redeemer of his people. These three characteristics of the exilic epoch are already manifest in the prophecy of Ezekiel, a Hebrew priest deported to Babylonia in 597, whose prophetic work belongs to the opening years of the captivity (592–570). His book leaves on the reader a strong impression of the unity of its structure, and it may be that it exists to-day very nearly as Ezekiel wrote it by the banks of the Chebar five and twenty centuries ago. Yet it is possible that, as some critics hold, part of the work was written in Jerusalem, and that portions (e.g. of the closing chapters) were added by a later hand. Unlike earlier prophecy, it is largely a literary composition rather than a collection of spoken utterances, though it contains some oral prophecies,[1] and comprises a sequence of discourses arranged in methodical order by his own hand. It abounds in vision and symbolism, and reflects throughout the temper of the priestly theologian.[2] Ezekiel (a) was uncompromising in his assertion of individual responsibility and retribution. He broke once and for all with the traditional conception of Yahweh as a jealous God, visiting the sins of the fathers upon the children. Each man stands or falls in Yahweh's sight by his own acts. 'The son shall not bear the iniquity of the father, neither shall the father bear the iniquity of the son; the righteousness of the righteous shall be upon him, and the wickedness of the wicked shall be upon him.'[3] There is no thought yet of retribution in a future life. Earthly prosperity and misfortune are apportioned in accordance with moral desert. We shall see in a later section how this exaggerated individualism failed to satisfy the developed moral

1. Ezek. xxxiii. 30, 31. On these disputed questions see the Introduction to Cooke's *Ezekiel* in the International Critical Commentary.

2. In Ezekiel we can trace the origin of the apocalyptic literature which later took the place of prophecy; see § 15 below. Unlike pre-exilic prophecy, that of the captivity and after assumes a literary form; it was written down by the prophet himself and not necessarily spoken at all.

3. Ezek. xviii. 20; see the whole chapter and xiv. 12–30, xxxiii. 1–20.

consciousness of the Hebrew people. But, in view of the exclusive insistence of the earlier religious teaching on the claims of the community, it was necessary and natural for Ezekiel to stress, with an equally one-sided emphasis, the complementary claim of the individual, that Yahweh's judgement should be determined by reference to his acts and to his alone. The prophet was confronted with the murmur of the exiles that God's ways were not equal, and his answer, in that it recognized the worth of individual personality, represents an ethical advance. No real progress was possible in moral reflection till the doctrine of personal retribution had been affirmed and found wanting. Again (b), the closing chapters of Ezekiel's book contain the promise of Israel's restoration. Yahweh will gather his scattered sheep out of all lands: 'I will make them one nation in the land, upon the mountains of Israel. . . . and David my servant shall be king over them. . . . My tabernacle also shall be with them; yea, I will be their God and they shall be my people. And the heathen shall know that I the Lord do sanctify Israel, when my sanctuary shall be in the midst of them for evermore.' [1] Ezekiel's horizon is limited to the future of the chosen people; the Gentiles have no place in the Messianic kingdom, but survive the triumph of Israel only to perish in the moment of their acknowledgement of Yahweh's omnipotence.[2] Zeal for Yahweh's honour dominates the whole sequence of Ezekiel's prophecies. Yahweh is bound to restore Israel, so runs his thought, for thus only will his honour be vindicated and his power be made manifest in the sight of all the earth. Hence he dwelt on the immeasurable gulf that parted man's impurity from the holiness of Yahweh. The restored Israel will be made clean. The priest in Ezekiel is clearly manifest in (c) this ideal of ceremonial purity. In the nine concluding chapters, he sketches the ideal constitution for the restored community. The formalism of his outlook and his conception of ritual holiness are obvious on every page. The governing idea was that of a priestly hierarchy, cham-

---

1. Ezek. xxxiii–xlviii, esp. xxxvi; the quotation is from xxxvii. 21–8.
2. Ezek. xxxviii, xxxix. But these eschatological chapters and considerable parts of chapters xl to xlviii may have been added later.

pioned by Messianic princes of the house of David, and regulating the religious life of Israel from a renovated temple. The measurements of the new sanctuary were prescribed in minute detail. Circumcision was commanded not as a national custom, but as a divine ordinance. Ezekiel was the forerunner of the theocratic ideal actually embodied in the institutions of the restoration epoch, and the true father of the Priestly code. Legalism and the conception of a church-nation had come to stay. The age of the prophets was about to give place to that of the law.

§ 12. As it is our purpose, not to review the history of Hebrew religious life in its varied manifestations, but rather to illustrate its bequest to modern civilization, we shall not trace the growth of legalism in the exilic and post-exilic periods, or dwell on the crust of pedantry and formalism which at times obscured the larger teaching of the great prophets.[1] Yet the influence of the prophets on the religion of Israel was never greater than in the centuries succeeding the restoration. 'The view that Ezra's lawbook turned Judaism into an arid ritualism and legalism is refuted by the whole literature of the following time.' So writes Dr Moore,[2] having in mind many of the finest of the Psalms, Proverbs, Job, and additions to the prophetic writings that date from the Persian and Greek periods. It was only very gradually that the prophetic inspiration was choked; it remained a living force until the ascendancy of Pharisaism. The centuries which followed the restoration were of crucial significance for the subsequent

1. After the law had established its autocracy as the complete system of divine commands in the restored community, there was no longer room for *personal* inspiration. Hence no new writer could come forward without the *imprimatur* of the law. Additions to the prophetic writings were ascribed to prophets (e.g. Daniel) anterior to the law. Pride of authorship was foreign to the Semitic temper and to the spirit of Hebrew prophecy; the titles ascribing prophecies to their authors are additions of later date. The apocalyptic that took the place of prophecy (see below, § 16) was pseudonymous. Rabbinical Judaism, which was legalistic, turned its back on apocalyptic in the first century A.D., leaving the field to Christian writers and apocalypses. Christian apocalyptic, freed from bondage to the law, threw over pseudonymity, but Jewish apocalyptic retained it through the early centuries of our era and the middle age. See Charles, *Eschatology*, pp. 196 ff., 403 f.

2. *Judaism*, I. 16.

history of Judaism. In them were determined the essential lines of its religious and moral practice for after-time. When Cyrus conquered Babylon, he granted leave to the exiles to return to their homes (538–7). A century later (458) the restored community was joined by a priestly company under Ezra, who brought with him a renovated law, the work of Babylonian Jews. This law, promulgated by Ezra in 397, served henceforward as the guiding rule of the community. The Deuteronomic law was transformed into the Priestly code and the traditions of the past were re-edited as the Priestly history. The Pentateuch ~umed a form virtually identical with that in which we read it in our Bibles to-day. The note of Ezra's reconstruction was that already sounded by Ezekiel, of sacerdotalism. An artificial Israel, a congregation rather than a state, inspired by the ideal of Levitical holiness, gathered under the presidency of the high priest around the temple-worship at Jerusalem.[1] Everything in Israel, so ran the post-exilic teaching, is Yahweh's by right; if the prescribed dues are paid, he will send his blessing on the remainder. The principle was a noble one; but its application by the casuists became well-nigh unbearable.[2] The breach of ritual prescriptions, often devoid of ethical significance, came to be regarded as sin of equal gravity with violations of the moral law; for both alike, as commands of Yahweh, were of unconditioned obligation.[3] In course of time the authority of the scribes, whose task was to edit and expound the law, tended to replace that of the priestly corporation.[4] Judaism became more and

1. The second temple was built in 516; the tone of this period is reflected in Haggai and Zechariah, i–viii. On external holiness, see Lev. xii.; xiv. 1–18, 33–53; xv. 16–30. It is well, however, to remember Kuenen's remark (Religion of Israel, ii. 285): 'We cannot but own that they were grand and beautiful designs which the lawgiver' (of the Priestly code) 'had in view. He formed broadly the idea of a holy people dedicated to Yahweh, and tried to realize it on a large scale'.

2. See Inge: Outspoken Essays, St Paul, pp. 211, 215–16, on the 'seminary education' under the Rabbis in apostolic times.

3. See, for example, Exod. xxx. 33, Lev. x. 1–16, xiv. 33–53, and Lev. generally.

4. After the close of the Persian period in 332, the scribes appear as a class distinct from the priesthood.

more the religion of a sacred book.[1] From this source sprang
the oral law, with its ever-growing burden. Above all, the bar
of separation between the Jew who observed the reconstituted law, on the one hand, and the heretic Samaritan and
heathen Gentile, on the other, was made absolute. The rite of
circumcision, the hall-mark of national particularism, was presented in the Priestly history as an integral part of the religion
of Yahweh, the sign of his everlasting covenant with Abraham.
We can see the reason that prompted the Jews of the restoration to prescribe this rigorous exclusiveness. Under the
Persian, and especially under the Macedonian empires, contact between East and West grew more intimate, racial barriers were gradually broken down, and the pious worshippers
of Yahweh might easily have lost their identity and been
merged in the heathen world around them, had they not fenced
in their distinctive faith, and therewith their distinctive
nationality, with a ring-wall of ceremonial law. They alone
were holy to Yahweh, all others were uncircumcised and pro-
fane. This consciousness of a peculiar vocation, and the unswerving resolve to be loyal to its obligations, were intensified
in the second century by the persecution of Antiochus Epiphanes (175–164), and subsequently by the conquest by Rome.
We can trace to this period the origin of the astonishing per-
sistency that marks Jewish religion and Jewish racial character
through all succeeding history. There is unquestionably a
grandeur in the spectacle of a small and despised people,
bereft of the natural and political bulwarks of unity, thus forg-
ing artificial stanchions, which availed to preserve their
nationality as a rock amid the storms that beat on every side.
The price paid was heavy, the imposition of a burden too
grievous to be borne, and the final closing of the door to
spiritual fellowship with the Gentile world. Henceforward, it
was only by a revolutionary breach with Jewish orthodoxy

1. The canon of scripture was not yet fixed even in the first century A.D.
Christianity took over the Jewish scriptures and therewith the doctrine of
literal inspiration; adding the N.T., which was much more homogeneous in
contents and in plane of spiritual teaching than the O.T. With the effects of a
book-religion on pre-Christian Judaism we may compare those of its revival
after the Reformation, still discernible to-day.

that the spirit of the religion of the prophets could permeate western civilization. We must look elsewhere than to the law for the main legacy of Israel to mankind.[1] The law was the shell rather than the kernel of post-exilic religious life. Side by side with ceremonial formalism developed a religion of inward piety and devotion. Side by side with the particularism of the orthodox congregation broke the vision of an ideal kingdom in Zion which should embrace all nations, and bring salvation not only to the Israelite, but to the Gentile.[2]

§ 13. It was entirely natural that this twofold expression of religious faith, the ideals of a personal communion with God

1. This statement must not be taken as a denial of the obvious influence exercised by the Mosaic law on the history of Christianity. For example, the moral precepts contained in the Pentateuch left a deep mark on Christian ethics. Christianity, when fused with Hellenism, preserved the lofty moral code which it inherited from Judaism. It is only necessary to mention the Decalogue. Again, the history of the priesthood and of Christian sacerdotalism was influenced by the Jewish priestly code and the Jewish conception of the priestly office. The epistle to the Hebrews is an early illustration of this influence, which left its mark also on the Christian doctrine of atonement. Yet the Christian priesthood, unlike the Jewish, was never hereditary and often celibate. Christian juridical thought was also influenced by the Mosaic law as is evident from Aquinas' tractate *de legibus* (S. Th. ii. 1. qq. 90–108). The Mosaic law served as a model for modifications introduced by Constantine and his Christian successors in the empire into the criminal law of Rome 'The laws of Moses', wrote Gibbon (c. 44), 'were received as the divine original of justice, and the Christian princes adapted their penal statutes to the degrees of moral and religious turpitude': e.g. adultery was made a capital offence. This juridical influence of the Jewish law received a strong impetus at the time of the Reformation. Prior to that time, it did not seriously affect the actual laws of western peoples. Alfred refers to Moses in the prologue to his Anglo-Saxon code, but the laws that follow show no trace of the influence On the other hand, Protestant communities frequently embodied Mosaic precepts in their legislation. In a manifesto issued by the German peasantry in 1525, we find the demand 'that all doctors of laws should be abolished and that justice should be administered according to the law of Moses, because it is not good for man to get better law than that proclaimed by God' (Vinogradoff Roman Law in Medieval Europe, p. 129). The early colonists in Massachusetts refused to adopt trial by jury on the ground that it was not authorized in 'Moses his judicials'. The death penalty for witchcraft and for sabbath-breaking, there and elsewhere in Puritan communities, was justified by reference to Mosaic authority. Of Luther's teaching, J. N. Figgis writes (From Gerson to Grotius, p. 209): 'law is for Luther, whether natural, moral, or civil, all embodied in the ten commandments, and anything else is mere administrative regulation, whether in state or church'.

2. See Additional Note at the close of this chapter, on post-exilic Jewish history.

and of his universal kingdom, should arise coincidently with the particularism of the law. An illustration of this tendency of the extremes of individualism and universalism to meet in intimate conjunction is afforded by contemporary Hellenism, where, on the decay of the free city-state after the Macedonian conquest, the Stoic philosophers insisted equally on the claims of individual virtue and on membership of a cosmopolitan society. Both ideals are prominent in Jewish religious literature of the exilic and post-exilic epochs. In regard to the former, it is very necessary to observe, especially after what has been said about the formalism that marked the institution of the Priestly code, how the rule of the law fostered in the Jewish community a lofty moral standard and a rich vein of piety. The strength of the religion of Israel was, in part, rooted in its very weakness.[1] The local synagogue, with its meetings for public prayer and for the reading and interpretation of scripture, proved a powerful stimulus to individual religion. Still more noteworthy is the fact that the temple-worship itself nurtured a spirit of fervent piety, which won enduring expression in the Psalter. The product of many successive compilations, ranging in date from the period of the captivity to the second century, these songs of unknown authorship, comprising the Psalter, have been called with good reason 'the hymn-book of the second temple'.[2] They testify on every page how the heart of the individual Jew beat in unison with that of his religious community. He lived and

1. Mr Claude Montefiore, in the Hibbert Lectures for 1892 on *Hebrew Religion*, has shown clearly how the law fostered the higher moral and spiritual life of the post-exilic community. The ethical results of 'legalism' were not what might *a priori* have been expected. 'One needs,' he says, 'to be very cautious in writing about the law' (p. 478, *note* 1). Chastity, benevolence, and, above all, joy in loving service marked the life of the orthodox followers of the law. It was not felt as a burden by the Jew; though from the point of view of universalism it was a burden. In this chapter the religion of Israel is treated exclusively from this standpoint; its value within the pale of Judaism lies beyond our scope. On Judaism in the first century A.D. see Mr Montefiore's chapter, entitled *The Spirit of Judaism*, in Jackson and Lake's *The Beginnings of Christianity*, vol. i.

2. Though, unlike our hymn-books, they were never in the hands of the congregation. It is possible that some of the Psalms are pre-exilic, but improbable that any are of Davidic authorship. See Driver, *Introduction*, and Cheyne, *Origin of the Psalter*.

moved and had his being in the life of the spiritual Israel. If
Yahweh is no remote divinity, but 'a very present help in
trouble', it is because he 'watches over Israel'. If his soul
panteth after Yahweh 'as the hart panteth after the water-
brooks', it is because he is parted from the temple-sanctuary,
where the God of heaven and earth has his peculiar dwelling in
the midst of his chosen people.[1] When the Psalmist speaks in
the first person, it is not in his own name but in that of the
spiritual corporation in which his private personality is
absorbed. Some of the Psalms are inspired directly by devotion
to the law; others, in a narrower vein, express the aspirations
and the sufferings of the champions of rigid orthodoxy, the
Chasidim (Asidaeans or 'pious', the forerunners of the Phari-
sees), who laid down their lives in resistance to Hellenism in
the days of Antiochus Epiphanes.[2] Side by side with the utterance of faith in Yahweh and of joy in his presence, we hear the
voice of ancient national memories, of hopes for national
deliverance, and of delight in the worship of the temple.
But the interest of the Psalter for us lies rather in its embodiment of a spirit of religious devotion transcending the narrow
bounds of the priestly worship and the law. The sway that these
poems have exercised over the human heart for more than
2000 years bears witness to the intensity and breadth of feeling
that inspired their nameless authors by the waters of Babylon
and in the restored community of Palestine. In certain Psalms
personal piety consciously breaks through the barriers of
external prescript, and appeals from the written law to that inscribed upon the heart.[3] It is this variety and wealth of religious
emotion, embracing all the moods in which the human spirit
turns towards God, alike in good and evil days, that has made
the Psalter the hymn-book, not merely of the second temple,
but of Judaism in all ages, and also of the Christian church.

1. Ps. xlii.
2. Devotion to the law, esp. Ps. cxix. Ps. i. expresses the feelings of the
'pious' or 'righteous', in contrast with the 'wicked', 'sinners', 'the scornful'
(cf. xii. 1). Reference to the temple is conspicuous in Pss. xxiv, xxvii, lxv,
cxxxviii. For an outline classification of the themes of the Psalter, see Driver,
Introduction, pp. 368–9.
3. E.g. Pss. xl, l, li.

§ 14. If the pious Israelite found satisfaction for his aspirations in the practical religion of the temple-service and in
observance of the law, he was at the same time confronted
with an ethical and theological problem which caused grave
searchings of heart. The doctrine of Ezekiel, echoed in certain
of the Psalms,[1] that each man is duly rewarded or punished
for his deserts in the course of his earthly life, could not maintain its hold in the face of facts. The fortunes of the individual
were manifestly dependent on those of his fellows; nor was the
meed of outward happiness proportional to his merit. It was
this practical contradiction, rather than any speculative inconsistency, that stirred men to question the divine justice.[2]
Some minds took refuge in the distinction between external
prosperity and inward satisfaction; others in the thought that
the sufferings of the righteous were not punitive, but disciplinary, while the good fortune of the wicked served only to
heighten the eventual catastrophe of his ruin.[3] But the conception of suffering as retributive for sin was too deeply
rooted in the Hebrew mind for such solutions to be acceptable.
The problem which thus arose forms the theme of the dramatic
poem of Job. Why do the wicked prosper and the righteous
suffer unmerited misery? The writer feels that it is unanswer-
able in terms of personal sin; but, while formulating the
difficulty, he offers no adequate solution. The Prologue seems
to give grounds for the suggestion that Job suffered as a
martyr-witness to God's justice while himself remaining unconscious of the purpose of his sufferings, viz., the vindication
of disinterested piety. His final appeal is from the facts of
outward circumstance to the dictates of moral faith; his
practical assurance of Yahweh's righteousness remains unshaken at the close.[4] In a single passage he gives a momentary
suggestion of the hope, which was destined, from the second
century onwards, to gain ground among the Jews, in a resur-

1. E.g. Ps. i. 3; xxxiv. 19–21; Prov. xi. 31.
2. Job xxi. 1–15.   3. Ps. xxxiv. 19; xxxvii. esp. 35, 36.
4. See Dr Robinson's booklet entitled *The Cross of Job* (Religion and Life
Books), pp. 64–69, and Charles, *Eschatology*, pp. 69–73. In the volume on Job
in the *International Critical Commentary* (Driver and Gray), the fifth century is
suggested as the probable date of the poem.

rection of the righteous to enjoy the personal vision of
Yahweh.[1] We shall return presently to this belief, merely
noting here that it emerges not as an inference from speculative premisses, but as a conclusion forced upon the mind by
the practical difficulties of life. This fact is sufficient of itself
to rule out the suggestion that the appearance of the new
belief was due to Hellenic influence. Despite the subjection of
the Jews to Macedonian rule from 332 onwards, the policy of
fusion between West and East fostered by Alexander's successors left little trace on Jewish thought, save at Alexandria
whe   Jewish colony enjoyed a position of peculiar privilege. The   t striking exception in the Old Testament is
offered by the book of Ecclesiastes, written probably towards
the close of the third century, where religious individualism
takes, under Hellenic stimulus, the form of sceptical inquiry.
The words, 'I applied my heart to seek and to search out by
wisdom concerning all that is done under heaven' reflect the
temper of Herodotus.[2] The writer's facile cynicism, 'I have
seen all the works that are done, under the sun; and, behold,

---

1. Job xix. 25–7: see Charles, p. 71, and Driver, *Introduction*, p. 418
('The thought of a future beatific life is *nascent* in the book of Job'). In the
volume on Job in the *International Critical Commentary*, the passage is thus
rendered by Gray:

v. 25.	But I know that my vindicator liveth,
	And that hereafter he will stand up upon the dust.
v. 26.	And . . . .
	And away from my flesh I shall behold God.
v. 27.	Whom I shall behold (to be) on my side,
	And mine eyes shall see (to be) unestranged.

The first half of v. 26 presents almost hopeless difficulty. The word translated
'redeemer' in A.V. means a vindicator from undeserved wrong (see R.V.
marg.). The *I* in v. 27 is emphatic. In his commentary, Gray interprets the
passage as expressing Job's conviction, not of a *continued* life of blessedness
after death, but of a momentary vision of God after death, revealing that God
is with him. On the belief in a resurrection, see below, § 15.

2. Eccles. i. 13, 14; cf. Prov. xxx. 2–4, for a similar scepticism. Greek
influence is traceable also in (possibly) Prov. i–viii and in the book of Eccle-
siasticus, where the ideal of the wise man is sketched, and the doctrine of the
mean and of the value of leisure for the life of wisdom are insisted on (e.g.
Ecclus. xxxviii. 24). The name *Ecclesiastes* is the Greek translation of the
Hebrew *Qohéleth*, which means a public teacher of wisdom. On the *Wisdom*
literature, to which the book of Proverbs belongs, see Driver, *Introduction*,
pp. 392 ff.

all is vanity and a striving after wind,' and his lack of speculative earnestness merely show how uncongenial a medium was the Hebrew mind for the reception of Greek philosophy. The views he affected were the prudential ethics of the Epicureans, the one of all the later Hellenic schools which attached least weight to metaphysical inquiry. The problem of Job is cursorily dismissed by the denial of moral retribution.[1] Ecclesiastes is an isolated figure in Jewish 'wisdom' literature. The sufferings of the martyred *hasidim* under Antiochus Epiphanes and the fierce patriotism of the Maccabaean revolt, provoked by his efforts to impose Hellenism by force, quenched the spirit of intellectual liberty in Palestine, and secured the victory of Jewish particularism.

§ 15. During the captivity the hope of the kingdom became a dominant force in the religious life of Israel. It was of gradual growth and took a variety of specific forms, now narrowed to square with the most rigid nationalism, now enlarged so as to break down every barrier that parted Israel from the Gentile world. It is often associated, especially in the years immediately preceding the birth of Christ, with the belief in the advent of a Messiah, the king of David's line who should deliver Israel and inaugurate Yahweh's kingdom.[2] But this feature is unessential; the core of the conception is the institution of 'a regenerated community, in which the divine will should be realized.'[3] The ancient expectation of 'the day of Yahweh', interpreted no longer as a visitation of wrath upon Israel but as a promise of redemption, was absorbed in the hope of the kingdom, heralded by Isaiah and Jeremiah, and

1. Eccles. viii. 14, ix. 2. Chance rules the world (ix. 11). Epicurean ethics of the less elevated type, akin to Cyrenaicism (iii. 12 f., v. 18 f., ix. 7–10). These and many other passages recall the tone of the *Rubaiyat* of Omar Khayyam.

2. *Messiah* means 'anointed'; its Greek equivalent is *Christos* (Christ). 'Yahweh's anointed' was a term frequently applied to the pre-exilic kings.

3. Charles, *Eschatology*, p. 84. The ideal kingdom is conceived by pre-Christian Judaism sometimes as the rule of a secular prince of Davidic lineage, sometimes as a theocracy under sacerdotal government. There is no mention of the Messiah in Amos, Zephaniah, Nahum, Habakkuk, Joel; nor in Daniel, nor in the late passages, Is. xxiv–xxvii, lxv–lxvi. The kingdom is often conceived as directly under the rule of Yahweh.

explicitly developed by Ezekiel.[1] In Ezekiel's prophecy the
conception is presented in its most exclusive form, as the
establishment of a priestly church, preceded by a merciless
judgement on the Gentiles and unfaithful Jews. The blessings
of the kingdom are reserved for the righteous in Israel, and for
them alone.[2] That this narrow interpretation eventually
triumphed among the Jews of the restoration was due, in part
to the fatal persecution under Antiochus, in part to their
inability to grasp the full meaning of their monotheistic faith.
They could not else have failed to draw the inference that the
God of the whole earth did not restrict his providential care
to a single privileged people, but willed that his knowledge
should, through Israel, be a light for all nations upon earth.
This larger conception of the kingdom did, in fact, receive
expression in exilic and post-exilic prophecy. There was that
in the spiritual life of Israel which would not brook confine-
ment within the bounds prescribed by Ezekiel. Such was the
vision of the kingdom that inspired the message of the Second
Isaiah.[3] He opens with the voice of consolation, 'Comfort ye,
comfort ye, my people', and of assurance of coming redemption, when 'the glory of Yahweh shall be revealed and all
flesh shall see it together'. Though the hope of speedy
deliverance at the hand of Cyrus the Persian is coupled with
remembrance of Israel's past infidelity and reproach for her
present lack of faith,[4] the dominant note is that of confidence
in Yahweh's mercy; He is the gracious Saviour who 'shall
feed his flock like a shepherd' and has freely pardoned the

1. On the 'day', see above, § 4; for Is., see above, § 7; Jer. xxiii. 5, 6,
Ezek. xxxiv. 23 ff., xxxvii. 24 ff. But there is no Messianic hope in Ezekiel
(see Cooke, op. cit., Introduction, p. xxx).

2. Contrast Jer. iv. 2, xii. 14–17, xvi. 19, where the nations are incorporated in the kingdom. The narrower view is reflected in, e.g., Is. lxvi, and
in the prophecy of Joel (c. 400 B.C.).

3. The prophecies of the Second Isaiah are found in cc. xl–lv. They date
from the time of Cyrus's conquest of Babylon (538). Included in these chapters are the four Songs of the Servant of Yahweh, possibly by another writer;
cc. xlii. 1–4, xlix. 1–6, l. 4–9, lii. 13–liii. 12. The last eleven chapters of the
book of Isaiah (lvi–lxvi) are probably by different authors and of later date.
In any case, it may be taken as established that cc. xl–lxvi contain no prophecies of Isaiah himself.

4. Is. xl. 27 f., xlii. 18–25, xlix. 14–21.

transgressions of his people. 'In a little wrath I hid my face from thee for a moment; but with everlasting kindness will I have mercy on thee, saith the Lord thy redeemer.'[1] The call of the Second Isaiah is to faith rather than to repentance. His theology is more conscious and reflective than that of earlier prophets; he enforces his monotheistic convictions as speculative truths, not by dogmatic assertion, but by persuasive argument. Yahweh is the acknowledged creator and sustainer of the universe, the one eternal and infinite God whose almighty hand is manifest throughout all nature and all history. 'Who hath wrought and done it, calling the generations from the beginning? I, the Lord, the first and with the last, I am he.'[2] The last traces of monolatry, as distinct from monotheism, have vanished. The gods of the heathen are idols, things of nought and vanity; 'beside me there is no God'.[3] In full accordance with this clear grasp of the divine unity, the vision pierces beyond the narrow bounds of nationalism, and sees the salvation of all peoples within the restored kingdom.[4] Jerusalem is conceived as the destined metropolis of a universal church; 'the Gentiles shall come to thy light and kings to the brightness of thy rising'[5] It is in the four *Songs of the Servant of Yahweh* that Israel's catholic mission receives its noblest affirmation. There is here no thought of political domination or human sovereignty. Righteous Israel is portrayed as a servant, suffering not for his own sin but for that of his people, 'despised and rejected of men, a man of sorrows and acquainted with grief', sent forth into alien lands to deliver those who are in bondage and to herald the coming of the

1. Is. xl. 11, xliii. 25, liv. 8.
2. Is. xli. 4, cf. xl. 12–end, xlv. 5–8, xliv. 24, li. 13.
3. Is. xliv. 6, cf. xliv. 9–20, xlvi, 1–7.
4. The relationship of the Gentiles to the kingdom is presented in various forms in the last twenty-six chapters of Isaiah. At one time, Israel appears as an imperial power to which all nations owe allegiance, Is. xlv. 14–17 (retribution visited upon the nations), xlix. 7, 22–3, liv. 3. At another, the nations accept Yahweh's kingdom of their own free will, Is. ii. 2–4 (= Mic. iv. 1–3), a post-exilic passage; xxv. 6, 7 (probably c. 300 B.C.).
5. Is. lx. 3; cf. Pss. xxii. 27–31, xlv, lxxxvi, lxxxvii and Is. xix. 18–25, a late and very striking passage, in which Assyria and Egypt are incorporated in the kingdom in complete equality with Israel. See also the allegorical narrative of Jonah.

kingdom. It is no exaggeration to say that these and similar passages from the later chapters of Isaiah left on men's vision an impress of an ideal order of society, that has endured through all after-time. Christians from the first saw in them the closest anticipation of the gospel-kingdom. It was on the *Songs of the Servant* that the Ethiopian eunuch was pondering in his chariot when the deacon Philip met him on the road from Jerusalem to Gaza. The song of Simeon, recorded by St Luke, is evidence that, despite the victory of particularism in the religion of orthodox Judaism, there were those at the time of Christ's coming who cherished the larger hope of the kingdom, as 'a light to lighten the Gentiles and the glory of thy people Israel'.[1] Moreover, it is surely possible that Christ, who took a passage akin to the *Servant* songs as his text when preaching in the synagogue, should have been consciously influenced by them in his own redemptive mission.

§ 16. The doctrine of the kingdom was transformed in a striking manner in the two centuries preceding the birth of Christ, through fusion with the belief, foreign to earlier Jewish thought, in the resurrection from the dead.[2] Alike in popular tradition and in the teaching of the prophets, the kingdom of Yahweh had been conceived as a deliverance of

1. Acts viii. 26 ff., Luke ii. 32.
2. See Charles, *Eschatology*, cc. v and vi. The Jewish belief in a resurrection to life, when it appeared thus late in the day, was in no sense a recrudescence of primitive ideas. It arose out of moral and religious problems that belong to the maturity of Jewish civilization. The religion of Yahweh had gradually killed ancestor-worship, with the associated belief in the continued life of the ghost in *Sheol*. Centuries elapsed before the new ethical faith in a resurrection arose, as explained in the text, out of the developed religion of Yahweh. The conception of a future life was closely connected in Judaism with that of a resurrection from the grave. Among the Greeks, on the other hand, it took shape as the belief in the deathlessness of the soul, whose immortality was intrinsic; there was no question of a resurrection. But the Platonic doctrine of the soul's immortality had this in common with the Jewish doctrine of resurrection, that it was independent of primitive survivals (though it utilized materials drawn from popular religious beliefs). Plato's conviction rested on scientific grounds (and in this stands in sharp contrast with that of the Jews). See below, c. iv. § 17, c. v. §§ 20, 21. The Christian belief in immortality, combined with that in the resurrection of the dead to eternal life, rests on a twofold basis, (a) on post-exilic Judaism (resurrection), (b) on Platonic philosophy (immortality). See C. C. J. Webb, Gifford Lectures (Second Course) on *Divine Personality and Human Life*, pp. 257–64.

Israel to be realized in the future history of the nation upon earth. It was late in the day and under the overmastering stimulus of personal suffering that the Jews were led to associate the hope of the kingdom with that of a resurrection of the righteous to share in its felicity, and, subsequently, with a belief in the immortality of the soul. The traditional view of the soul, for the Hebrews as for other races, was crude and material, closely associated with the cult of ancestors, and devoid of ethical significance. At death the wraith passed to *Sheol*, where it persisted in quasi-bodily form; while the spirit or breath of life, which was distinguished later as the source of the higher psychical faculties, returned to God who gave it. There is here no question of personal immortality or of moral retribution after death.[1] It took long, as we have seen, for the Hebrew mind to grasp the thought of individual responsibility;

1. On the interesting and too much neglected subject of Hebrew psychology, see the Essay (XI) under that title by Principal Wheeler Robinson in *The People and the Book* (ed. Peake), pp. 353–382. For the Hebrews the individual human being (the self) is 'the body as a complex of parts drawing their life and activity from a breath-soul which has no existence apart from the body' (p. 366). The life-principle, including conscious powers, is assigned both to the bodily substance as a whole and to its several members (heart, reins, flesh, bones, eye, hand, etc.). Hebrew psychology knows no dichotomy of soul and body, and *a fortiori* no trichotomy of body, soul, and spirit. The body is the man; personality is animated body, not incarnate soul. The Hebrew word for the life-principle is *néphesh*, usually mistranslated 'soul' in A.V. and R.V. Another term *ruach* (normally translated 'spirit', which originally meant 'wind', regarded as the 'breath' of God) is frequently used with an inspirational implication, to indicate the life-principle as an afflatus or in-breathing of the divine energy acting on man from without, esp. in prophetic inspiration and other exceptional manifestations of life-power. Of man's conscious activities, feeling and emotion are commonly referred to *néphesh*; intellect and (esp.) will (conscience) to *leb* (lit. 'heart'); will being primary in Hebrew ethics, both in God and in man (see above, p. 54, n. 1). The ghost or wraith passed to Sheol as a replica of the whole man and continued his existence in a ghostly state. To regard Sheol as the *habitat* of 'departed spirits' is therefore a grave error; Sheol was peopled solely by these 'shades' (*nephaim*). When, as in the case of Samuel at Endor, the dead are supposed, quite exceptionally, to return, the bodily guise borne when living is continued. So in Homer (Od. xi), the wraiths in Hades need to drink blood in order to recover consciousness and converse with Odysseus. Consequently, when the Hebrews came to conceive a future life, it was as a true resurrection of the body, to provide a renewal of bodily life on earth. The Christian doctrine of the resurrection of the body is strictly faithful to the Hebraic tradition, though it was fortified by opposition to Manichean dualism (the view that matter, and especially the human body, is inherently evil and due to a superhuman evil creator).

until the eve of the exile, the nation was accountable for the sins of its members, and innocent and guilty alike suffered from the retribution which befell the community. Then, with the exile, came a change; the claims of the individual on Yahweh's justice pressed more and more urgently for satisfaction. We have seen how thinkers like the author of Job struggled vainly to find an answer to the problem. It was the stress of persecution under Antiochus that forced the belief in resurrection upon the mind of the Jewish people. Prior to that time it had been confined to a small minority, influenced possibly by contact with Zoroastrian ideas during the epoch of Persian rule. The passages in the Old Testament that allude to it are few and late.[1] When the conviction took root among the Jews, it was in a distinctively Jewish form, in close alliance with the national expectation of the kingdom. The righteous Israelites would rise from *Sheol* to share in the realization of the kingdom upon earth. Thus a solution was reached which vindicated Yahweh's justice towards the individual sufferer, and satisfied the cherished aspiration for the eventual deliverance of Israel. The apocalyptic writings of the second and first centuries show that this belief was no stereotyped dogma, but appeared in a diversity of forms in dependence on the changing course of Jewish history.[2] Many questions were stirring, which admitted

1. The two passages in the O.T. where the belief appears are in the remarkable (late) prophecy in Is. xxiv–xxvii (esp. xxvi. 1–19, resurrection of righteous Israelites, c. 300 B.C.), and the apocalyptic book of Daniel (c. 165 B.C.). In Dan. xii. 2 we find resurrection of (*a*) the eminently righteous, (*b*) the eminently wicked (i.e. apostates from Judaism). In neither passage is there mention of a *general* resurrection. The resurrection is viewed as the return of the ghost to renewed bodily life on earth, the only kind of life conceivable by the Hebrew mind. They never entertained the idea of a disembodied soul.

2. On the nature of apocalyptic (Greek *apocalypsis* = revelation) and its distinction from prophecy, see Charles, *Eschatology*, pp. 173 ff., 387–8. The main differences are that apocalyptic is later in date, pseudonymous, and more comprehensive in range. It essayed a philosophy of religion and of history, seeking to penetrate behind events to their divine purpose, and embracing past, present, and future in a single supernatural scheme, culminating in the advent of the divine kingdom, that last judgement, and the resurrection of the righteous to a blessed future life. It showed a taste for fixing the dates of coming events with chronological precision. Millennarianism is the product of Jewish apocalyptic. It furnished an imaginative outlet for the patriotic spirit among the Jews, who were too weak to realize their national aspirations in action. The numerous Jewish apocalyptic writings are translated by Charles

of varying answers. Was it the righteous Israelites only who rose, or did the wicked and the heathen share in the resurrection? In the latter case, what was the fate of the unfaithful Jew and the Gentile at the judgement preceding the institution of the kingdom? Were the Gentiles admitted to its privileges or reduced to bondage to Israel? These problems were met normally in a spirit of rigorous particularism. Again, of what nature was the intermediate state, between death and the advent of the kingdom? Was the resurrection of the soul only or of the embodied spirit, and what was the form of the resurrection body? Was the kingdom eternal on earth, or of limited duration? What was the function of the Messiah in relation to its institution and to the judgement? As the first century drew on, a further and far-reaching development made its appearance. The conviction grew that this earth was unworthy to be the scene of the consummation of the kingdom, that at the coming of the Messiah, or at the close of his earthly reign, Yahweh would create a new heaven and a new earth, and that, after a final judgement, the soul of the righteous Israelite would pass to an eternal life in the heavenly kingdom. Moreover, the Messiah is sometimes figured as a supernatural 'Son of Man', sometimes as a prince sprung from the lineage of David, who should deliver the Jewish people from the Roman yoke, and inaugurate the earthly kingdom as a prelude to the heavenly and eternal.[1] It would be interesting to follow out these conceptions in Jewish apocalyptic literature after the

in his great work: *The Apocrypha and Pseudepigrapha of the O.T.*; on Christian apocalyptic, see the same writer's edition of the Book of Revelation in the *International Critical Commentary*; and, for a brief survey of the whole subject, his volume entitled *Between the Old and the New Testaments* in the Home University Library. The importance of Jewish apocalyptic for an understanding of the religious environment under which Christianity appeared is very great, and its influence on Christian eschatology proved deep and lasting; e.g. the conceptions of the final judgement, of heaven, and of everlasting punishment have their source in apocalyptic literature.

1. The supernatural Messiah is to be clearly distinguished from the Davidic. Christ's adoption of this title 'Son of Man' gives a peculiar importance to its history. There is no supernatural implication in its frequent use by Ezekiel (cf. Ps. viii, where it stands for humanity in general). In Dan. vii. 13, it is used of Israel as the ideal type of humanity, in contrast to the beasts = heathen kingdoms. In the apocalyptic Enoch i (second century B.C.) it is applied to the supernatural Messiah.

coming of Christ; but enough has been said to show how decisively the spirit of national exclusiveness had triumphed by that date over the larger outlook of earlier prophecy. Rarely in the Jewish writings of the first century B.C. or the first century A.D. is any trace discoverable of the admission of the Gentiles to the kingdom.[1] Monotheism and particularism persist henceforward, despite their essential inconsistency, in the faith of the Jewish community.

IV. CONCLUSION

§ 17. We have traced the course of the prophetic teaching and its issues to the eve of the foundation of Christianity. Two conclusions can be gathered from our survey. In the first place, the religious life of Israel, even in its highest developments, is inseparably blended with characteristic limitations. The strength of Hebrew religion lay in the belief in one sole God and his moral government of the world. Its besetting weakness was the ineradicable presupposition that the divine purpose was concentrated on a single people, chosen out of all the nations to be the peculiar recipients of Yahweh's favour, and that the whole course of nature and of human history revolved, by Yahweh's will, around the life and destiny of Israel. That the policy of artificial isolation intensified religious loyalty, and fostered a moral elevation that forms a contrast to the prevalent laxity of Graeco-Roman and Graeco-Oriental practice, is undeniable; but it excluded the Gentile from any share in the spiritual inheritance. Jewish religious history is full of these strange anomalies and paradoxical contrasts. The humility which springs from the sense of personal sin was coupled with a fierce and intolerant pride in membership of a righteous community, the spirit of inward piety with a meticulous scrupulosity in regard to external observances. The faith in God's continual presence and in his providential ordering of every incident of common life gave rise to an equal respect for the essentials of moral duty and for the puerile regulations of a

1. But IV Esdras is an exception.

ritual code.[1] Thus the Hebrew people failed to realize effectively the larger hope of the prophets, or to complete their appointed mission in the spiritual education of mankind. If we seek the underlying reason of this failure, if we ask why it was that they never grasped the incompatibility of particularism with the faith in a single moral ruler of the universe, we must point in answer to their intellectual limitations. Unlike the Greek, the Hebrew did not think things out. He never attained to the plane of intellectual development at which reason claims a voice in the determination of religious and ethical beliefs.[2] This is why the noblest utterances of Hebrew piety defy systematization in a coherent body of theological truth, and are riddled with inconsistencies and contradictions, of which their authors remain entirely unaware. Thus again we can explain what may be termed the contingency of Hebrew religious thought, the fact, noted frequently above, that its utterances are determined by the sequence of historical incidents which happened to affect the Hebrew nation. These incidents suggested not only the occasion, but in large measure the content, of Hebrew prophecy. The more bitter the humiliation, the more intense the sufferings, of the chosen

1. So also God's transcendence and his immanence as indwelling in the heart of the righteous, his justice and his mercy, the doctrine of strict retribution and that of free forgiveness, the hope of future reward for meritorious acts and the pursuit of goodness for its own sake, determinism and freedom, the wrath and the love of God, are combined in Jewish religious thought, though the *speculative* difficulties are never thoroughly grasped.

2. When the intellect did come into play, it tended towards casuistry, formalism, and the barren logic of the schools. At the same time, continuity was preserved between the highest spiritual teaching and the religion of the people. The Jewish prophets succeeded here, where the Greek philosophers failed (see Webb, Gifford Lectures, First Series, on *God and Personality*, pp. 85, 86.) The personal relationship of Yahweh to his Jewish worshipper was unimpaired at all levels of religious apprehension. We may note also that while the close connexion between Hebrew prophecy and the historic crises of the nation tied Yahweh's purposes and will down to temporal events, it gave the Jews a strong sense of the moral significance of history. They were never tempted, as Greek philosophers were often tempted, to divorce ideal values from the course of facts. 'The whole of history is an unfolding of the divine purpose; and so history as a whole has for the Jew an importance which it never had for the Greek thinker, nor for the Hellenised Jew, Philo. The Hebrew idea of God is dynamic and ethical; it is therefore rooted in the idea of time' (Inge, *Outspoken Essays*, St Paul, p. 215). This sense for the value of historic fact impressed itself strongly on Christian thought; see Vol. 2, c. ix.

people, the stronger grew their certainty of eventual redemption. The spiritual vision of Israel expanded in inverse ratio to her secular achievement. The logic, for a logic it needs must have, was in part that of historic circumstance, in part the inward logic of the conscience. Only it was never, from first to last, the logic of the intellect. Thus, finally, it was granted to the prophets to see truths, now one and now another, in their isolation and independence; it was not granted them to know the truth. This is the reason why, even apart from the restrictions of the law, the Hebrews were incapable of conveying the import of their spiritual vision to the people of the West. For this to be possible, the several truths needed to be moulded into a coherent whole, the essential to be distinguished from the irrelevant, the implications unfolded, and the relative validity of each truth defined, by a process at once of clarification and of enlargement. Thus only could the prophetic teaching issue in a religious faith that appealed not merely to the heart, but to the mind. Was it credible that so radical a transformation should take effect save at the cost of a breach with Judaism?

§ 18. In the second place, the religious life of Israel furnished the historical antecedents of Christianity. Christ himself recognized this affiliation when he declared that he came not to destroy the law, but to fulfil. For St Paul, the apostle of the Gentiles, the law was a schoolmaster to lead men to Christ. It was through the mediation of Christianity that the spiritual inheritance of Israel was transmitted to the western world. In the process of transmission it was remoulded and transformed; much that was distinctive of Judaism was dropped, and what was assimilated became the groundwork of a new structure. Henceforward the two religions went their several ways; the consciousness of historical relationships served but to widen the chasm that parted them. The continuity is most apparent in the conception of the divine kingdom. It was natural that the disciples of the new faith should turn for anticipations of the gospel to the prophets rather than to the law. For to the prophets had been revealed the vision of 'the day of Yahweh', when justice shall prevail

and oppression and wrong shall vanish, when men 'shall beat
their swords into ploughshares and their spears into pruning-
hooks: nation shall not lift up sword against nation, neither
shall they learn war any more', when 'they shall not hurt nor
destroy in all my holy mountain; for the earth shall be full of
the knowledge of the Lord, as the waters cover the sea'.[1]
Their reception of these truths had been trammelled by limitations, by their prejudice for the prerogatives of the peculiar
people, their failure to reconcile the spiritual claim of the
individual with that of the community, their imperfect
realization of divine immanence, and their relegation of the
ideal society to future time. In the teaching of the gospel, the
thought of the kingdom was freed, once and for all, from
these restrictions. The individual could find salvation and win
eternal life only through incorporation in the divine society,
whose members were bound one to another in their personal
relationship to its head. The barriers of nationalism were at
length and for ever broken down; the doors of the kingdom
were opened to Jew and Gentile, Greek and barbarian, bond
and free; and a faith that bridged the gulf which had severed
the divine from the human united all mankind in the bonds of
universal brotherhood. Once more, the institution of the
kingdom was conceived as no remote event, but as a present
fact, a living reality, actual in the hearts of men, 'on earth as
it is in heaven'.[2] But the seeds of this doctrine, so fruitful for
the spiritual regeneration of humanity, were planted in the

1. Is. ii. 4 = Mic. iv. 3; Is. xi. 9 = Hab. ii. 14.
2. On the kingdom as present fact: Mark iv. 11, 30 ff. (the grain of mus-
tard seed), x. 14, xii. 34; also Matt. v. 3 = Luke vi. 20, Matt. vi. 33 = Luke
xii. 31.

On the kingdom as not yet come: Mark i. 15 ('at hand'); also Matt. viii. 11,
xxii. 2 ff., and the parables of the treasure hid in a field and the pearl of great
price.

On the kingdom as eternal life in the age to come: Mark ix. 43 ff.,
x. 17 ff.; also Matt. vii. 21 ff.

See Jackson and Lake, *Prolegomena I.* to the *Acts of the Apostles*, pp. 278 ff.,
whence the above references are taken. They all occur either in Mark or in
the portions of Matthew and Luke that can be assigned to a common source,
styled Q, co-ordinate in value with Mark. Charles (*Eschatology*, pp. 364 ff.)
cites Matt. xii. 28, Luke iv. 18–21 (kingdom as present), Mark ix. 1 (future,
in heaven), Matt. xviii. 3, 4 and Luke xviii. 17 (both present and future).

soil of Hebrew prophecy. It is for this reason that not the Jew only, but the Christian, can admit the claim of Israel to the title of the chosen people. 'You only have I known of all the families of the earth.' To Israel alone of the peoples of the pre-Christian world was vouchsafed the vision of the kingdom of God; and her record of that vision constitutes her legacy to mankind.[1]

ADDITIONAL NOTE

ON POST-EXILIC JEWISH HISTORY

It will be useful to summarize briefly the salient facts of post-exilic history. It falls into three periods.

(i) The restored exiles were subject to the mild sovereignty of Persia from the middle of the fifth century till the conquest by Alexander the Great of Macedon (332).

(ii) For nearly two centuries they were ruled by Macedonian overlords. Palestine was once more the bone of contention between the Ptolemies in Egypt and the Seleucid kings of Asia. The gates were thrown open to

---

1. A further difference between Christianity and contemporary Judaism must be indicated. Christ came to preach 'good tidings of great joy', and it was as such that his message appealed to the peoples of the Mediterranean world. But in the Jewish apocalyptic writings of the period 200 B.C.–A.D. 100, the dominant thought is that of the divine vengeance. For the world at large, and even for the ungodly among the Jews, the message was one of terror, not of hope. The Jews believed in the efficacy of fear and punishment, and taught God's implacable enmity to unrepentant sinners. Even the *Testament of the Twelve Patriarchs* (second century B.C.), which contains the nearest approach to the Christian doctrine of forgiveness, falls short of the Christian ideal of love towards enemies. Mr Montefiore (in Jackson and Lake's *Acts*, i. 79) notes that contemporary Judaism lacks the distinctively Christian precept of a love that seeks out the sinner and the fallen. If this be man's duty, it must be as the expression of divine love, extending even to the unthankful and the evil. The apocalyptic writers came to marvel why God created the mass of men for eternal punishment; but they never questioned the fact. Doubtless, Christian theology absorbed much of this Jewish tradition. In Dante's poem, we read that shoals of spirits are driven into hell before the poet's eye, while only one (Statius) passes, during his journey, from Purgatory into Paradise. Yet this baneful legacy has never obliterated Christ's new and essential teaching of the universal love of God, as enshrined, e.g. in the parables of the lost sheep and the prodigal son.

Hellenism. Under the Seleucid Antiochus Epiphanes, civil tumult broke out (168) between Hellenizing Jews, supported by the Greek king, and the orthodox party, leading to Antiochus' forcible intervention, the violation of the temple, and frequent martyrdoms. The 'godly' found a champion in Judas Maccabaeus, of the priestly tribe of the Hasmonaeans (*Hashmunai*), who secured national independence and established a theocratic state, which lasted till Rome appeared on the scene.

(iii) In 63–61, Pompey, having conquered Mithradates of Pontus, Rome's great enemy in the East, reorganized that part of the Mediterranean area. The Jews were placed under Roman suzerainty, with a considerable measure of self-government under the high priests. In 40, the government passed into the hands of Herod the Great, an Idumaean ruler of exceptional ability, who consistently supported, and was supported by, Rome. He rebuilt the temple with great splendour and founded Caesarea. Among the mass of the Jews he was unpopular as an alien. On his death (4 B.C.) the kingdom, always under Roman suzerainty, was divided; in A.D. 6, Judaea became a province of the second rank, administered by a *procurator*, who was responsible to the *legatus* of Syria. This mode of government lasted (except during the three years A.D. 41–4, when Herod Agrippa I ruled Judaea as king) till the great revolt of 66 and the destruction of Jerusalem by Titus in 70. Pontius Pilate was one of the series of *procurators* in the reign of Tiberius. Lastly, after the second rising of the Jews against Rome in the time of Hadrian (132–5), the community received its final blow: the name Judaea was suppressed, and the subsequent history of the Jews is that of the Dispersion.

It should further be noted: (*a*) that Jewish national patriotism grew in intensity and exclusiveness with the increasing stringency of foreign sovereignty, Persian, Greek, and Roman. Every attempt to impose western ideas provoked a passionate outburst of resistance. The nationalist party gained strength under Roman rule, despite the studied respect of the imperial government for Jewish religious sentiment, and the wide judicial and administrative powers granted to the Sanhedrin (Greek *synedrion* = council). The Jewish people were always on the verge of revolt throughout this period: Galilee was the chief storm-centre. (*b*) That the Jewish communities of the *Diaspora* (= Dispersion) grew steadily in numbers and importance during the Macedonian and Roman periods. There was always a large and very important Jewish colony in Babylon; Jews settled in the towns of Asia Minor, Syria, and Egypt, especially at Alexandria, where they occupied two of the five quarters of the city and enjoyed extensive privileges. There the Greek version of the O.T., known as the *Septuagint*, was compiled in the second century B.C. Alexandria was the chief meeting-ground of Judaism and Hellenic thought; we find Judaism bending to western influence, but never breaking under the strain (see below, c. vi. § 8 and c. ix. § 2). The Jews made many proselytes (also half-proselytes, who accepted the Jewish faith without circumcision and other Mosaic observances) in the Hellenized provinces. Acts ii. 9–11 conveys some idea of the range of the *Diaspora*; the presence, there indicated, of Jews in Parthia and other eastern lands outside of the Roman empire accounts for the preaching of Christianity in those parts in early times (though very little is known about these missions). The desire expressed by St Paul to preach in Spain (Rom. xv. 28) suggests that Jews had penetrated to the extreme west of the Roman world. (*c*) That it was in the Greek, Persian, and Roman periods that Judaism, as distinct from the pre-exilic religion of Israel, developed as a religion to the complete and definitive form in which it has persisted ever since the latter half of the second century and the beginning of the third. This process, which, as we have seen, began with the promulgation of the Law by Ezra, and which, through the prophetic influence in its earlier phases, preserved unbroken continuity with pre-Judaic religion, was marked by the increasing dominance of the traditional *Torah*, as interpreted in the schools and synagogues by the 'scribes' and subsequent professional expositors, whose work was

eventually embodied in the *Mishnah*, the body of traditional
law as promulgated at the close of the second century and
later in the *Talmud* ('Learning') compiled in Galilee (late
fourth century) and Babylonia (late fifth century). The *Torah*,
thus codified, provided a catholic Jewish faith, based on community of observance, penetrating to every detail of the com-
munal life of the Jews, secular as well as religious, personal
and domestic as well as national. Particularism had replaced
universalism; legalism had triumphed, and living prophecy
had ceased; but the creation of Judaism in its final and permanent shape remains a truly notable achievement of the
religious genius of the chosen people.[1]

1. See Moore, *Judaism*, Vol. I, Introduction; Chap. I, Vol. IX.

CHAPTER FOUR

THE RISE OF HELLENISM

*

I. INTRODUCTORY

§ 1. THE origins of the Greek people are hard to trace. We have seen how, far back in the third millennium, Crete was the home of a rich civilization, which reached continental Greece, the Aegean islands, and the Mediterranean. It is generally thought that the makers of this civilization differed from the Greeks of later history in race, character, and language. Further, the evidence both of ancient tradition and of modern archaeology points to a catastrophic overthrow of Cretan power, some time towards the close of the second millennium, and to a subsequent period of anarchy and chaos, analogous to that which intervened between the downfall of the Roman empire in the west and the emergence of a new order of society in the Middle Ages. Antiquity too had its Dark Ages; and from it issued the Greece of history. In Crete, for example, the great Minoan buildings were destroyed by conflagration; then, after centuries of which but slight record is left, we find Dorian Greeks in occupation of the island. Greek religious story told of conflict between older and younger gods, and of the victory of the latter; Greek poets and historians have preserved memories of migrations by land and sea, of struggle and of fusion between Achaean and Dorian invaders on the one hand, and pre-Achaean 'Pelasgians' on the other. The little that we know of this age of transition suggests problems rather that conclusions. But this much at least is certain, that late in the second millennium tall, yellow-haired, fair-complexioned warriors of Indo-European stock descended in successive waves upon the Aegean world from the inland regions of the north. Some, bearing with them their families and chattels, like the Goths and Franks of a later time, forced their way southwards by land into Thrace and

Macedonia, Thessaly, and Epirus, and on into central Greece and the Peloponnesus. Others, possibly at an earlier date, crossed the Hellespont into Asia Minor. Others, again, like the ninth-century Northmen, raided by sea the coasts and islands of the Aegean. We may picture these rude northerners as not dissimilar, in their manners and culture, to the Macedonians of the age of Philip and Alexander, or to the Albanians of the present day. It was not wholly as destroyers that they mastered, in the course of centuries, the ancient civilization of Crete. It left its traces on their development; and it is possible that the superiority of Greek culture as compared with that of the Romans was due in part to this fact of early contact with Minoan civilization. In any case, the Greeks of history were the product of gradual fusion between Achaean and other intruders from the north and the older inhabitants of the Aegean world. It is natural that the latter, being far more numerous, should have impressed their culture upon the conquerors. The settlements of the invaders in European Greece were accompanied or followed by migrations of Greek colonists to the islands and Asiatic shores of the Aegean, and by conflicts with their own kinsmen, who had earlier passed thither by another route. Very possibly it is the memory of such struggles that is preserved in the story of the Trojan war.[1] One of these groups of colonists, the Aeolians, sailed from Thessaly to the north-west of Asia Minor and the islands that lay off the coast. Other settlers, farther to the south, united in a federation, called the Ionian league, round the sanctuary of Apollo at Delos. It was by the name Ionians (*Javan* in the Old Testament) that the early Greeks were known to the peoples of the East. We may date these maritime migrations across the Aegean between 1300 and 1000 B.C.; they are very probably connected with the troubles which Egypt suffered from sea-rovers under the twentieth dynasty.[2]

1. The traditional date of the Trojan war is B.C. 1184. The opinion of scholars at the present day is more conservative than a generation ago. These commotions in the Aegean and eastern Mediterranean world may have caused the Hittites to lose their influence in western Asia Minor. See above, c. ii. § 12, and Cowley's Schweich Lectures on *The Hittites*.

2. See above, c. ii. § 4. Some of the later invaders carried iron swords of

Finally, at the very close of the second millennium, the last wave of northern invasion broke upon European Greece, when the Dorians, a hardy warlike stock, the forefathers of the Spartans of later history, occupied parts of Central and Western Greece, and, pressing southwards, gradually mastered the greater part of the Peloponnesus. Dorian emigrants also crossed the Aegean, colonizing Crete, Rhodes, and the south-western shores of Asia Minor. As the outcome of these move-ments, which covered several centuries and terminated about 900 B.C., the Greek race and the Greek language were estab-lished on both sides of the Aegean.

II. THE HELLENIC CITY-STATES

§ 2. The life of the Greek people during the early centuries of the first millennium, as in the preceding period of the migra-tions, is veiled in obscurity, and our knowledge of its character consists largely of general conclusions, based upon inference from the succeeding age. This, at all events, is clear, that from the dawn of its history Hellenic civilization extended beyond the limits of continental Greece. We shall see presently how in the eighth and seventh centuries it spread beyond the Aegean area round the Euxine (Black Sea), and over the coast-lands of northern Africa, southern Italy, and Sicily. Southern Italy came to be known to the Greeks as 'Great Hellas'. Wherever in the Mediterranean world we find Greek cities and the Greek speech, there for purposes of history is Greece. But the fact of cardinal importance for Hellenic civilization is that, when the veil is partially drawn in the eighth century, the Greeks, with the exception of backward island communities, are already grouped in city-states. The patriarchal monarchies of which we read in the Homeric poems have mostly given place to hereditary aristocracies; and in the more advanced of the civic communities laws and constitutions are beginning to appear. Each of these small cities enjoyed complete political independence and developed its own distinctive institutions

improved design, against which the bronze rapiers of their Cretan antagonists could avail little.

and rule of life. It is essential to realize that free Greece was
never united in a single state. The national bond was that of
common race and language, not that of political union. We
must think of Greek history as the record of hundreds of
independent cities scattered over the islands and shores of the
Mediterranean, each possessed of a small tract of civic territory. That of Athens, for example, which was exceptionally
large, comprised the peninsula of Attica, with an area equal
to that of an average English county. Its citizen-levy in the age
of Pericles was 30,000, representing a free population of about
250,000, including women and children, to whom must be
added many slaves and resident aliens.[1] Like the Italian republics
of the later Middle Ages, these Greek cities were passionately
jealous of their independence. Whenever any one of them,
such as Athens or Sicilian Syracuse, acquired sovereignty over
others, the empire was invariably transient and, while it lasted,
provoked deep resentment among its subjects. Greek
patriotism was civic rather than national. This does not mean
that they were insensible to the common bond of Hellenic
kinship; on the contrary, they realized clearly the gulf that
parted their own standards of morality and civilization from
those of the 'barbarians' who surrounded them; but the tie
was one of feeling, speech, and culture.[2] It found peculiar
expression in the great athletic festivals, held under religious
auspices, and open to all Hellenes, and to them alone. Of
these the oldest and most celebrated was that which took
place every four years at Olympia on the borders of Elis in
honour of Zeus; from the early sixth century others were instituted at Nemea, near Argos, on the isthmus of Corinth, and
– the Pythian – on the plain of Crisa, near Apollo's shrine of

1. See note to c. v. § 5. Sparta, a strictly limited conquest-state, had some
8,000 citizens able to bear arms at the time of the Persian war; this number
had declined to about 1200 to 1500 by 371, and in Aristotle's day to less than
1000. Argos and Thebes had about 20,000 citizen-soldiers at the end of the
fifth century.

2. Professor Gilbert Murray points out (*Five Stages of Greek Religion*, p. 81)
that the consciousness of Hellenism takes its rise among the Ionian Greeks in
Asia Minor, where the contrast with the surrounding barbarism was most
evident. 'Hellenic' means 'like the Hellenes', not 'descended from Hellenes'
(*ibid.*, pp. 58 f.).

Delphi. The religion of the Greeks, despite a multitude of local variations, constituted a common inheritance; the chief Olympian deities, such as Zeus, Poseidon, Athene, and Apollo, were reverenced throughout the Hellenic area, and in the epoch of commercial expansion the oracle at Delphi developed into a pan-Hellenic religious institution. Thanks to easy communication by sea between all parts of the Hellenic world, the art, the poetry, and the science, that arose in various centres of culture, became rapidly a common possession of them all. Thus the need of political union as an instrument of civilization was not felt by the Greeks through the great creative period of their history; even when, in the fourth century, the cities of central and eastern Greece were dominated by the Macedonian kingdom, those of Italy and Sicily retained their independence, and the Macedonian overlordship was won and held by force.

§ 3. The *Polis* or city-state was the peculiar creation of the Hellenic people.[1] Its significance for the future of civilization is incalculable. In the first place, in its life and structure are presented, in a simpler form than in the large states of modern times, the data and problems, both moral and economic, which confront man in all ages as the member of a social community. As, in their philosophy, the Greeks formulated in comparatively simple terms the essential issues of human thought, obscured to our later view beneath a complex mass of material, so, in the field of public action in the *Polis*, they set themselves to realize the essential conditions of a worthy civic life. Again, the problems of civilized society were worked out by the Greeks to the full solution possible under that form of organization; the history of the Hellenic *Polis* can be followed from its beginnings until its decline and fall. Thirdly, the

1. The Phoenicians, both at home and in their colonies, especially Carthage, founded city-states; but nowhere do we find the free public life associated with the institution as in the case of the Greek cities or of Rome. Fowler (*City-State*, p. 5) sees in the *Polis* the key to the sense of a common inheritance of civilization left by Greeks and Romans (e.g. by the Greek historian Polybius in the second century B.C.). It may be questioned whether the Italian urban communities were fully-formed city-states. The towns of Latium and Campania were rather urban centres within a tribal group. On Rome, described by Polybius as 'a state most like the Hellenic', see below, ch. VII.

Greeks furnished their own theory of politics; they not only created the *Polis*, but reflected upon it; in their philosophy we find both the ideal and the speculative analysis of their public action. The Hellenic city-state stands in contrast, on the one hand, to the early empires of the East, on the other hand, to the states of modern times. The modern state is the fatherland, not its capital town; the capital may be changed, as in Russia from Moscow to St Petersburg, and later from Leningrad to Moscow, while the state remains the same. A state may come into being, like the Australian Commonwealth, even before the site of its future capital has been fixed. But in Greece, and in Rome under the republic, the capital city was itself the state. In distinction from Oriental kingdoms, the city-states of Greece achieved the union of civilized life and political liberty. In the East, freedom of government is found, but only among rude tribes living in small communities. Advance in culture is possible only through the formation of large aggregates of such communities under despotic rule, and is therefore purchased at the cost of liberty. So the Israelites, struggling against their neighbours, placed themselves voluntarily under a monarch, as the only hope of national salvation. 'And they said, Nay; but we will have a king over us, that we also may be like all the nations, and that our king may judge us, and go out before us, and fight our battles.' [1] Throughout antiquity, a large state meant despotism. Till the Greeks appeared, progress in civilization meant the creation of a large state. They were the first to solve the problem of uniting culture with freedom in a small community, and solved it through the city-state. They willed to resemble one another and achieved a unique result, realizing in the free public life of the *Polis* a history that contrasts dramatically with the monotonous tale of despotism, caste-privilege, and servitude recounted in the records of the East.

§ 4. The *Polis* furnished at once the basis and the ideal of

---

1. See Bevan, *House of Seleucus*, vol. i. c. i, whence the illustration from I Sam. viii. is taken. The passage was appealed to frequently by political writers of the Middle Ages, to support the doctrines of the popular basis of sovereignty and of the social contract.

Hellenic civilization. We know little of the process by which
the primitive settlements developed into city-states. We can
picture the northern invaders, dwelling as conquerors amid a
hostile population, in days when the sea was thronged with
free-booters, and erecting rude forts at points of vantage on
hills a little distance from the shore, whither they might take
refuge with their herds in moments of danger. At Athens in
historic times the citadel of the Acropolis was still the 'City'.
Village communities may have come together for self-defence
or have united round a common sanctuary for religious worship. In Homer the *Polis* was first and above all else a defensible
fortress.[1] We must think ourselves back into a time when,
among the Greeks as among other early races, gods, men, and
even their animals were bound together by a tie of kinship.
With the migrations, the bond weakened, and family attach-
ments began to give way to devotion to the group. The *Polis*
became the concrete symbol of this loyalty; it stood there
visible to the naked eye of every clansman as he farmed his
holding in the outskirts, or foregathered with his fellows for
barter and for worship within its walls. In the precincts of
the city everything that met his view was intimate and familiar. In the little community of a few hundred citizens, grouped
in families and clans, with the sense of kinship still alive within
them, there prevailed a real equality of comradeship.[2] Everyone knew everyone by sight; rich and poor, rulers and ruled,
stood in direct personal relationships one to another. Kings
and nobles were not hemmed in, as at eastern courts, by
etiquette and state-ceremony; no formalities of introduction
served as a barrier to human intercourse. The Greek lived his
life in the open, under the sun; lounging in the market-place
(*agora*) or wrestling ground (*palaestra*), as the southerner still
loves to lounge, in leisurely conversation with his neigh-

1. It is 'sacred' (*hieros*) in Homer; e.g. *Il.*, i. 366. The earliest temples
were, naturally, on the rocky citadel, hard by the chieftain's place; later, as
commercial activities developed, temples arise around the *agora*, or market-
place.

2. So, in the *Odyssey* (Book vi, 1–109), Nausicaa, a king's daughter, washes
'the' clothes with her maidens; Herodotus (iii. 42) represents the pirate-
despot Polycrates as asking a fisherman to dine with him.

bours.[1] The Greeks were an agricultural people, cultivators of
corn, vine, and olive; their occupation and the climate rendered
possible a life spent largely out of doors, with stretches of
leisure for social intercourse.[2] No contrast more complete
can be imagined to the life of a modern industrial city, where
everyone is hustling to his business, and moments of relaxa-
tion are few and regular, than the free informal life of the
Greek *Polis*. But leisure meant to the Greek anything rather
than idleness; it furnished an escape from the pressure of
material claims, and an occasion for the display of intellect and
talent. We must think of the Greeks as men of action, even
more than as artists or thinkers; their art and their science
were closely bound up with the interests of practical life.
Sculpture and architecture arose naturally among them out of
the need of houses for gods and men; and their philosophy out
of the need for intelligent control of the world in which they
lived. The Greek admired efficiency above all things; his
word for virtue (*arete*) covers not only moral excellence, but
intellectual talent and the capacity to win success in every
field of public life.[3] The ideal of the strong man, who knows
what he wants from the world, and has the power to get it,
was ever luring him away from the path of moderation. For
this restless energy of mind and body the *Polis* provided a
natural field. The only life worth living in the eyes of the
Greek was that of citizen service. The family possessed little
interest and no serious moral value. The son, when of age,
left his father and mother; in his own household, the wife

1 See Zimmern, *Greek Commonwealth*, c. i. The Greek of to-day likes to
overwhelm a stranger with eager questions. The ancient Greek prided himself
on his 'boldness of speech' (*parrhêsia*): he was free from all shyness or reserve.
Plato (*Rep.*, viii. 557) indicates *parrhêsia* as a symptom of extreme democracy.
Zimmern suggests that the short question and answer attending the entry of a
new character in the Attic drama reflects this national characteristic.

2. The Greek word for leisure was *scholê*, whence our 'school'. For leisure
meant to them opportunity for pursuits of intrinsic worth, such as a man
would choose for their own sake (e.g. the pursuit of knowledge). This idea is
at the root of their distinction between 'liberal' pursuits and 'necessary'. This
distinction is of fundamental importance in Aristotle's *Politics*. See below,
ch. xii. § 9.

3. The Greeks would have regarded Napoleon as a man of pre-eminent
aretê. Themistocles possessed *aretê* in a remarkable degree.

had no soul and did not count. Hence the inferior status of women and children, and the failure of Greek education. The *Polis* and, in the *Polis*, the *agora* with its surrounding porticos and public buildings, formed his home and his world. Hence, as the intellectual and moral horizon of the Greeks expanded, the culture in which it found expression was at every point associated with the city. The tone of public opinion, which determines insensibly and yet so powerfully men's character and habits, was the distinctive tone or *ethos* of the *Polis*.[1] To play his part worthily in its life formed the highest ambition of the citizen and the measure by which he gauged his success and his happiness. *Spartam nactus es; hanc exorna*. To be born into a mean *Polis* was accounted a grievous misfortune. Moreover, the *Polis* determined the content not only of his moral, but of his religious, obligations. The Greeks knew no distinction between church and state; from Homeric times onwards, the magistrate presided over the religion of the community, while the priesthood was confined to the discharge of ceremonial duties.[2] The *Polis* furnished also the stimulus to intellectual progress. Alike in the formal assemblies of the people and in the daily intercourse of the market-place or the dinner-table, it gave opportunity for freedom of thought and speech. Such liberty of criticism is something quite independent of democratic institutions and the machinery of political self-government. Soldiers canvass the acts and characters of their officers behind the scenes, juniors those of their seniors at school or college, without possessing any right of voting for their election. Democracy in Greece was the effect, not the cause, of free discussion. The Greeks were a nation of talkers, and their talk was often childish and insincere, such as to rouse scorn in the breast of the Roman, who was wont to act in silence. What distinguished the Greeks

1. We may bear in mind the moral atmosphere of a school, college, club or regiment. Plato (*Rep.*, vi. 492) asserted that no individual, however gifted, could resist the force of the public tone of his *Polis*.

2. As the gods could not compel, but only warn and punish, so the priest could only warn and protest. He was the housekeeper and watchman (ὑπηρέτης) of his god, and only occasionally his spokesman. When a χρησμός is given, it is because a man ἐχρῆτο, i.e. accepted the god's help.

above other nations who have loved talking is that they talked
also about what was most worth discussion : law and freedom,
moral duty and the end of government, the nature and causes
of things, art and poetry, virtue and the good for man. Above
all, their talk was reasoned and logical, the expression of clear
thinking and grasp of fact. No people have ever thought so
deeply or talked so well on these high subjects as did the
Greeks. No people have ever drawn with so firm a hand the
line between illusion and reality, or set themselves so resolutely to understand and master the world of nature. And all
this was the outcome of the free play of mind with mind,
fostered by common intercourse as citizens of the city-state.

§ 5. The Greek ideal of life was conceived in terms of the
Polis. Alike for statesmen and for philosophers, happiness
(*eudaimonia*) lay in the honourable discharge of civic duty.[1]
The dramatists and historians of the fifth century reflect on
almost every page of their writings their sense of the value of
the *Polis* as furnishing scope for the realization of the good life.[2]
The philosophers who sought to determine by scientific reasoning the nature and standard of human goodness, were unswerving in their conviction that the only life worth living was that
of the citizen in the Hellenic city-state. When Socrates after
his condemnation by the Athenians was offered escape from
prison, he replied that to evade the law of the *Polis*, even when
unjustly exercised, was as morally wrong as for a son to do
violence to an aged parent. Plato condemned all existing
Greek states as hopelessly corrupt, yet sketched in his *Republic*
the ideal community as a reformed Hellenic *Polis*.[3] For him,

1. *Eudaimonia* (lit. having a good 'daemon' or guardian-spirit) was the
Greek term for 'happiness' or 'felicity', i.e. the *summum bonum* or ideal of
human life. For the interpretation of this ideal by a cultured Greek of the
fifth century, see Herodotus's tale of Solon's conversation with Croesus
(i. 30 ff.). To the popular mind happpiness consisted in good fortune (*eutychia*);
the philosophers consciously rejected the view that the chief good depended
on external circumstances, or on the arbitrary caprice of the gods, or on luck.

2. Compare especially Herodotus, *loc. cit.* and iii. 80 ff. In the latter passage the Persian grandees are represented as debating the merits of democracy,
aristocracy, and monarchy respectively. The speeches, of course, reflect
Greek sentiments, just as Shakespeare's Romans are really Elizabethan Englishmen. See also the conversation of Xerxes with Demaratus, vii. 101 ff.

3. Plato, *Rep.*, v. 470. For Socrates' refusal, see Plato's *Crito*.

as for Aristotle in the succeeding generation, the good city afforded at once the condition and the complement of the good life for its members. Aristotle defined the *Polis* as 'an association formed for maintenance of complete and self-sufficient life'; other forms of association enabled man to live, but the *Polis* alone enabled him to live well.[1] Man he defined as 'a political animal', a living creature whose nature marked him out for the life of civic activity.[2] The main function of the lawgiver and the statesman was the development of moral goodness in the citizen, his education to the complete achievement of the capacities of his nature in the city-state. Even the Stoics, writing amid the shattered fragments of Greek political independence, strove to reconstruct the fabric of moral duty by teaching men to live as citizens of the cosmopolitan republic, a *Polis* grounded in pure reason, the city of God.[3]

§ 6. Thus the civilization of the Greek people was rooted deep in the soil of the city-state. It was 'the rock whence they were hewn', 'the hole of the pit whence they were digged'. Architecture and sculpture, the dramatic festivals and lyric song, science and philosophy, religion and morals, craft-gilds and the arts of peace and war, the structure of the constitution and the maxims of public policy, the forms of social intercourse, speech, and manners, were branches of a single organism, the *Polis*. But there is another side to the picture. Freedom has a two-edged sword; and the life of the *Polis* gave play alike to the temper of civic patriotism and to that of personal ambition. In ancient Greece, as 2000 years afterwards in Dante's Florence, the disintegrating forces of party faction and individual self-seeking seethed close beneath the surface. *Stasis*, civil discord, was the chronic malady of the Hellenic *Polis*. Both the forms which it assumed, the inability of cities to combine in political union even in face of a common foe, and the internal strife of men, families, and parties

1. Arist., *Pol.*, iii. 9, 1280 *b*; i. 2, 1252 *b*.
2. Arist., *Pol.*, i. 2, 1253 *a*. Writing as late as the middle of the second century, the Greek historian of Rome, Polybius, insists that a constitution is good or bad according as it produces citizens of good or bad moral character (*Polyb.*, vi. 47).
3. Cosmopolis means 'the city (*polis*) of the universe (*cosmos*)'.

within the walls of a single town, worked for the eventual dissolution of Greek independence. We read continually, it is true, of confederations of cities for purposes of religion or of defence. Greek history is largely the history of Leagues, from the Amphictyonic league of the seventh century to the Achaean and Aetolian leagues of the fourth and third. But these combinations lacked permanence and solidarity; they were effective only for transient purposes and within the narrow bounds of Hellenism, and proved wholly unavailing when matched against the forces of Macedon and Rome.[1] In the event, excess of liberty issued in bondage to an alien power. The Greeks, with their keen sense of the facts of life, were not slow to diagnose their own disorder, but they were powerless to cure it. Plato's unerring insight into human nature traced the source of public tyranny in the state to the tyranny of lawless passion within the individual. He saw that it was the most gifted of the citizens, a Themistocles or an Alcibiades, who, because of their great possessions, were the most tempted to fall victims to the lust for power, and to shatter, first the economy of their own souls, and then that of the community.[2] For all its splendour of achievement, Greek history is full of tragedy. Its pages are strewn with the wreckage of ruined lives. They represent the sacrifice by which the mind of man purchased its freedom to think and act. But they must not deceive us into thinking for an instant that the triumph was not worth the sacrifice.

III. THE EXPANSION OF GREECE

§ 7. The influence of the city-state, for good and for evil, becomes clearer as we study its development in Greek history. The eighth and seventh centuries saw its rapid diffusion over the islands and coast-lands of the Mediterranean. This expansion of the Greek race was favoured by geographical and

1. Federations and empires alike appeared to the Greeks to mark a retrograde step from the independent *Polis*.
2. See *Rep.*, vi. 490 ff. (where the reference is undoubtedly to Alcibiades), and viii. 562 ff. (where tyranny is shown to arise out of excess of democratic liberty).

climatic conditions. The cities of the Aegean area were situated
either on islands or in valleys parted by high mountain ridges,
and were thus protected from aggression on land. But they
were not shut off from mutual intercourse; else, like the
Swiss of modern history, they would have preserved their
independence at all costs. The bond of union was the sea.
The gulf of Corinth and numberless bays and inlets secured
for the European Greeks a great length of coast-line; there
was hardly any Greek state that had not easy access to the sea.
The Greeks were a maritime race from early days; intercourse in trade both among themselves and with other peoples
combined with the freedom and individuality of their cities to
promote a rich and varied culture. Rarely has any race been so
lavishly endowed by nature with the physical conditions of
civilization.[1] Mountains and sea, a temperate and bracing
climate, a soil that called forth and rewarded energy and skill,
fostered the qualities of love of adventure and free action that
the northern invaders brought with them when they descended
into the Aegean world.[2]

§ 8. The eighth and seventh centuries were marked by
commercial enterprise, great activity in colonization, the
growth of wealth and social refinement and widespread
political unrest. By 600 B.C. the Greeks had planted commercial colonies on the shores of the Propontis (Sea of Mar-
mora) and the Euxine (Black Sea), on the northern coast of
Africa, round the south of Italy, and over the whole Sicilian
coast-line, save where the Carthaginian strongholds commanded the extreme west of the island. We saw how, early in
the sixth century, Greek traders secured from the friendly
princes of the twenty-sixth dynasty a permanent foothold at
Naucratis in the Egyptian Delta. The trade of the Mediterranean from Sicily to the Levant had passed from the Phoenicians to the Greeks. In the extreme west Carthage enjoyed an
unchallenged monopoly. But elsewhere the Greek trader and

---

1. But they had no resources of natural power (hence the necessity of slave-
labour on a large scale), no glass (hence no chemistry or optical instruments),
no coal (hence no boiler-plates or steam).
2. But the Minoans as well as the Northerners showed maritime enterprise.

colonist, with a natural genius for making himself at home amid new conditions and alien peoples, ousted earlier races from the markets of the Mediterranean. This commercial expansion carried with it far-reaching effects on social and political life. Splendid cities arose, such as Miletus in Ionia, Syracuse in Sicily, and Sybaris in southern Italy; a 'Sybarite' is to this day a term for the lover of luxurious ease. A class of merchant princes sprang into existence, who were liberal patrons of art and poetry. In the field of politics there seethed perpetual ferment and revolution. The new plutocracy struggled for power and privilege against the monopoly of the old nobility. Keen party struggles proved a stimulus to fresh colonization. Not infrequently, and often under the guidance of the Delphic oracle, which rose to importance in this epoch, the malcontents were despatched as colonists to some unoccupied region favourable to trade, where they founded a self-governing *Polis*. The Greek colony was politically independent of the mother-city; such bonds as existed were those of religion, of sentiment, or of commercial alliance.[1] Thus the age was one of rapid political transition. The rivalry of birth and wealth, of land and trade, prepared the way, now for democracy, now for despotism. The most remarkable phenomenon of the times was the rise of the form of government known to the Greeks as 'tyranny'. Though short-lived in any single city, it is henceforward a standing feature in the commercial centres of Greece. Often, as in the days of the Italian renaissance, a rich merchant would overthrow the oppressive nobles with popular aid, and establish himself as despot. The 'tyrants' were frequently enlightened and humane rulers, e.g. Pisistratus at Athens in the sixth century, but they deeply offended the Greek love of freedom, and their rule excited bitter resentment. They set themselves above the law, and thereby renounced all claim to its protection. Their authority

1. Yet we read of colonies that were bitter commercial rivals of the parent-city, e.g. Corinth and her colony Corcyra. See Thucydides, iii. 82 ff., where the revolutions at Corcyra are described as an illustration of the moral and political effects of party struggles in the Hellenic world of the later fifth century. On the Delphic oracle and colonization, see Her., iv. 150–8 (Cyrene).

was a violation of the *ethos* of the Hellenic city-state. More-over, the Greeks shared to the full the dislike, felt in all ages by free people, towards power based on possession of wealth. 'To lay low a tyrant who consumes the people is no sin and will not be punished by the gods,' wrote Theognis of Megara. The poet Simonides celebrates the praise of the murderers of Pisistratus' son in these words: 'A great light broke upon the Athenians when Harmodius and Aristogiton slew Hipparchus.' The issues of this epoch in the public life of Greece are seen also in the development of law and political institutions, and in the advance towards democracy through the breaking-down of hereditary privilege.[1] Of still greater moment was the expansion of culture in the domain of poetry, art, and science.

IV. EARLY POETIC LITERATURE

§ 9. The literature of Greece, like that of many nations, opens with song; and the earliest poems that we possess are two epics ascribed to Homer, the *Iliad* and the *Odyssey*. The *Iliad* tells the story of battles 'on the ringing plains of windy Troy', of the wrath and prowess of Achilles, and his slaying of Trojan Hector. The *Odyssey* narrates the ten years' wandering of Odysseus over sea and land after Troy had fallen, his return to Ithaca, and his slaughter of the suitors who had wasted his home.[2] They are the two survivals of many early epics, and

1. The intervention of Persia, which could always co-operate with oligar-chies, cut sharply across the normal development to democracy. This accounts for the persistence of oligarchy into the fourth century.

2. In neither epic is the sequence of incidents presented as the fulfilment of a single large design. As Mr C. S. Lewis has recently pointed out in his illu-minating *Preface to Paradise Lost*, it is characteristic of the early heroic epic, in Greece, as among the peoples of northern Europe, that unlike the later 'secondary' epic it has no great subject, such as the founding of Rome (Virgil) or the fall of man (Milton). 'That kind of greatness,' he writes (pp. 28–29), 'arises only when some event can be held to effect a profound and more or less permanent change in the history of the world. . . . The mere endless up and down, the constant aimless alternations of glory and misery, which make up the terrible phenomenon called a Heroic Age, admit no such design. No one event is really very much more important than another. . . . Nothing "stays put", nothing has a significance beyond the moment. Heroism and tragedy there are in plenty, therefore good stories in plenty; but no "large design. . . ." The total effect is not a pattern, but a kaleidoscope.'

represent the ripe fruit of a long period of poetic creation.
The first Greek settlers in Asia Minor, of Aeolian stock,
brought with them from southern Thessaly ballads and lays in
praise of gods and tribal ancestors, composed in hexameter
verse – 'the stateliest measure ever moulded by the lips of
man'.[1] These were wrought into great epics in the island of
Lesbos or on the shores of north-western Asia between about
1200 and 800, and brought into their present form, with later
modifications, accretions, and expurgations among the Ionian
settlers further south.[2] We can trace in them changes of
language, thought, and custom, and the growth of moral
ideas; the *Odyssey*, which on the whole is the later of the two,
perhaps reflects the romantic temper of the age of maritime
adventure. We cannot enter here upon the disputed problems,
how far the two epics or either one of them was the work of a
single poet, and merely note that to-day scholars are more disposed to take a conservative view on these questions than they
were half a century ago. The view that Homer was an actual
individual and that the *Iliad* and the *Odyssey* are to be ascribed
to his authorship can no longer be ruled cavalierly out of
court. For us, as for the Greeks, Homer stands as the per-
sonification of the whole body of epic saga. The marvel is that
the race could thus early give birth to a school of consummate
poets. No extant literature opens so gloriously as that of
Greece with these two poems. Alike in content and in form,
they reign in unquestioned sovereignty over the epic poetry of

1. Tennyson, *To Virgil*. The verse of ancient poetic literature was un-
rhymed; Dante was the first great world-poet to use rhyme. Greek (and
Latin) metres rest on the quantity of the syllables rather than on stress. Hence
modern imitations of, e.g., hexameter verses give a very inadequate impression
of the metre as used by the ancients. The following from Clough's *Bothie of
Tober-na-vuolich* may serve as an imperfect illustration:
'So in the | golden | morning they | parted and | went to the | westward.'
'There hath he | farmstead and | land, and | fields of | corn and | flax fields.'
The normal scheme of the six feet line is:

$$ - \cup\cup \mid - \cup\cup \mid - \cup\cup \mid - \cup\cup \mid - \cup\cup \mid - \cup $$

the long syllable being reckoned as having double the value of the short
($\textbf{d}$ and $\textbf{J}$).
2. They are in the Ionic dialect, but were originally composed in the
Aeolic. On the Homeric theology, see Nilsson, *History of Greek Religion*.

every race and time. Their significance for the after civiliza-
tion of Greece and of the world is threefold. Their beauty and
splendour have been a perennial source of poetic inspiration.
We can trace their influence through the whole course of
Greek literature and art. Roman poetry, and especially the
Aeneid of Virgil, is shaped in large measure on the model of the
Iliad and the *Odyssey*; and the spirit of Homer still breathes in
the poetry of the modern world. Aeschylus is said to have
called his tragedies 'fragments from the great banquet of
Homer'; poets of all ages might echo his words.   The parting
of Hector and Andromache; Helen's remembrance of her
dead brothers as she watches the Achaean host from the walls
of Troy; the supplication of Priam to Achilles for Hector's
corpse, when the aged king 'dared what none other man on
earth has dared before, to stretch forth my hand toward the
face of the slayer of my sons'; stir a like emotion in readers of
every nation and language, in the unlettered peasant as in the
scholar or the poet.[1] From the dawn of Greek poetry its
theme is what is most universal in human life and feeling.
Secondly, as time went on, the Homeric poems came to be
read and taught as a storehouse of moral and religious truth.
Lines such as the words of Achilles to the envoys, 'hateful to
me as the gates of hell is he who speaketh one thing with his
lips but hideth another in his heart', or Odysseus' 'endure, my
heart: far worse hast thou endured', served as texts, which
Greek children learnt much as those of modern England learn
verses from the scriptures.[2] The Homeric poems did much to
shape and fix the religious and moral ideas of subsequent

1. *Il.*, vi. 390 ff., iii. 234 ff., xxiv. 505–6 (*tr.* Lang, Leaf, and Myers).
2. *Il.*, ix. 312–13, *Od.*, xx. 18. On the other hand, there were many passages which struck the developed moral sense of later Greeks as ill-suited for
the education of the young. Such were the incidents from the *chronique scan-
daleuse* of the gods, which were probably later additions, reflecting the
persiflage and religious scepticism of the seventh-century Ionians: e.g. the
tricking of Zeus by Hera (*Il.*, xiv. 153 ff.); the surprise of the amours of
Hephaestus and Aphrodite (*Od.*, viii. 266 ff.), condemned by Plato (*Rep.*, iii.
390); and the fight of Athena with Ares and Aphrodite (*Il.*, xxi. 391 ff.),
which might be paralleled with the parody in *Tom Jones* (Bk. IV, c. 8 – Molly
Segrim's encounter with the village women), 'a battle sung', Fielding tells us,
'by the Muse in the Homerican style'. On these later additions, see Murray,
Rise of the Greek Epic, Lect. X. They have their value for history, e.g. Hera's

generations.[1] Thirdly, these poems have a value for history. They depict with substantial fidelity the life of the chieftains and warriors of the Aegean world in the later centuries of the second millennium. We cannot indeed affirm that the persons actually lived or that the incidents actually took place, though a siege of Troy is no historic improbability. The poets, it is true, are singing of a past age, and the picture is coloured by an infusion of later custom. Yet we learn much of early usage, of marriage and religious worship, of modes of house-building and habits of domestic life, of the manner of warfare, of agriculture and faring on the sea. When we read the description of the institutions of king, council, and assembly of the folk (e.g. in the second book of the *Iliad*), of the shield of Achilles (in the eighteenth book), of the palaces, the armour and the dress, we find striking confirmation of their accuracy in the discoveries of Schliemann and his successors. The word of Homer was a real world. Two features, among others, stand out in prominent relief. The life portrayed is that of a feudal aristocracy. We hear but little of the common people; they bear no part in the action, and the very slaves are captives of princely birth. The poetry before us was not popular poetry, any more than its religion was popular religion; it was composed for noble chieftains by minstrels who sang to the honour of their families and clans. Yet, despite this undemocratic character, we breathe an air of freedom in the Homeric world. There is no political despotism, no priestcraft; intrigue and magic alike are rare; women live on an equality with men to a degree unknown in later Greece, and enjoy high dignity in the household; slaves speak to their masters, and are spoken to, as men to men.[2] Common humanity reaches

---

toilet (*Il.*, xiv. 170 ff.) is highly instructive. Plato's strictures on Homer and the poets generally in his *Republic* (ii. 377–iii. 392) are directed not against their merits as poetry (which he fully recognized: *Rep.*, x. 607), but against their claim to be a bible of religious and moral instruction. He expressly singles out for approval (*Rep.*, iii. 390) the words of Odysseus quoted in the text.

1. Herodotus (ii. 53) recognizes this: the passage is quoted in § 11 below. The Olympian religion, as distinct from more primitive popular worships, owed its enduring triumph largely to Homer.

2. On women, see the *Odyssey*. The relations between the sexes are handled

nearer to the surface in Homeric society than in our more complex modern world.

§ 10. The early epics were tales of heroic action, of the deeds of famous men. Later poets struck a new subjective note, and in a more romantic spirit uttered their passion in lyric verse. Their interest was centred, not on the past, but on the present, on the poets' personal experience of life. The age of commercial expansion saw the birth of lyric and elegiac poetry, richly varied in subject and metrical form, comprising poems of love and war, sorrow and *ennui*, the dirge and the marriage-song, choric odes, and political and personal satire. 'Age cannot wither' the imperishable beauty of these poems. They defy translation, but an echo of their charm may be caught in Rossetti's adaptation from Sappho –

1

Like the sweet apple that reddens upon the topmost bough,
A-top on the topmost twig – which the pluckers forgot somehow –
Forgot it not, nay, but got it not, for none could get it till now.

2

Like the wild hyacinth flower which on the hills is found,
Which the passing feet of the shepherds for ever tear and wound,
Until the purple blossom is trodden into the ground.

The elegiac vein may be illustrated by the famous couplet inscribed by Simonides early in the fifth century on the tomb of the Spartan dead at Thermopylae : 'Go, stranger, and tell the men of Lacedaemon that we lie here, obedient to their charge.' Lyric poetry, as the name implies, was written to be sung to music. The choric ode, developed to great perfection in this same age, was accompanied both by music and dancing. The chorus celebrated the praises of gods or heroes or victors in the games ; the extant odes of Pindar (early fifth century), one of the glories of Greek poetry, are mainly in honour of athletic victories. In the next chapter we shall see how the

with delicacy and restraint. On slaves, see Eumaeus in the *Odyssey*; he is of noble birth, captured in war, and is treated as an honoured retainer of the family. See later, c. v, Additional Note.

lyric genius of the Greeks was interwoven with the epic in the Attic drama.

§ 11. Side by side with these forms of lyric verse, the growing interest in moral reflexion gave rise to gnomic poetry (*gnome* = a maxim), expressive of naïve criticism of life, counsels of policy or prudence, and precepts of private and public action. Didactic poetry had arisen in yet earlier times among the peasantry of central Greece, as the counterpart of the Homeric epics among the Aeolian and Ionian aristocracy; it survives in the poems ascribed to the Boeotian Hesiod.[1] The gnomic poetry of the later seventh and sixth centuries may be compared with the works of Piers Plowman, or of the 'moral' Gower, in English literature. Theognis of Megara voiced in elegiac metre the Dorian noble's scorn for the vile demos who had robbed his class of wealth and power; the Athenian statesman, Solon, sang of loyal service to the city, and of the duty of restraint in the use of power, to a people ever prone to overstep the bounds of moderation. This new type of poetry is of special significance, when we remember how in the Greek view poets rather than priests were the recognized teachers of moral and religious truth. This does not mean that the Greeks failed in piety; the Athenians of Solon's day, like their descendants at the time of St Paul's visit, were if anything too 'god-fearing',[2] and their attachment to the worships of the *Polis* broke out on occasion into frenzied extravagance.[3] It was part of the poets' function to narrate and

1. The *Works and Days* of Hesiod give an interesting picture of life in the later part of the dark age that followed on the northern immigrations into the Aegean. See Ure, *The Greek Renaissance*, c. ii.

2. Acts xvii. 22. The Greek term, translated 'superstitious' in A.V. and R.V., means literally 'daemon-fearing'. Daemons were divine beings, like Heracles and other children of the gods in Greek religious story.

3. E.g. on the occasion of the mutilation of the statues of Hermes, on the eve of the sailing of the Armada to Sicily in 415: see Thuc., vi. 27 f. The effect on the populace may be compared to that which a desecration of the images of the Madonna would have produced in a Spanish town at the time of the Armada of 1588. On the Homeric theology, see Nilsson, *History of Greek Religion*. The society of the Olympian gods was feudal in character, after the fashion of human societies in the heroic age. The gods were conceived anthropomorphically, as differing from men only in *degree* of knowledge and power, but as immortal. They were not omniscient nor omnipotent; yet everything in human life was regarded as subject to their influence.

interpret the tales of gods and heroes, and considerable latitude was allowed them in selection and reconstruction.
Herodotus said that the early epic poets, Homer and Hesiod,
'gave the gods their titles and distributed among them honours
and arts and set forth their forms'. He meant that they brought
some measure of system and co-ordination into the multitude
of local cults, and thus helped to crystallize the leading outlines of religious tradition for after times. No one can realize
the part that poetry played in the life and education of the
Greeks, who does not keep in view its intimate association
with their religion.[1]

§ 12. The gnomic poets heralded the work of Pindar and
the fifth-century dramatists, in that they attempted to adjust
poetic teaching to the growing moral consciousness of the
time. The prevalent unrest led inevitably, among a people endowed with rare powers of intellect, to changes in men's
views of life, and to the substitution of new moral values for
the old. A symptom of this reflective temper was the circulation in this epoch of proverbial maxims, such as 'know thyself', 'nothing in excess', 'rule will reveal the man', which
represent popular inductions from moral experience. The
conception of an ethical standard took shape in the ideal of
sôphrosynê, a term which defies translation by any single
English word, and means literally 'keeping the mind safe', or
as we might say, 'the head clear'.[2] Its primitive nucleus is the
Homeric aidôs or respect, the inner feeling which in the days
of barbaric warfare stayed a man's hand from outrage of the
orphan, the aged, the suppliant or a fallen foe; checked his
impulse to cowardice or to disloyalty, and kept him dutiful
towards parents, rulers, and the gods.[3] The essential meaning
of sôphrosynê, as it developed in the Greek mind, was self-

1. See Plato, Rep., ii, iii, on the place of poetic tales about gods and
daemons and men in the moral instruction of the young rulers of the ideal city.

2. Aristotle (Ethics, vi. c. 5) interprets the term as meaning literally the
virtue 'which keeps safe practical wisdom (phronêsis)'. Phronêsis means the
power of right judgement in matters of human conduct.

3. See Murray, Rise of the Greek Epic, pp. 78 ff. In the Iliad (iv. 402 ff.), when
Agamemnon chides Diomedes for slowness in gathering his men to battle,
the latter answers not back 'from aidôs for the voice of the reverend (aidoios)
king'; and when Sthenelus answers angrily in his stead, Diomedes rebukes

restraint and obedience to law, whether of the state or of inward principle, in face of the besetting temptation to abuse wealth and power, and to subordinate civic loyalty to the claims of personal ambition. Over and above this negative obligation, it implied the positive quality of clear vision, born of self-knowledge, that enables an individual or a community to act with a balanced judgement in the critical moments of their history. The well-known phrase, 'a right judgement in all things', furnishes perhaps the closest expression of its meaning.[1] The antithesis to this saving wisdom was *hubris*. The term is found already in the early epics; its root-meaning is the violent overstepping of the mark, the insolence of triumph, and the pride of life that tramples under foot the unwritten law of gods and men. *Hubris* is the closest Greek equivalent for 'sin'. Its most characteristic application was to the insatiable thirst for power which drives a man or a nation headlong, as though possessed by a demon, on the path of unbridled self-assertion. This blinding passion, outraging alike personal liberty and public law, lures the victim in a frenzy of self-confidence towards destruction. It provokes *nemesis*, the feeling of righteous indignation, in the gods and in his fellowmen. 'An ancient *hubris* ever breeds a fresh and living *hubris* to add to human woes';[2] so the Greek poet, striving to give their due both to inherited fatality and individual desert, pictured the gathering cloud of doom that visited the sins of the fathers upon the children, through successive generations of a sinful race. When tyranny made its appearance, it was regarded as the crowning manifestation of *hubris* in the public

him, 'For I do not feel *nemesis* at Agamemnon, shepherd of the people, when he urges the well-greaved Achaeans to the fight.'

1. See especially the analysis of *sôphrosyně* in Plato, *Rep.*, iv. 430 ff., and Aristotle, *Ethics*, bk. III. In these philosophers the term represents the reflective outcome of *aidôs*, the primitive feeling developed into a clearly defined form of moral excellence. The phrase quoted in the text is from the collect for Whitsunday in the English *Book of Common Prayer*.

2. Aesch., *Agam.*, 760 ff. In this play, when Clytemnestra bids her lord Agamemnon tread the purple on entering his home on his return from Troy, preparatory to the doom she has prepared for him, he does so with fear: 'As I tread these sea-stuffs, may no jealousy (*phthonos*) from a god's far eyes strike me. For I have much *aidôs* in wasting substance, ruining by my tread riches and textures bought with silver' (*Ag.*, 946–9).

life of the city-state.[1] Later on, the conception is applied to
the collective action of a nation uplifted by pride of empire to
menace Hellenic independence, as in the case of the Persian
invasion and the maritime sovereignty of Athens.[2] The Greek
knew full well his weakness and the evil passions that were
ever on the watch to lure him to assert his individuality
beyond the bounds prescribed by reason and law. It was hard
for him, with his great possessions, to enter on the kingdom of
his own soul. Of temptress-passions the chief were Persuasion
(*Peitho*), Hope (*Elpis*), and Passion (*Eros*). They were conceived
as personal agents rather than as abstract motives. 'Miserable
Persuasion wreaks her might, the insufferable child of fore-
counselling Doom (*Ate*); and all cure is vain.'[3] 'Hope,'
wrote Hesiod, 'is an ill guide for a needy man'; and Sophocles,
'Far-roving Hope, though many have comfort of her, is to
many a delusion, that wings the dream of Love; and he whom
she haunts knows naught till he burn his feet against hot
fire.'[4] Poets and philosophers alike hold Love to be a tyrant,
who enslaves his blinded victims to wild passion. 'Love rules
even gods at will, and me also,' cries the hapless Deianira,
'how then rules he not others such as I?'

> For mad is the heart of Love,
> And gold the gleam of his wing;
> And all to the spell thereof
> Bend, when he makes his spring.[5]

1. Soph., *O.T.*, 873, 'hubris begets a tyrant'.
2. For Persian *hubris* and its resulting *nemesis*, see Aeschylus' 'Persians'
and the history of Herodotus, esp. Her. vii. 7–18 (conversation of Xerxes
and Artabanus). On Athenian *hubris* in the closing third of the fifth century
towards her subjects, see Thucydides, i. 75, 76, iii. 37 ff., and especially the
Melian dialogue, v. 89 ff., followed immediately by the Sicilian expedition
(*nemesis*). A Greek would have readily interpreted the rapid development of
German nationalism into a policy of Germanizing the world by force as an
example of national *hubris*. On *nemesis*, see Murray, *op. cit.* The idea is definitely ethical. While *aidôs* expresses my sense of the inconceivability of such
behaviour, *nemesis* expresses my conviction that I (or another person) *should*
not act thus.
3. Aesch., *Agam.*, 385.
4. Hesiod, *Works and Days*, 494; Soph., *Antig.*, 616; cf., on Hope, Aesch.,
Agam., 990 ff., Soph., *Trach.*, 666, Thucydides, iii. 45, v. 103, and Cornford,
Thucydides Mythistoricus.
5. Soph., *Trach.*, 443–4; Eur., *Hipp.*, 1268 ff. (*tr.* Murray). See also

A later age came to see in these three powers, Faith, Hope and
Love, a triad of graces, the crowning glory of man's spiritual
pilgrimage. But to the Greek of the great days they were evil
daemons, luring the gambler in the game of life to stake his all
blindly on one fatal throw, and to rouse thereby the *nemesis* of
heaven. For the Olympian gods were jealous, and visited their
wraith on the insolent mortal who dared to outrage their prerogative.[1] Greek poetic literature is full of reflexions which
centre round these conceptions of *sôphrosynê* and *hubris*; they
form the Hellenic counterpart to the ethical teaching of the
Hebrew prophets, and exemplify the conscious recognition
by the poets of their function as the moral educators of the
Greek people. But already in the sixth century another voice
was audible; philosophy was asserting in opposition to poetry
a rival claim to teach the truth about the world and human
life.

V. THE BIRTH OF PHILOSOPHY

§ 13. 'The desire of knowledge,' wrote Aristotle, 'is natural
to all men'; and, again, voicing Plato, 'It was wonder that
first led men to philosophy.' [2] The desire he has in mind is
the disinterested love of truth, the impulse to think for
thinking's sake, not merely as a means to practical ends. 'The

Plato's picture of the soul mastered by a tyrant *Eros* in *Rep.*, ix. 572–3, and the
opening of the choric song in Soph., *Antig.*, 781 ff., thus rendered by Swinburne (*Ode to Athens*):

> 'Love in fight unconquered, love with spoils of great men laden,
>   Never sang so sweet from throat of woman or of dove;
> Love whose bed by night is in the soft cheeks of a maiden,
>   And his march is over seas and low roofs lack not love;
> Nor may one of all that live, ephemeral or eternal,
>   Fly nor hide from love; but whoso clasps him fast goes mad.'

1. On the jealousy (*phthonos*) of the gods, see Her., iii. 40–43 (the tale of
Polycrates) and vii. 10 (Artabanus' speech). Plato's passionate denial that God
is jealous, echoed by Aristotle and all later philosophers, marks one of the
great advances made by scientific thought on popular religion (Plato, *Phaedr.*,
247; Aristotle, *Met.*, i. 2).

2 Aristotle, *Met.*, i. 1, 980 *a* 21 and i. 2, 982 *b*, 11 ff., *tr.* Ross (with
very slight alteration); cf. Plato, *Theaet.*, 155 d. Plato illustrates by the tale
that Iris, the messenger of the gods, was the child of Thaumas (Wonder).

man who is puzzled and wonders is conscious of his ignorance; therefore, since they philosophized in order to escape from ignorance, it is clear that they studied science for the sake of knowledge, and not for any utilitarian end.' To the Greeks the curiosity to know the causes of things and to probe their inner nature came naturally; already in the childhood of their history they had all the child's desire to know how and why. 'At first they wondered at the obvious puzzles; little by little they advanced to inquire into the larger problems, the phenomena of the moon and sun and the stars, and the origin of the universe.' [1] In this disinterested curiosity, as Aristotle was aware, science and philosophy had their birth. The Greeks drew no distinction between the two, for knowledge had not yet been mapped out into provinces; the world of human experience, in its entirety and in its detail, formed the common theme of their inquiry. The speculative impulse, thus grounded in the Greek genius, was stimulated to effective exercise by the age of expansion. Miletus, a great centre of Ionian commerce and colonial enterprise, was the birthplace of Greek philosophy.[2] The unrest, which we have noted in the field of politics, seethed also in the minds of thinking men. A larger world had been unfolded to view, traditional customs were seen to vary with local and temporal conditions, and old tales were disproved by wider experience – the Scylla and Charybdis of the *Odyssey* were found to be mere natural phenomena, a rock and a whirlpool. The frequent migrations of the period broke down the links that bound early faiths to special localities. For the first time in the history of human civilization the scientific spirit swung free from entanglement with popular religious beliefs.

§ 14. The attempts of the first Milesian philosophers to explain the universe were distinguished by three features from any that had gone before. In the first place, they bore, like all other creations of the Hellenic genius, the stamp of individu-

1. Aristotle, *Met.*, i. 2.

2. Miletus was in contact with Mesopotamian civilization by the great road that led from the Aegean coast eastwards through Asia Minor, and with Egypt by the recently established Milesian settlement at Naucratis.

ality. Eastern science, if we may dignify it with that name, was, in the main, anonymous, the inherited achievement and possession of a caste or gild.[1] But Thales, Anaximander, and Anaximenes, the first philosophers of Miletus in the sixth century, stand forth as personalities, each with his distinctive contribution to the development of thought.[2] Like Plato and Aristotle at a later day, they founded schools; but the corporate tradition was based on the creative work of individual thinkers, whose names have survived, and whose personality dominated, in an increasing degree, the course of intellectual progress. In the second place their procedure was thoroughly scientific; observation was broadened by experiment[3] and illumined by hypothesis; limited as were the range of accessible facts and the instruments of research, their aim was the discovery of principles of necessary connexion amid the changing diversity of phenomena. 'Nothing can arise out of nothing'; 'naught happens for nothing, but everything from a ground and of necessity'.[4] Unlike the Chaldaean astronomers, who merely utilized their store of observed facts as a basis for fantastic interpretation, the Greek thinkers set themselves to understand the world as a world of rational law, with system and unity of structure. They pursued this path with unswerving confidence and courage, displaying rare genius alike for scientific hypothesis and for logical procedure. 'No sooner,' writes Professor Burnet, 'did an Ionian philosopher learn half a dozen geometrical propositions, and hear that the phe-

1. See Burnet, *Early Greek Philosophy*, pp. 28 ff. The Hebrew prophets, as has been shown in the previous chapter, were in no sense scientific thinkers. The remark in the text applies to the wise men in Egypt and Babylonia, and also to the annalists and codifiers of the law among the Hebrews. Even prophecy became anonymous as it became reflective, e.g. in Is. xl–lxvi, while the later apocalyptic was either anonymous or attached itself to earlier teachers (e.g. Enoch); see above, c. iii. § 11, *note* and § 15, *note*.

2. Thales flourished *c.* 585, Anaximander *c.* 565, Anaximenes *c.* 550–545.

3. Cf. Anaximander's observations in marine biology and Empedocles' experiment with the water-clock to prove that air is a physical body; Burnet, *Early Greek Philosophy*, 71, 229.

4. Parmenides, *fr.* 8, Empedocles, *fr.* 12, Leucippus (Burnet, *Early Greek Philosophy*, p. 340). The fragments are referred to according to the numbering in the translations given by Burnet.

nomena of the heavens recur in cycles, than he set to work to look for law everywhere in nature, and, with an audacity almost amounting to *hubris*, to construct a system of the universe.' Thus it was that they were enabled to discover, in the course of two or three generations, the true theory of eclipses, the sphericity of the earth, and the fact of its revolution, like the other planets, round the centre of its system.[1] Such were the firstfruits harvested by the spirit that took to itself two watchwords, to 'save the phenomena' and to 'give a reason'. Thirdly, the scientific genius of the Greek philosophers is evident in their clear conception of the problem they set themselves to solve. Renouncing once and for all the fruitless quest after a first beginning of the universe in primeval chaos, which in Greece as elsewhere had tortured the ingenuity of earlier generations, they sought for the underlying reality of that which *is*. What, they asked, is the bottom truth of the world as we know it now? The desire to find unity and principle amid the restless variety of nature took the form of the search for a primary substance which remains permanent amid change, for an active energizing matter whose motions, determined in accordance with necessary law, give birth to the phenomena of sense-experience. Such a primary substance, called by them *physis* (nature), formed the theme of their inquiry and the title of their treatises.[2] Thales held it to be water, others found it in vapour or in fire or in a combination or harmony of opposite principles. They differed also in their explanations of the process by which our world arises from this ultimate reality. But all alike start from observed facts and advance by logical reasoning towards the conception of an ordered universe, wherein, by operation of necessary law, the One generates the Many and the Many are resolved into the One.[3]

1. *Early Greek Philosophy*, pp. 23, 25.

2. To translate *physis* by 'nature' may be misleading, since it transfers attention from process to origin. *Physis* is always a verbal substantive, meaning a process like the growth of a plant.

3. Our knowledge of these early thinkers is derived from scattered fragments of their writings and from notices in later Greek authors. Thales alone left no writing behind him. Anaximander, his successor, held that *physis* was

§ 15. We cannot do more than indicate the trend of these early speculations, in order to show how they present an ordered sequence of scientific thought.

(i) The first efforts of the Ionian thinkers referred to in the preceding section led, at the beginning of the fifth century, to the philosophy of Heraclitus of Ephesus,[1] whose central doctrine was that the life of nature consisted in a strife of opposite forces, in tension one against the other, and constituting by their reciprocal action the harmonious unity of the world. Fire, the most active element, passes into air and is fed by moisture in equal measures; summer and winter, waking and sleeping, day and night, life and death all exemplify the ceaseless and universal conflict of the 'way up' and the 'way down'. 'War is the father of all and the king of all'; 'the way up and the way down is one and the same'; 'men do not know how what is at variance with itself agrees with itself. It is an attunement of opposite tensions, like that of the bow and the lyre.' Heraclitus realized that nature's law is one of ceaseless change, that the world as it appears to sense is ever a becoming and a ceasing to be, nowhere a *being*, nowhere a thing of which we can say 'it *is*'. 'You cannot,' he said, 'step into the same river twice'; 'No,' added one of his followers, 'nor even once.' The issues of this thought of the ceaseless flux of the sense-world are apparent, as we shall see later, in the philosophy of Plato.

(ii) Coincidentally with this development among the Ionian

a boundless material substance containing in fusion all the opposite principles (moist and dry, hot and cold), which were separated out from the boundless mass by a sifting process, and thus gave rise to innumerable worlds of which ours is one. Anaximander was the first to realize that the earth swings free in space, needing no material support. Early Greek medicine (Alcmaeon, see below, p. 125, n. 2) was based on Anaximander's opposites; health was conceived as the *isonomy* or equilibrium of the hot and the cold, the moist and the dry, disease as the despotism of one of the opposites over the other. Anaximenes, the third in time of the Milesian philosophers, held that *physis* was vapour, from which our world arises by condensation and rarefaction. For details on these and the other early thinkers, see Burnet, *Early Greek Philosophy*, and *Thales to Plato*.

1. Heraclitus flourished between 500 and 480; he was influenced also by early Pythagorean science. The quotations that follow are from *Fr.* 44, 69, 45, 41 (cf. 81).

Greeks, the impulse to scientific inquiry had been stirring in
the west. (a) Already in the sixth century Pythagoras and his
followers in southern Italy had founded the study of mathematics, both in the field of pure geometry and in the application of mathematics to other branches of science, especially to
the theory of musical sounds, and to philosophy in general.[1]
Their doctrine that 'things are numbers' was no fantastic
analogy, but the reasoned conclusion of thinkers, who in their
analysis of experience found themselves confronted at every
turn by laws admitting of mathematical formulation. They were
feeling their way towards a system like that of Descartes, who
determined the independent reality of the physical universe,
in terms of its geometrical properties, as figured extension.
This was precisely the position taken up by Plato in the *Timaeus*,
under the influence of his Pythagorean predecessors.[2] (b)
Another school of thought, the Eleatic, founded by Parmenides of Elea, also had its home in southern Italy.[3] Par-

1. Pythagoras flourished about 530; he was a native of Ionian Samos who
settled in Italy. Little is known of his life or of his personal teaching apart
from that of his school. The Pythagoreans combined scientific research with a
religious rule of life, and played an active part in south Italian politics. Henceforward Greek philosophy is never merely intellectualist; it directs *praxis* as
well as *theoria*. The school continued its work well on into the fourth century.
In contrast to the eastern Greek philosophers, their inquiries were predominantly mathematical. See Sir T. Heath, *History of Greek Mathematics*, especially
pp. 2, 166 ff., where the mathematical achievements of the Pythagoreans are
summarized (covering Euclid, books I, II, IV, VI and probably III).

2. The Pythagoreans interpreted numbers in terms of geometry, the unit
being a point having position in a spatial field; hence arose the term (mathematical) 'figures'. See Burnet, *Early Greek Philosophy*, pp. 99 ff., and *Thales to
Plato*, pp. 51 ff. Burnet shows how the discovery that the notes of the lyre
depend on mathematical ratios influenced mathematical speculations. Pythagorean science also stimulated the study of medicine and of rhetoric in southern Italy and Sicily. Its importance was thus very great. The thought that the
physical world is built up of spatial (or spatio-temporal) elements and that its
nature can be explained in terms of mathematical equations, is prominent in
modern physics and philosophy. The most recent metaphysical system in this
country, that of Professor S. Alexander (*Space, Time and Deity*, Gifford Lectures at Glasgow, 1916–18), interprets the universe as generated from pure
spatio-temporal elements, viz. point-instants. The scientific studies of the
Pythagoreans led them, in the very dawn of scientific development, to conceptions that were extraordinarily fruitful.

3. Parmenides flourished between 480 and 450; about the latter date he
visited Athens, see Plato, *Parm.* 127. Burnet's view of his place in Greek
philosophy is followed in the text.

menides unfolded with inexorable logic the conclusions that
follow from the assumptions which previous thinkers had
accepted without question. All had taken for granted not only
that *physis* or reality was one, but also that it was corporeal; all,
moreover, had conceived this one body as possessed of inherent motion, and had thus derived from it the manifold
phenomena of experience. Parmenides showed that, if the
real is one and is corporeal, the many and motion are alike
illusory. He accepted this refutation of the reality of the changing world of sense, but in effect his logic proved the *reductio
ad absurdum* of the received assumptions. Henceforward the
unity of *physis* was sacrificed by all thinkers who retained their
faith in the other Parmenidean tenet, viz., that the real was of
the nature of body.[1]

(iii) As a result of Parmenides' philosophy, there arose in
the middle of the fifth century a number of pluralist systems.
Empedocles of Agrigentum in Sicily, Anaxagoras of Clazo-
menae in Asia (the first philosopher to take up his abode at
Athens), and Leucippus of Miletus (the teacher of Democritus
and founder of the Atomic school), all agree with the later
Pythagoreans in holding two positions, the traditional view
that reality is corporeal, and the new view, to which they were
driven by Parmenides, that it is not one but many.[2] Empedocles and Anaxagoras further sought for a cause of motion; the

1. Zeno's famous paradoxes, e.g. that of Achilles and the tortoise, were put
forward in support of his master Parmenides' denial of motion. There was, of
course, another way out of the quandary, viz. to maintain that reality was one,
but that it was a spiritual, not a material, unity. This view appears first with
Socrates and Plato, see c. v. §§ 17, 20.

2. Empedocles flourished *c.* 460, Anaxagoras and Leucippus *c.* 450; Democritus belongs to the next generation and was influenced by the Sophists, on
whom see c. v. §§ 13–15. The middle of the fifth century was a time of great
creative activity in Greek thought. It should be observed also that the biological sciences were assuming increasing importance during the fifth century.
Schools of medicine also flourished, at first, in close connexion with philosophy, as that of Alcmaeon of Croton in southern Italy, who dedicated his work
to the Pythagorean community, but later, in independence, as in the case of
the fifth-century Hippocratean school in the island of Cos. Alcmaeon was the
real founder of psychology (see on this and generally on early Greek psychology, Beare, *Greek Theories of Elementary Cognition*, and Brett, *History of Psychology*,
esp. pp. 24, 25, and c. v). Later Greek sculpture (the school of Pergamos)
shows some knowledge of anatomy. See Burnet, *Early Greek Philosophy*, pp. 26,
193 ff.

latter found it in *nous* or mind, though he interpreted its
action mechanically as that of an external physical agent.[1] The
entire course of speculative development was summed up by
the Atomists, who were the first to affirm the reality of empty
space, and who reduced the universe to a congeries of innumerable atoms, homogeneous, and differing only in size,
shape, and position, drifting through infinite space in ceaseless
motion.[2] With the publication of this system, the effort to
conceive the world in terms of its material elements had
worked itself out to fulfilment.

§ 16. It was entirely natural that the problems as to the
nature of reality, and whether it is one or many, should have
been answered by these early philosophers in physical terms.
By *physis* they meant either one body or a plurality of bodies,
and, in the latter case, bodies either limited or unlimited in
number, and either differing in quality or homogeneous. A
time would come when the thought of a spiritual reality
would arise in the mind of Greek thinkers, but for this the
hour was not yet ripe. Each successive phase of Greek philosophy appears in order of logical development, in obedience to
a law imposed, not by external circumstances, but by the
intrinsic nature of human reason. We must not suppose that
these physical inquirers ignored the facts of man's mental and
moral life. The distinction, so familiar and yet so puzzling to
modern thought, between the material and the spiritual had
not yet been clearly drawn. Anaximenes of Miletus, for
example, held that the soul is vapour.[3] To call this materialism
in the modern sense would be less true than to say that his
vapour was something not merely physical. So, again, Heraclitus spoke of fire convicting all things and of the sun as
observing the bounds of justice;[4] while love and strife, the

1. For Socrates' dissatisfaction with the concept of mind as a mechanical
force, to the exclusion of purposive action, see the remarkable account of his
early intellectual history in Plato, *Phaedo*, pp. 96 ff.

2. Leucippus' more famous successor, Democritus of Abdera in Thrace,
wrote in the last third of the fifth century, when the new ideas of the Sophists,
raising problems of the theory of knowledge and of ethics, were abroad. The
Atomism of Epicurus (see c. vi. § 18) is based on Democritus's system.

3. The 'air' of Anaximenes included the 'breath' of life, wind and vapour.

4. *Fr.* 27; cf. *fr.* 29. 'The sun will not overstep his measures; if he does,

motive forces of Empedocles, were conceived as corporeal masses, and the *nous* of Anaxagoras as filling space. But it was not till well on in the fifth century that men's thinking and conduct claimed equal attention with the problems of physical nature. Then first the question arose: since moral standards, religious beliefs, and the laws and institutions of the *Polis* present, like physical nature, a scene of instability and change, are they in consequence only of local and transitory value, 'conventions' artificially set up by human ordinance? Or is there some *physis* or natural morality, some unchanging law of God or man, of which the changing conventions are the passing embodiment? Such questions were inevitable in a time of political unrest, when men's minds had already been disciplined by more than a century of intellectual inquiry. They were asked by the Greeks of the middle years of the fifth century, and, when once asked, gave birth, as we shall see in a later chapter, not only to moral and political philosophy, but to a new and enlarged conception of the nature of reality, and of man's place and destiny in the universe.

§ 17. It remains for us to notice the double relationship, of hostility and of fusion, between the new-born philosophy and the old religion.[1] On the one hand, the broadening of men's

the Erinyes, the handmaids of justice, will find him out.' So Anaximander: things 'make reparation and satisfaction to one another for their injustice in an order of time' (Burnet, *Early Greek Philosophy*, p. 52).

1. In conformity with our purpose of concentrating attention on those factors which have most directly influenced later times, we have omitted the interesting subject of Greek religion, save in so far as it bears on the history of Greek philosophy. Recent investigations have done much to throw light on this field, which is important not only for an understanding of Greek poetry, law, and daily life, but also, of course, for the comparative study of early religions. A point of special interest to readers of this book is the distinction between the Olympian gods, represented by Apollo, and the Mystery gods, represented by Dionysus. The former were idealized superhuman beings, dwelling in remote transcendence, with whom anything of the nature of personal communion was hardly conceivable; the latter were directly accessible to the initiated in the state of emotional ecstasy, and through sacramental food and drink. The mystery-religions furnished materials to the philosophers (see below, § 17 and c. v. § 21); that of the Olympians provoked only hostility. See C. C. J. Webb, Gifford Lectures on *Personality, Human and Divine*, i. 77ff. Nietzsche's *Birth of Tragedy* should be read; see also Gilbert Murray, *Five Stages of Greek Religion*, and other works mentioned in the bibliography appended to Vol. 2 of this book.

range of experience, the growth of the critical temper, and the awakening of higher moral aspirations were bound to provoke scepticism. But this effect was confined to the few who thought seriously about such matters, or, at most, to the cultured public. Anaxagoras might proclaim that the sun was not a god, but a stone 'about as large as the Peloponnese'; the fifth-century Athenian felt a shock to his devotion, and condemned the philosopher for impiety. Such hostility was due, not to any distaste for speculation, but to inbred loyalty to the traditional worships of the city. This was the main reason for the distrust of science and philosophy that found brilliant expression in the satire of the Old Attic comedy. One of the charges brought against Socrates by his accusers was that of introducing new divinities, and teaching men to disbelieve in those whom the city worshipped. It is thoroughly significant of Greek life that the opposition to philosophy was led, not by priests, but by poets and politicians. The philosophers, on their side, were uncompromising in condemnation of the traditional beliefs. Especially in Ionia, the birthplace both of science and history, where the merchant-princes formed a cultivated public, the spread of the sceptical spirit was rapid and general. 'Homer and Hesiod,' wrote Xenophanes of Colophon, 'have ascribed to the gods all things that are a shame and a disgrace among men, thefts and adulteries and the deception of one another.' 'Homer,' said Heraclitus, 'should be turned out of the lists and whipped, and Archilochus likewise.' The 'quarrel between poetry and philosophy' was referred to by Plato in the *Republic* as of long standing; he meant the quarrel, not of art and knowledge, for these have no ground of conflict, but between the rival claims of religious tradition and scientific reason to teach the truth.[1]

§ 18. In the matter of the relationship of the new science to the established faiths of the *Polis* there was thus from the first a clear issue. The case was different and less simple in regard to the wave of revival of primitive popular religion that swept over Greece in the sixth century. Beneath the cult of the Olympian deities, fostered by the Homeric poets and the aristocracy of

1. Plato, *Rep.*, x. 607. Xenoph., *fr.* 11. Heracl., *fr.* 119; cf. *fr.* 16, 35, 43.

the Dark Ages, there may have persisted in the minds of the common people a mass of ancient belief, the survival probably of pre-Hellenic Minoan religion.¹ These primitive faiths, traces of which appear in the Hesiodic and even in the Homeric poems, were associated with the cult of the dead, with the divinities of the under-world, and especially with the incarnation of the non-Homeric god, Dionysus. Dionysus and Orpheus were alike associated closely with Thrace. They received official recognition in the mystic rites of Eleusis in Attica, which consisted of dramatic representations of sacred incidents, and of initiatory ceremonies to purify the soul of the worshipper from guilt. Purification was the essence of the sixth-century revival. Prophets and purifiers of cities, such as the Cretan Epimenides, who was called in to cleanse Athens, appear in the Hellenic world, as do also organized confraternities, analogous to churches, and detached from the bonds, of kinship or of the *Polis*, which formed the basis of the established worships. They possessed sacred poetic writings, ascribed to the legendary hero Orpheus, and containing distinctive theological doctrines, especially in regard to the destiny of the soul in the world beyond the grave. The Orphic brotherhoods taught the soul's pre-existence and inherent immortality, resting upon its kinship with the divine, its successive incarnations in the bodily forms of men and animals, and its purification from guilt through ecstatic union with the god.² For the initiated they held out the hope of everlasting felicity; in this life the soul suffers imprisonment and the body is its tomb; through the series of incarnations it works out

1. The worship of Apollo and the Olympian religion generally were probably introduced by the northern (Achaean) invaders, though the new cult may have been coloured by assimilation of the beliefs of older Aegean peoples. The close association of the tyrants of the sixth century, both with the religious revival and with the early development of the drama (which arose in connexion with the worship of Dionysus), is explicable, if we regard their power as that of wealthy capitalists resting on popular support against the feudal aristocracy. The latter were naturally attached to the traditional Olympian religious cults.

2. The belief in immortality depends on that in the kinship of man with God; only by becoming God can immortality be attained. In Orphic teaching the soul is conceived as a fallen god which can be released by purifications and sacraments from the prison of the body (ecstasy, Greek *ecstasis*, means

its cycle of destiny. In practice, these doctrines were preached and accepted in a crude and material form; purification meant the observance of weird taboos and external ceremonies; the future life a paradise of sensual enjoyment – in Plato's scornful phrase – 'eternal drunkenness'.[1] Yet the ideas which lay at the root of Orphic teaching were capable of a higher interpretation. Poets like Pindar and Aeschylus made use of them in their effort to accommodate religious authority to the claims of the more elevated moral consciousness of their day.[2] Of the response which they could evoke from philosophy the *Phaedo* of Plato is an imperishable monument. In this, and in others of his writings, the same thinker who poured the vials of his anger upon the pardon-mongers and stewards of superstitious mysteries transformed the Orphic doctrines of the soul's imprisonment in the body, of its pre-existence and immortality, and of its judgement in another world, into an instrument of the loftiest metaphysical and religious teaching.[3] Herein Plato was treading in Pythagorean steps.[4] The scientific researches of this school were intimately bound up with their religious tenets and ascetic rule of life. Pythagoras himself had set the

'stepping out' of the body) and regain its divinity (see Burnet, *Early Greek Philosophy*, c. ii. pp. 80–4). For the Homeric (Olympian) religion, gods and men are different orders of being; no man can become a god, and therefore there is no human immortality. Only a favoured few were carried by the gods to Olympus *during their life*, none after death. Hesiod holds that heroes might go at death to Elysium instead of Hades. It was far otherwise in the primitive religion and in its sixth-century revival. It should be observed that the Greek belief in immortality utilized materials drawn from primitive religion, while that of the Hebrews arose in complete independence of it; see above, c. iii. § 15, p. 84 *note*. Consequently the Greek conception, unlike the Hebrew, implied pre-existence, i.e. immortality *ex parte ante* as well as *ex parte post*. On the whole subject, see Guthrie, *Orphism*.

1. See the whole passage in condemnation of the mysteries and of Orphic teaching, *Rep.*, ii. 363 ff.

2. See Pindar, *Olymp.*, ii. 62 ff. and *Fragments*, 129–33; Aeschylus, *Eum.*, 269 f. (judgement after death); and (of special interest for the problems it raises) the *Bacchae* of Euripides, one of his latest plays.

3. Especially in the eschatological myths in the *Gorgias*, *Phaedo*, *Republic*, *Phaedrus*. See Stewart, *The Myths of Plato*, and Adam, *Religious Thought in Greece*.

4. The *Phaedo* is dedicated to a Pythagorean coterie in European Greece. Socrates had been closely associated with several Pythagoreans who took refuge in Greece after their expulsion from Italy during the last half of the fifth century.

example of this fusion, teaching that science was the true purification of the soul, and that salvation was to be attained through initiation into its mysteries. From that time onwards, philosophy meant for the Greek thinker a 'way of life'.[1] The philosopher, in the eyes of the Pythagoreans and of Plato, was the saint of rationalism. In the *Symposium*, the Orphic faith in the ecstatic union of the devotee with his god is moulded into an intellectual intuition of absolute beauty, the crown of a laborious pilgrimage up the mountain-chain of scientific reasoning.[2] We shall see further fruits of this conception when the time comes to speak of Neo-Platonism in the early centuries of the Christian era. From the same Pythagorean source flowed the distinction, derived by analogy from the Hellenic games, of the three types of human life. Some, like those who came to these festivals to sell their wares, choose the path of material satisfaction, of gain and pleasure; others, like the competing athletes, aspire after honour in the field of action, in politics or war; while there are those who, like the lookers-on at the games, prefer the life of the spectator, contemplating, with a mind untrammelled by the cravings of its bodily prison-house, the vision of perfect truth. This conception of intellectual contemplation (*theoria*) as the highest human activity, akin to the divine, realized first by the Pythagoreans and developed by Plato and Aristotle, carries us into the very heart of the Hellenic genius.

VI. CONCLUSION

§ 19. The process of expansion recorded in this chapter illustrates the intellectual quality of Hellenism. There is a logic inherent in all the creations of the Greeks. A glance at their architecture, with its mastery of form and function, and its mathematical symmetry, suffices to show how the scientific spirit informed imaginative art. The belief that 'God ever geometrizes' dominated both their theory of nature and their aesthetic production. Art for the Greeks is regarded always as a form of wisdom (*sophia*). Not only the Greek thinker, but

1. Cf. Plato, *Rep.*, x. 600.   2. Plato, *Symp.*, 210.

the Greek artist, possessed the sense of truth that led them to distinguish clearly between the ideal and the actual, giving both their due. They felt, too, the inspiration of that power to which the one among modern poets who has entered most fully into the spirit of ancient Greece dedicated his life, the vision of intellectual beauty.[1] Severity and truth are marks of Greek art. When, for instance, Homer says 'Helen,' he means 'Helen'; when Virgil says 'Dido,' he means 'Cleopatra', or 'Carthage'. A like logic is discernible in the process of their development. We have seen above how the records of political history, of poetic literature, and of scientific thought, reveal an ordered sequence of forms.[2] What the Ionian philosophers remarked in nature is true also of the mind of Greece; everywhere there is variety and change, nothing is at rest. But the changes, though ceaseless and pervasive, were guided throughout by rational law. Type succeeds type, school follows upon school in logical sequence, till the range of possible forms has been exhausted, and the cycle of development is complete. The cardinal service of Greece to civilization was to create in action and to define in thought the essential characters of human experience. The terms in use to-day to express the distinctions and groupings that form the basis of our understanding of the world; in politics – monarchy, aristocracy, democracy; in literature – epic, lyric, dramatic, tragedy, and comedy; in knowledge – the names of the arts and sciences, poetry, physics, astronomy, mathematics, history, philosophy itself – are all terms invented by the Greeks. The forms which they thus distinguished and named were evolved by them in the process of their own life-history. No race has ever grasped with so clear an insight, and defined with such precision, the truths of life and knowledge.[3] It is because of this marvellous gift of

1 See Shelley, *Hymn to Intellectual Beauty*.

2. See especially the study of defective forms of political government in Plato, *Republic*, books viii and ix, where the logical order in which Plato treats of them presents many analogies to the actual course of development in Greek history.

3. The Hippocratean clinical records, for example, are concise statements of facts, unencumbered by any superfluity of language. Even the Greek orators show a wonderful economy in their speeches.

intellectual judgement, enabling them in thought and deed to realize the objects for which these terms stand, that all succeeding generations have been content, and in fact obliged, to build on the foundations which they laid.

CHAPTER FIVE

THE GREATNESS OF ATHENS

*

I. THE ATHENIAN STATE

§ 1. IT was at Athens in the fifth century that Greek civilization reached its zenith. Athens was then the chief political and commercial city of the Hellenic world, whither flowed all the currents of literature, art, and knowledge. In the famous phrase of her statesman Pericles, she became 'the school of Hellas'. History affords no parallel to the wealth and variety of creative genius that Athens in this century produced or gathered to herself from all quarters of Greece. In a single city, whose free population was not greater than that of a moderate-sized English town, there dwelt, within three generations of human lifetime, statesmen such as Themistocles and Pericles; the three tragic poets Aeschylus, Sophocles, and Euripides, and the comic poet Aristophanes; Phidias and his marvellous school of sculptors; the historians Herodotus and Thucydides; the philosopher Anaxagoras; Socrates, the greatest of all human teachers; and Socrates' immortal disciple Plato. There were numberless others, statesmen and poets and thinkers, many of them little more than names for after time, who yet, in a less brilliant epoch, would have been among the famous men of history. It seems as though the individuality of Greek civilization strove for the brief period of its maturity to surpass the bounds of possible achievement.

§ 2. Though Athens developed into a great commercial city, the basis of her civic life was agricultural. By the seventh century the population of Attica had been united in a single commonwealth, monarchy had given place to the rule of a landed aristocracy, class distinctions of nobles, farmers, and craftsmen had become definite, and the evils of debt and personal bondage were already acutely manifest. The smaller landholders had become hopelessly indebted to the larger, and

were allowed to pledge their personal freedom to their
creditors. The close of that century saw the publication of a
code of laws, an event of moment in the history of all early
communities, and especially so in the case of Athens, where
'equal law' (*isonomia*) was the pride of her citizens, and the
science of jurisprudence attained a level of perfection unequalled in the Hellenic world.[1] Thanks to her proximity to
the sea and her harbour of Piraeus, Athens was enabled to take
her full share in the expansion of trade; here, as elsewhere,
the influx of wealth and the rise of a plutocracy of merchants
intensified the prevalent unrest. The root of the trouble was
that political privileges had been confined to landholders.
Solon first allowed men with mercantile capital to purchase
land from impecunious landowners and so to qualify for active
citizenship and public office. Early in the sixth century, called
to power in order to solve the economic crisis, he succeeded,
by reform of the criminal law, and, above all, by the institution of popular tribunals to which the magistrates were
accountable, in laying the foundations of democracy. In ancient
society the law court rather than the assembly was the home of
political liberty, where the people won control over the executive. Constitutional changes followed in rapid succession
throughout the sixth century. Pisistratus' tyranny, resting
probably on the support of his employees in the mines of
southern Attica, was remarkable in its respect for law and
constitutional procedure, its encouragement of agriculture
and trade, and the stimulus it gave to art and culture. He also
encouraged the small reclaimer of waste land in Attica.
Athens now extended her commercial and diplomatic relations over both shores of the Aegean.[2] The tyranny of the

1. On *isonomia*, see Herod., iii. 80 f.; cf. v. 78, where the term employed
is *isêgoriê*, 'equality of speech'.
2. See Professor P. N. Ure, *The Greek Renaissance*, c. vii, on the connexion
of tyranny in general and that of Pisistratus in particular with capitalism and
employment of labour. The argument is developed more fully in his later
work, *The Origin of Tyranny*. Pisistratus' rule was of epoch-making importance
for Athens in art, literature, and religion. Athens then became the centre of
Homeric influence in Greece. On this, see Murray, *Five Stages of Greek Religion*,
p. 61. As her population grew, Athens drew her food supply from Euboea
and the Euxine; hence the extension of her maritime power to the east and

Pisistratids was short-lived; for the thirst for political equality, once aroused in the Athenian citizen-body, was uncompromising and unquenchable. Pisistratus' family were expelled by a popular revolution backed by Spartan force, but their real enemies were the Alcmaeonidae, a rival noble family; and in the closing years of the century Clisthenes dealt a death-blow to the territorial influence of the aristocracy and reorganized the government on a frankly democratic basis. He not only admitted alien residents to full citizenship, but broke up political groupings based on local land ties, replacing them by new tribes, whose members were drawn from various parts of Attica. Thus, when the tide of invasion burst upon Greece at the dawn of the fifth century, Athens was able to confront the crisis with an outfit of political institutions worthy alike of the temper of her citizens and of her new-won status in the commonwealth of Hellenic city-states. Alike in capacity for political development and in freedom of intercourse with other cities, Athens presented, at this time and henceforward, a notable contrast to the state then dominant on the Greek mainland, Sparta.[1] From their home in the secluded valley of the Eurotas, the Spartan aristocracy held the southern Peloponnesus in absolute subjection, and, thanks to their unquestioned courage and skill in arms, were recognized as the leading military power in Greece. But Sparta was a barrack rather than a state: the training and life of her citizens were governed by the one aim of efficiency in war; she retained her primitive institutions for centuries almost unchanged; and, scorning trade, guarded her borders rigorously from the intrusion of strangers. She contributed little or nothing of lasting value to the structure of Hellenic civilization. Her strength lay in her support of the *ancien régime* everywhere in Greece, in her *Herrenvolk* policy, and the separatism that ensured her supremacy. She produced brave soldiers, but few statesmen of dis-

north-east was essential to her existence. It was with her as with Holland in the later sixteenth and seventeenth centuries. This explains why the Athenian democracy consistently advocated imperial expansion.

1. Thucydides gives expression to this contrast in the speech of the Corinthian envoys at Sparta in 432, i. 70, and also in the Funeral Oration of Pericles, ii. 35–46, extracts from which are quoted in § 5 of this chapter.

tinction; her more gifted citizens were objects of suspicion at home, and, when freed from the atmosphere of Spartan tradition, became easy victims of corruption. We wonder at the fame that Sparta won in the eyes of contemporary Greece, and at the moral authority that she wielded over many of the best Hellenic minds. When Plato despaired of the political salvation of Athens, it was towards Sparta that he looked for a remedy. The reason lay in this: that, narrow and unfruitful and oppressive as was the Spartan aristocracy, its stability, unity of principle, and loyalty to the state seemed to furnish the needed complement to the restless and emotional democracy of Athens.[1]

§ 3. The war with Persia afforded Athens her supreme opportunity. We have already told the story of the rapid rise of the Persian empire, and of the subjection of the Asiatic Greeks to its yoke. Its navy, recruited from the merchant cities of Phoenicia, threatened to convert the Aegean into a Persian sea. The autonomy of the Greek city-states clashed with Persian imperialism, while democratic movements, threatening the political and economic *status quo*, threw its conservative defenders into the arms of Persia. Greek nationalists stigmatized this way of escape as 'Medism', for it dates from before the rise of Persia. The sea-power of Polycrates of Samos had endangered Persian control of the coasts of Asia Minor. Darius' Thracian conquests opened the eyes of Miletus which at first had 'medized'. The revolt of the Ionian Greeks in the first years of the fifth century impressed upon the government at Susa the need for consolidating their western frontier, and in 490 a punitive expedition was despatched by sea against the Athenians, who had aided the abortive rising of their Ionian kinsmen with an armed contingent. The Persian force was faced and beaten on the plain of Marathon, on the north-

1. Plato's picture of the timocratic state in *Rep.* viii. 547–8 is admittedly analogous to the Spartan. Its guiding principles are 'honour' (*timê*) and 'victory'. It is the least corrupt of the types of 'unjust' states. Later, in the *Laws*, Plato is much less tolerant towards Spartan institutions. Aristotle criticizes Sparta severely in the *Politics*, ii. 9, vii. 14, 15. Polybius (vi. 48–50), in his examination of Spartan institutions, pronounces them unequalled for preserving independence and self-sufficiency at home, but most inadequate for the conduct of external relations and empire.

eastern coast of Attica. It is difficult, in view of subsequent events of greater magnitude, to realize what this victory meant to Greece. For the first time, the Persian Colossus had been countered in the open field. For Athens, Marathon furnished an imperishable memory; long afterwards, when her greatest orator told how his fellow-citizens rallied to the death-struggle against Macedon, his thought reverted to those who fell gloriously at Marathon.[1] To the Persians, doubtless, it meant little more than an awkward set-back to their forward frontier policy. It rendered necessary operations on a large scale; but the imperial levy took time to muster, and a revolt of Egypt and the death of king Darius involved several years' delay. It was not till 481 that the host assembled under Xerxes at Sardis, with the fleet in the Aegean hard by, for the definite conquest of Greece. The critical moment for Hellenic civilization had come at last; as the Persians advanced, half of the Greek cities gave in their submission, and the oracle at Delphi played traitor to the Hellenic cause. Sparta, the back-bone of defence on land, thought, as ever, chiefly of the Pelo-ponnese. It was now that Athens stood forth as the champion of Hellenic freedom. Twice her citizens witnessed undismayed from their island refuge at Salamis the ravaging of their lands and the destruction of their city. Her navy secured the deci-sive victory of Salamis (480); and in the year following her soldiers fought side by side with the Spartan infantry at the 'crowning mercy' of Plataea. Athens found a leader of com-manding ability, both in war and statesmanship, in the person of Themistocles. Greece was saved, and her salvation was due primarily to the patriotism of Athens.[2] Never again was Hel-lenic liberty menaced from the East. The danger had been two-fold. In the West also Carthage had attacked the Greeks of Sicily in the year of Xerxes' invasion, to meet with a crushing defeat on the Himera at the hands of Gelo, the tyrant of Syracuse. Gelo's triumph inaugurated a brilliant epoch of

1. Demosthenes, de Coronâ, § 208.
2. See Herod., viii. 143 f., on Athenian patriotism at this crisis. The expedi-tion of 490 is related by him in vi. 94–120; that of Xerxes in vii–ix. Aeschylus dramatized the defeat of Xerxes in his Persians.

Syracusan sovereignty. Indeed, Syracuse henceforward stands second only to Athens as a centre of Hellenic art and culture.[1]

§ 4. The Greek victory was magnificent, but in no wise miraculous; it affords the first clear illustration in history of the secular triumph of quality over quantity. The Greeks had done at Salamis and Plataea what Alexander did afterwards at Issus and Gaugamela, and Clive in modern times at Plassey.[2] Human history belies at every point the foolish epigram that 'God is on the side of the big battalions'; if Napoleon ever said this, it must have been with the implicit reservation, 'quality being equal'. The true marvel lies in the use the Athenians made of their victory. In the hour of triumph, they displayed the same insight into facts and breadth of vision as in that of overwhelming danger. When Sparta and other Greek states were content to rest upon their laurels, Athens resolved to prolong the struggle till every Greek city in the Aegean area had been freed from the Persian yoke. Policy as well as patriotism doubtless pointed in this direction, but it is to the eternal honour of Athens that at this moment she identified the call of civic interest with that of Hellenic independence. She reaped her reward a thousandfold; in political greatness, alike in her internal civic life and in her commerce and empire upon the seas; and also, as we shall see, in the noblest fruits of intellectual culture that have ever fallen to human kind. The war of liberation (478–470) left her the unquestioned mistress of Aegean waters. The fortification of the city and of its port, the Piraeus, secured her from Spartan rivalry on the land. Her fleets policed the Aegean, henceforward closed, as were the coast-lands of western Asia, to the Persians. These facts formed the basis of the understanding which

1. Pindar addressed several of his finest odes to Sicilian princes, including Gelo's successor Hiero; Aeschylus visited Sicily more than once, and died at Gela; Gorgias of Leontini was a famous sophist and master of rhetoric; in the fourth century Plato visited Syracuse on two, if not three, occasions. Gelo was Captain-general of an exclusive Capitalist oligarchy. The Ionian cities in W. Sicily had in despair called in Carthage. Syracuse offers a striking contrast to democratic Athens.

2. The Athenians themselves saw clearly that the victory was due to the strength and skill of their navy, the sagacity of Themistocles, and their spirit of unwavering patriotism (see Thuc., i. 73, 74, 144).

terminated in 448 the long conflict of more than forty years. Athens was left in possession of a monopoly of eastern trade. The liberated cities were still organized in a league under her presidency, with a common treasury at the sacred island of Delos, to which each city contributed an appointed quota for the maintenance of the protecting navy. So brilliantly had Athens made good her avowed intention. But, as the century wore on, her policy underwent a change. The presiding state of the Delian confederacy developed into the sovereign city of a subject-empire. Her former allies became tributaries, their claim to secede from the league was sternly trampled down, the treasury was removed to Athens, and their internal institutions were remodelled in the interest of Athenian sovereignty. Since Athens was a democracy, the subject cities must also be democracies. It is characteristic of Greek political history that friendships and enmities between states depended largely on the political complexion of the party in power. Democratic governments allied themselves with Athens, aristocratic governments with Sparta. In the time of Pericles (460–430) the Athenian empire comprised the islands of the Aegean, the coast-cities of Thrace and Asia Minor, the Hellespont and the sea-passage to the Euxine, though Naxos revolted in 465 and Samos in 440. Athens further displayed her activity in vain attempts to master central Greece, and in a military expedition to Egypt, which ended in disaster. The city grew in wealth and population, as the natural result of her extensive and varied trade. Bitterly as her empire was resented by its subjects, there is no evidence that it was unjustly governed. Our verdict must be guided by two considerations. By the centralization in the Athenian courts of commercial suits involving different cities and of the most serious criminal causes, the most highly developed system of judicial administration then existing in the world was thrown open to the whole of eastern Greece. Moreover, Athens fully recognized the obligation imposed on her by sovereignty. Her citizens, so at least her foremost statesmen felt, were bound to live worthily of their empire. The efforts of Pericles to realize this ideal won the confidence of a democratic people. The dream of a pan-

Hellenic union under the leadership of a single city never came so near to fulfilment as in the Athenian empire in the Periclean age.

§ 5. When we turn from the external power of Athens to consider her inner public life, we find that from the time of Clisthenes the government was controlled by the will of the free citizen-body.[1] We have seen how to the Greek the true life of the citizen was the service of the state in peace and war. At Sparta this conception was realized by the governing aristocracy; endowed with estates worked by the subject population, they had leisure to devote their whole lives to military service. Pericles and his successors in the fifth century strove to make such a life possible for the democracy of Athens. The introduction of pay for attendance in the assembly and the law courts, which were occupied largely with political causes, was the means employed to effect this end. Over and above the business of local government, it was open to every citizen to attend in person, to vote and to speak, at the weekly meetings of the sovereign assembly (Ecclesia), where questions of foreign and imperial policy and of finance were determined, magistrates elected, and their reports discussed and scrutinized. The Boule was charged with the preparation of legislation for the Ecclesia; and a tenth of the number (the *prytany*) sat as a permanent executive in the town hall during each month of the year. Panels of several hundred jurors, chosen by lot from the citizen body, adjudged on political and religious impeachments; the conservative poet Aristophanes pours bitter scorn on the litigious excess of these Athenian 'wasps'.[2] The spirit of faction ran high; the aristocratic party advocating peace and friendship with Sparta, the democratic party, with its strength in the maritime population,

1. The free population of Attica in the Periclean age may have numbered about 250,000. Thuc., ii. 31 asserts that *c.* 430 the Athenian citizen force numbered 30,200. To these must be added some 20,000 of the lowest property class, making 50,000 adult male citizens; women, children and the aged, would be more than double this number, making up perhaps 200,000 free persons, *plus* 50,000 *metics* or resident aliens. The census of 309 B.C. shows a decrease of adult male citizens to 21,000, *plus* 10,000 *metics*.

2. Aristophanes, *Wasps, passim*.

championing the extension of the empire over sea and land. But when all allowance has been made for excesses of party spirit and individual ambition, the Athenian democracy was not unworthy of the ideals of the great statesman who established its supremacy. Pericles gave expression to that ideal in his speech in praise of the soldiers who fell in battle in the campaign of 431. The speech is recorded by the historian Thucydides, and the following passages may be quoted in illustration of Pericles' conception of Athenian democracy:

'Our form of government does not enter into rivalry with the institutions of others. We do not copy our neighbours, but are an example to them. It is true that we are called a democracy, for the administration is in the hands of the many and not of the few. But while the law secures equal justice to all alike in their private disputes, the claim of excellence is also recognized; and when a citizen is in any way distinguished, he is preferred to the public service, not as a matter of privilege, but as the reward of merit. Neither is poverty a bar, but a man may benefit his country whatever be the obscurity of his condition. There is no exclusiveness in our public life. . . . While we are unconstrained in our private intercourse, a spirit of reverence pervades our public acts; we are prevented from doing wrong by respect for authority and for the laws, having an especial regard for those which are ordained for the protection of the injured, as well as to those unwritten laws which bring upon the transgressor of them the reprobation of the general sentiment. . . . We are lovers of the beautiful, yet simple in our tastes, and we cultivate the mind without loss of manliness. Wealth we employ, not for talk and ostentation, but when there is a real use for it. To avow poverty with us is no disgrace; the true disgrace is in doing nothing to avoid it. An Athenian citizen does not neglect the state because he takes care of his own household; and even those of us who are engaged in business have a very fair idea of politics. We alone regard a man who takes no interest in public affairs, not as a harmless, but as a useless, character; and if few of us are originators, we are all sound judges of a policy. The great impediment to action is, in our opinion, not discussion, but

the want of that knowledge which is gained by discussion preparatory to action. For we have a peculiar power of thinking
before we act, and of acting too, whereas other men are
courageous from ignorance but hesitate upon reflexion. . . .
To sum up, I say that Athens is the school of Hellas, and that the
individual Athenian in his own person seems to have the power
of adapting himself to the most varied forms of action with the
utmost versatility and grace. This is no passing and idle word,
but truth and fact; and the assertion is verified by the position
to which these qualities have raised the state. . . . For we have
compelled every land and every sea to open a path for our
valour, and have everywhere planted eternal memorials of our
friendship and of our enmity. Such is the city for which these
men nobly fought and died; they could not bear the thought
that she might be taken from them; and every one of us who
survives should gladly toil on her behalf.' [1]

§ 6. Both the empire of Athens and the rule of the democracy which created and fostered it were short-lived. Athenian
history in the fifth century falls into three periods; the first
marked by the rise of her power in the Persian war, the second
by its consummation under Pericles, the third by its decline
and fall. Greek public life is everywhere a record of kaleido-
scopic change, and the halcyon days of Pericles' leadership
were clouded even before the great statesman's death (427).
The rivals of Athens were waiting an opportunity to combine
in an attack upon her supremacy. The impulse came from the
Isthmus states and especially from Corinth, whose commercial
interests in western Greece were menaced by the growing
ambition of Athens. While the Corinthians stirred into
activity the powerful though sluggish forces of Sparta, the
subject-cities of the Athenian empire watched eagerly for a
favourable occasion for revolt. In 431 broke out the conflict
known to history as the Peloponnesian war.[2] In reality all
Greece was involved in the struggle; the maritime power of
Athens on the one side was ranged against a coalition of her
enemies under Spartan leadership. It lasted with intermissions

1. Thuc., ii. 37-41 (tr. Jowett).
2. It had been anticipated by an earlier war (460 to 445).

till 404, when the destruction of the Athenian navy was followed by the fall of the imperial city. The story of the war has been told by Thucydides, himself an actor in its earlier scenes, in a work which remains for all time a magnificent creation of reflective history. To him the conflict was a drama, centring round the growing *hubris* of the Athenian democracy and culminating in the retribution (*nemesis*) that ensued when, in the effort to conquer Sicily, they overstepped the mark. As his predecessor Herodotus had traced the hand of a jealous providence in the *nemesis* that overtook the Persian empire, when in pride of power she hurled her hosts against free Greece, so Thucydides, in the spirit of a riper philosophy, saw in the catastrophe that befell his native city, at the instant when her thirst for universal empire seemed to have achieved its goal, the inexorable operation of the laws that determine the destiny of nations. The dialogue in which he narrates the ultimatum of Athens to the islanders of Melos, with its uncompromising assertion that necessity knows no law, that political expediency overrides all claims of moral obligations, and that the tyranny of the strong over the weak is the natural right of gods and men, is followed without a break by the story of the sailing of the Armada against Syracuse, its initial successes, its subsequent disasters, and its annihilation.[1] Athens never recovered from the blow. Alcibiades, the friend of Socrates and the most versatile and brilliant political personality of the age, finding himself discredited by the disaster, joined her enemies, and counselled the alliance with Persia, which furnished them with unlimited resources for the creation of a naval power. Athens could be conquered only on the sea. Her people fought on with marvellous tenacity and courage against overwhelming odds; but their life-blood had been drained, and eventual ruin was inevitable.[2] When the end came, a garrison of the hated Spartans was lodged in the

1. See Thuc., v. 89 ff. for the Melian dialogue. The sentiments remind us forcibly of the German defence for their violation of Belgian neutrality in 1914. Thucydides writes as a clinical observer of political disease.

2. The aristocratic and pro-Spartan party worked within the city for the enemy. They had been active from 415 (the revolution of the Four Hundred); their political battle-cry was 'Back to 460', i.e. before Pericles.

Acropolis, and the subject-cities, who had risen against Athens in hope of regaining their independence, lay helpless in the victor's grip. Though Athens was able to shake off the Spartan yoke, though the democracy was restored, and trade again flowed into the Piraeus, her empire was no more; the genius of the city, after a brief period of political and military splendour, found its true and enduring home in the fields of literature and of thought.

II. ART AND LITERATURE IN FIFTH-CENTURY ATHENS

§ 7. We remarked above that all forms of creative activity in which the Greek genius found expression were gathered at Athens in the great days of the fifth century. This is true, in the first place, of the allied arts of architecture, painting, and sculpture. The motive of all three was religious, the erection and adornment of temples for worship of the gods. Both the Doric and the Ionic styles of temple-architecture, the one massive and severe, the other more elegant and ornamental, had developed in the preceding epoch out of primitive forms of building in wood.[1] Sculpture too had its origin in wood-carving; wooden temple-figures gave place, in the age of commercial expansion and under the patronage of wealthy despots, to statues of stone. In the sixth century, the schools of Argos, Sicyon, Aegina, and Athens rapidly advanced in mastery of technique, in knowledge of anatomical structure and in freedom of treatment, and the art of sculpture was freed from exclusive association with religious subjects. Statues of athletes illustrate the growing interest in types of masculine beauty. The climax of these earlier developments was attained in the Athenian school in the Periclean age, under the leadership of Phidias. To Athens came also Polygnotus of Thasos, the foremost painter of the time, famous for his large monumental compositions, e.g. the sack of Troy and Odysseus in

---

1. Of the Athenian temples of the Periclean age, the Theseum and the Parthenon (see § 8) were the chief examples of the Doric, the Erechtheum and the Temple of Wingless Victory (*Nike Apteros*) of the Ionic, style.

Hades, and commended by Aristotle for his skill in the representation of human character.[1] The buildings of Athens had been destroyed by the Persian invaders, and in the two succeeding generations her statesmen set themselves to make the new city worthy of her imperial position. Pericles in particular strove to train the citizens to a love of the beautiful through his buildings and the sculptures that adorned them. For an age when books were comparatively inaccessible, it is impossible to overestimate the value in education of noble buildings. The Acropolis of Athens, with its entrance portal, its temples, and its statues, rendered the same service to the Athenians of that day as the richly carved cathedrals to the towns of medieval Europe. In a passage of the *Republic*, Plato concludes his argument that the young rulers of the ideal city shall be surrounded with an environment of grace and beauty with these words:—

'Ought we to confine ourselves to superintending our poets, and compelling them to impress on their productions the likeness of a good moral character, on pain of not composing among us; or ought we to extend our superintendence to the professors of every other craft as well, and forbid them to impress those signs of an evil nature, of dissoluteness, of meanness and of ungracefulness, either on the likenesses of living creatures, or on buildings, or any other work of their hands; altogether interdicting such as cannot do otherwise from working in our city, that our guardians may not be reared amongst images of vice, as upon unwholesome pastures, culling much every day by little and little from many places, and feeding upon it, until they insensibly accumulate a large mass of evil in their inmost souls? Ought we not, on the contrary, to seek out artists of another stamp, who by the power of genius can trace out the nature of the fair and the graceful, that our young men, dwelling as it were in a healthful region, may drink in good from every quarter, whence any emanation from noble works may strike upon their eye or their ear, like a gale wafting health from salubrious lands, and win them imperceptibly, from their earliest childhood, into resemblance,

1. Aristotle, *Poet.*, c. 2, c. 6; *Pol.*, viii. 5.

love and harmony with the true beauty of reason?' [1] No one who has passed his youth under the shadow of some noble cathedral or within the walls of one of our ancient colleges will dispute this judgement on the subtle and unconscious influence of the arts on the character and mind of man.

§ 8. The chief of the buildings raised by Pericles on the Acropolis was the temple of the maiden Athene, the Parthenon. The sculptures that adorned the temple, the work of Phidias and his fellow-craftsmen, have never been equalled in any age. Early in the nineteenth century most of those that remained were brought to England by Lord Elgin and are now in the British Museum. In the pediments were represented the birth of the goddess Athene from the head of Zeus, and the struggle between Athene and the sea-god Poseidon for the possession of the soil of Attica. On the metopes that adorned the outer band of stone, surrounding the temple above the line of Doric columns, were sculptured scenes of conflict from the heroic legend of the contest of Centaurs and Lapiths. In contrast to the scenes depicted on the outside of the temple, the frieze that girt the outer wall of the *cella* (nave) presented in low relief the civic life of contemporary Athens, the religious procession of the Pan-Athenaic festival, men in chariots and on horseback, sheep and cattle led to sacrifice, the magistrates of the city, musicians and the maidens who bore the sacred woven robe, as an offering to Athene seated among the Olympian deities. The central figure of the whole, the colossal statue of Athene, wrought in gold and ivory by Phidias, has perished. But the marbles in our national museum, more than any other monuments of antiquity, reveal to the Englishman of to-day the qualities of energy and repose, lofty idealism and serene beauty, that marked the art of the age of Pericles. [2]

§ 9. In the domain of literature, fifth-century Athens is memorable for the creation of two new forms of expression, the drama in poetry and history in prose. The impulse to

---

1. Plato, *Rep.*, iii. 401 (*tr.* Davies and Vaughan). Note Plato's recognition of the significance of the sub conscious.

2. It must be remembered that both the exterior of temples and the sculptures were coloured.

dramatic impersonation is common indeed to all mankind, for, as Aristotle has observed in his *Poetics*, both the habit of imitation and delight in its products are rooted in human nature.[1] But there is a wide gulf between the rude improvisations of the early Greeks and other races, and such finished masterpieces of dramatic art as the tragedies and comedies of Periclean Athens. To survey and interpret this rich treasure of dramatic literature lies beyond the scope of this volume. It will suffice to indicate certain distinctive characteristics, a knowledge of which is prerequisite for the intelligent study of the plays themselves.[2] The modern reader, when he thinks of the drama, inevitably thinks of Shakespeare; but a Greek play differed strikingly, both in atmosphere and structure, from the Shakespearian type, and the difference is partly due to the historical conditions under which the Attic drama came into existence.[3] Thus, for example, tragedy and comedy were composed by different poets and performed at different festivals; the one treated of ideal subjects, the other portrayed human nature on a lower plane than the normal, and excited laughter by ridiculing human imperfections.[4] They differed in the circumstances of their origin; tragedy (*tragos*, a goat) arose out of hymns sung by a chorus clad in goat-skins among the Dorians in

1. Aristotle, *Poet.*, c. 4. This treatise illustrates how in poetry as in other fields the Greeks not merely produced works, but thought out the theory of their production. The extant portion of the *Poetics* treats mainly of tragedy. The second book, dealing with comedy, is lost. Aristotle notes (1449a 10) that both tragedy and comedy originated in improvisation.

2. For suggestions as to English translations see the Bibliographical Appendix.

3. The difference between the Shakespearian and the Hellenic drama was due mainly to the sense of order and rule characteristic of the Greek mind. This tradition was canonized later by the French in the doctrine of the dramatic unities, which, however, was never formulated by the Greeks, and which won little hold in this country where Shakespeare had done his work without it. 'The unities were effective in France because the French drama had proved itself, in practice, not very effective without them. Shakespeare, without them, had made wonderful theatrical patterns of his own, perfect, some of them, in form and symmetry' (W. P. Ker, on *The Humanist Ideal*, *Essays and Studies by members of the English Association*, vol. vi.).

4. See Aristotle, *Poet.*, c. 2 and c. 5 *init*. Aristotle, be it noted, ignores a strictly realistic drama. At the close of Plato's *Symposium* (223) Socrates is pictured as arguing that the tragic poet must also be a comic poet. Milton, in the preface to *Samson Agonistes*, speaks of 'the poet's error of intermixing

the northern Peloponnese, while comedy was of Sicilian growth, and had its birth in the untutored jests of rustic revellers (*komos*, a band of revellers) who enlivened their processions at the vintage and harvest seasons by flinging personalities at their fellow-yokels in the surrounding throng. Three further characteristics, arising out of the history of the Attic drama, call for special notice. (i) In the dramatic 'episodes' or acts, and in the choric odes sung in the intervals of the action, we see conjoined in a higher unity the two main streams of earlier Hellenic poetry, the epic and the lyric. It is the presence of the latter element, with its accompaniments of music and dancing, so that the three arts form a single aesthetic product in which the words of the song are the determining factor, that strikes us on first acquaintance as unfamiliar.[1] Now the choric hymn or dithyramb was the original nucleus of the drama; the element of narration was gradually detached and transformed, first, in the form of interludes spoken by the chorus-leader between the parts of the hymn, then by the introduction of one answerer (*hypocritês*) or actor speaking from a stage (here we have the beginning of dialogue and action), then by the addition of a second, and finally of a third, actor. Thus the dramatic factor developed at the expense of the lyrical, until the part of

comic stuff with tragic sadness and gravity'. Shelley, in his defence of poetry, says, on the other hand, that 'the modern practice of blending comedy and tragedy, though liable to great abuse in point of practice, is undoubtedly an extension of the dramatic circle', and instances *King Lear*. Aristotle's famous definition of tragedy, in *Poet.*, c. 6, 1449b, 24 f. is as follows: 'A tragedy is the imitation of an action that is serious and also, as having magnitude, complete in itself: in language with pleasurable accessories, each kind brought in separately in the parts of the work; in a dramatic, not in a narrative form; with incidents arousing pity and fear, wherewith to accomplish the *catharsis* of such emotions' (*tr.* Bywater). The second clause refers to the admixture of choric song with music and dancing; the word 'serious' and the reference to 'pity and fear' distinguish tragedy from comedy; *catharsis* is a medical term signifying 'purgation'. Bywater discusses the various interpretations of the term in the notes on the passage in his edition of the *Poetics*. The emotions are expelled as by a purge, through their very excitement in the drama; the spectator, in Milton's words, 'With peace and consolation is dismiss'd, And calm of mind, all passion spent' (closing lines of *Samson Agonistes*).

1. See Plato, *Rep.*, iii. 398. The arts of music and dancing developed in Greece in strict relationship to lyric poetry, which was always meant to be sung to an accompaniment and danced.

the chorus, originally dominant, became thoroughly sub-ordinate to the dialogue and the action.[1] In this, and in the almost universal selection of plots from the heroic sagas, we see the influence of epic poetry. Aristotle, who was fond of tracing the early anticipations of later forms, noted that 'all the parts of an epic are included in tragedy; but those of tragedy are not all of them to be found in the epic'.[2] Both the earlier types of epic and lyric poetry, as well as music and dancing, were thus blended under the form of dramatic representation in this sovereign creation of the Greek poetic genius.[3] (ii) The external conditions under which the plays were produced also had an influence on their character. For one thing, they were performed in the open air, in a theatre hewn out of the slope of the Acropolis, hard by the temple of Dionysus, and were witnessed by a vast concourse of spectators, perhaps as many as 30,000, seated in concentric curves rising above the orchestra and stage, which were situated at the base.[4] This rendered necessary the use of artificial devices to aid sight and hearing, the buskin to raise the actor's height, padding and masks symbolic of the part enacted, fitted with speaking tubes to enable the voice to carry its full distance. These instru-ments necessarily intensified the conventional character of the

1. The *Suppliant Maidens* of Aeschylus, probably the earliest extant Greek drama, shows the chorus as still predominant. The decisive innovation was that of the second actor; it is associated with Aeschylus, who later employed a third. There were never more than three actors with speaking parts employed in the course of a Greek tragedy, though a single actor might appear in dif-ferent parts in different scenes. The messenger-speeches frequent in Greek tragedies are reminiscent of the earlier narrative interludes.

2. *Poet.*, cc. 5, 26; cf. cc. 4, 23, 24.

3. The whole play was in verse, lyric metres being employed in the choric songs, and the unaccompanied iambic metre ($\cup - \acute{} = $ ♪ ♩) is the iambic foot) of six feet ('the most speakable of metres', says Aristotle) in the dia-logue and speeches. Coleridge illustrates the iambic measure by the line, 'Iambics march from short to long.' Mr Vernon Rendall suggests: 'English quantities are seldom clear, but might be more so in foreign words anglicized, e.g.

"A rose, acanthus, asphodel, chrysanthemum." '

Euripides was fond of introducing solos from the stage in lyric verse.

4. The plays were thus visible, and (thanks to the devices referred to in the text) audible, to a concourse as large as that which assembles to-day to witness a test match or an international football contest.

Greek drama, which represented types in the persons of individuals. Yet the Greek dramatists and actors succeeded through mastery of technique in largely overcoming these limitations, and we can trace the growth of individual characterization as we pass from Aeschylus to Sophocles and from Sophocles to Euripides. But, even in its latest development, the Greek drama was far more simple in plot and structure than that of modern Europe.[1] (iii) The dramatic poets, like the athletes at the games, contended one against the other for a prize. When we remember that each competitor presented four new plays at a single festival, and that the contests were many and frequent, we can appreciate the wealth of dramatic creation in fifth-century Athens. The extant plays, seven tragedies of Aeschylus, seven of Sophocles, eighteen of Euripides, and eleven comedies of Aristophanes, form but a small fragment of the body of dramatic works produced by these and many other poets of the age. The constant attendance at these festivals, and the practice there acquired of judging the awards, furnished, in a time when books were rare, an educative influence of extraordinary value to the Athenian public. We know from Plato's insistence on the moral significance of right standards of dramatic composition for the training of youth how deeply the teaching of the poets impressed itself upon the minds of the audience.[2] As in politics, so in literature, the Athenian citizen must have been, if not 'an initiator', at all events 'a sound judge' of aesthetic merit.

§ 10. The poet Shelley, in an essay from which we have already quoted, remarks of the Athenian drama that 'it is indisputable that the art itself never was understood or practised according to the true philosophy of it, as at Athens'. Stressing thus what we called above the intellectual quality in Hellenic art, he continues: 'For the Athenians employed language, action, music, painting, the dance and religious institutions, to produce a common effect in the representation of the highest idealism of passion and of power; each division in the

1. E.g. there was far less scope for underplot than in modern drama.
2. Plato, *Rep.*, ii, iii.

art was made perfect in its kind by artists of the most consummate skill, and was disciplined into a beautiful proportion and
unity one towards the other. On the modern stage, a few only
of the elements capable of expressing the image of the poet's
conception are employed at once. We have tragedy without
music and dancing; and music and dancing without the highest
impersonations of which they are the fit accompaniment, and
both without religion and solemnity. Religious instruction has
indeed been usually banished from the stage.'[1] It is this
intimate association with religious observance that constitutes
the most striking peculiarity of the Attic drama. The dramatic
festivals were held in honour of the nature-god Dionysus,
under the presidency of Dionysus' priest, in the vicinity of his
temple and with the accompaniment of religious ceremonial.[2]
In the centre of the *orchêstra* or dancing-place stood the altar of
the god. Attendance was a pious duty incumbent on every
good citizen. As an integral part of the worship of the *Polis* the
festivals were directly under the charge of the civic magistrates,
and the plays themselves furnish frequent illustration of the
poet's patriotic feeling. The plots, at least in the case of
tragedy, were usually drawn from the traditional tales of gods
and heroes; the range and variety of this material may be
gathered from the fact that more than 200 different themes are
known to have been handled by the fifth-century dramatists.
Thus Greek tragedy dealt with ideal situations, and with events
which, despite the freedom allowed to the poet in the treatment of characters and detailed incident, were thoroughly
familiar to the audience, who believed them to have actually
happened in the heroic past. From all this there arose in the
mind of the Athenian public a close association between
dramatic poetry and the teaching of moral and righteous truth.
That this was so even in comedy is evidenced by Aristophanes'

1. Shelley, *A Defence of Poetry*.
2. Note that tragedy and comedy both belong originally to Dionysus, i.e. to
the mystery-religion as distinct from the Olympian. In the fifth century,
Apollo, the typical Olympian god, whose service is not mysticism but clear
self-knowledge, comes by his own in the drama; Sophocles' religion centres
round Apollo. See Wilamowitz-Moellendorff, Lecture on *Apollo* (Oxford,
Clarendon Press, 1908).

claim that the dramatic poet was the moral teacher of the adult citizen.[1] But it was the three great tragedians, Aeschylus (525–456), Sophocles (496–406) and Euripides (480–406), who invested the religious traditions of the Greeks with a new spiritual meaning. Aeschylus, in language that has often suggested an analogy with passages in Hebrew prophecy, sought to 'justify the ways of God to men', to interpret the almighty sovereignty of Zeus so as to harmonize divine righteousness with the facts of suffering and sin, and to reconcile the inexorable laws of destiny with freedom of the human will.[2] In Sophocles, the divine decrees are represented as working through the subtle medium of human character; the unwitting transgression, the rash act that springs from blindness and ignorance, brings down unsuspected doom on an otherwise noble nature.[3] The poet's religion is that of Apollo, the god of purity and light, with its watchword, 'know thyself'. His ethical ideal is that of *sôphrosynê* in opposition to self-assertion and pride of life (*hubris*). With equal moral earnestness, though voicing a religious scepticism that contrasts with the conservative piety of his predecessors, Euripides rent asunder the veil of reverence which had concealed from critical analysis the acts and characters of the gods, and with relentless realism showed them for what they actually were. You demand fact, he seems to say, and here I give it you; if, as you believe, these things really happened, the gods who did them were not good, but evil, not ideal divinities, but cruel and vindictive, with the worst passions of human kind. It was a

1. Aristophanes, *Frogs*, ll. 1009, 1055. Cf. 686: 'Well it befits the holy Chorus to counsel and teach the city what is good,' and 1500 ff., where Aeschylus is called upon by Pluto to save the Athenian *Polis* by good counsels. In the preceding Chorus (1482 ff.) his wisdom is explicitly contrasted with Socrates' idle prattle. The whole of the closing scene (1418 ff.) turns on the vocation of the tragic poet to preserve the state.

2. See, especially, the *Prometheus Bound*. Probably the sequel, *Prometheus Freed*, showed Zeus as schooled to humanity by suffering.

3. Such was the fate of Oedipus in the *Oedipus King*; see Arist., *Poet.*, c. 13. Analogous tragedies following on error of judgement and blind impulses form the theme of *Othello* and *King Lear*. For subtlety of character, see the *Philoctetes*. The fate of Deianira in the *Trachiniae* well illustrates how hope and fear unite to blind the judgement of a weak woman and to lure her to destruction. See above, c. vi. § 12.

disturbing picture that he drew, reflecting the changed temper of a rationalist age. Euripides was profoundly serious alike in this merciless analysis of the orthodox faith, in his unflinching resolve to see the truth and face the facts of life, and, above all, in his pity for the weak and suffering, for women, children, captives, and slaves, for all the numberless victims of human injustice and natural law.[1] The time had come when the super-natural powers of earlier belief were yielding place in thinking minds to the forces of nature. But when once this was evident, the vocation of the poet as a teacher of knowledge was doomed; men looked to science, not to poetry, for guidance in the search for truth.

§ 11. Tragedy had established itself at Athens already before the Persian wars. But it was that crisis and the consequent expansion of Athenian public life that gave the impulse to its development. Each of the three great tragedians represents one of the three epochs into which the history of fifth-century Athens naturally divides. Aeschylus had fought at Marathon, and in his *Persians* dramatized the naval victory at Salamis. Sophocles' art is the perfect expression of the idealism of the Periclean age. Euripides, as we have noted, voices the intellectual unrest which gathered over Athens in the years of the Peloponnesian war. But it is in Attic comedy that we find the most direct relation between the drama and Athenian civil life. Aristophanes, like most of the comic poets, was a conservative, who idealized the tempered democracy of the time of the Persian wars; in his plays, personal and Rabelaisian to a degree inconceivable under the conditions of modern life, he satirized the new currents in poetry, philosophy, and politics which were stirring in the last third of the century.[2] In the

1. The *Hippolytus* illustrates these points. On the other hand, the *Bacchae* shows that Euripides could enter into the spirit of Dionysiac religion. As the fifth century wore on, the stories of the gods were taken less seriously and the cultured Athenian public, while conforming to the worships of the *Polis*, was frankly sceptical. In the vase-painting of the time we can trace the transference of interest from religious subjects to matters of technique in grouping of figures and execution. So in the art of the Renaissance epoch the devotional motive yields place to purely aesthetic motives in the treatment of the Madonna.

2. The coarseness of the Old Comedy had a ritual significance; here as

Knights (424) he held up to ridicule the democratic statesman Cleon; in the *Wasps* (422) the jurors in the popular law courts; in the *Birds* (414) the wild dreams of empire that led to the Sicilian catastrophe; in the *Frogs* (406) the modernist art of Euripides, the representative in tragedy of the new culture; in the *Clouds* (425) the speculations and teaching of Socrates; in the *Lysistrata* (411) and the *Ladies in Parliament* (392) the claims of women to share in the public life of the city, claims advocated by the Cynic followers of Socrates and, later, by Plato in his *Republic*.[1] The lyric songs interspersed in his plays are of an extraordinary beauty. A feature of this Old Comedy, which furnished the poet with a peculiar opportunity for personal satire, was the *Parabasis*, a survival from the early village-revels, when the chorus turned round in the middle of the play to address the audience in a song reflecting on persons and topics of the day. The fall of Athens and the ruin of her democratic policy dealt the death-blow to such outspoken political criticism. It is with peoples as with individuals; they can enjoy ridicule only so long as their consciousness of security remains unshaken. In the hour of strength, the Athenians cherished the right of every citizen to speak his mind unfettered by laws of libel, and this characteristic freedom of speech found its frankest expression in the Old Comedy. With the fourth century, on the other hand, comedy ceased to be personal or to concern itself with politics; the New Comedy was a comedy of manners, depicting types of social life, on lines followed by the Romans, Plautus and Terence, and in modern times by Molière, and by English dramatists of the Restoration. The same epoch witnessed the decline of tragedy. But the works of the fifth-century dramatists abide with the Phidian sculptures among the highest achievements of the Hellenic genius in the field of aesthetic creation. In the words of a modern poet, thinking at once of the colossal statue of Zeus wrought in gold and ivory by Phidias for the temple at Olympia

everywhere in the drama it is necessary to remember its intimate connexion with religious cults.

1. See *Rep.*, v. The Greek title of Aristophanes' play is *Ecclesiazousai*, lit., 'female members of the *ecclesia* or popular assembly'.

and of the tragedy in which Aeschylus pictured the mighty
Titan, giver of fire and the arts to men, enchained on 'the
frosty Caucasus' by the restless tyranny of the self-same God:

> Dead the great chryselephantine god, as dew last evening shed:
> Dust of earth or foam of ocean is the symbol of his head:
> Earth and ocean shall be shadows when Prometheus shall be dead.[1]

§ 12.   Greek prose literature had its home in Ionia, where it
developed two forms, philosophy and history.[2] Of the early
Ionian philosophers we have already spoken; Anaximander
was the first who is known to have composed a book. The
literature of western Greece was poetic until well on in the
fifth century, when the rhetorical studies of the Sicilian
Gorgias led to important developments in prose writing;
though both Parmenides and Empedocles had expressed their
philosophy in verse. The earliest critical historian, Hecataeus,
was a native of Miletus and figured prominently in the Ionian
revolt against Persia. The opening words of his book, preserved in a fragment, show that he struck a new and scientific
note, in comparison with the municipal chronicles of an earlier
generation. 'Hecataeus of Miletus thus speaks. I write as I
deem true, for the traditions of the Greeks seem to me
manifold and laughable.'[3] The Greeks created history, as they
created the drama; for they were the first to grasp its two
essentials, the distinction, never clearly realized by Oriental
annalists, between fact and fiction, and the necessity of a
reasoned interpretation of recorded fact.[4] To say that they

1. Swinburne, *Athens*. The drama referred to is, of course, the *Prometheus
Bound*. The reader will be aware of the influence exercised over European
dramatic literature in the seventeenth and eighteenth centuries by the models
and canons of composition furnished by the Greek dramatists, and by Aristotle in his *Poetics*, an influence issuing in many respects in artificial formalism.
The dramas of Calderon, Corneille, Racine, and Voltaire illustrate this influence at varying levels of excellence. Milton's *Samson Agonistes* and Goethe's
Iphigenie may also be referred to in this connexion. But the spirit of the Greek
drama is far more adequately represented by Shelley's *Prometheus Unbound*.

2. So also the speech-verse of the drama, the iambic metre, was of Ionian
origin.

3. Murray, *Ancient Greek Literature*.

4. Thus the Semites, for all their sense of the religious significance of
historical events, left no history that deserves the name. The historical books
of the Old Testament (e.g.) are mere chronicle, the expression of corporate
rather than of individual judgement. The Greeks were the first to exercise a

threw their personality into their writing and recorded their individual impressions and judgements, is only another way of stating the same claim. Hebrew history was anonymous, the product of a group; even the prophets preface their message, not with 'Thus saith Isaiah, the son of Amoz,' but with 'Thus saith the Lord.' The Greek historian, like the Greek philosopher, spoke in his own name; 'this is the exposition of the inquiry of Herodotus of Halicarnassus', and 'Thucydides the Athenian wrote of the war of the Peloponnesians and the Athenians'. They did so with right; for history and philosophy alike express the reflective criticism of the individual thinker on the facts of life. Two great historical compositions of the fifth century have come down to us, and both are closely associated with Periclean Athens. Herodotus took up his abode there for some years before joining Pericles' colony at Thurii in southern Italy; Thucydides was Athenian born, and absorbed in youth the great traditions of Periclean statesmanship. Herodotus was a keen traveller and visited Egypt, Phoenicia, Babylon, and the Euxine coasts as well as all quarters of the Hellenic world; his eager curiosity and desire to understand what he heard and saw, 'the wonderful works of Greek and barbarian, and especially that the causes may be remembered for which these waged war on one another,' make him perhaps the most characteristically Greek of all Greek writers.[1] In Hellenic politics his sympathies are strong for Athens and for democratic government; again and again he defends equality of laws and liberty of speech against the claims of tyranny.[2] In temper of mind he is typical of a genera-

reasoned judgement on the past. Their word *historiê* was originally of wide comprehension; it meant 'inquiry' and covered all research into matters of fact, natural history, geography, and anthropology, as well as political history. We are told that a Greek historian of the fourth century (Ephorus) explicitly censured the introduction of legend (*mythos*) into *historiê*.

1. Herodotus was born *c.* 484 at Halicarnassus in S.W. Asia Minor; visited Athens *c.* 450, settled at Thurii 443. He was Carian in stock, Ionian in culture, Athenian in sympathies. The latest reference in his book (vii. *c.* 233) is to events in 431–430 at the beginning of the Peloponnesian war. The words quoted are from the opening sentence of Book I.

2. See c. iv. § 5, *note* 1 above; cf. with the passages there referred to, v. 78 and 92 f. (on tyranny at Corinth as illustrative of its evils), and on Athenian democratic patriotism vii. 138 f., viii. 143 f.

tion that wavered on the border line between credulity and
scepticism. It is constantly on his lips to tell us that the
religious traditions of his people are old wives' tales, but he
never can quite bring himself to say so; and behind all nature
and human history he sees the hand of a mysterious 'divinity
that shapes our ends, rough-hew them how we will'. With
justice he has won the name of 'the father of history', not
merely because his is the first extant history that discriminates
truth from fiction and seeks to know the causes of things that
happen, but also because he first sought to co-ordinate his
story under a single purpose, namely, to exhibit the rise of
Persia and the judgement that overtook her *hubris* through the
agency of Greece.[1] Thucydides' theme was more concentrated
and his outlook on affairs more scientific. His purpose was to
record the Peloponnesian war to the fall of Athens in 404.[2]
While Herodotus tells the tale of Persian *hubris* with all the
geniality and diffuseness of a literary artist exulting in the
glamour of splendid triumph, Thucydides records that of
Athens with austere and sombre gravity, moved by the single
desire to unfold the truth in its bitter reality. Between the
two writers lay not only the downfall of Athens, but the age
of intellectual enlightenment. In language, and still more in
thought, Thucydides is of the lineage of the Sophists. Writing
as a statesman for the instruction of statesmen, he analyses
minutely the causes and effects of moral and political phenomena.[3] We have referred already to his narrative of the

1. On Xerxes' *hubris*, see vii. 7 ff., on the jealousy of Providence and the
instability of human prosperity, i. 5, 30 ff. Books i–v bring the history
up to the Ionian revolt, Book vi to the victory of Marathon, while Books vii–
ix tell the story of Xerxes' invasion. Herodotus intended to cover the war of
Liberation (see vii, 213), but left his work unfinished. Thucydides embodied
a summary of the years 478–432 in Book i, 89–117 of his history.

2. Thucydides was an exile from Athens for twenty years, in consequence
of his failure as commander of the fleet to save Amphipolis in 423. He was no
friend to the post-Periclean democrats (e.g. Cleon) and stood for the moderate
Periclean liberalism. He survived the fall of Athens (iv. 104–7, v. 26), but
carried his history only as far as the year 411. Xenophon in his *Hellenica*, an
inferior work to Thucydides', continued the narrative from this point up to
the battle of Mantinea (362).

3. See especially the Prologue (i. 1–22), the account of the plague at
Athens and its moral effect (ii. 47–54), the analytic study of political revolutions (iii. 82–4), the exposition of Athenian *hubris* and imperial tyranny

THE GREATNESS OF ATHENS

Sicilian expedition, recorded with a dramatic intensity un-equalled in historical literature. For Thucydides, as for Euri-pides, the course of human life is determined, not by super-natural agents, but by natural law; he exhibits a thoroughly sceptical reluctance to accept the plea of disinterested motive for human action, and he has all the intellectualist's faith in reason as the key to unlock the secrets of men's characters and conduct. Finally, in the speeches which abound in his work, we can trace the influence of the new art of rhetoric, which had its home in Sicily, but was quickly acclimatized at Athens.[1] In the last quarter of the fifth century it began to exercise a decisive influence upon Attic prose. Oratory, forensic and political, took a recognized place as a form of literary art. In the fourth century we find not only the high-water mark of Greek oratory in the speeches of Demosthenes; but, in the philosophical dialogues of Plato, the most perfect achievement in prose that Greece, and possibly the world, has ever known.

III. THE SOPHISTS AND SOCRATES

§ 13. We have noted that the history of Thucydides, the tragedies of Euripides, and the comedies of Aristophanes alike in their various ways bear the mark of the new speculative movements that were stirring in the Periclean age. The growing tendency of thought was towards questions of moral theory and conduct. This was due in part to a sense of disil-

(i. 74–8, iii. 37 ff., vi. 83 ff., and, above all, the Melian dialogue, v. 84 ff.), and the contrast of Athenian and Spartan character and policy (i. 70, ii. 35–46); also Cornford, *Thucydides Mythistoricus*.

1. On Thucydides' speeches see his *Prologue* (i. 22) and Jebb's essay in *Hellenica*. The Funeral Oration, quoted above (§ 5), can hardly be other than an accurate report of Pericles' argument and phrases, probably heard by Thucydides himself.

In reading the works of Greek (and Roman) historians, the close affinity to poetry, and especially to dramatic poetry, is noticeable, alike in form, content, and purpose. They understood by history something very different from our twentieth-century conception. It was an art rather than a science, and was never taught, like the sciences, in universities. Further, it was written for the edification of men of affairs. Quintilian observes (*Inst. Orat.*, x. i. §§ 31, 34): 'history is closely allied to poetry and may be likened to a poem in prose; its aim is narration rather than proof . . . its chief value is in furnishing examples for our instruction.'

lusionment with the physical inquiries of the preceding epoch; the various lines of speculation had been worked out to a finish and men were faced with a maze of conflicting conclusions which seemed to defy reconciliation. They despaired of attaining certainty in such matters, and turned to seek a knowledge more immediately related to practical life. Physical science too was becoming more departmental, and the specialists were inclined to resent the intrusion of the philosopher into their preserves. In any case, the moral problem was clamouring for treatment on rational methods of inquiry. We saw in the last chapter how a criticism of moral standards and institutions was the logical outcome of the effort to find a permanent substance beneath the changes of physical nature. This newly awakened interest in ethical questions was fostered by the special conditions of public life in democratic Athens, and by the general aspiration after a higher standard in religion and morality which the poets strove to satisfy. The time from 450 onwards was one of extraordinary fertility, both of criticism and of construction, in ethical and political thought, and preluded a momentous revolution in the intellectual life of Greece, and, through Greece, of mankind. For the first time in history the clear light of reason was directed upon the problem of human conduct. It was an epoch of enlightenment, like that named as such in the Europe of the eighteenth century, of which Voltaire was the central figure; and just as the modern enlightenment led forward to the great constructive philosophy of Kant, so the earlier prepared the way for that of Plato. The saying of Protagoras, 'Man is the measure of all things,' may be taken as its watchword.[1] A widespread con-

1. Protagoras of Abdêra in Thrace, born c. 500, died c. 430, legislated for Pericles' colony of Thurii. The best brains of Greece were enlisted in this undertaking; Hippodamus of Miletus, the greatest living architect, designed the city, and Herodotus, as has been noted above, was one of the colonists. Protagoras' saying, quoted in the text, meant that the judgement of each individual was the measure of what it was desirable to do or not to do in any practical situation. Later, the doctrine was applied by others to support a theory of the relativity of knowledge, viz. that what each man perceives is true for him when perceiving it, and that this is the only truth attainable. See Plato's *Theaetetus* for this development and a criticism of it as conclusive as anything in philosophy.

viction arose in the Hellenic world that, alike in the special professions and arts and in the art of living in general, an outfit of reasoned knowledge was an indispensable condition of success. Virtue (*aretê*), depended not merely on natural talent or on gifts of fortune, as men had commonly supposed, but on an equipment of acquired theory. A demand arose for a new type of education, and it was met and fostered by a body of eminent teachers. The professors of the new culture brought their knowledge to bear on the practice of war, music, and agriculture, as well as on more specialized training in horsemanship, stagecraft, and cookery. Manuals of instruction, called *technai* (arts), were composed on a multitude of such subjects. Above all, they taught rhetoric, the art of public speech, indispensable to the aristocrat who found himself constantly threatened with impeachments before the popular tribunals, and to the young aspirant after political honours in the law court and the assembly. The rise of rhetoric affected, not merely the character of Greek public life, but the development of Greek literature through the kindred arts of grammar and style. But its chief importance lay in the training it afforded in the general conduct of public and private life. When Protagoras, in the dialogue of Plato which bears his name, was asked by Socrates what benefits his young pupil would receive, he answered that he would teach him to speak, and thereby make him day by day a better citizen, more competent to handle the affairs whether of the *Polis* or of his domestic household.[1] In fact, the founders of rhetoric inaugurated a new era in ethical inquiry. Words are the symbols of thoughts, and the study of the expression of moral ideas involves analysis of the ideas themselves.

§ 14. The teachers of the new learning were called Sophists. The term meant simply 'professors of wisdom (*sophia*)'; it had not yet received from Plato the implication

---

1. Plato, *Protag.*, 318–19; cf. 328 and *Rep.*, 600. The whole dialogue should be studied as illustrative of the teaching of the Sophists. Isocrates in the next century said that the Sophists claimed that those who learnt from them would 'know what ought to be done and through this knowledge achieve happiness'.

that the wisdom professed was illusory.[1] They hailed from all quarters of the Hellenic world, travelling from city to city and giving lectures and informal instruction in all branches of knowledge.[2] Hippias, one of the company of Sophists introduced in the *Protagoras*, claimed to be a master of every art; in addition to researches of real value in mathematical and astronomical science, he taught chronology, mnemonics, phonetics and the study of rhythms, the theory of sculpture, painting and music, and industrial crafts – the story runs that he appeared at the Olympic games dressed in clothes entirely of his own making. He was also a moralist and a poet, and served his native state as an ambassador. It would be an error to suppose that the Sophists' learning was superficial, for in those days it was easier to be a polymath than now, when the vast mass of material entails specialization; beneath Plato's hostility to the type we can detect his real respect for great thinkers like Gorgias and Protagoras. 'Culture,' said the latter, 'does not flourish in the soul unless one reaches a great depth.' The Sophists were not a sect, bound to a uniform doctrine; if we seek a modern parallel, we should find it in the journalists of to-day, or in the influence on intelligent public opinion of writers like Huxley, Ruskin, and Matthew Arnold in the last half of the nineteenth century.[3] Plato might

1. The primary suggestion of the term is that of professional teaching, though it is also used in a wider sense of any wise man, e.g. of a poet. Herodotus calls Solon a Sophist. The Sophists frequently taught for pay; Protagoras is said to have allowed his pupils at the end of the course to give what they thought his instruction was worth. Plato (*Protag.*, 317) says that Protagoras was the first to call himself a Sophist. Plato sharply distinguished the true philosopher from the Sophist, applying his favourite contrast of 'real' and 'seeming'; see *Gorg.*, 463, cf. *Soph.*, 221, 'the practiser of an art of deception, who without real knowledge of what is good can give himself the appearance of that knowledge'. So Aristotle, e.g. *Rhet.*, I, i. 4, 'an impostor who pretends to knowledge employing what he knows to be false for the purpose of deceit and monetary gain'. It was George Grote (*Hist. of Greece*, viii. c. 67) who rescued the reputation of the Sophists from the stigma inherited from Plato and Aristotle. In this he had been in some measure anticipated by Hegel.

2. E.g. Gorgias from Leontini in Sicily, Hippias from Elis, Prodicus from the Aegean island of Ceos, Thrasymachus (cf. Plato, *Rep.*, i) from Chalcedon.

3. Or again, Herbert Spencer. Among recent writers, Mr Bernard Shaw and Mr H. G. Wells might be compared to the Greek Sophists. We may also think of the rapid extension in our universities of the application of theory to practice, in agriculture, engineering, commerce, domestic science, and

scorn the Sophist as 'a wholesale exporter of spiritual goods manufactured by others,' and in certain cases the scorn was doubtless justified; but there were not a few who united in their persons the gifts of the intellectual middleman with those of the original thinker.

§ 15. The ethical discussions, provoked by the teaching of the Sophists, were focussed round the terms nature (*physis*) and convention (*nomos*).[1] Individual Sophists differed widely in their conclusions; some, like Hippias, based moral duty upon unwritten natural law, eternal and divine; others held, like Thrasymachus, that by law of nature Might is Right, or, again, that social justice was an artificial compromise imposed by the weak in self-defence against the strong. Others, again, like Protagoras, denied the existence of any unchanging natural principle, and taught that the conventions of the city should be accepted and observed by the citizen.[2] The tone of these discussions affords a striking parallel to those of the later eighteenth-century enlightenment, embodied in the writings of Rousseau, Tom Paine, and William Godwin; in the preamble to the American Declaration of Independence, and in the manifestoes of the French Revolution; as also to those evoked in our own day by the advocates of the claims of the superman and of the super-state against the restrictions of conventional moral valuations.[3] They exemplify the genius of the Greeks for grasping the essential and enduring problems of human conduct. The same topic of nature and convention was

especially welfare work and social service. The problem of present-day education is to do for the many what the Sophists claimed to do for the few.

1. *Nomos* = 'convention' and also 'law', i.e. what is posited by human will, can be made and unmade, and varies in different times and places. It is used often in the sense of 'law *and custom*', as when Aristotle (*Ethics*, v. c. ii. § 1) lays down that what *nomos* does not enjoin it forbids.

2. On Hippias' views, see Xenophon, *Mem.*, iv. 4; cf. Sophocles, *Antigone*, 449–57, for a similar doctrine. For Thrasymachus, see Plato, *Rep.*, i. and cf. Glaucon's speech at the opening of Book ii. Plato's final verdict on the historic controversy between *physis* and *nomos* is given in *Laws*, 889.

3. The superman was a common theme in Greece in the last half of the fifth century. He was typified by the hero Heracles; see Euripides' play, *The Mad Heracles*. For the super-state, see the Melian dialogue in Thucydides, v. 84 ff.

threshed out in its various applications to the origin of society and language, the social position of women and slaves, the institution of private property and the validity of religious tradition.[1] The outcome of the controversy was to elicit a truer conception of nature and of the natural, as meaning, not an imaginary primitive condition devoid of all social acquisitions, but rather the full realization of the capacities of man's social nature. To unfold this ideal of a developed human personality, and thereby to heal the crude divorce between the interest or good of the individual and that of society, was the aim of Plato's *Republic*. We shall return later to his solution of the problem, which was rendered possible by the critical inquiries of the Sophists. Though their teaching made for scepticism, and, as such, aroused the bitter antagonism of conservatives like Aristophanes, yet its issues proved essentially constructive. A thorough analysis of the traditional beliefs was necessary, if moral values were to be remoulded on rational principles. The trenchant criticism of the Sophists bore fruit in the speculative systems of Plato and of Aristotle.

§ 16. Incomparably the most notable thinker of the age was Socrates of Athens (469–399), the greatest human teacher who ever lived.[2] Amid the wealth of genius that adorned Athens in the last half of the fifth century, his personality was the most

1. On the origin of society, Plato, *Protag.*, 320 ff., *Rep.*, ii. (Glaucon's speech). In regard to slavery, see Additional Note to this chapter. It must be borne in mind that while Greek culture undeniably rested on a slave basis, the Greeks were the first people to question its justifiability. On communism, see Plato, *Rep.*, iv. 416–17 and v. Arist., *Pol.*, ii. criticizes these views and Phaleas of Chalcedon's schemes for equalizing real property and state ownership of slaves, involving state control of industry. On the position of women, see Additional Note, p. 182.

2. The three main sources of knowledge about Socrates are Xenophon's *Memorabilia*, the *Clouds* of Aristophanes, Plato's dialogues. The account in the text is based primarily on the last-mentioned source. It is not possible in this work to discuss the grounds for refusing to regard Plato's Socrates as a dramatic fiction; the reader is referred to the writings of Professors Burnet and Taylor (whose views have largely influenced the account here given) with the caution that their conclusions are by no means universally admitted. The author is, however, convinced that, unless Plato is accepted as the main authority on Socrates, it is impossible to give an intelligible explanation either of Plato's philosophy, or of Socrates' influence, or of the satire of Aristophanes. See Burnet, *Thales to Plato*; Taylor, *Varia Socratica*; and the Introduction to Burnet's edition of Plato's *Phaedo*.

unique and impressive. Grotesque in gait and features – the stout figure, with bald head, snub nose, thick lips, and protruding eyes, reminded Plato of the images of the satyr Silenus – he strutted barefoot and ill-clad through the streets of Athens, 'like a water-fowl', says Aristophanes. His habits and bearing were strangely disconcerting, when he broke in upon a company of Sophists or revellers at a banquet, or of young nobles in the *palaestra*, or when he stood stark and silent for long stretches of time in the thoroughfare or the portico, wrapped in a mystic trance.[1] The inward voice, too – the *daimonion* (divine thing) he called it – which counselled him audibly against peril at critical moments of his life, forbidding him for instance to enter politics, singled him out from other teachers of his day.[2] He lived in comparative poverty, scorning to take pay for the fulfilment of what he regarded as a divine mission; and held aloof from the recognized avenues of civic distinction, save on two occasions, towards the close of his life, when he was forced into political prominence, and showed his wonted independence in resisting the mandates alike of democracy and of despotism.[3] On the other hand, he served on several occasions with conspicuous valour in the field, and his personal courage was proverbial throughout Greece.[4] Socrates was no recluse, nor was there in his nature anything of the rigidity of the intellectual aristocrat or the puritan ascetic; like another, he came eating and drinking, and his geniality was as characteristic as the self-control which provoked the wonder and the envy of his contemporaries. The secret of his influence lay in his force of personality and in the magic of his talk. In this, as also in his weird appearance and demeanour, his breadth of human interest, his passion for argument and his love for the city whose walls he never quitted save under protest – 'I am a lover of knowledge, and the men who dwell in the city are my teachers, and not the trees or the country'[5] – he reminds us at times of Doctor Johnson. He left

1. Plato, *Symposium*, 215–22; on the trances, *Symp.*, 174–5; cf. Arist., *Clouds*, 150.
2. On the *daimonion*, see *Apol.*, 31, 40; *Rep.*, vi.
3. The two occasions were in 406 and 403; see Plato, *Apol.*, 32.
4. See *Symp.*, *loc. cit.*   5. Plato, *Phaedr.*, 230.

no written word, but lived for seventy years in the public eye, spending his days in conversations with all sorts and conditions of his fellow-men, rich and poor, statesmen and generals, poets and thinkers, humble craftsmen and women of the world, conversations which Plato describes as 'ridiculous at first hearing; his talk is of packmen and smiths and cobblers, and he is always repeating the same things in the same words, so that any ignorant or inexperienced person might feel disposed to laugh at him; but words which in their heart are the only words that have a meaning in them, and also the most divine, abounding in fair images of virtue, and of the widest comprehension, or rather extending to the whole duty of a good and honourable man'.[1]

§ 17. When Aristotle summarizes Socrates' contribution to the history of thought in the words 'induction and general definitions', we are apt to feel a shock of disillusionment.[2] His life-work must surely have meant more than that. Aristotle, of course, is concerned with Socrates' service to philosophic method, and every student knows how reform of method heralds each decisive advance in the history of science. Moreover, the Socratic induction implied the recognition of the real natures of things embodied in their sensible appearances; while definition, for him as for Aristotle, was no matter of mere words, but the precise expression of the essence of the things defined. In youth, as we learn from the *Clouds* and from the biographical passage in Plato's *Phaedo*, Socrates had been a keen student of the physical systems which then held the field. But they failed to satisfy him, for they spoke only of the 'how' of things, and his desire was to know the 'why'; and he 'came out by the same door wherein he went'.[3] The Pythagoreans alone, who had been led by mathematical inquiries to the thought of an intelligible reality behind the show of sensible phenomena, seemed to point the way to the goal of his endeavour, the reasoned knowledge of ideal good. Socrates was

1. In the mouth of Alcibiades, praising Socrates, *Symp.*, 221–2.
2. Ar., *Met.*, i. 6, xiii. 4.
3. See *Phaedo*, 96 ff. In his early manhood, Socrates met Parmenides and Zeno, and also Protagoras: Plato, *Parm.*, 130, 135; *Protag.*, 361.

at once a scientific thinker and a religious mystic. His faith in reason was unquenchable; he was a true child of Greece in his conviction that only by intellectual labour can man's soul attain to the vision of perfect truth. Hence the discipline of philosophy was at the same time the fulfilment of a religious vocation. The tale is preserved how, when he was between thirty and forty years of age, the Delphic oracle declared Socrates to be the wisest of men, and thereby summoned him to the mission to which he devoted the remainder of his life.[1] How could this be, he asked himself, since God alone is wise, and he, Socrates, knew no wisdom? We have here the key to the Socratic conception of Eros or Love, child of Plenty and of Want, round which he played in his conversations, now in jest, now with deep seriousness – the thought of man as a creature of two worlds, midway between ignorance and knowledge, whose salvation lies in the passionate thirst for wisdom (*philosophia*) that guides the soul upwards from the love of the transitory things of sense to the intuition of an intellectual beauty, whose 'light alone gives grace and truth to life's unquiet dream'.[2] Socrates justified the oracle by saying that, though he knew nought else, he knew one thing – his own ignorance; while others thought themselves wise when they were not so. This is the 'irony' of Socrates, which aroused such astonishment and irritation in his questioners.[3] How could he save their souls by revealing a knowledge for which he was still a seeker, or otherwise than by convincing them of their own ignorance, and thus wakening in them the desire to know? This indeed was the mission to which he set his hand with unwearying loyalty; to examine into men's standards of conduct, the ends they loved and lived for, and to test them by a fierce annihilating logic, till the hearer was shaken out of his complacency and confessed himself paralysed and impotent. 'An unexamined life,' said Socrates, 'is not worth living'.[4] He

1. *Apol.*, 21 ff.
2. Shelley, *Hymn to Intellectual Beauty*; see *Symposium*, 210 f.
3. *Symp.*, 216. *Eirôn* = 'sly' (Burnet, who compares the Scotch word 'canny'). There was a great common sense in Socrates. It follows from the irony that he refused to be called a teacher, *Apol.*, 33.
4. *Apol.*, 38.

compared himself to a gadfly sent by God to sting a noble horse, the Athenian *demos*, out of indolent slumber; and again to a spiritual midwife, who brings to birth true thoughts in the souls of men.[1] So we may fancy him asking the modern Englishman what precisely he meant by such terms as 'honour' or a 'gentleman' or a 'Christian', why he aspired to enter Parliament, and why he sent his son to the university or to a public school. He would show relentlessly the vagueness of men's notions about such matters, and that they had never thought them out or envisaged the alternatives; above all, that their views and their practice were but a pale reflexion of the average opinion of the world around them. And this, moreover, in the one concern of surpassing moment, the pearl of great price, the chief good and end of life! Socrates' teaching thus assumed a negative form which belies its real significance. He disclaimed the title of teacher; for he knew that the saving wisdom must be won by each man for himself, and that his own task lay solely in tearing aside the veil of ignorance which hid men from themselves. Self-knowledge, the Delphic watchword, was the one thing needful in life, and constituted virtue; vice, he said, was ignorance, or, to quote his seeming paradox, 'no one errs of his free will'.[2] He knew that prosperity without self-knowledge lay at the root of half the misery and evil in human life. He knew also, only too well, how men will pardon anything rather than being shown their folly, and how bitterly they resent the shattering of the self-satisfaction with which they have entrenched their souls. 'I was not unconscious,' he told his judges, 'of the enmity which I provoked, and I lamented and feared this; but necessity was laid upon me -- the word of God, I thought, ought to be considered first.'[3] His central prescript to his fellow-citizens, that they should 'take care of their souls', carried with it an implication that marks an epoch not merely in

---

1. *Apol.*, 30, 31; *Theaet.*, 150, 151; see also *Meno*, 79, 80, for the effect on his hearer.

2. Self-knowledge, *Phaedr.*, 229; Xen., *Mem.*, iv. 2, 24 ff. Goodness is knowledge; *Laches*, 194, *Protag.*, 345, *Apol.*, 25; see Xen., *Mem.*, iii. 9, 4, and Arist., *Ethics*, vii. 3, 1145b, 21.

3. *Apol.* 21e.

tion, to those writings which have best preserved the memory of Socrates' mind and personality. It lies beyond our scope to track the golden stream of thought that flows through the Platonic dialogues.[1] These are consummate masterpieces both of scientific reasoning and of dramatic art; we can well appreciate how Plato in youth had been drawn to write poetry. The dialogue form not only gave free play to the imagination of the artist, but reflected naturally the living movement of the Socratic conversations, and Plato's own conception of philosophic method as the upward endeavour of kindred spirits, by challenge of mind to mind, in the search for absolute truth.[2] Of these writings the *Republic*, composed after his return to Athens and in the full maturity of his genius, affords the best approach to the study of Plato's philosophy.[3] It is the most comprehensive in range of all the dialogues. Opening with the question 'What is justice?' it portrays the ideal society and the progress of the soul to philosophic wisdom, and closes with a picture of the life

1. All Plato's writings have come down to us. The grounds on which their chronological order has been determined with a high degree of probability cannot be mentioned here. The results may be stated as follows for the reader's guidance in a first acquaintance with Plato. The order within each period is more doubtful.

Period I (between 399 and *c.* 387): the *Euthyphro, Apology, Crito, Charmides, Laches, Lysis, Cratylus, Euthydemus, Protagoras, Gorgias, Meno* (the last three being towards the close of the period).

Period II (*c.* 387 to *c.* 375): *Symposium* and *Phaedo* (early); *Republic, Phaedrus.*

Period III (*c.* 367 to *c.* 360): *Theaetetus, Parmenides, Sophist, Politicus* (or *Statesman*).

Period IV (*c.* 360 to 347): *Philebus, Timaeus, Critias, Laws.*

The *Republic* marks the turning-point when Plato's thought, which was always on the move, began to travel beyond the lines of Socrates' philosophy. In the later dialogues, Socrates is (except in the *Philebus*) no longer the chief speaker. On the whole question, see Burnet, *Thales to Plato,* and *note* 1 to § 16. The *Epistles* of Plato are either genuine or at any rate contemporary documents of high value.

2. Plato's term for philosophy, both as science and as method, is *dialectic*: it is derived from the verb *dialegesthai* (= to converse) and is allied with 'dialogue'. Plato says that, even when a man is engaged in solitary thought, the soul carries on a dialogue with itself (*Soph.*, 263; *Theaet.*, 189). Plato himself preferred oral teaching to the written word, see *Phaedr.*, 275 f.

3. The *Republic* was probably completed at the time when Plato was engaged in founding the Academy, between *c.* 387 and *c.* 378. He was then forty to fifty years old.

beyond the grave. The problems of ethics and politics, psychology and education, literature and art, religion and science, are handled in a living unity, as factors in the single problem of the universe, by a thinker whose proud boast it was to be 'the spectator of all time and all existence'.[1] But Plato was inspired, not only by the impulse of philosophy to know the truth, but also by an ardent passion for practical reform. From his youth, when he looked to enter the public life of his native Athens, up to his last vain journey in old age to Sicily, he was possessed with a burning desire to save the souls of men, and to build, as far as earthly conditions allowed, the city of God on Hellenic soil. For him, as for his master Socrates, philosophy was always a 'way of life'. From Socrates too he had learnt that goodness was knowledge, and that the only sure basis of practical conduct was a reasoned apprehension of the principle of good. Thus both problems, the speculative and the practical, found for Plato their common solution in philosophy, in a knowledge that should reveal the inner truth of the world as ideal goodness, and form the goal of individual and social action. What is this knowledge? And how can man attain to it? These are the cardinal questions of Plato's philosophy.

§ 20. That knowledge must be knowledge of what *is*, that its object must have true being, was never questioned by Plato; for him not merely must reality be knowable, but knowledge can be only of the real. Where, then, is true being to be found? Heraclitus had held that all in the sense-world was in ceaseless change, ever coming to be and ceasing to be, never abiding in being. The followers of Protagoras had applied this doctrine to show how, at least in the field of sense, each passing appearance was true to the individual percipient in the instant of his perception. Such views robbed truth of all its meaning, and Plato could not rest content with them. He was driven, therefore, like Socrates before him, to seek for being elsewhere than in the world of sense. Reflection on our actual thinking shows it to involve objects of a very different order from sense-data; for these can be known only by aid of general concepts, apprehended not by the senses but by thought.

1. *Rep.*, vi. 486.

This is especially evident in mathematical judgements, and in those that express moral and aesthetic values. No sensible lines or circles are perfectly equal, and to call an action good or a picture beautiful implies a single standard of goodness or of beauty, to which the particular instances are imperfect approximations.[1] Thus Plato was led to the belief in an intelligible world, wherein there existed in unchanging being, as substantial realities, the Forms or Ideas, the perfect archetypes, 'shared in' or 'imitated by' their manifold and changing copies in the world of sense. These Forms alone were the proper objects of scientific 'knowledge'; the particular instances of them in the sense-world, on the other hand, were objects of fallible and fluctuating 'opinion', the source alike of speculative error and of moral delusion. He who thinks and lives in bondage to the body and to things of sense, for all his keen insight into the particular circumstances around him, is as one walking amid dream-phantoms in his sleep; the philosopher, with his mind's eye fixed on the intelligible realities, alone has waking vision.[2] Plato proclaimed the doctrine of two worlds and, perhaps for the first time in the history of western thought, ascribed true being to immaterial substances. Moreover, the Forms are not isolated spiritual atoms but constitute an intelligible economy or order, which it is the philosopher's main task to trace. Supreme in this super-sensible hierarchy is the Form of Good, the source both of knowability and of being in all the other Forms, itself 'transcending knowledge and being'.[3] In the *Republic* Plato evinces reluctance to expound directly this 'highest object of knowledge', nor does he supply the deficiency anywhere in his writings; indeed, in a

1. See the *Phaedo*, which shows how Plato (Socrates?) was led to the doctrine of Forms (or Ideas) by the study of mathematical, moral, and aesthetic judgements.

2. See *Rep.*, v. 471 ff. vi, vii. It is very possible that the doctrine of Forms or Ideas (Plato employs both words, *Eidos* (Form) and *Idea* – the latter is ambiguous in English) had been held by Socrates and derived by him from Pythagorean speculation. Plate subjected the theory, as presented in the *Phaedo* and the *Republic*, to criticism and radical modification in later dialogues (especially the *Parmenides*).

3. *Rep.*, vi. 509. This expression formed the text from which, later, the Neo-Platonists drew the thought of the super-essential One = the Good, which is the highest member in Plotinus' spiritual triad (see Vol. 2, c. ix, § 12).

letter he states explicitly that 'There is no writing of mine on the subject nor ever shall be. It is not capable of expression like other branches of study; but, as the result of long intercourse and a common life spent upon the thing, a light is suddenly kindled as from a leaping spark, and when it has reached the soul, it thenceforward finds nutriment for itself.' [1] We know, however, that the Good formed the goal of all Plato's intellectual endeavour, and that he lectured on the subject in the Academy to the close of his life. [2] It gave unity and system to the intelligible world, harmonizing the Forms in one sovereign and universal purpose. As in the sense-world the sun is the source of light and life to all created things, so in the thought-world the Forms derive their rationality and being from the Form of Good. [3] Such in outline was Plato's answer to the two questions, What is knowledge? and What is being? which form the burden of metaphysics in all ages. His solution is liable to misinterpretation, and in three directions. (i) The Forms, though apprehended by the mind through general concepts, are no thought-abstractions, but substances, existing independently of the mind of any thinker in an objective spiritual world. [4] (ii) The Form of Good is not identified by Plato with God. God is not a Form, but a living and active soul, the self-moving source of the motion of the heavens and, as Plato relates in semi-mythical language in the *Timaeus*, the creator of the sensible universe, after the pattern of the Forms and in accordance with mathematical law. The doctrines that God is himself the supreme good, and that the Forms are his eternal thoughts, having their being in the divine intellect, were not Plato's, but modifications of Plato's theory which naturally suggested themselves to Neo-Platonic and medieval thinkers. [5] Finally (iii) it must not be supposed that in

1. *Epp.*, vii. 341 (*tr* Burnet).

2. Aristotle published his notes on Plato's lectures on the Good, but these unfortunately have not been preserved.

3. *Rep.*, vi. 504 ff.

4. In the *Parmenides*, 132, the suggestion that the Forms are concepts in the mind is brusquely rejected.

5. God endowed the sensible world with a world-soul, so that it might, as far as may be, resemble his own goodness. This conception was influential in later speculation. Philo (first century A.D.), the Jewish Hellenist of Alexan-

denying scientific knowledge of things of sense, Plato rejected them as illusory or worthless. It is not because the sense-world has no truth, but because its partial truth is visible only to the mind that grasps its dependence on the Forms, that Plato insists that the latter are the true objects of scientific study. Plato, in fact, conceived the sense-world as fashioned by God in space out of geometrical figures, a theory not so far removed from Descartes' reduction of physical body to terms of figured extension. Plato was a deep student of the mathematical sciences, which he held to be the proper approach to philosophy; and there is a tradition that over the portals of the Academy were inscribed the words, 'Let no one who is not a geometrician enter here.' In his view, mathematics furnished the key to physical nature; his later theory of Forms was in all likelihood a doctrine of mathematical relations, akin to that of modern physics, save only that, for Plato, the mathematical interpretation, far from precluding explanation in terms of purpose, required for its foundation the essential Form of Good.[1]

§ 21. In the nature of man, the distinction between the intelligible order and the sensible appears as that between the soul and the body. For Plato, as for Aristotle after him, soul (*psyché*) is the principle of life and motion, so that, wherever these are present, there is soul; and the human soul, far from being the only or the chief expression of soul, is but one form of its manifestation. Greek philosophy stands in sharp contrast to the modern tendency to regard the human mind as the pivotal fact of experience. Beside human and infra-human souls, there is in Plato's universe the soul of God, the world-

dria, was the first to treat the Forms as thoughts of God. Burnet, *Thales to Plato*, c. xvii, holds that Plato was the first philosopher to base theism on a scientific foundation.

1. On the mathematical sciences, see *Rep.*, vii. 522 ff. Plato's philosophy, like that of Socrates, was through and through teleological; the being or reality of each fragment of the universe lay in its function, i.e. in its realization of a purpose or good. The Form of Good is best thought of as a single supreme purpose which gathers up all fragmentary and individual purposes into a systematic unity. All the laws of the being of special parts of the world can be deduced from this single supreme purpose. Thus Plato's doctrine is far removed from that of mechanical determinism; wherever he finds law, and he finds it everywhere, he finds rationality and the Good.

soul, and the divine souls that move the stars. With a passionate
intensity of conviction, Plato believed all souls to be inherently
immortal; his final proof, stated in the *Phaedrus* and again in his
latest dialogue, the *Laws*, argues from the fact of motion to the
necessity of a cause of motion which is self-moved, and therefore can never begin or cease to move.[1] Consequently, human,
like all other, souls existed before incarnation in the body,
and will survive the body's death. Thus Plato explains how the
imperfect copies of the Forms in the world of sense 'remind'
the soul of the perfect archetypes which it had known before
its embodiment, and solves the difficulty how man comes by a
knowledge that transcends the limits of sense-experience.[2]
It enables him also to account for present suffering as expiation
for evil done in a previous incarnation and to develop the
genuinely ethical doctrines of rewards and punishments after
death, and of progressive purification in a series of lives.[3]
Here Plato is building on the soil of Orphic teaching, which
came to him through the Pythagoreans and Socrates. The body
is the prison-house and tomb of the soul; its death is the soul's
liberation; the life of philosophy, which fixes the mind's
thought on the super-sensible Forms, is the prelude to this
liberation and, in literal truth, the study of death.[4] In temporal union with the body, the human soul appears, not in its
native purity, but like the sea-god Glaucus in the tale, 'en-
crusted with shells and seaweed', so that its essential nature,
reason, is concealed from outward view.[5] In our actual experience, the soul forms a composite unity of three powers:
reason, the philosophic faculty, the rightful authority in the
soul's economy, whose rule ensures harmony within, and also
with the kindred reason in other souls and in the universe; the
'spirited' or passionate faculty, impulsive and pugnacious, a
willing servant of reason but liable, if undirected, to lead the

1. *Phaedrus*, 245 C, *Laws*, 893 b ff. The earlier arguments in the *Phaedo*
and *Republic* were dropped in later dialogues; they were possibly Socrates' own
as distinct from Plato's proofs.

2. See the *Meno*, 81 ff., on this doctrine of recollection (*anamnēsis*).

3. See the myths in the *Gorgias*, *Phaedo*, *Republic*, x, and *Phaedrus*, and
Stewart's *Myths of Plato*.

4. See the *Phaedo*, 64 f.   5. *Rep.* x. 611.

soul astray on the path of self-assertion; and the appetites, associated with bodily pleasures, some lawful, others unlawful, but all alike insatiable in their thirst for satisfaction, and, unless sternly disciplined by reason, ever plunging the soul into a riot of anarchy and disunion. Under the outward semblance of a man, we can picture a creature compounded of three natures, those of a man (reason), a lion (passion), and a many-headed hydra (appetites).[1] The ethical and educational scheme of the *Republic* is largely based on this threefold psychological distinction; for example, the picture of three types of life, inspired respectively by love of pleasure, love of honour, and love of wisdom; the analysis of moral virtue into the specific forms of wisdom, courage, and temperance, which have their common root in justice, the principle enabling each part of the soul to do its proper work in the economy of the whole, and ensuring a harmony or 'music' through the entire soul; the division of education into music and gymnastic, the disciplines of the appetites and of 'spirit', forming the requisite moral basis for the use of reason in maturer years; and, finally, the conception of philosophy as a conversion of the soul from the darkness of the sense-world to the light of the world of Forms, and as a lifelong preparation for the unfettered exercise of reason in the world beyond the grave.[2]

§ 22. Against those who maintained that morality was mere convention and that the individual finds his true happiness in a life of self-assertion, Plato showed how man in the very core of his being was marked out for social co-operation. He formulated two positions in intimate conjunction, namely, that each individual has by nature a unique capacity which determines his particular function in society, and that this function can only be efficiently discharged, so as to bring happiness to the agent, when it is regulated by the general good.[3]

1. *Rep.*, ix. 588–9; cf. the simile of the chariot of the soul, *Phaedrus*, 246 f.
2. For Plato's psychology in application to ethics and the education of the young, see *Rep.*, ii–iv; for the higher training of reason, *Rep.*, vii (especially the allegory of the prisoners in the cave); also Nettleship's essay on *The Theory of Education in Plato's Republic* in the volume entitled *Hellenica*.
3. See *Rep.*, ii. 369 ff. The claims of individual self-assertion are voiced by

The economy of the state is dependent on the psychology of the citizens, and this analogy between the *Polis* and the individual governs the picture of their good and evil types throughout the whole of the *Republic*. Social functions will be apportioned on the basis of the individual characters of the citizens; those in whose souls appetite is dominant will perform physical labour, supplying the material needs of the community as artisans or farmers; the 'spirited' souls will constitute the military class; the philosophic souls, which have proved in repeated trials their capacity for the life of reason, will be intrusted with the highest task of government. Thus Plato is brought by logical steps to his famous paradox, that 'until philosophers are kings and kings philosophers there will be no salvation for states or for the souls of men'.[1] There will be none for the state, since reason is the power in the soul that makes for unity, and the realization of reason in the philosophic life is the only safeguard against social anarchy. Nor will there be for the individual soul; for, unless reason be sovereign in the community, no private person can resist the corrupting influence of public opinion and the allurements of the world.[2] Believing that it was possible for the philosopher to attain in the course of his earthly life to the culmination of speculative knowledge in the vision of absolute Good, he drew the natural corollary that failure to conform in conduct to that vision was inconceivable. Knowledge on this exalted plane entailed conformity of conduct. It was impossible to sin against the light. Christianity at once endorsed and modified the Platonic doctrine. On the one hand, it held for the redeemed in Paradise, who enjoyed the direct vision of God, the absolute Good (*non posse peccare*); on the other, that direct vision was unattainable by men in this life, even on the highest level of mystic contemplation. The saint, for all his saintliness, remains a sinner; he sees God only 'through a glass darkly' (*per speciem in aenigmate*), never 'face to face'. Plato's Form of Good was not identified by him with God (who was a 'soul',

Thrasymachus in Book I, by Glaucon and Adimantus at the beginning of Book II, and by Callicles in the *Gorgias*.

1. *Rep.*, v. 473.   2. *Rep.*, vi. 492.

not a 'form'), but it was knowable by the philosopher 'face to face'. Thus, inspired partly by the conviction that in a perfect society all things must be in common, and each member feel joy and sorrow in the joy and sorrow of every other, partly by a sense of the danger even to the chosen few of the curse of private interests, Plato denied to the ruling classes the possession of private property and replaced the private household by a single state-family, regulated with uncompromising rigour by the philosopher-kings. In these provisions we see at once Plato's passionate longing for unity, and his clear grasp of the forces of evil that are ever ready to assert their claims in the life of the individual and of the community. His austere idealism and unrelenting logic combined to lead him, in the temper of a monastic founder, to banish all temptations, such as private possessions and the dramatic art, that might possibly provoke to moral licence. The world of his day, and especially the political and ethical tone of fourth-century Athens, is, in the *Republic*, unreservedly condemned. The individual Athenian seemed to him to have been swept off his bearings on a tide of emotional debauchery, the Athenian state to have been rent asunder by party faction and the self-aggrandisement of its leaders. If the souls of men or human societies were to win salvation, it must be through a radical change of heart, carrying with it the institution of severe self-discipline and a revolution in the principles of life and government. Plato's keen insight into the evil of human nature and his bitter sense of the hopelessness of actual society reminds us frequently of Tolstoy. But he differed from Tolstoy in that he was always also a philosopher. His remedy for the evils of the world was to place power in the hands of those who know. They alone, who, as the fruit of long moral and intellectual training, have attained to knowledge and love of the sovereign good, are qualified to mould the citizen's character and direct the policy of the state. In contrast to the ideal of Periclean democracy, Plato preaches professorial socialism. In a famous simile in the sixth book of the *Republic* he likens the Athenian people to the captain of a ship, good-natured but sluggish, and easily influenced by the flattery of artful mariners who vie with one another in cajoling him to entrust the helm to one of themselves. None of them has ever learnt the pilot's art or has the true knowledge that alone avails to guide the ship aright. All the while, the true pilot who is master of his craft remains neglected and alone. Thus in Plato's view the Athenian *demos* had fallen into the hands of unscrupulous and incompetent adventurers, while the philosopher, by right of nature the true-born ruler, was condemned to the inactivity of private life.[1]

§ 23. Needless to say, Plato failed to convince his fellow-citizens, and Athens pursued her course until the advent of the Macedonian conqueror. Unwearying in his efforts after practical reform, he thrice visited Sicilian Syracuse, in the hope that as a despot's counsellor he might succeed in instituting the philosophic state. But already in the *Republic* he had come to see that the ideal city was 'a pattern set up in heaven', incapable of perfect realization upon earth.[2] In two of the later dialogues, the *Statesman* and the *Laws*, he evinced a more tolerant temper towards existing forms of government and, in the last-named writing, sketched a second-best polity as an accommodation of the ideal to the facts of life. But his true vocation, during the last forty years of life, lay in the Academy, the college for scientific and philosophical research which he founded and endowed. The Academy can justly claim to be regarded as the earliest university in history. Students flocked thither from all quarters of the Hellenic world, notably Eudoxus,[3] a mathematician and astronomer from Cyzicus, and the young Aristotle from Stagira on the Macedonian coast. The members of the school shared a common life, residing in the Academy, and engaging not only in strictly philosophical studies but in inquiries into mathematics, biology, and problems of morals and jurisprudence. Amongst its achievements was the development of solid geometry, and Plato, in sketching his programme of higher studies in the

1. *Rep.*, vi. 488, 496.   2. *Rep.*, ix. 592.
3. On Eudoxus, see Heath in *The Legacy of Greece*, pp. 117 ff. He discovered the theory of proportion expounded in Euclid, Book V; and also the method of exhaustion for measuring curvilinear areas and solids, developed later by Archimedes.

Republic, advocated state support for this new science.[1] The subsequent course of educational thought and practice, alike in Graeco-Roman and in medieval times, is grounded on Plato's institution of the Academy. It became a custom to seek for legislative reformers in the ranks of the school. Plato's latest writing, the *Laws*, is an example of this branch of its inquiries.[2] The Academy had a long and memorable history; it served as the model for subsequent foundations, such as Aristotle's college in the Lyceum, and those of the Stoics and the Epicureans, and continued in being as the central home of Platonic teaching for a thousand years, until the pagan schools were finally disendowed and disestablished by the Christian emperor Justinian (A.D. 529).

§ 24. The philosophy of Plato, because of its other-worldliness and uncompromising idealism, has seemed to many minds more akin to the spirit of Christianity than to that of Greece, which looked to this life and its opportunities for the satisfaction of man's intellectual and moral aspirations. There is truth in this assertion, though the differences are more vital than the likeness. Plato's doctrines of the soul's salvation through laborious intellectual discipline, and of the spiritual direction of society by a scientific aristocracy, carry us a long way from the ideal of a spiritual kingdom to be entered, not by the wise and prudent, but in the spirit of a little child. Moreover, the root-conceptions of Plato's thought proved fruitful beyond expectation in moulding the Hellenic ideal of life. The conviction, expressed in the *Republic*, that the highest life is that not of pleasure or power, but of philosophical contemplation, remained the governing ideal of ancient thought. When the city-state lost its independence and the career of free public activity was closed to the Greek citizen, the best minds busied themselves more and more with the pursuit of knowledge. Aristotle, who, though often contrasted with Plato, yet builds at every point

1. *Rep.*, vii. 528.
2. His codification of Greek, especially of Athenian, law, as developed subsequently, exercised a great influence on Hellenistic and, through Hellenistic, on Roman, law. See below, c. vii, § 6, *n.* 2.

on his master's foundations and is rather to be regarded as the first great Platonist, shared his belief that the life of philosophy is that in which the soul finds fullest satisfaction and approaches most nearly to the divine. In the centuries that followed, the same conviction was held alike by Platonists and Aristotelians, by Stoics and Epicureans.[1] Nor was it confined to the Pagan world. Stripped of its peculiarly intellectual interpretation as the life of philosophy, the ideal of contemplative activity dominated medieval Christianity.[2] The Mary and Martha of the Gospels became the types of the theoretic and active life; and the former had chosen the better part. The institution of monasticism, the writings of Dante, and the sculptures that adorn the cathedrals of the Middle Ages, are evidence of the hold which this thought, the product conjointly of the Christian and the Hellenic genius, had won over the spiritual aspirations of mankind. Plato, like all the greatest of the Greeks, whether in literature or philosophy, stands for something of universal value. Whenever the spirit of man turns from the world of sense and change towards that which is eternal, unchanging, and one, whether it be in intellectual or religious contemplation, it has claimed kinship with the spirit of Plato.

ADDITIONAL NOTES

Among the ethical questions which the thinkers of the fifth-century enlightenment in Greece asked themselves, were two that possess a special interest for the modern reader. These are (i) the question of the status of women in the community, (ii) the question of slavery.

1. The Status of Women [3]

In the Funeral Oration as reported by Thucydides, Pericles addressed the female mourners in well-known words: 'If I am to speak of womanly virtues to those of you who will

1. And especially by the Neo-Platonists: See Vol. 2, c. ix, §§ 10–14.
2. See below, c. xi.
3. See, in addition to other references given below, Xenophon, *Oeconomicus* (tr. Dakyns); Benecke, *Women in Greek Poetry*; Zimmern, Part III, c. 12.

henceforth be widows, let me sum them up in one short admonition: to a woman not to show more weakness than is natural to her sex is a great glory, and not to be talked about for good or for evil among men.' [1] This sentiment, inconceivable on the lips of a modern statesman offering public condolence to the bereaved in war, must have seemed entirely becoming to the majority of Pericles' hearers of both sexes. A century before, Theognis had written: 'I hate a woman who is a gad-about'; a century later, Menander declared that 'the house-door is the bound for a free woman'. Women played no part in the recorded public life of Athens. Yet in art and poetry, as in religion, they are present everywhere; objects now of pity, now of terror, idealized in awe or analysed with subtle discernment, they are never ignored. The Homeric heroines enjoyed a dignity and freedom which contrast with their subjection and seclusion in after times; though it may be that Achaean, like medieval, chivalry invested the wives and daughters of chieftains with a halo of romance denied to women of ignoble birth.[2] No dramatic literature is so rich in portraits of women as the Greek, which left no aspect of feminine humanity, save (until Hellenistic days) the love of youth and maiden, unexplored.[3] Clytaemnestra, Antigone, Medea, Phaedra, and Alcestis stand on a plane with the great heroines of Shakespeare's tragedies. In actual Greek life we detect little that answers to this interest. The only woman of note in Athenian history, Aspasia, was an alien and bound to Pericles in a left-handed union.[4] At Athens the sphere of

1. Thuc., ii. 45; *tr.* Jowett.
2. Possibly, too, as Professor Murray suggests (*Rise of the Greek Epic*, p. 75), the tradition of the matriarchal system once prevalent in the Aegean world survived the Achaean conquest. The same writer (p. 124) points out how in the *Iliad*, as an epic of warfare, we hear little of women (save in two great passages, *Iliad*, iii and vi, 237 to end) in Troy. On a military expedition, he thinks, women may have been taboo. Samuel Butler maintained the interesting paradox that the *Odyssey* was written by a woman, perhaps by Nausicaa (see his *Authoress of the Odyssey*).
3. The sole exception in an extant play of the classical age is the love of Haemon and Antigone in Sophocles' *Antigone*. It is in the New Comedy of the fourth century that the love of youth and maiden, culminating in marriage, becomes a prevalent theme.
4. After the law of 451, which laid down that both parents must be

woman was the home. The man's sphere, on the other hand, was the *Polis*; the home counted for little in his life. At Sparta, for military reasons, women were allowed greater freedom; they were trained in public exercises that they might grow up to be strong mothers of soldiers. The result, we are told, was that, though handsome, they were hoydens, prone to luxury, avarice, and rebellion, and apt to engage in political intrigue.[1] The exclusion of women from Greek public life evoked many protests in the fifth and fourth centuries. That projects of reform were in the air is witnessed by the two comedies, the *Lysistrata* (411) and the *Ecclesiazousae* (392 or 389), in which Aristophanes lashed their claims to emancipation. Women missionaries were to be found among the Cynics. Euripides was stirred to pity and indignation by the lot of women, who in childbirth were called upon to endure worse sufferings than men in battle.[2] Plato was impressed by the waste of good material for the service of the state. He held that the difference between the sexes was one not of kind but of degree; women were indeed weaker than men, but none the less capable of sharing their civic functions, including that of philosophic sovereignty. Women might be found in each of the three classes in his ideal city. As they shared in the vocations, so they shared also in the education of men. There is no thought here of 'women's rights'; they were to be trained on masculine lines and for the advantage, not of their sex, but of the community. The whole passage, in the fifth book of the *Republic*, is strongly utilitarian. Moreover, Plato proposes to abolish the private household and embody all the citizens of both sexes in a single state-family. Marriage unions, the rearing (or exposure) of infants, and nurture in early childhood are to be controlled exclusively by the

citizens, if the children were to be legitimate, these second marriages with non-citizen women were frequent. No obloquy attached to them.

1. Later, they owned a large part of the Spartan lands. On the Spartan women, see Aristotle, *Politics*, ii. 9; also Plato, *Laws*, 780 ff., *Protag.*, 342; and Euripides, *Andromache*, 595 ff.

2. Eur. *Medea*, 248 ff. The soliloquy of *Alcestis*, in the play that bears her name, is very instructive. On her death, her boy-child will get his chance; but what about the girl?

government.[1] His avowed motives were (a) eugenic, to preserve the quality of the ruling class, (b) fear of disunion and civic faction (stasis), the source of which lay in private interests and possessions, and (c) an ideal aspiration after a society which should know no divorce of 'mine' and 'thine', but throb with a single pulse of all its members.[2] Finally, Aristotle set himself to confine the projects of radical reformers within the bounds of common sense. Women, he held as against Plato, differed from men in kind; they were defective, though not entirely lacking, in intellectual and moral capacity; hence, while debarred from full citizenship, they must be ruled by men constitutionally, not despotically like slaves. They would enjoy a limited freedom and receive an education adapted to their subordinate vocation in the Polis. What seems to have impressed him was their lack of scientific intelligence and of the quality of mind that carries authority.[3] We can hear him echo the voice of male superiority in every age: 'Be good, sweet maid, and let who can' – the men – 'be clever'. He kept in close touch with current Greek opinion, leavening it with a spice of liberalism; but in his handling alike of ideal values and of the facts of human nature he fell far short of Plato.

11. Slavery [4]

Among the Greeks, as generally throughout antiquity, slavery formed part of the traditional order, and, as such, was accepted without question. We read in Homer, and especially in the Odyssey, of slaves in relatively small numbers, captured in piracy or war. It was a fate that might befall any man: Eumaeus and Eurycleia were of noble lineage; though it reft the victim of 'half his manhood', it entailed no disgrace. Eumaeus

1. Infanticide, sanctioned possibly by Plato in certain cases, was prevalent in many ancient societies, though probably not at Athens. The speeches of Isaeus furnish evidence to the contrary. It was generally the female infants who suffered this fate.
2. See Rep., v.
3. See especially Politics, i. cc. 12, 13, and the criticisms on the Republic in ii, cc. 2–4.
4. See, on the subject, Zimmern, c. xv, and Smith's Dictionary of Antiquities, art. servus.

enjoyed 'a good life' as an honourable retainer, who spoke to his master's family as man to man; lines of social cleavage were less rigorous in those simpler times.[1] In the next age, with the Dorian invasion, a new type of slavery appears; the slaves are a conquered population, bound to the soil, like the Spartan Helots and the *Penestae* in Thessaly. Later still, the spread of industry and commerce brought in its train the slave-trade over the Aegean world; the chief recruiting areas were among the barbarians of Asia Minor, Thrace, and the lands around the Euxine; the chief markets, in maritime states which controlled the carrying trade, like Chios and, subsequently, Athens. At Athens, slaves were employed (*a*) in the household for domestic work rather than, as later at Rome, for luxury; (*b*) in large industries, especially in the silver mines at Laurion; (*c*) as state-slaves, etc. as rowers on ships of war.[2] The census return for the year 309 gave 400,000 slaves in Attica. The great majority were barbarians; Greek captives were always open to ransom. The lot of the ordinary Athenian slave had its alleviations and compares favourably with that of a later age at Rome or in the plantations of Christian slave-owners in modern times. The slave was protected by Attic law; his life was not in his master's hands, and slave torture was restricted within precise limits. There was no distinction of dress between slaves and free men; though excluded from the temples, gymnasia, and the public assembly, they were often allowed wide liberty of speech and action. Xenophon calls the slave the 'fellow-worker' of the citizen, who should be ruled by persuasion rather than by force, and induced to work willingly by hope of emancipation. He comments on the leniency shown towards slaves at Athens, a verdict confirmed by the pictures drawn in the New Comedy and by Plato's scornful censure of the licence

1. For Eumaeus, see *Odyssey*, xv. 380 ff.
2. A poor man would have only one domestic slave, a rich man as many as fifty. The abuses of slavery were most evident in the mines; Nicias owned 1,000 slaves at Laurion. Cf. Thuc., vii. 87, on the sufferings of the Athenian captives in the Syracusan quarries. The tale that certain of these won their freedom by reciting Euripides has been woven into Browning's poem, *Balaustion's Adventure*.

characteristic of slaves in the democratic state.[1] It was a
common practice for a master to give domestic slaves their
freedom, either in his lifetime or by will on his death. Doubtless the slave's lot varied greatly according as he was a family
servant or an apprentice in trade or, again, for his misfortune,
an employee in the mines. The ugly fact was present throughout Greek history. But the assertion that Greek civilization
rested on slavery as its basis is true only under reservations.
The two things do not vary proportionately to one another.
Slavery on an extended scale was subsequent to the rise of
Hellenic art and science, and increased as that art and science
passed into decline. Other nations, such as Egypt and Assyria,
who employed slaves in far greater numbers, failed to achieve
a culture comparable to that of Greece. The unique quality of
Greek civilization cannot therefore be explained as due to
slavery. Above all, the Greeks were the first to question its
moral justification.[2] Even if their culture were due to slavery,
so also was the thought of those who, like the Sophists, struck
at the roots of the evil. That slavery was grounded not on
nature but on convention was a common topic among the
poets and philosophers of the fifth and fourth centuries. The
Cynics declared boldly for emancipation. The Sophist Alci-
damas preached throughout Greece that 'the deity has made all
men free; nature has enslaved no man'.[3] Plato condemned the
enslavement of Greek by Greek.[4] So likewise did Aristotle,
who in his *Politics* handled the subject, after his wont, in the
spirit of a conservative reformer.[5] Only those, he held, were
slaves by nature who, like most barbarians, were disqualified
by lack of reason and moral capacity for participation in the
life of the *Polis*. Such 'natural' slaves were doomed to servitude,

1. Xen., *Mem.*, ii. 3, 3; *Rep. Ath.*, i. 10–12; Plato, *Rep.*, ix. 563.
2. See Murray, *Rise of the Greek Epic*, pp. 16 ff.
3. So Euripides, *Ion*, 854–6.

> 'The name alone is shameful to the slave;
> In all things else an honest man enslaved
> Falls not below the nature of the free.'

4. *Rep.*, v. 469. There appear to be no slaves in the *Republic*. In the *Laws*,
where slavery is recognized, provision is made for mitigation of its evils.
5. See especially *Politics*, i, cc. 3–7, 13.

as necessary instruments to the 'good life' of the free Hellenic citizen. They were means to another's ends, not ends in themselves; in the language of a later day, they were 'things', not 'persons'. The slave should be governed despotically, for his master's interest, not (save accidentally) for his own. True, he should be treated with humanity; and Aristotle went so far as to admit that though, *qua* slave, he is incapable of rational life, and cannot stand in any relation of friendship (*philia* = bond of social union) with his master, such association may be possible for him *qua* man. His attitude offers an obvious contrast to the Christian ideal of humanity. For Aristotle, the individual human being as such has no intrinsic worth. The view that inferior races may be trained to capacity for fuller and relatively self-determined life never crossed his mind. Their highest function was to minister to the material wants of the Hellenic citizen. These limitations lie open on the surface. They led, among the Greeks as elsewhere, to moral abuses, the gravity of which no one will desire to palliate. The fact that the Greek thinkers realized the existence of the problem and attempted to offer a solution implies an immense advance upon anything hitherto achieved in history. In restricting slavery to those who were incapable of free life, they formulated a principle which could be indefinitely extended in its application, e.g. by the Stoics. Analogous problems exist for the modern world, though the status and style of slavery have passed away, e.g. how to achieve a high level of culture without sacrifice of the many to the leisured few, and how to spread knowledge among the masses without peril to the stability of society.[1] The practice of the present day, as is evidenced alike in the treatment of lower races and in the monotony and squalor of industrial conditions in civilized lands, stands in glaring contrast with the avowed ideal. It ill becomes the critic to cast a stone at the ancient Greeks because their actual performance fell short of the precepts of their greatest thinkers.

1. The readers of the novels of the late Henry James may well wonder how the cultured and charming world there portrayed could subsist apart from the virtual, though not actual, slavery of the uncultured purveyors to its comfort.

CHAPTER SIX

GRAECO-MACEDONIAN CULTURE

*

I. ALEXANDER

§ 1. WITH the dawn of the fourth century we enter a changed world. Political power is no longer focused in Athens and Sparta, but shifts to new centres in the north; dreams of world-dominion on a scale unprecedented in Greek history are stirring the ambition of statesmen and military leaders. The brief sovereignty of Sparta that followed the downfall of the Athenian empire has little or no interest for civilization; the maritime cities quickly realized the hollowness of the victor's claim to be their liberator from the Athenian yoke, and that the little finger of her tyranny was thicker than the loins of Athens had ever been. The Greek world burned with shame and indignation when by the peace of Antalcidas (387) she handed back the Asiatic cities to the Persian king. Of far greater significance was the northward trend of political gravity, first, to Boeotian Thebes, whose serried phalanx shattered the once formidable Spartan infantry at Leuctra (371); then, by way of Thessaly, to Macedonia. The rise of the Macedonian kingdom is the central fact in the history of fourth-century Greece.[1] The Macedonians were akin to the Greeks in race and language; hardy mountaineers, born fighters, full of turbulent energy and devoted to their clan-chieftains, they had preserved the primitive habits of the early invaders of the Aegean world, despite the veneer of culture surrounding a court which had welcomed the trage-dians Euripides and Agathon. A strong and politic sovereign, able to win and hold the devotion of the wild nobles and their retainers, had in this people a splendid instrument for a policy of military aggrandisement. Such a king, in fact, was Philip,

1. Macedonians, who had fought with the Greeks against Persia, were admitted to the Olympic games in 476.

who ascended the Macedonian throne in 356 at the age of
twenty-two. In youth he had been trained at Thebes to appreciate Hellenic culture and, what was more to his purpose, to
master the tactics of the phalanx. Like Peter the Great of
Russia, who utilized western civilization for the consolidation
of a semi-barbarous empire, Philip moved his capital from
the interior to a site of vantage near the coast, reorganized his
kingdom, and trained his warrior subjects in the science of
war. With the weapon thus forged, he conquered Thrace to
the east, profited by the everlasting disunion of Greek states to
subjugate the cities of the northern Aegean, and, partly by
force, partly by the acts of diplomacy, of which he was a consummate master, won control of Thessaly and central Greece.
A crowning victory at Chaeronea (338) over the combined
armies of Thebes and Athens laid all Greece at his feet.
Chaeronea meant more than the failure of the heroic efforts
of Demosthenes, the patriot-orator of Athens, to save the
cause of Hellenic liberty. On that fatal field was sounded the
death-knell of the independent *Polis*. Henceforward the political history of Greece is that of her Macedonian conquerors.

§ 2. The subjugation of Greece was for Philip merely the
initial step to the realization of a project of empire which had
been working in the minds of the statesmen and thinkers of
Greece for more than half a century. The defeat of the Persian
invaders of 480 had made manifest the superiority in war of a
trained citizen army, animated by loyalty to the free city-
state, over the vast but ill-disciplined levies whose sole bond
of union was their common subjection to an Oriental despot.
Persia learnt to recognize this superiority, and before the
close of the fifth century had welcomed Greek condottieri
into her service, while by her diplomacy and her gold she
kept Greece disunited at home. The retreat of 10,000 Greek
mercenaries from the heart of the Persian empire to the
Euxine, through a difficult country, amid a hostile population,
and harassed by a host of enemies, had shown that it was
not merely on Hellenic soil that Greece was unconquerable;
from that moment (401–400) the thought of a war of revenge,
of a Greek invasion of Persia, loomed in the minds of Greek

captains.[1] Philosophers and political idealists, like Plato and
Isocrates, saw in a national crusade against the barbarian the
opportunity for Hellenic union and the remedy for domestic
strife.[2] But the city-states of Greece cherished their independence too dearly to tolerate political solidarity. The union
was imposed from without by the Macedonian sovereign.
Philip, supreme after Chaeronea by force of arms, declared
for the long-projected enterprise; his army was already
marshalled for war, when he died at the hand of an assassin
(336). The task of realization fell to his son Alexander.

§ 3. Alexander stands at the close of an old, and at the beginning of a fresh, chapter in world-history. The invasion of
Greece by Xerxes had opened a new phase in the secular
contest between East and West. The conquest of the Persian
empire by Alexander terminates this episode in the historic
drama. The catastrophe was blinding in its swiftness. In the
spring of 334 Alexander crossed the Hellespont, routed the
advanced guard of the Persians on the Granicus, conquered
the coast-lands of Asia Minor, and secured the control of the
great highway leading through the mountains of the interior
to the Cilician gates. In the following year he won his first
great victory over king Darius in person at Issus, at the north-
east corner of the Levant. The beaten king offered him the
western half of his empire to the Euphrates; the compromise
was haughtily refused. The capture of Tyre in 332, after a
resistance that forecasts that of Carthage or of Jerusalem – the
Semites were terrible when besieged – gave Alexander the
sea-power in the eastern Mediterranean, and was followed by
the conquest of Canaan and Egypt. In 331 he advanced to the
heart of the Persian empire, and won his crowning triumph
over Darius at Gaugamela in the valley of the Tigris. The death
of the fugitive king in the succeeding summer made manifest
Alexander's true purpose to the world. Hitherto the king of
Macedon and captain-general of the Greeks, he now stood
forward as the inheritor of the Persian kingdom, as the 'King

1. E.g. King Agesilaus of Sparta and Jason of Pherae, the powerful Thes-
salian chieftain.
2. This seems to be the implication of Plato, *Rep.*, v. 470–1.

of Kings' in Darius' stead. The next five years witnessed a
series of marvellous campaigns and marches, in which Alexander subdued the eastern satrapies to the Oxus and Jaxartes
and beyond the Hindu-Kush, pierced the Khyber Pass,
conquered the Punjâb and traversed the valley of the Indus to
its mouth. On the refusal of his army to march eastwards to
the Ganges, the fleet returned by the Persian Gulf, the land
forces through the terrible desert of the Mekran. Alexander
was back at Susa, the old Persian capital, in the spring of 324.
A few months were devoted to the organization of the vast
empire. By June 323 he had gathered at Babylon a great army
for the conquest of Arabia. There, stricken suddenly by fever,
he died after a ten days' illness, at the age of thirty-two.

§ 4. The campaigns of Alexander opened a new world to
Greece and by extending the range of knowledge had important results on scientific thought. But his great achievement
was the diffusion of Hellenism over the eastern world. The
political genius of Alexander is most evident in his deliberate
purpose to fuse into one the Hellenic and the Oriental spirit.
On the one hand he adopted Persian state, Persian dress,
Persian customs; he practised and encouraged intermarriage,
recognized the religions of the conquered peoples, and became
in all things an Eastern to the Easterns. On the other hand, he
incorporated Persians into the phalanx, trained their youth in
Hellenic culture, and promoted their nobility in his service.
Recognizing clearly that this policy of fusion must rest on an
economic basis, he strove to create a system of world-commerce, linking the Nile, the Tigris, and the Indus with the
Mediterranean.[1] Few of his Macedonian followers were able
to share these great ideas; we read of periodic resentment and
mutiny in the years following 330, provoking Alexander to
the rare acts of severity that present a striking contrast to the

1. Everywhere Alexander presented himself as the champion of native
religions and customs. He showed special favours, e.g. to the Jews. It is probable that the Jews, who were spread in large numbers over the Persian empire
and kept up channels of intercommunication (especially with Jerusalem),
rendered him great service as guides in his marches into what must have been
practically unknown lands. Mahaffy, *The Empire of the Ptolemies*, p. 85, speaks
of them as his 'natural intelligence department'.

habitual generosity and humanity of his nature. His chief instrument in welding together East and West was the foundation of cities on the Hellenic model. The cities of the Persian empire were few in number, a fact that explains the decisive finality of his victories in the field. Alexander planted cities everywhere on his marches, Alexandria, the most famous of them all, in Egypt, in the Euphrates valley, in the far northeast in Turkestan, on the Indus banks, and on the shores of the Persian Gulf. These cities, with their colonies of Macedonian and Hellenic settlers, formed abiding centres of Greek culture. As the outcome of this policy, which was followed out by his successor, the life of the vast region from the Aegean to the Indus, from the Caspian to Ethiopia, was transformed in a greater or less degree by the Hellenic spirit. Greek science took root in Babylon; the art, religion, and political government of India received the impress of the Greek mind. When we reflect that this achievement represents a mere fragment of Alexander's policy, accomplished in the few spare months between his campaigns, we realize that it has hardly a parallel in human history.

§ 5. The royal family of Macedonia claimed Greek descent, and Alexander was in all the essentials of character a Greek. At moments wild passions would break the bounds of his natural humanity and self-discipline, though for his few recorded acts of violence he showed an equally passionate remorse. Greek culture was not with him, as with many of his officers, a thin veneer that veiled the barbarian; its poetry and thought had stirred deeply his ardent and enthusiastic nature. For three years of his youth, between the ages of thirteen and sixteen, he had been the pupil of Aristotle, the greatest thinker of the age; his imagination was nourished on the poems of Homer; his court and camp were the scene of athletic and dramatic festivals; in the hour of vengeance on Thebes he spared the house of Pindar from the flames. When he sat as 'king of kings' on the throne of the great Darius, or assumed in Egypt the divine honours that marked the Pharaoh, he was never the victim of his own glory, but remained in heart and mind a Greek. He possessed great physical strength and courage, risking his life with apparent recklessness in the field; on one occasion in India he leapt with three companions into a besieged city and was wounded nearly to death. The king of the rude and warlike Macedonians had to hold their loyalty by personal prowess. Few great historical personalities are so free from meanness of spirit as Alexander. Open-hearted, truthful, ardent in personal friendship, chivalrous alike to friends and enemies, possessed of a noble pride and love of honour, he bound both generals and soldiers to his service by a strong tie of personal magnetism. The purity of his moral character was a proverb and a marvel to the age. With these qualities of mind and person were combined a clearness of insight, a capacity of adjusting means to ends, a supreme mastery of the art of war, and the rare union of political imagination and consummate statecraft. His hero of romance was the Achilles of the *Iliad*; but in Alexander we see grafted upon the ardour, courage, and love of glory of the Homeric hero, the rich heritage of moral and intellectual culture evolved by the Hellenic race in the long course of its history.

§ 6. Tradition tells that the dying Alexander, when asked by his marshals to whom he bequeathed his empire, made answer, 'To the strongest.' For twenty years they plotted and fought for the inheritance, till the battle of Ipsus in Phrygia (301) determined the broad lines of partition for the succeeding age. The Balkan peninsula fell to Lysimachus, forming a separate Macedonian kingdom with suzerainty over European Greece. Ptolemy had occupied Egypt immediately upon the great conqueror's death, and his dynasty continued to rule that country till its incorporation within the Roman empire. The bulk of Alexander's dominions, the Asiatic provinces from the Aegean to the Indus, passed to Seleucus, henceforward king of Asia. We cannot trace the detailed history of the conflicts among these dynasts through the two following centuries of storm and change. The politics of the eastern Mediterranean world were in the hands of Hellenic autocrats, often competent leaders in war and statesmanship, often romantic in their personality and fortunes, often, on the other hand, mere mediocrities, the puppets of chance and circumstance, selfish adventurers or shallow dilettanti or the slaves of debauchery and vindictive passion.[1] In an age which afforded unbounded opportunity to individual genius we find no leader of men of the front rank, save when for a moment, at the dawn of the second century, the heroic figure of the great Carthaginian passed to his doom across the panorama of the eastern world, cherishing to the bitter end undying hatred against Rome. But Hannibal was a Semite and an exile in alien lands, whose rulers, the Antigonids, Ptolemies, and Seleucids, were cast in a very different mould. Their interest for history lies almost solely in their furtherance of Alexander's policy of Hellenizing the East. Otherwise they pursued a path of personal aggrandizement, or followed in their methods of administration the models established by the former rulers of Macedon, Egypt, and the Persian empire. Greeks in race, speech, and manners, they ruled in Hellenic courts by the aid of Hellenic soldiery and Hellenic ministers, and with deliberate intention diffused and preserved Hellenic civilization, anticipating in their generation the historic mission of the Rome of a later day. The influence of this policy alike in East and West was incalculable. Its success was largely independent of the personality of the monarch, who, as we have noted, was often a *fainéant* or a ruffian; Polybius expressly brands the Ptolemies as persons of no importance.[2] Yet it was these very Ptolemies in whose case the habit of deifying the ruler became habitual. The old Egyptian kings had been worshipped as incarnations of Ammon (= Re). Even Alexander had been worshipped as a god during his life. The practice quickly

1. The first Seleucus, the first Ptolemy, and the Attalid rulers of Pergamos are examples of able sovereigns; Demetrius the Besieger of cities (*Poliorcetes*) and Pyrrhus of Epirus of romantic condottieri; Antiochus *Epiphanes* (the God-manifest) of the dilettanti. The 'tigress-princesses' of Macedonian blood add materially to the personal interest of the epoch (see Bevan, *House of Seleucus*).

2. He contrasts their 'nothingness' (*oudemeia*) with the superior capacity of the Seleucids, xxxiv. 14. Though Alexandria was an important centre of Hellenic culture (see the next section), the Ptolemies governed Egypt on the lines of the old Pharaohs, treating the country as a lucrative personal estate, with an exclusive eye to their own sovereignty and profit. Of the ministers of the Seleucids we hear little ; but the government appears to have been efficiently carried on, even under indolent dynasts. Bureaucracy had by this time established itself in the Mediterranean world.

spread, e.g. among the Seleucids. In origin it was Hellenic rather than Oriental. The Olympian religion as we have seen conceived the gods anthropomorphically, in a manner alien to the religions of the East; their difference from men was one not of kind but of degree, save in the fact of their immortality. In the Hellenistic age, the need of salvation was urgently felt, and the philosophic gospels (of which we shall speak presently) were too abstruse to appeal to popular imagination. Why, then, should not a living saviour be regarded as a god? Moreover, the centralized monarchies established in the generation after Alexander needed a visible symbol of unity and of personal loyalty to the ruler. The practice of deification met these new requirements in the period of Macedonian overlordship as later in that of the Roman Empire. To Jews and Christians, nurtured in the pure monotheistic tradition, it seems a blasphemous abomination, but the Greek and the Roman viewed it with very different eyes. To them it meant very little more than canonization means for Catholic Christiantiy to-day. It was a natural way of expressing gratitude for saving benefits. Were our records more ample than they are, we should probably find that the task of Hellenization was in the hands of a competent bureaucracy, and that, as subsequently under the Roman empire, the administrative machine preserved its efficiency despite the vagaries of individual rulers. A noteworthy illustration of this efficiency is the systematic development of Egyptian agriculture under the Ptolemies, a task which had been neglected by the Persian rulers. As a result, Egypt became the chief granary of the Roman empire. Moreover, the Hellenic city, the great instrument of the policy, tended when once founded to flourish by its own organic vitality. Of the nature of the culture thus developed at Alexandria at the Nile mouth, at Antioch on the Orontes, at Seleucia on the Tigris, and at a hundred other cities which owed their existence to Alexander and his successors, we shall speak in a later section of this chapter. Of the three Graeco-Macedonian dynasties, it was the Seleucid kings of Asia who bore the heaviest burden and yet carried forward the work of Hellenization most effectively. Macedon and Egypt were compact states, homogeneous and comparatively easy of defence, while the Asiatic empire was hampered by the same lack of internal unity and cohesion as that of Persia in days gone by. Its monarchs proved unequal to contend at once against their rivals in the West and in the East, the Ptolemies and Macedonians on the one side, and on the other the Parthian power which arose in the third century in Iran.[1] The Punjâb soon recovered its independence,[2] the satrapies east of the Tigris fell to the Parthians, and early in the second century the descendants of Seleucus found themselves restricted to the lands between the Euphrates and the Levant, cooped up between Parthia and Rome. A hundred years more and their rule vanished even from Syria, and the Roman legions confronted the Parthians on the Euphrates. Yet in the course of these few generations the house of Seleucus achieved great things for civilization. By founding a multitude of cities in Syria and Babylonia, in Asia Minor and the lands around the Caspian, they planted Hellenism in the Middle East and prepared a meeting-ground for Greek and Oriental thought.[3] The debt was not merely one-sided; if Hellenic culture took root in Asia, the religions of the East also began to win a hold over the Mediterranean world. The fusion was pregnant with momentous issues. It was at Antioch, the Syrian capital of the Seleucids, that the disciples of the faith which the East gave to the West were first called by the Greek name of Christians.[4]

1. The Parthian kings were a Scythian dynasty who established themselves on the Iranian plateau.

2. It must be remembered that Greek cities with Greek colonists were planted in the Punjâb, and that Greek influence in that part of India did not cease with the recovery of independence. A native prince wrote to Antiochus I, asking him to send a Greek sophist to the Punjâb; Antiochus replied that sophists were not for sale (Bevan, i. 297).

3. Seleucia on the Tigris replaced Babylon, which henceforward was merely a religious centre; Seleucia continued as a Greek city under the Parthians (Tac., Ann., vi. 42). Strabo (xi. 509), who lived in Augustus's time, attributed the lack of development of the resources of Hyrcania and the Caspian district in his day to the fact that it had never been ruled by Greeks. The Graeco-Macedonian government, like our Egyptian and Indian civil service, eagerly fostered material and economic improvements, roads, irrigation, drainage, etc. On the above, see Bevan, i. 281, and, generally, chapters xi to xiv of his work.

4. Acts xi. 26. Mithraism began to spread in western Asia under the successors of Alexander; see Vol. 2 c. ix. § 8.

§ 7. We remarked above that the advent of the Macedonian power meant the downfall of the Hellenic *Polis* as an independent political unit. This was the price paid by Greece for the opportunity of extending Hellenism over the East. That achievement was possible only for a large state, and throughout all antiquity a large state meant despotism. We shall see how Rome, too, ceased to be a republic when she had acquired a world-empire. The devices employed by modern nations in order to reconcile an extended territory with the maintenance of political freedom, the printing-press, steam transit, communication by electricity, and, above all, representative government, were unknown to the ancients. But our assertion, though true in the main, must be accepted with certain reservations. For one thing, the free city-state died hard. The Graeco-Macedonian period witnessed repeated struggles between the forces of republicanism and of autocracy, and in not a few cases the republics were able to hold their own. This was so, beyond the limits of Alexander's empire, in the West, where communities like Syracuse, Tarentum, and Massilia remained independent till they were absorbed under the sway of Rome. Elsewhere we find that individual cities preserve or recover independence, in accordance with varying circumstances of time and place. In European Greece, Athens, Sparta, and the Aetolian and Achaean leagues secured a transitory autonomy; the like is true of Byzantium, Heraclea on the Euxine, Chios, and certain Aegean towns. The island-city of Rhodes, especially, enjoyed a brilliant epoch of commercial prosperity under a republican government, which suppressed piracy, protected weaker states without exaction of tribute, founded a remarkable code of maritime law, and fostered both religion and culture, preserving its freedom from international complications until the middle of the second century.[1] Pergamos, again, flourished as a home of art and culture under dynasts of its own, the house of Attalus, rich merchant princes who valiantly defended Hellenism against the inroads into Asia of barbarian Gauls. But the

---

1. Rhodes was founded in 408, and was the middleman between Alexandria, Syria, the Euxine, and European ports.

majority of Hellenic cities were subject politically to one of
the three Macedonian kingdoms. These cities, for the most
part, were allowed entire liberty of local government, and
many, like Smyrna, or the chief cities of Cilicia, Phoenicia, and
the Orontes valley, were recognized as ' sacred and invio-
late', standing outside of the ordinary system of administration. Their position under Macedonian rulers, as later under
Rome, was analogous to that of the free Hanseatic towns in
the days of the Holy Roman empire. The dynasts were careful
to observe the forms of courtesy due to the high traditions of
the Hellenic *Polis*, to speak not of 'subjects' but of 'allies', of
'voluntary contributions' in place of 'tribute', to foster their
material welfare by generous largesses, especially to the civic
temples, and generally to veil under a guise of acknowledged
liberty the hard reality of subjugation. The cities in their turn
were ready to flatter the despots with divine honours, a clear
sign of degeneration from the temper of the fifth-century
Polis.[1] The Seleucids at all events were sincerely phil-Hellene
and knew well that Hellenization could be accomplished only
through the civic organism. Yet, when all allowance has been
made for the independence of individual cities, for the multi-
plication of new municipalities in the Seleucid kingdom, and
for the indulgent policy of its rulers towards old and new alike,
the truth remains that the sovereignty of the Greek *Polis*, and
with it the fountain head of the spirit of political liberty, had
passed away. We can therefore appreciate the passionate
resistance offered to Philip by Athens under Demosthenes,
and the refusal of the Greek states to be blinded, by the
dazzling splendour of Alexander's victories, to the real
sacrifice which those victories entailed. They felt instinctively
that a blow had been struck at the roots whence Hellenism
had sprung. So in fact it was; slowly but surely the Greek race
lost its ancient energy during the Graeco-Macedonian and
Graeco-Roman epochs. The Greeks 'were like the freeholder
of an ancient family, who has mortgaged and lost his inheri-

1. The restored democracy of Miletus conferred divine honours on the
degenerate Antiochus II (*Theos*). On the apotheosis of princes, see Murray,
Five Stages, pp. 133 ff.

tance, but is still allowed to live on in the old home. The essential charm of ownership was gone for them, and with it all the joy and intensity of social life; and though this very calamity might widen their mental horizon, and find them new interests and fresh work to do, the stream of their intellectual effort would never again run so clear and strong as in the days of the perfect freedom of the individual city-state.' [1] Doubtless at the same time new possibilities were opened out for Hellenism. The transformation of economic conditions carried with it far-reaching social and political consequences. With the eastern trade largely in the hands of Greece, business enterprises developed on a new and expanded scale, the old methods of banking were superseded, and the cleavage between the capitalist and the industrial worker was widened, with the inevitable results that the security of the leading commercial cities was menaced by the fear of revolution. Prices everywhere rose out of all proportion to the increase of wages; between the fourth and third centuries the drachma lost half its value; the masses were in constant danger of starvation; nor did there exist an extensive middle class to bridge the gulf that parted the very prosperous from the miserably poor. Hence the cries for the stock revolutionary panaceas, cancellation of debts, equal division of land, confiscation of personal property and liberation of slaves, which drew theoretical support from Stoic ideas, now rapidly spreading among the *intelligentsia*. [2] Moreover, the conquests of Alexander brought a larger world within the field of man's vision than was compatible with the maintenance of a merely civic patriotism. The despotism of Macedon and Rome, breaking down the barriers that severed Greek from barbarian, Western from Oriental, paved the way for the ideal of cosmopolitanism which found expression in the Stoic philosophy, in Roman jurisprudence and, ultimately, in the religion of Christianity. There was that in the creations and in the

1. Warde Fowler, *City-state*, pp. 301–2.
2. See Tarn, *The Hellenistic Age*, pp. 108–40, on 'The Social Question', with detailed illustration from revolutionary movements at Sparta during the fourth and third centuries (Agis, Cleomenes, and Nabis).

spirit of the Greek genius which transcended the limitations of the race that gave them birth. Hellenism was a light, not only for the Hellene but for mankind, and the hour wherein it set in its native skies saw its dawn among the non-Hellenic peoples.

II. HELLENISTIC CULTURE

§ 8. The decay of Hellenism was very gradual; for Greek culture preserved its freshness and distinction through the long period of decline. The well-springs had been sapped; but the stream still flowed, though with scantier and more sluggish volume; and the waters were those of Greece. Our purpose here is to outline the general character of that culture in the so-called 'Hellenistic' period, between the dominion of Alexander and that of Rome (330–30 B.C.).[1] In a later chapter we shall speak of Hellenism under the Roman empire. Two governing facts must be stated at the outset. First, the loss of civic independence meant that the serious business of government was no longer a concern of the individual citizen; literature and thought henceforward move in an atmosphere of personal interests, and of social, as distinct from public, life. Secondly, Greece is more and more conscious of her accomplished past; hitherto creative of the present and the future, she now becomes historical and reflective. It is when the impulse to creation is decaying and energy begins to flag that a race turns towards its past achievements to analyse and to record. 'The owl of Minerva does not start upon its flight till the evening shadows begin to fall.' [2]

§ 9. Hellenistic literature and Hellenistic art are the product of the changed conditions of life and thought. Broadly speaking, the literature is marked by scholarship and learning, by criticism and reflection, by imitation of old models, the pouring of new wine into old bottles, or, again, by the

1. The term 'Hellenistic' is inadequate, but in current use. 'Graeco-Macedonian' is a better term. 'Alexandrian', which is often employed, is very misleading. The import of the term 'Hellenistic' is much narrower than that of 'Hellenism'.

2. Hegel, Preface to the *Philosophy of Right*.

desire to furnish social entertainment for a cultured public, in close dependence on the patronage of the great. In this field, as in that of action, it was an age of clever second-rate men; the really eminent scientist, Eratosthenes, was nicknamed *Beta* (i.e., in Class II), though this was probably the expression of the jealousy felt by specialists for a colleague of wider intellectual outlook than their own. If we except Rhodes and Athens, the chief centres of literary and scientific activity were the courts of despots. Poetry of course was freshest where life was most free, as in Sicily, beyond the range of the Macedonian empire, or at Athens, the home of great traditions, where at least the show of political independence was zealously preserved. The idylls of the Syracusan Theocritus (*c.* 270) were the last achievements of the Greek poetic genius deserving of mention in the same breath with Homer and the Attic dramatists.[1] Theocritus created a new form of literature and was the source of inspiration to the pastoral poetry of all succeeding times, including the *Eclogues* of Virgil, Milton's *Lycidas*, and Shelley's *Adonais*. At Athens flourished the New Comedy of manners (330–250), that portrayed typical characters and situations of Greek social life. In place of the living personages lampooned by Aristophanes, Menander and his fellow-dramatists brought upon the stage the querulous father, the spendthrift son, the parasite, the confidante and the courtesan, the miser and the braggadocio adventurer, the Harpagons and Dugald Dalgettys of the age. In comedy, epigram, and epic, the love interest between man and woman, conspicuously absent from earlier Greek poetry, became a dominant motive;[2] the Rhodian poet, Apollonius, for example, imitating the earlier epic form, wrote in hexameter verse the story of the Argonauts and the passion of Medea for Jason. The spirit of romance found beautiful expression in elegies that had their home in Alexandria. The

1. Though Theocritus lived at Alexandria under the second Ptolemy, the spirit of his poetry is Sicilian.

2. Euripides was the first of the Greek dramatists to make the love of the sexes a central theme. Love, however, in the ideal modern sense is rare in Greek literature. (See *Antimachus of Colophon and the Position of Women in Greek Poetry*, by E. F. M. Benecke.)

same city, under the patronage of the Ptolemies, was the centre of Hellenic erudition. Two great libraries, one of which contained 700,000 manuscripts, testified to the ardour with which princes and scholars collected the classics of the past. Schools of critics and commentators laboured at the tasks of editing and interpretation. By the side of the scholar arose his parasite, the pedant. It was an age at once of general culture and of specialist research. Thanks to the papyrus, there came into being a cultured reading public. Philological and aesthetic criticism flourished at Alexandria; the departmental sciences were pushed forward by the aid of new data and appliances; and among the learned men who had their home in the Museum were the geometer Euclid; Archimedes, who discovered the principle of the lever; the geographer Eratosthenes of Cyrene, who first measured a degree of latitude on the earth's surface; and the Homeric scholar, Aristarchus of Samothrace. Eratosthenes' estimate of 28,000 miles for the earth's circumference was a truly astonishing approximation to the truth. It was Eratosthenes, too, who embodied in his map the fruits of the famous voyage of Pytheas of Marseilles (late fourth century) along the Atlantic coast of Europe to Britain and by the shores of the North Sea to the mouth of the Elbe. In fact, the Greeks of the fourth and third centuries may be regarded as the creators of geographical science. In the middle of the third century the great mathematician and astronomer, Aristarchus of Samos (c. 310–230), formulated the heliocentric hypothesis, following the tracks of Pythagorean and Platonic science.[1] It was at Alexandria too that anatomy first became the basis of medical science (Herophilus, c. 300 B.C.). In the Jewish colony at Alexandria, which enjoyed peculiar privileges, the contact of eastern and western culture bore fruit in the production of the Septuagint, the Greek version of the Old Testament scrip-

1. See Burnet, *E. Gk. Ph.*, p. 299, and Heath, *Aristarchus of Samos*. Burnet remarks that Copernicus, in a letter to Pope Paul III, admitted that his studies of Pythagorean science had given the impulse to his rediscovery of the heliocentric theory. Euclid lived in the reign of Ptolemy I; Archimedes and Eratosthenes belong to the third century, Aristarchus of Samothrace to the first half of the second century.

tures.[1] The period is noteworthy also for its historical works, of which the best-known is that of Polybius (second century), a Greek republican statesman, who was carried as a hostage to Rome at the time of the conquest of Macedonia, and enjoyed the friendship of the celebrated Scipionic circle. He recorded in his own tongue the expansion of the Roman power, inspired by the conviction – a rare tribute from a Greek author – of the fitness of the Roman race to rule the world. Significant of the success of the policy of Hellenization were the histories of Egypt by a native priest Manetho, and of Babylon, also by a native priest, Berosus. It was a Babylonian scientist, bearing the Greek name of Seleucus, who championed the new heliocentric theory of the heavens in the second century. The freer political atmosphere of Athens and Rhodes gave a stimulus to famous schools of rhetoric. Of the philosophy of the age we shall speak in a later section. The period was also one of the organization of knowledge in schools and libraries. University centres, on the model of Athens, arose over the Hellenic world, as at Rhodes, Pergamos, and Tarsus in Cilicia. At the close of its history, Greek culture perished of inanition in learned academies; but it was in learned academies that it rose again to life in the Italy of the Renaissance. One more feature of Hellenistic literature deserves remark. Authors wrote no longer, as the Athenian dramatists had written, for their fellow-citizens; but, in conformity with the new world outlook, for a public that was at once cosmopolitan and trained in the culture of the past.

§ 10. The art of the period likewise, from the beginning of the fourth century onwards, reflects the altered outlook upon life. If the architecture and sculptures of the age of Philip and Alexander lack the repose and grandeur of the earlier style, there is gain to compensate the loss in an increased mastery of technique, a freer rendering of human emotion, and a wonderful power of individual characterization. As time

1. The Septuagint (LXX), so called because it was supposed to have been the work of seventy translators, was produced in the third and second centuries. The early Christian church knew the Old Testament chiefly through this version.

went on signs of degeneration become visible in the love of
florid elegance and the conscious effort after archaism.
Among the noblest monuments of fourth-century sculpture
two may be studied in the British Museum, the *Mausoleum*, the
tomb erected at Halicarnassus to king Mausolus of Caria
(*c.* 350), a work in which Scopas of Paros bore a part, and the
Nereid shrine from Xanthus in Lycia. Both are evidence of the
hold that Greek culture had won among the non-Hellenic
races of Asia Minor. At Olympia may still be seen the *Hermes*
of Praxiteles, a sculptor of the Athenian school, whose statues
of the goddess Aphrodite created a new type of female beauty
in art. Perhaps the most characteristic artistic development
of the time was the rise of portraiture. Alexander sat frequently to the sculptor Lysippus and to the great Greek painter,
Apelles of Colophon. No paintings of this age have come
down to us; but the features of the leading dynasts are preserved on a large number of gems and coins. In architecture,
the fourth century saw the adoption of the florid Corinthian
capital (e.g. in the *Choregic monument of Lysicrates* at Athens, *c.*
335), and the supersession, in Greece proper, of the severe
Doric by the richer Ionic style. When we pass on to the
third century we find the best art, like the best poetry,
flourishing where life was most free. At Alexandria there was
little worthy of record save an artificial revival of native
Egyptian art under the patronage of the Ptolemies. Town-
planning, a favourite interest of the Greeks since Pericles
employed Hippodamus of Miletus to lay out Thurii in squares,
and Dionysius I remodelled Syracuse, naturally flourished
under the Macedonian dynasts; Alexandria and Antioch were
built on systematic and elaborate designs. The most beautiful
of all cities, in site and structure, was Pergamos, the creation of
the princes of the house of Attalus. Both Pergamos and Rhodes
were centres of living art in the third and second centuries.
The former grew around a hill-fortress into the capital of
cultured princes, who, like the Medici of the Renaissance,
gathered about them philosophers and artists. The Per-
gamene sculptures, commemorating the victories of Attalus I
(241–197) and Eumenes II (197–159) over the Gauls, were

the finest of the age.[1] Rhodes at an earlier date had crowned its heroic resistance to the forces of despotism by the erection of the Colossus, a statue of the sun-god over 100 feet in height, the work of a pupil of Lysippus. The famous Laocoon group was modelled in the Rhodian school, and the Rhodian Protogenes was one of the great painters of the day. Subsequent developments of sculpture are represented by such well-known works as the *Apollo Belvedere* and the *Venus* (*Aphroditê*) of Melos. Genre-painting, pictures of interiors like those of the great Dutch artists of the seventeenth century, had also a vogue, and furnishes an analogy to the scenes from social life in the New Comedy. Under the Seleucids, Greek art spread eastwards over the Asiatic continent; modern scholars assure us that it was from the Greeks who ruled for a brief span in the Punjâb that the Indians learnt to build and carve in stone. We must remember, too, how the literature and art of the Hellenistic age directly set its mark on those of Rome, and thus, through Rome, influenced later civilization even more deeply than the great master-works of the age of Pericles.

III. ARISTOTLE

§ 11. When Israel lost her national independence she sought a refuge in religion. The decline of the Hellenic city-state left the Greeks without that source of consolation. We have seen that the popular faiths of Greece had ceased to influence the more thoughtful and earnest of the race; these – the aristocracy of culture – turned to philosophy for guidance and support. It is the philosophy of this age that has most profoundly influenced later generations of mankind. The greatest of Plato's pupils, Aristotle, had for three years been Alexander's tutor – perhaps the most impressive conjunction of personalities in human history. Aristotle, like Alexander, stands at the parting of the ways. His philosophy is rooted in that of Plato;

1. E.g. the *dying Gaul* of the Capitoline Museum (often erroneously called the *Dying Gladiator*). The art of Pergamos was remarkable for its dramatic realism and mastery of technique; it was more truly alive than any other art of the age.

there is hardly one of his leading ideas of which the germ is not to be found in the Platonic dialogues.[1] Even more than Plato, whose attitude to the life of his age was one of remorseless condemnation, he is representative of Greek life as embodied in the city-state. That the knell of the free city had sounded at Chaeronea, Aristotle seems scarcely to be aware. It is his strong grasp of the actual in nature and human life, and his interest in the social and physical phenomena of the Hellenic world, that make his philosophy such an illuminating commentary on Greek culture. Plato saw deeper into the springs of human action, but Aristotle was the more typical Hellene. His political ideal was the Hellenic city-state reformed rather than revolutionized; his ideal for the individual was the life of reason, informing, as a principle of proportion and measure, the rich and varied field of citizen duty presented in the life of the Greek state. It is this sense of the value of attained fact, of the necessity of realizing the ideal form amid the material of actual conditions, that distinguishes Aristotle from Plato. Like Plato, he held the contemplative life to be the highest; like Plato, he held that to be most real which is most knowable, and sought this reality in the eternal truths which are objects, not of sense, but of thought. But these eternal forms were not in his view denizens of a world remote from that of actual experience; they were the governing principles of the world in which he lived.[2]

§ 12. To indicate the scope and value of Aristotle's philosophy in a brief compass is an impracticable task; especially as there is no single writing of his which, like Plato's *Republic*, furnishes a comprehensive groundwork of study. His works were specialized treatises, frequently pre-

1. Aristotle was, in fact, the first Platonist. To interpret his philosophy as an original development of Plato's is far more accurate than to stress the contrast, as has too frequently been done in later times. Aristotle was, of course, anxious to make clear to his own generation the points wherein he diverged from the dominant system. This has given a handle to misinterpretation.

2. In Raphael's cartoon of *The School of Athens*, Plato is portrayed as pointing upwards to the heavens, Aristotle as pointing downwards to earth. Jaeger's *Aristotle* makes clear the development of his thoughts away from Platonic otherworldliness towards concentration on positive science.

served in the form of lecture notes by himself or his pupils, addressed to minds versed in the several subjects and presupposing a knowledge of other parts of the system. Science, as we have noted, was already in process of differentiation into departments, and Aristotle's writings abound in technical terms and formulas divorced by a wide gulf from the language of common converse. It is not that Aristotle is really harder to understand than Plato. Plato soars on strong wings towards the sun, and few there are that can attend him on his flight. 'The thyrsus-bearers are many, but the inspired are few.' [1] Yet his genius draws the reader irresistibly into the upper air, dazzled and confounded though he be by the unwonted splendour. Aristotle wields no such magical attraction. To study his philosophy there is need from the first of patient effort and of the full strength of that 'desire to know' which he tells us is natural to man.[2] The range of his learning was unequalled in that or any other age. The extant treatises alone comprise works on logic or scientific method, on *first philosophy* or *metaphysics*,[3] on physical nature and on moral science, on psychology, on rhetoric, and on poetry, together with a large number of remarkable writings on biological science. Aristotle may be reckoned the founder of zoology, and his pupil, Theophrastus, the founder of botany. It is these last that Charles Darwin had in mind when he wrote, 'Linnaeus and Cuvier have been my two gods, though in very different ways, but they were mere schoolboys to old Aristotle.' [4] In one sphere alone was he outshone by others of his age, in mathematics, where his deficiencies, because of his immense authority over succeeding times, long proved a hindrance to progress in those sciences, such as astronomy, which rest on mathematical foundations. In view of the impossibility of

1. *Phaedo*, 69.
2. *Met.*, i. 1; the opening words.
3. The name *metaphysics* (i.e. after the *physics*) was assigned to this treatise by later editors in antiquity, for the purely accidental reason that it followed next after the *Physics* in the published order of Aristotle's works. Hence the general use of the term metaphysics to signify the science of being, which is the matter of this treatise. Aristotle himself called the science *first philosophy* or *theology*.
4. Darwin, *Life and Letters*, iii. 252.

surveying this vast body of speculative inquiries, we shall select two problems, which will serve to illustrate both the cardinal tenets of Aristotle's philosophy and its divergence from that of Plato, and to introduce the reader to conceptions which deeply influenced the subsequent course of Hellenic and medieval thought. These are his doctrine of Being and his ideal of the chief Good for man.[1]

§ 13. (1) *The Doctrine of Being.* It was the fact of change, manifest alike in physical motion, in the growth of living organisms, and in man's intellectual and moral development, that constituted for Aristotle the main problem of speculative science. Change implies that which changes, i.e. permanent subjects of change, concrete things and persons which become now hot, now cold, now good, now bad, taking on the forms of heat and cold, virtue and vice. Cold does not become heat, nor virtue vice; it is not the form which changes, but the individual recipient of the forms. These concrete individuals, this stone or this tree or Socrates, are compounds of matter (*hylê*) and form (*eidos*); they are not reducible to mere form, for, as we have said, form cannot change; nor are they reducible to matter, for nothing exists save as a definite somewhat, endowed with a character or form, as stone, or tree, or man. Mere matter, wholly indeterminate and void of form, is no actual existent, but a limiting conception, necessary to explain becoming and change; how indeed could anything come to be out of that which was not already something definite? The forms, again, do not exist, as Plato had supposed, in a super-sensible heaven, cut adrift from the actual world of our experience; for what could such separate forms contribute either to the being of our world of change or to our knowledge of it? Thus for Aristotle it is the concrete individual, not the mere universal, that has substantial being. When asked, What is *substance* (*ousia*)?, he answered, 'this stone', 'this tree', 'you' and 'I'.[2] All other modes of being are

1. For the sections that follow, the reader is referred to the works on Aristotle mentioned in the Bibliographical Appendix to Vol. 2.

2. In fact, Aristotle gave divergent answers to this question: but the text states the main drift of his solution of the problem.

qualities, affections, or relations of this fundamental mode, and can exist only in dependence on substantial being; 'black' or 'equal' can be only if there be a black thing or equal things. Now philosophy has for its business to discover the *causes* of these individual substances and thus to explain the changes which they undergo, and Aristotle shows how such explanation demands the co-operation of four kinds of cause. In order that anything may come to be, say, a statue, there are required (*a*) the matter (*hylê*) out of which it arises, e.g. the marble block; (*b*) an external principle of motion that starts the process of change, e.g. the mind, hand, and tool of the sculptor; (*c*) the form (*eidos*) realized in and through the process, e.g. the form of the Phidian *Zeus* or the *Hermes* of Praxiteles; (*d*) the aim and end of the process, e.g. the completed statue as the goal of the sculptor's work. Thus we must posit a material, an efficient, a formal, and a final cause. It is obvious that the three last-mentioned causes tend to coalesce. It is the form (*c*) of the statue which is the sculptor's aim (*d*), and the thought of this aim in his mind is the motive impulse (*b*) that initiates and guides the process of his work. The conception of form as the end or purpose of development, in contrast to undeveloped matter, is the fundamental thought of all Aristotle's philosophy. Alike in biology, in psychology, in ethics, and in the theory of art, his explanation, like Plato's, is teleological. The cosmic process, through all its detail, is interpreted as the progressive actualization of the capacity to receive form, and in each case the process attains its end in the realization of the appropriate form. The undeveloped must thus be explained in the light of the developed, not *vice versa*; the man is prior to the child, the oak to the acorn, and to begin at the beginning is simply to begin at the wrong end.[1] Thus Aristotle expresses the dis-

1. This shows how different, despite his insistence on the idea of development and his genius as a biologist, was Aristotle's interpretation of organic nature from that of modern evolutionary science. Nor did he apply the idea of development to species, which he regarded as separate and fixed. His teleology led him to reject with contempt the hints at an evolutionary process by natural selection and the survival of the fittest which had been thrown out by Empedocles. 'We may suppose that all things have fallen out accidentally just as they would have done if they had been produced for some end. Certain

tinction of matter and form more fruitfully in dynamic terms as that of potency (*dynamis*) and actuality (*energeia*). The child is the potency of the man, the acorn of the oak; when the forms of man and oak are actualized in the respective individuals, the process is complete, the end achieved. But, be it observed, for the process to start at all, form and actuality are presupposed, though in another individual of the species; the child can come to be only through the agency of an actually existing human father. By this line of thought, Aristotle is led to the eternal being of *God* as pure form. Since only in the strength of an already existing actuality (form) can an individual's potency move towards actualization, since 'man only can beget man' and the production of the statue demands the prior existence of the form in the sculptor's thought, so is it also with the primal fact of change, the motion of the universe. If we are to escape from an infinite regress of causes, there must be an eternal first mover, to account for the eternal and primary motion of the heavens; and since the cause is ever other than the effect, the mover than the moved, the first mover cannot, as Plato held, be self-moved, but must be himself unmoved.[1] This unmoved first mover is pure form, eternally actual and divine. In Aristotle's theism there is no place for a Creator, because the universe has no beginning in time, and the act of creation would imply movement and change and potency in God; nor for a Providence, for God is beyond and apart from nature, and his life is not one of practical activity but of simple contemplation (*theoria*). He does not even know the universe, but is pure self-conscious intelligence, at once the subject and the object of his own most

things have been preserved because they had spontaneously acquired a fitting structure, while those which were not so put together have perished and are perishing, as Empedocles says of the oxen with human heads.' This, in Aristotle's opinion, would be to explain nature as due to chance, whereas nature does not work in vain and achieves the goal normally ('for the most part'). See *Phys.*, ii. 8, and Burnet, *E. Gk. Ph.*, p. 243 (on Empedocles), whose translation of the passage I have here given. Cf. also (on Anaximander), *E. Gk. Ph.*, p. 71.

1. The influence of Aristotle's argument to God as Pure Act and as unmoved mover of the universe on medieval Christian philosophy was profound, as any reader of Dante knows.

perfect thought. Alone in this absolute transcendence, God draws the world towards himself as the goal of its desire. 'The final cause produces motion as does an object of love, and through that which it moves (the outer sphere of the fixed stars) moves all things else.' 'On such a principle, then, depend the heavens and the world of nature. And its life is such as the best which we enjoy and enjoy but for a short time. For it is ever in this state (which we cannot be), since its actuality is also pleasure. . . . If thus God is always in that good state in which we sometimes are, this compels our wonder; and if in a better, this compels it yet more. And God *is* in a better state. And life also belongs to God; for the actuality of thought is life, and God is that actuality; and God's essential actuality is life most good and eternal. We say therefore that God is a living being, eternal, most good, and that life and duration continuous and eternal belong to God; for this *is* God.' [1]

§ 14. (II) *The chief Good for man.* Aristotle's argument to God's existence from the fact of motion furnishes the philosophical groundwork to the theology of the Middle Ages. It held the chief place among the proofs formulated by Aquinas, and will be recognized as the source whence Dante drew his conception of 'the Love that moves the sun and the other stars '.[2] The passage from the *Metaphysics*, quoted above, suggests Aristotle's answer to the second of our problems, that of the *summum bonum*, or chief good for man. Whereas Plato had insisted uncompromisingly that knowledge of absolute good was essential to true virtue and felicity, and that the goal of man's nature was realizable only in a life of devotion to philosophy, Aristotle turns from the search for the Absolute to that for the specific form of human goodness, an end attainable by the good citizen of the Hellenic *Polis* within the compass of his earthly life. It is to be found here or nowhere; for the individual soul, as the form of the organic body, lives in union with the body, its matter, and can have no separate

1. *Met.*, xii. 7 (*tr.* Ross).
2. Aquinas, *Summa Theol.*, i. q. 2, art. 3, *Summa contra Gentiles*, i. c. 13; Dante, *Paradiso*, xxxiii. 145.

claim to immortality. To determine the form of the good life, wherein consists human felicity (*eudaimonia*), is the problem of political science, which treats of the development of man's natural capacities towards the realization of this end. It is handled by Aristotle in two treatises, the (*Nicomachean*) *Ethics* and the *Politics*.[1] For Plato, political science was inseparable from metaphysics, the philosopher must be king and the king a philosopher; Aristotle, on the other hand, distinguishes sharply between knowing and doing, and between theoretical and practical science. He approached the problems of morals in an empirical and inductive spirit. Both works were designed as manuals for the legislator in his practical task of educating the citizen to the complete form of social virtue.[2] He defined felicity (*eudaimonia*), the chief good for man, as 'activity of the soul in accordance with virtue (*aretê*)', and virtue as 'a settled disposition of will, being in the relative mean, determined by rational principle, and as the man of practical wisdom would determine it'.[3] By the 'relative mean' must be understood not a standard of mediocrity or compromise with evil, but the observance of the due proportion, as against excess and deficiency of feeling and purpose, in each of the varying situations that call for action. The nerve of the definition lies in the appeal to a reasonable principle (*logos*), by which is meant, not an abstract formula of conduct, but a 'right judgement in all things', constituting in the soul of the citizen the sovereign excellence of practical wisdom (*phronêsis*). Aristotle discusses a host of problems arising out of this conception of human goodness, such as the formation of moral principle by habituation in right conduct, the nature of voluntary action and responsibility for wrong

1. The reader, if unfamiliar with Aristotle's works, is advised to commence his study of them with the *Ethics*; for English translations, see Bibliographical Appendix to Vol. 2.

2. Hence the interest of the *Ethics* as reflecting current Greek ideals and types of conduct. 'Aristotle's system,' writes Eucken, 'is wholly rooted in the classical world; its fundamental views, its valuations, work on uninterrupted in him. . . . Aristotle's system brings the substance of the classic world of Greece to marvellously perfect scientific expression, and so hands it down to future humanity' (*The Problem of Human Life*).

3. *Ethics*, i. 7, ii. 6.

done, the specific forms of virtue and their corresponding vices, the standard of justice in reference to its application by the law, the relation of felicity and pleasure, and the ideal of human friendship.[1] He devotes particular attention, in view of Socrates' and Plato's identification of virtue and knowledge, to the intellectual requirements of goodness and the good life. Though he does not question the need of intellectual excellence as essential to moral goodness, the fact of the man of weak will, who knows what is right yet does what is wrong, precludes their identification; the wisdom, moreover, that is requisite is not the theoretic wisdom (*sophia*) of the philosopher, but the practical wisdom (*phronêsis*) of the statesman.[2] It would be hard to exaggerate the influence of Aristotle's discussion of these questions on the thought of later times. The ethical doctrines of the Stoics, the Neo-Platonists, and even the Epicureans, are in large measure developments of those of Aristotle. His treatment of responsibility for crime affected Roman jurisprudence; the ethical sections of Aquinas' *Summae*, and the structure and content of Dante's *Divina Commedia*, show the impress of the *Ethics* at every turn.[3] If Christian speculation on man's ultimate felicity followed naturally in the track of Plato's other-worldliness, it drew freely on Aristotle's ethical teaching in the application of that ideal to man's life on earth. Aristotle himself, despite his emphasis on the points where he diverged from his master, strikes, at the close of the *Ethics*, a strong Platonic note. Since felicity consists in the exercise of the soul's highest activity, and since in the human soul reason is by nature supreme, it must needs be that the form and end of man's development attains its most complete expression in the life of philosophic contemplation. In that life, he can enjoy, if only intermittently, a fragment of the satisfaction which God, as pure reason, enjoys eternally. When Aristotle speaks of man's

1. Habituation, *Ethics*, ii; responsibility, *Ethics*, iii. 1; the specific forms of virtue and vice, *Ethics*, iii. 6 ff. and iv; *Ethics*, v; pleasure, *Ethics*, vii. 6 ff., x. 1–5; friendship, *Ethics*, viii and ix.

2. On weakness of will, *Ethics*, vii. 1–5; on the intellectual excellences (especially *sophia* and *phronêsis*), *Ethics*, vi.

3. See Vol. 2, c. xi. §§ 10, 11, 14.

obligation to direct his life by that in him which is most like to God, and of the wonderful felicity that such whole-hearted devotion brings with it, and identifies this free service with the life of philosophic study, we cannot fail to recognize in his language the direct reflexion of a personal experience. 'A man should not, in accordance with those who so advise, think human thoughts, because he is a man, or mortal thoughts because he is mortal, but as far as in him lies he should put on immortality, and do all to live in accordance with the highest there is in him; for though this be small in bulk, yet in power and worth it rises above all else.' [1]

§ 15. Aristotle was not merely the disciple of Plato but the herald of a new era in the history of thought. The material available for knowledge had been immeasurably enriched through the campaigns of Alexander, and vast collections, gathered by the scientists who accompanied those expeditions, lay at Aristotle's disposal. He utilized them freely both for his biological researches and to assist a reconstruction of philosophy which should correlate the special sciences in a comprehensive system. Two achievements were his especially; he determined the method of scientific inquiry, and mapped out the provinces of human knowledge. Aristotle was the real founder of logic, not in the sense of John Locke's celebrated epigram that 'God had not been so sparing to men, to make them barely two-legged animals, and left it to Aristotle to make them rational', [2] but in that, building always on Plato's foundations, he analysed the processes of scientific reasoning, and formulated the method by which demonstrative, as distinct from merely probable, truth could be attained. The formalism and artificiality of the pseudo-Aristotelian logic of the later schoolmen provoked a natural reaction among the great pioneers of science in the sixteenth and seventeenth centuries, which still cumbers the minds of many who are ignorant of the history of thought. In fact, Aristotle, who was never the slave of formulas, would have recognized in Galileo and in Descartes the true fulfilment of his own principles of scientific method. Every fresh epoch in the progress of speculative science has been inaugurated by a reform in logic. So it was, not only with the *Organon* or logical 'instrument' of Aristotle, but with the *Discours de la Méthode* of Descartes, the *Novum Organum* of Bacon, the Critical Method of Kant, and the Dialectic Method of Hegel. Philosophy and science differ from popular thinking not so much in being busied with different objects as in their handling of the same objects in a different way. The plants and animals which form the object-matter of botany and zoology had been already grouped and distinguished and vaguely understood before these sciences arose; the task of science was to correct and systematize these popular classifications, and to fix with precision the essential characters of things and their laws of growth. Aristotle, in his generation, realized that the problem of method was of decisive moment, and set himself to analyse the logic of science with unrivalled insight into the nature of the process of human thought. Secondly, he defined the various provinces of the sciences as parts of a single whole. No philosopher has so justly balanced the proportion of whole and part in knowledge, or has kept so firm a grasp on the real distinctions of things, while comprehending them in a unified system. It was his genius for systematization combined with the universal range of his inquiries, his appreciation of the variety of ruling principles in the world of our experience, his unerring eye for the differences and affinities of type throughout the universe, and his precision in the formulation of philosophic method, that justify Dante in styling Aristotle 'the master of those who know '. [1] They explain why the philosophy of the western world moved for 2000 years largely on the lines that he laid down. His authority in all matters of secular knowledge was sovereign throughout the later Middle Ages. [2] Even when the spirit of the new learning proclaimed the supersession of

---

1. *Inferno*, iv. 131.
2. See, on the authority of Aristotle, Dante, *Convivio*, iv. 6. This influence was not without its hindrances to progress, especially in the field of physics; e.g. the Aristotelian distinction between the upper heavens and the sublunary world lay like a burden on astronomers and physicists till the sixteenth and seventeenth centuries.

authority by free inquiry and abjured the Aristotle of the schools, it followed unwittingly in his steps. As the great organizer of knowledge, he holds in things of the mind a place analogous to that of the Roman empire in the field of government and law.

IV. STOICS AND EPICUREANS

§ 16. To Plato and Aristotle philosophy was a 'wave of life', by which alone man could attain knowledge of the highest good and therein find salvation. But its appeal was to the few who felt the call to intellectual contemplation; and even for these, philosophy tended to degenerate into sceptical indifference or arid formalism. The cultured layman needed something less abstruse and more directly practical than was offered him in the Academy and the Lyceum. The old landmark, the city-state with its religious worships and moral obligations, was fast vanishing from sight; cut adrift from his moorings, he sought a creed which should save his soul from shipwreck and pilot him to a haven of refuge from the ills of life.[1] In satisfaction of this demand there appeared, in the generation succeeding that of Aristotle and Alexander, the Stoic and Epicurean systems. Both were predominantly ethical in aim and doctrine; theory of knowledge (logic) and of nature (physics) served rather as the scaffolding than as an integral portion of their philosophic structure, while metaphysics, the kernel of Platonic and Aristotelian speculation, receded altogether into the background. Within the field of ethics, again, both claimed to furnish guidance for the soul of the individual, to show him how to live wisely and attain peace from the turbulent world without and the storms of passion within. Both portrayed the character of the wise man as a model for imitation, and taught how this ideal was to be attained. But here the resemblance ceases. When we ask as to the nature of the philosophic life, the two schools give

---

1. Of course, the traditional religious conceptions and worship persisted among the masses, but they were no longer effective to direct men's lives, as did the *Torah* of the Hebrews.

widely different answers. To the Stoic, it consists in following virtue, in obedience to an authoritative law of nature or reason; the sage, by subjugating emotion, and by detachment from the restless world of circumstance, disciplines his soul to self-sufficiency and inward independence. To the Epicurean, the good life is that of rational enjoyment of all the satisfactions which the world affords; the sage masters circumstances by using them as means to his convenience; the good is pleasure, i.e. not the momentary gratifications of the senses, but the fruits of 'cool self-love', above all, the delights of intellectual study and of social intercourse. Taken at their best, Stoicism was the more exalted, Epicureanism the more genial and human, of the two ideals. The Stoic was a moral aristocrat, somewhat prone to pride himself on his ascetic fortitude and to despise his weaker brethren; while the Epicurean creed, especially in its recognition of the equality of the sexes and its insistence on the pleasures of friendship, was less exclusive and more democratic. On a lower plane, Stoicism degenerated into puritanic formalism and casuistical compromises with the world that squared ill with its lofty professions; Epicureanism into a complacent acquiescence in the coarser satisfactions of life. But both were alike indifferent to the course of society and government. That rested in the hands of the despot, his army, and his civil service; the business of the individual lay elsewhere, in ordering aright the city of his own soul.

§ 17. Both schools had a long history, extending well into the Christian era. Of the two, Stoicism exercised by far the greater influence, alike in antiquity and over the modern world. Its doctrines appealed naturally to men of affairs, and were patronized, and sometimes even practised, by the dynasts and statesmen of the Graeco-Macedonian age. It became popular, as we shall see later, with the republican nobility of Rome; there was something in the practical Roman temperament that was repelled by other philosophies but responded readily to the Stoic creed. It left its mark both on Roman jurisprudence and on Hellenic Neo-Platonism, wherein Stoic teaching is blended with that derived from Plato and Aristotle. Christian thinkers were attracted by its moral elevation and uncompromising idealism. In modern times, it stirred the admiration of such different philosophers as Descartes, Bishop Butler, and Immanuel Kant.[1] What, then, was the secret of the hold which Stoicism won and kept so long over the hearts of men? The answer lies in its appeal to man's power of will, and in its resolute assertion both of human freedom and of divine providence. The Stoic taught that, impotent as man seemed to be in the face of hostile circumstance, of slavery, torture, disease, and death, in reality he was absolute master of his will, and that on this mastery of will alone depended all the value and good of life. 'Nothing is good without qualification but the good will'; this dictum, uttered more than twenty centuries later by the philosopher of Königsberg, would have been recognized by the Stoic as his own.[2] For the Stoic, as for Kant, the good will is unconditionally good. There are no degrees of goodness; if you are right you are absolutely right, if wrong, absolutely wrong. Whether you are right or wrong depends solely on the inner character of your volition. Further, the will is good when it wills the good, and the good is – what is. The order of the universe, the truth of all its happenings, the nature (*physis*) which is its creative energy, is perfect, is law, reason, God.[3] Therefore the wise man, the Stoic saint, recognizes willingly in whatever suffering may befall him the fulfilment of the providential purpose, and asserts his unconditional freedom in the face of it by willing it to be – what it is. His reason gladly goes forth to meet the kindred reason of the world. Thus, by strength of inward self-determination, he conquers passion and wins tranquillity of soul: '*e la sua*

1. Descartes, who wrote no work on ethics, when asked in 1645 by the Princess Elizabeth for his views on the subject, replied by recommending the Stoic treatise of Seneca *de vita beata* as sufficient for the purpose. See Descartes, *Œuvres*, ed. Adam and Tannery, vol. iv, pp. 251 ff., 263 ff.

2. Kant, *Grundlegung zur Metaphysik der Sitten*, Sect. I. *init.* (tr. Abbott, p. 9).

3. Professor Gilbert Murray, in his lecture on *Stoicism*, compares the *physis* of the Stoics to M. Bergson's *élan vital*. Stoicism, alone of Greek philosophical systems, approached near to Pantheism.

voluntate è nostra pace'.[1] Hence the Stoic precepts, Follow nature, Follow reason, Follow virtue, are merely different ways of saying the same thing. The Stoic said also, Follow God: for, despite the somewhat crude materialism of his physical theories, he held that the law which governs the course of nature was no blind mechanism, but the rational working-out of a divine purpose which was essentially good. In its thoroughgoing teleology, Stoicism fell into line with the traditions of Plato and Aristotle.[2] Its originality as an ethical creed lay partly in its appeal to the will, partly in its entire independence of the historic traditions of the *Polis*. From first to last, its message is addressed to the individual, bidding him stand, free from all conventional ties of human ordinance, foursquare in his own strength against all the winds that blow. In this personal appeal, as also in the trenchant dogmatism with which it was delivered, we catch the spirit of the first founder of the school. Zeno was a Semite of Citium in Cyprus, who settled while still young at Athens (*c.* 320) and taught there for more than half a century in the Painted Porch (*Stoa Poikilê*). Many of the most famous among his followers were natives of the islands and coastlands of the Levant, and the impress of the Semitic mind is clearly visible beneath the Hellenic setting of the system.[3] Stoicism, in fact, was the intellectual first-fruits of Alexander's policy of fusion. There was not a little about Zeno that recalls the Hebrew prophet; the latter's 'thus spake Yahweh' seems to be echoed in the form 'thus spake Reason'[4] The voice must needs be that of

1. 'And his will is our peace'; Dante, *Par.* iii. 85.

2. For Stoicism, all is determined, yet determined as the working-out of a rational purpose. The doctrine of correspondences in nature, which fitted in with this conception, afforded a basis for the accommodation of Stoic philosophy to the belief in divination and other features in the popular religion. Plutarch (see Vol. 2 c. ix. § 7) illustrates this tendency. The Stoics made free use of allegory and myth; their allegorical method of interpretation was taken over by Christianity. The Stoics were, in fact, experts in accommodation.

3. Chrysippus, the second founder of Stoicism (*d.* 206) was a native of Soli in Cilicia; he gave the doctrines of the school the systematic form which persisted for centuries. Cleanthes (third century) came from Assos in the Troad, Panaetius (second century) was a native of Rhodes, Posidonius (early first century) of Syria. Tarsus, the chief city of Cilicia, with a university, was a flourishing centre of Stoic teaching.

4. See Bevan, *Stoics and Sceptics*, Lect. I.

GRAECO-MACEDONIAN CULTURE 221

reason, for Zeno preached his gospel to Greeks, the one
people of history from whom it was idle to expect a hearing
unless you addressed yourself to their intelligence. But, this
step once taken, the appeal was bound to embrace more than
the private judgement of the individual hearer. Reason, as
Plato had shown, is common ground; and a teaching that
was in accord with it could be no gospel of purely personal
salvation. Thus with the same breath the Stoic proclaimed a
cosmopolitan ideal; the city that claimed the wise man's
loyalty was that of nature, of reason, of God. This conception
of a community comprising all mankind tallied with the wider
outlook of the age and with the actual establishment of world
states, first under Macedonian rule, and, later, under Rome.
It helped to shape the doctrine of a law of nature (*jus naturae*),
underlying the positive enactments of particular communities,
which was assimilated by Roman jurists, and through them
wielded far-reaching influence on the ethics and jurisprudence
of medieval and modern times. St Paul, a native of Tarsus, one
of the chosen seats of Stoicism, used the language of that
school to express the spiritual community of which all Christians are members. The thought of a heavenly citizenship recurs
constantly in his letters; in his sermon at Athens he quoted
from the Stoic Cleanthes' hymn to Zeus and declared, in
words that echo cardinal tenets of the Stoic system, that
God 'dwelleth not in temples made with hands', and that he
had 'made of one blood all nations of men for to dwell on all
the face of the earth '.[1]

§ 18. Stoicism, it has been said, 'ended in moral fervour
and logical bankruptcy'.[2] The doctrines of the Epicureans
were from the first of less speculative interest, and their
influence on the world was less widespread than that of the
Stoics. Epicurus was a pure Hellene, probably a native of
Samos, who came to Athens a little later than Zeno, and
founded there a small community of personal disciples. The

1. The quotation from Cleanthes (Acts xvii. 28) is 'For we are also his
offspring.' Cf., for Stoic ideas, Phil. iii. 20, Eph. ii. 19, etc.; and for the
parallel between the Christian and the Stoic sage, 1 Cor. iv. 8, 2 Cor. vi. 10,
Phil. iv. 12, 13.

2. Brett, *History of Psychology*.

history of the sect is marked throughout by devoted adherence
to the memory and the teaching of its founder.[1] Epicurus'
theory of nature was not original; having an ethical gospel to
preach, he took over, as a speculative foundation, the atomic
philosophy of Democritus, the most logical and complete
materialist system in existence. Democritus taught that the
universe, and all that therein is, is reducible to terms of homogeneous atoms, in eternal motion in empty space.[2] Mechanical
necessity determines alike the course of nature and that of
human action; every trace of freedom and of purpose is
rigorously excluded. Such doctrines were admirably adapted
to serve as a basis for the ethical message which constitutes
Epicurus' true claim to originality. His aim, pursued with a
passionate fervour of sincerity, was to destroy the last strong-
hold which the traditional religion still retained in the popular
mind. The terrors of a future life, of the bogey-land beyond,
where so-called gods wreaked their inhuman will on impotent
shades, were, in his view, the source of all disquietude and
suffering to men in life. 'It was fear that first made the gods.'
If, on the other hand, it be true that man's soul is but a
transitory concourse of atoms, dissolved at death to form part
of new aggregates, with total discontinuity of personal life
and consciousness, fear is dispelled, and man may possess his
soul in peace.[3] Pleasure, for Epicurus, is really to be interpreted as freedom from passion and disquiet (*ataraxia*), and this
negative rendering of the term brings his ideal, despite
many points of difference, into line with that of the Stoics.[4] It

1. See Lucretius' poem *de rerum natura*, opening lines of Books iii, v, vi,
for praise of Epicurus.

2. See above, c. iv. § 15. Though Epicureanism had but little influence in
later times, it may be noted that in the seventeenth century Father Gassendi, a
friend of Descartes, published a system of philosophy which comprised a physical
atomic theory and an ethical hedonism, analogous to Epicurus' doctrines.

3. See the great passage, Lucretius, iii. 830–end. The popular idea of God
and immortality were the bugbears of Epicureanism. But the Epicureans were
not atheists. They believed, on the evidence of abnormal psychical experiences,
that gods existed in a remote region of the universe, heedless of mankind,
enjoying a life of blessedness and perfect self-sufficiency. See also the aphorisms
translated in Wallace, *Epicureanism*, p. 110.

4. See Lucretius, ii. 22 ff., iii. 59 ff., 995 ff., iv. 1037 ff., v. 1152 ff.; on
the ideal of the wise man, iii. 322 ff.

is entirely misleading to treat the saying 'Let us eat and drink for to-morrow we die' as anything but a parody of Epicurean doctrine. Epicurus and his companions lived a life of charming simplicity, marked by strong mutual affection; and his followers in later generations copied their example. Their rule and habits won a warm encomium from the satirist Lucian in the second century A.D. There can be no question that Epicureanism brought peace to many a troubled spirit in the stormy times that followed the partition of Alexander's empire. That it, as well as Stoicism, could inspire and exalt is shown by the magnificent poem in which the Roman noble, Lucretius,[1] embodied the physical tenets and the religious gospel of its founder.

V. CONCLUSION

§ 19. We shall return to the Stoic philosophy when the time comes to speak of the conflict between the spirit of Hellenism, as reflected in the teaching of the schools, and the new spirit of Christianity. Here we need only remark that both ideals of life, the Stoic and the Christian, had their birth in the new world opened out by Alexander and his successors. This in itself is sufficient to belie the view that the force of Hellenism was extinguished with the downfall of the independence of the city-state. But it is equally the case that Hellenism had by that time well-nigh finished its work on purely Hellenic soil, and that its constructive energy was henceforward conditioned by fusion with the civilization of other lands. By the close of the fourth century, the structure of Hellenic civilization was already organic and complete. We have endeavoured to convey some idea of its character and history in this and the two preceding chapters. Its importance for human progress, both intrinsically and in its issues, is obvious and incalculable. The epoch which witnessed its creation, from the eighth to the third centuries before Christ, is among the

1. Lucretius died in 55 B.C.

most memorable in the history of mankind. For within it falls, not only the creation of Hellenism, but the transformation of primitive Hebrew religion into a faith of universal value. The first of the higher prophets, Amos and Hosea, were contemporaries of the pioneers of Greek colonization in the Mediterranean. The Babylonian exile and the writings of the second Isaiah synchronize with the birth of philosophy in Ionia and the development of the Athenian state under Solon and Pisistratus.[1] The Psalmists were writing at Jerusalem during the Persian wars and the age of Pericles. Nor were Hellas and Israel alone in thus laying the foundations of the civilization of the coming time. More than once in these chapters we have carried forward our story to the point when Mediterranean culture was gathered into a single state under Roman rule. 'Rome was not built in a day.' Long after Alexander set forth to win the East for Greece, and to inaugurate the policy of which Stoicism and Christianity were alike the fruits, nameless statesmen and soldiers had been fashioning the weapons of war and government, and the fabric of institutions and of law, that enabled a small Italian township to acquire a Mediterranean sovereignty, and establish the world-empire of Rome.

1. Murray, *Five Stages*, p. 57, cites Bevan to the effect that in Greece, nearer Asia (e.g. Palestine), China, and India, the sixth–fifth centuries saw the rise of a new age.

CHAPTER SEVEN

THE ROMAN REPUBLIC

*

I. THE FOUNDATIONS OF THE ROMAN STATE

§ 1. ON a ring of hills by the banks of the Tiber, fourteen miles from its mouth, there stood in the early centuries of the first millennium groups of rude huts surrounded by a stockade, where shepherds took refuge with their flocks when raiders descended on them from the Sabine hills. As time went on, several of these hamlets were united within a single ring-wall, and a town came into being.[1] It occupied a favoured spot as the natural market of the plain of Latium, where the river still was navigable, and beyond the reach of the Etruscan pirates that harried the coast.[2] At the dawn of its history, this settlement formed one of the members of a league sanctioned by religious ceremonial under the presidency of Alba, in which the inhabitants of the plain united for mutual trade and defence against the highland tribes. The league was called the Latin league; the city on the Tiber banks was Rome.

We can trace in broad outline the beginnings of the growth of Rome. The first clear landmark in her story is the expulsion of the kings and the establishment of an aristocratic republic at the close of the sixth century (509). Already before that date she had risen to the chief place in the Latin confederacy, had secured the Tiber bank to the port of Ostia at its mouth, and

---

1. There are clear traces of the early fusion of two settlements, one of Latins on the Palatine hill and one of Sabines on the Quirinal; the Sabines appear to have won the mastery and to have been the forefathers of the patrician families. The citizens of Rome in the regal period were called *Quirites*, a name probably of Sabine origin.

2. Rome was most favourably situated; the site, in Livy's phrase, was 'uniquely marked out for the expansion of the city' (*ad incrementum urbis natum unice locum*): v. 54, 4. Rome held a central position in Italy, the central peninsula of the Mediterranean, equi-distant from Cadiz and Alexandria, fronting Africa, at once linked to and protected from central, western, and southern Europe. The port of Brindisi connected Italy with the East.

had developed political institutions and an organized citizen-army. It appears that some time in the sixth century Rome became the capital of princes of alien stock who bore sway over southern Etruria and the whole plain of Latium.[1] The expulsion of the kings meant the overthrow of this foreign dominion. Yet the Etruscan occupation had permanently changed the position of Rome in relation to her Latin neigh-bours. She never relapsed into her former position as one of many confederate Latin towns, but retained an effective suzerainty. Had it not been for the Etruscan domination, her constitution might well have taken a different form, with a Latin as one of the Consuls. In fact, rather than yield to this demand on the part of the Latins, Rome eventually wiped out the League. The Etruscan overlords had laid the foundations of the future splendour of Rome; fragments of their archi-tecture, such as the stone wall ascribed to Servius Tullius, remain to this day as witness of their skill; in the words of Montesquieu, 'Already they had begun the building of the Eternal City.' [2]

§ 2. How Rome rose from these humble origins through centuries of growth to the lordship of the Mediterranean world is one of the most memorable episodes in human history. Her empire was no brilliant creation of individual genius, but the slow and measured outcome of the national energy of a people of mixed origin, but united in purpose. It is because of this that it endured; its foundations were so surely laid in the character of the Roman people. '*Tantae molis erat Romanam condere gentem*,' wrote Virgil; he knew well that the 'mighty work' was not the conquering of the Roman empire but the 'building of the Roman race.' [3] The record of their early history is for the most part legendary, for such rude annals as were committed to writing were destroyed

1. The Tarquins, possibly Greek colonists of Etruria, who acquired wealth and power in the pottery industry and trade. They are analogous to the Hel-lenic tyrants of the same epoch. See Professor P. N. Ure's *Origin of Tyranny*, c. viii.

2. *Grandeur et décadence des Romains*, c. 1.

3. Virgil, *Aeneid*, i. 37. 'So mighty a work was it to build the Roman race.'

when the Gauls burnt the city in 390; but the national character is clearly reflected in the legends that won belief. They were a race of iron-hearted warriors; it was the Roman people, not the fabulous Romulus and Remus, that were true nurslings of the she-wolf, sprung of the lineage of Mars. Tradition told, too, how the first Romans lived the life of freebooters, and how the state and the family alike had their origin in force.[1] The first of their kings gave them political union; the second, Numa, instituted the religious worships which throughout Roman history played the part of instruments of public policy. One legend may be quoted as peculiarly significant, the tale how three Horatii championed Rome in combat against three Curiatii of Alba. Two of the former were slain; the unwounded Horatius held the field alone against his three antagonists. Feigning flight, he vanquished them singly, crippled as they were by wounds. As he returned to Rome bearing the spoils, his sister, betrothed to one of the slain Curiatii, broke out in lamentation; her brother slew her on the spot. He was condemned for murder, but acquitted of guilt by the voice of the people, in that he had wrought justice on one who mourned the enemy of Rome. Thus, as after-ages believed, arose the time-honoured right of the Roman citizen to appeal on a capital charge to the popular assembly (*provocatio*). Let us mark the significance of the story. The fortune of the Roman people, as Montesquieu observed, throughout their history brought their enemies upon them one by one.[2] Their wars open almost always with disaster, but invariably close in victory. Above all, the Roman never questioned that the claims of personal interest must be subjected to those of civic loyalty. The instinct of subordination and the habit of reverence for public authority were ingrained deeply in his nature. To think and act as a typical Roman citizen and soldier, to 'do at Rome as Rome does', was virtue (*virtus*) and fame.[3] To live and die for

1. E.g. the legend of the rape of the Sabine women. See Hegel, *Philosophy of History*, Part III, Sect. I, c. i. Polybius, i. 37, remarks how the Romans employed force in all their undertakings.
2. *Gr. et déc*, c. 4.
3. *Virtus* = valour, manliness, from *vir* = a man.

Rome was his loftiest ambition. This spirit of sacrifice for the good of the commonwealth is what ennobles Roman republican history. The average Roman understood the meaning of public responsibility and civic obligation. After-ages seized upon and magnified this quality of Roman character. Late in her story, when she was on the eve of disruption at the hands of barbarian invaders, Augustine saw in it the justification of Rome's world-empire. The Roman devotion to an earthly state was an example to the citizens of the celestial city. Her fall from splendour was equally the just penalty for the lapse from her ancient virtue. Augustine's eulogy was echoed nine centuries after by Dante. In the *de Monarchia* he claims that 'the Roman people were ordained by nature for empire', in that, 'contemning greed, and loving peace with liberty, they had foregone their own advantage to secure the public safety of mankind'. He points to the sacrifice of the individual Roman citizen, who endured 'toil, poverty, exile, bereavement, loss of limbs and life, in the effort to enrich the public good'.[1] Both the saint and the poet saw the facts idealized through the haze of intervening time; nor did their vision pierce beyond the bounds of Mediterranean history; but when all deductions have been made, their verdict rests on a foundation of truth. In 'love of the fatherland and an unmeasured thirst for renown' lay, as Virgil knew, the secret of Rome's sovereignty among the nations.[2]

§ 3. Such a people was destined to excel in the tasks of law and government. Already in the regal period the foundation-stones of the Roman state had been well and truly laid. Thanks to the innate conservatism of the Roman character, it preserved through all developments the principles which had been silently evolved in prehistoric days as the unwritten customs of the race. The same forms and methods of procedure that regulated the life of the civic community in the seventh century before Christ survive, though modified and rationalized by Greek jurisprudence and Christian ethics, in

---

1. Augustine, *de Civitate Dei*, Book V (see Figgis, *Political Aspects of St Augustine's City of God*, p. 11); Dante, *de Mon.*, ii. 5.
2. *Aeneid*, vi. 823. '*Vincet amor patriae laudumque immensa cupido.*'

the *Digest* compiled 1200 years later by Justinian. We are
thus enabled to reconstruct, not the acts of individuals or the
detailed incidents of political history, but the general features
of Roman society in the days of the monarchy. The Roman
state was the family writ large. The Romans understood the
meaning and the value of home-life and gave expression to it in
their literature. The home-pieties (*Lares and Penates*) provided
a religious sanction. Plato had proposed in his *Republic* to
abolish the private household, on this ground, among others,
that it divided the citizens' loyalty with the state.[1] But the
Roman family was at once the mirror and the training-ground
of civic patriotism. The same word 'piety' (*pietas*) denoted
the conscientious devotion of son to parent, of citizen to
magistrate, of man to the gods. The civil personality of the
Roman comprised three essential factors, freedom, citizenship and membership of a family. The Roman type of family is
unique, when compared not only with the modern family but
with that in other ancient societies, in its extreme assertion of
patriarchal authority.[2] Its root-ideas of unity and power were
realized exclusively in the person of its head. The father
(*paterfamilias*) possessed throughout his life absolute authority
(*patria potestas*) over the persons and goods of wife, sons,
unmarried daughters, clients, and slaves. Within the
family he was sole owner of property, sole priest and
guardian of the family *sacra*, and sole judge. He had the right
to put to death his wife or child. In his hand alone it lay to
rear or expose his new-born offspring. Family relationships
were reckoned through the male line; a son was not regarded
in law as a kinsman of his mother's relatives, and his relation
even to his mother lay through the father.[3] Roman law took

1. *Rep.*, Book v.
2. The Romans were fully conscious of this; 'the right of authority which
we exercise over our children', we read in Justinian's *Institutes*, I. ix, 'is the
peculiar prerogative of Roman citizens'.
3. The *patria potestas* was, of course, restricted to citizens. The son, on
his father's death, became a *paterfamilias* even though unmarried, but acquired
patria potestas only on marriage. The wife, if married under strict form of law,
passed into her husband's 'hand' (*manus*) and became subject to his *potestas*,
ranking as a daughter (*loco filiae*). A daughter was under her father's *potestas*
(or, if he were dead, under that of a male kinsman) till marriage, when she

no cognizance of natural, as distinct from legitimate, paternity;
the legally adopted son was reckoned as fully a son, one born
out of lawful wedlock as not a son at all. On the death of the
paterfamilias the sons became straightway heads of families,
while the wife and unmarried daughters passed – 'because of
the inconstancy of a woman's disposition', says Gaius – into
the guardianship of the sons. Thus a Roman woman of free
citizen birth was either in the power (*potestas*) of her father, or
(after marriage) of her husband, or (in widowhood) under
guardianship of a male kinsman. In the well-known phrase
of the Digest, 'a woman is both the beginning and end of her
own family'; for her motherhood was unrecognized by law
and she could exercise no power over her children.[1] The
father and the father alone represented the family; his relationship to the other members was unilateral, all the rights
being on his side, all the duties on theirs. In the eye of the
law, the *patria potestas* was as absolute in the family as was the
imperium of the magistrate in the state.[2] But we should entirely
misconceive the order of Roman society if we imagined that its
conduct was determined solely, or even mainly, by considerations of theoretical right. In the case of the father as in that of
the magistrate, legal theory was in practice modified at almost
every point by ancestral custom. Chief among the restrictions
on the *patria potestas* was the customary tradition that, in

passed into her husband's family. A striking peculiarity of the Roman family
was the restriction of legally recognized kin to the *agnati*, i.e. those who would
have been in the *potestas* of a single male ancestor had he survived. For
example, A's son was an 'agnate' of A's brother or brother's son, not of his
mother's father or brother. Later law gave increasing recognition to *cognati*,
i.e. blood-relations whether through the male or female. On the whole
subject, see Maine, *Ancient Law*, c. v. The chief capital offences on the wife's
part were adultery and drunkenness; we hear of a Roman matron being put to
death for stealing the key of the wine-cellar.

  1. The reference to Gaius is i. 144, to the *Digest*, 1. 16, 195, 5. '*mulier
familiae suae et caput et finis est*'. A woman's family began with herself, for on
her father's death she became *sui juris* ('of her own right'); it ended with
herself, for directly she tried to continue it by marriage, she passed into her
husband's *jus* and family. She could, of course, be *sui juris*, and yet under
guardianship, e.g. of son or brother.

  2. A son, though in his father's power, could act as a citizen as if he
were a *paterfamilias*, e.g. he could hold magisterial office and in that capacity
exercise public authority over his father. The *patria potestas* did not extend to
the *jus publicum*.

cases of serious disciplinary action within the family, the father must call the adult male members into counsel. When the wife was accused, her male kinsfolk also were summoned. Quite early in republican times we find the censor degrading a senator for divorcing his wife without taking advice from the domestic council.[1] The exercise of the power to expose an infant was severely limited, and that of the power to sell a wife absolutely prohibited, by religious custom. Sons and even slaves were allowed by custom to amass under the name of *peculium* what in time became virtually, though not in the eyes of the law, equivalent to private property. In actual fact, the father normally administered the family wealth in the spirit, not of a private owner, but a trustee. So again the moral obligations of the father towards wife and child were fully recognized in practice. Cato the censor, an unbending champion of conservative tradition, felt it his duty every morning to see his baby properly bathed. The Roman matron enjoyed a position of dignity denied to mothers at Athens and in most other lands, a position all the firmer in that it rested on inviolable custom. As time went on, the advance of public opinion, the gradual disuse of the old forms of marriage which placed the bride in her husband's 'hand' (*manus*), and the introduction of new methods of evading the law of tutelage, combined to secure for Roman women a freedom and independence hardly paralleled in ancient or modern society.[2] In one respect, indeed, the *patria potestas* remained unchanged; whether unrestricted, as in theory, or limited, as in practice, it endured throughout the lifetime of its holder. But even in early days its exercise, though rigorous, was rarely tyrannical, and gross cruelty was the exception, not the rule. Moreover, it must be remembered that the standards of domestic purity and of fidelity to family obligations, thus sternly inculcated, were long maintained in the Roman household and proved of

1. The father was not legally bound to follow the advice of the domestic council, any more than the magistrate was legally bound to follow that of the senate; but the authority (*auctoritas*) in both cases carried great weight.

2. The recognition of marriages whereby the wife did not, as under the old forms, pass into the husband's *manus*, constituted the first serious breach in the *patria potestas*; it dates from before the close of the third century B.C.

incalculable service to the moral stability of the Roman state.[1]

§ 4. Rome was a city-state, and her early institutions, the king, the council, the assembly of the people, were those common to other branches of the Indo-European family. Already at the dawn of their recorded history the Romans had developed these germs of social organization into a body of clearly defined organs and principles of civic government. The king (*rex*) as supreme magistrate possessed by right an absolute executive authority (*imperium*). Throughout Roman history the *imperium* of the executive magistrate persists as the pivot of constitutional development. Conferred by a formal vote of the community on one of their members nominated in their presence by the king (or, if there were no king, by an *interrex* appointed by the senate), and ratified by the authority of the senate, the *imperium* was legally absolute both in peace and war, and formed the source whence all other executive power was derived by delegation.[2] The king was at once leader in war, supreme judge, and head of the state-religion. Criminal

---

1. This finds expression in Virgil's lines (*Aen.*, ix. 448–9):

> *Dum domus Aeneae Capitoli immobile saxum*
> *Accolet, imperiumque pater Romanus habebit.*

'While the house of Aeneas shall dwell by the Capitol's immovable rock and the Roman father bear his sovereignty' (*tr.* Mackail).

2. The *imperium*, in the regal period, was conferred by the following procedure, which illustrates admirably the formalism of Roman constitutional procedure. On the death of the king (*rex*), the senate (fathers of clans, entrusted with the charge of the religious observances of the community) appointed an *interrex*, who in turn appointed a second, for the *imperium* could be transferred to the new king only by nomination of one who already possessed it (sometimes a third or even a fourth *interrex* was appointed, to veil the breach of continuity by a plausible fiction). The last *interrex* of the series selected a king in consultation with the senate; the king-designate was then nominated by the *interrex* to the assembly for acceptance, and, if accepted, his appointment was finally ratified by the senate. Thus personal nomination, the senate's co-operation and popular election were all combined in the process. The same procedure was followed under the republic in the case of magistracies carrying with them the *imperium*, e.g. the consulship and praetorship only; (*a*) the need for an *interrex* was normally absent, since magistrates with *imperium* were already in being to nominate the new candidate, and (*b*) after 336 the consent of the senate had to be given prior to the popular election, and thus became as purely formal as is the royal assent to an act of the legislature in Britain at the present day. It was as if the royal assent were given to every Bill introduced into Parliament prior to its acceptance or rejection by the two Houses.

jurisdiction was concentrated in his hands. The close analogy
with the position of the father in the family is obvious at a
glance. But in the state, as in the family, custom provided a
limit to the exercise of absolute authority. It was a fundamental
maxim of the Romans that the holder of power must fortify
himself by counsel. The senate of heads of families, in theory a
consultative body, meeting only at the magistrate's summons
to discuss what the magistrate willed to lay before it, became
in practice an august council of state, whose opinion could be
ignored only by an act of virtual revolution. The *imperium* of the
king was balanced by the *auctoritas* or moral authority of the
senate.[1] Lastly, when any situation arose in the life of the
community which necessitated a departure from established
precedent, such as a declaration of war, the adoption into a
new family of the last male survivor of an old one, or the election of a successor to the throne, it was obligatory to obtain
the assent of the sovereign people.[2] They assembled for this
purpose by 'curies' or wardships, to vote on what was laid
before them by the presiding magistrate, without amendment
or debate. Self-government was thus the exception rather
than the rule in early Rome, and the monarchical and aristocratic elements in the constitution far outweighed the popular.
But, despite all contrary appearances, one conviction, rooted
in the primordial tradition of the community, never wholly
passed into oblivion; the citizen-body was the ultimate and
sovereign source of all rightful power.

II. THE ESTABLISHMENT OF THE REPUBLIC

§ 5. The opening of the fifth century saw Rome a republic.
The last Etruscan kings had exceeded the bounds which

1. *Auctoritas* means 'moral influence'; the English word 'authority' in the
sense of executive power would be expressed in Latin by *imperium* or *potestas*.
2. Adoption was frequently practised at Rome, for it was of primary
concern to the Roman to leave male posterity behind him and thus maintain
his family in being. Failing a son of his body, he could adopt a son, who
became in all respects the equal of one born in lawful wedlock. But if the
adopted son was himself a father of a family, his transference to the family of
his new father involved the extinction of a family and of its *sacra*, a matter of
grave religious moment, requiring the special sanction of the community.

custom prescribed to the exercise of the *imperium* and had been expelled by their Latin subjects (*c.* 509 B.C.). This revolution, if such it may be called, involved no change in the governing principles of the constitution; the *imperium*, hitherto vested in the king alone for life, was now conferred on two equal and supreme magistrates, elected annually by the people with the sanction of the senate.[1] The dual magistracy served as an effective check on the *imperium*; for, though each consul possessed it in its full scope, this very fact enabled one to veto the act of the other, and at Rome, as between two equal magistrates, the negative voice always prevailed. Moreover, a consul was hardly likely to override the will of the senate which had ratified his election, and into whose ranks he would pass, on the expiration of his year of office, for the remainder of his life. Thus the transition to the republic meant that the government of Rome fell into the hands of an oligarchy of patrician families. The hated title of king vanished, though provision was made for the temporary restoration of regal power in time of crisis in the person of a *dictator*. During the two following centuries (509–287) the small republic was beset by foes without, and torn inwardly by political conflicts. Chief among the latter was the long struggle of the plebeian citizens for equality of social, political, and religious rights with the patricians, which closed by the end of the fourth century with the victory of the former all along the line. The distinction of the two orders may well have arisen out of racial differences, like that of Norman nobility and Saxon commons in English history.[2] Early landmarks in the struggle were (*a*) the law that no magistrate might execute a capital sentence on any citizen without its ratification by the assembly; (*b*) the establishment, as a result of a general strike of the plebeian body against the state (494), of ten plebeian

1. The two magistrates were originally called 'praetors', later 'consuls', the praetorship becoming a distinct office.

2. We cannot discuss here the vexed question of the origin of this distinction. Both patricians and plebeians were members of the citizen-body; but owing to the fact that the former were sole masters in religion, the latter were in practice excluded from privileges depending on religious ceremonial, e.g. marriage with equal status, membership of the senate, tenure of office that carried with it the *imperium*.

officers (*tribunes*), for protection against patrician magistrates, and of a plebeian assembly; and (*c*) the publication in the middle of the fifth century (451–450) of the Twelve Tables, the earliest code of Roman civil law. The tribunate was an institution which had far-reaching results on later constitutional history. The tribunes were not magistrates, but plebeian officers, whose persons were declared sacrosanct (taboo, inviolable in religion), with the power of interposing a veto (*intercessio*) on any act of magisterial oppression within the city boundary.[1] In course of time their powers widened; they became, first, the recognized popular political leaders, and, later, virtual masters by their right of veto of the whole machinery of the state. The gradual extension of magistracies as the duties of administration grew more numerous and complex involved a customary partition of spheres of authority (*provinciae*), and, by consequence, mutual checks of colleagues one upon another. The Canuleian law (445) removed social inequality between the orders by legalizing the marriages of plebeian and patrician; the next century (367) saw the termination of the long contest for admission to the supreme magistracy by the law that one consul henceforward must be a plebeian. The other offices were opened in rapid succession, the victory of the plebeians culminating in their capture of the religious colleges (300). In 336, a plebeian dictator reduced the senate's control over the popular elections to a barren formality (*lex Publilia*); another in 287 (*lex Hortensia*) did likewise in regard to the laws passed in the plebeian assembly, which henceforward were *ipso facto* binding on the whole community.[2] The distinction of plebeian

1. Neither the veto of the tribune nor the right of appeal to the people on a capital charge availed against the military exercise of the *imperium*. When a dictator was appointed all restrictions vanished; the appointment was equivalent to a declaration of martial law.

2. We have purposely omitted details as to the different assemblies in the Roman state; suffice it to say that the oldest assembly of the 'curies' ceases to be important after the regal period, that the assembly of the centuries (originally a military assembly in which the propertied classes had preponderating influence) elected the consuls and magistrates with *imperium*, while the democratically organized assembly of the tribes became in the period under review the chief legislative body.

and patrician was thus deprived of any practical significance. Moreover, these same reforms implied, to all appearance, that the Roman state had passed from the form of oligarchy to that of democracy. That the event proved otherwise was due to causes which had their source in the external life of the community and will be considered in a later section. But the political struggle above outlined was far from being the only motive of internal ferment in the early republican period. We read also of the constant demand on the part of the poorer plebeians for allotments on the lands of conquered enemies, and for relief from the ever-present pressure of debt. The Roman of early times was at once citizen, soldier, and farmer, and both his political and his social status rested on tenure of property in land. The military and political strength of the state was rooted in the soil, and the agrarian problem is of the first importance throughout the course of Roman history. It was the growing tendency of the wealthier citizens, patrician and plebeian alike, to acquire large tracts of conquered territory, to the detriment of the wise policy of allotting such land in free holdings to the poorer population, that stirred the repeated agitation of the commons. Nor did the Licinio-Sextian law of 367, which limited the acreage of any such 'occupied' lands in a single owner's family, do more than afford partial and temporary relief from evils which we shall find recurring, in a far more acute form, at a later stage of republican history. As for the problem of debt, the Roman law was terribly severe, entailing the enslavement of the debtor's person in the creditor's prison cells. Here, too, the legislation of 367 afforded some redress; in course of time the rigours of the law were modified so as to satisfy the demand for more humane treatment, while the growing commercial prosperity of the state rendered the citizen less liable to insolvency.

§ 6. Among these measures, one stands out as fraught with peculiar significance for Roman civilization. The code of the Twelve Tables, compiled by the decemvirs in 451 and 450, was the earliest written law of Rome. As such, it was regarded throughout the history of the republic and of the empire as the basis of the civil law (*jus civile*), i.e. of the law regulating the relations of Roman citizens (*cives*).[1] When Cicero was a lad, schoolboys still learnt its rhythmic sentences by heart, much as English children used to learn their catechism; though a generation later it was already yielding place to the praetorian formulas. Nowhere was the aptitude of the Romans for right judgement in practical affairs more conspicuously displayed than in the field of law, their most enduring contribution to world-civilization.[2] Elsewhere their functions were those of the policeman and the middleman, to preserve order in the Mediterranean area and to hand on the culture of other peoples to after-time; their philosophy, such as it was, and their poetry, though instinct with the spirit of Roman manners and national history, were stimulated and inspired by Hellenic models. But their law was largely their own creation; the framework of Greek jurisprudence being implemented by praetorian *formulae* and Roman case-law. Thus early were laid the foundations of the majestic structure that arose, stone upon stone, in unbroken continuity during a thousand years of workmanship, till its final completion in the *Corpus juris* of the emperor Justinian in the sixth century A.D. There had been indeed a rich development of earlier customary law solidified into definite form in the period of the kings. Custom was always held by the Romans to be an authoritative source of law, and the Twelve Tables themselves represent a selection from recognized custom, concentrating on points which were socially liable to abuse or had given rise to dispute. Though Livy could still regard the Twelve Tables as 'the

1. The *jus civile*, being the local law of the city-state (*jus proprium civitatis*, Gaius), applied to none but citizens. Full citizenship carried with it the public rights (*publica jura*) of service in the army, voting in the assembly, and eligibility to public offices, and the private rights (*privata jura*) of intermarriage and trade with Roman citizens. Under the republic there were grades of partial citizenship involving certain of these rights apart from others (see below, §§ 10, 17). 'Latin' rights, again, enabled the possessor to share in the civil law. The same is true when the right, e.g. of trading with Roman citizens was granted to members of another community by special treaty. On the *jus gentium*, see below, § 20.

2. Tradition records that the decemvirs studied Greek models. This may be so, though the influence is not obvious in the Twelve Tables. We shall see presently how Hellenism set its mark on later Roman jurisprudence.

fount of all public and private law', Roman law, like our own, was not so much the product of legislative statutes as of unenacted custom, interpreted and formulated by the steady tradition of a learned class of practising lawyers (*prudentes*), as well as by the praetorian edicts. Though Greek influence is present from the outset and increases during the republican period, the legal method (*prudentia*) is the expression of the distinctively Roman genius.[1] In many particulars, for example, plebeian customary law was preferred to patrician, with the aim of healing class-strife in the civic community. Thus the enactments of the code presuppose an organized state-law as already in being. Many of the primitive customs familiar to early Hellenic, Germanic, and Scandinavian law had long vanished at Rome; hardly a trace survives of blood-vengeance or wife-purchase, or of the conflict between the jurisdiction of the clan and the state. Moreover, the Romans had early drawn the distinction between *fas*, the religious law regulating men's relation to the gods, and *jus*, the secular law of the human community; close as was the union between the religious and the political machinery of the city, infractions of *fas* were but rarely punished by the secular arm. With equal precision, they distinguished (i) public law, determining the constitution of the state and the organization of public power, from private law, determining the mutual relations among individual citizens; and consequently (ii), among offences, between injuries to the public interest, including the crime of murder, where action lay with the executive magistrate, and injuries to private individuals, where the law intervened only on the complaint of the aggrieved party. In the former case, the state needed not to employ legal process, but redressed instantly its own wrongs; e.g. the quaestor could distrain on goods owed to the state without a judicial warrant. Public vengeance was thus self-executed; against the community the individual had no rights, and could bring no action at law. The law relating to private offences, as disclosed by the Twelve Tables, illustrates the gradual advance

1. See de Zulueta in *The Legacy of Rome*, pp. 186 ff. and Cicero, *De Oratore*, i. 44, 197, there quoted (p. 187).

from (a) the primitive custom of personal vengeance, through the stages of (b) voluntary compensation by monetary payment dependent on the wills of both parties, and (c) obligatory compensation determined by law, to (d) entire prohibition of personal redress and the inclusion of all private injuries in the category of public injuries, under cognizance of the law of the state. In the Twelve Tables, murder alone comes under the last-mentioned head. Elsewhere, private redress is tolerated where not expressly forbidden. Voluntary compensation is allowed for flagrant theft and grave injuries to the person; for minor offences the payment is fixed by law. Certain crimes, e.g. the ill-treatment of parents by children, the removal of boundary stones, and the destruction of standing corn, were dealt with by religious law. But except in a few special cases there were no regular courts of criminal justice; the wrongdoer must be haled in person before the magistrate, who referred the case to a private citizen (*judex*) for his decision on the issue of fact.[1] Here again we have an illustration of the Roman sense for clear distinction; they entrusted the ruling in law to the magistrate, as the depositary of state-*jus*, and the hearing of the facts to the *judex*.[2] This procedure applied equally to civil causes, with which the Twelve Tables were primarily concerned. The civil law regulated the whole mass of relationships between citizens, marriage and the family, guardianship, emancipation of son or slave, testamentary succession, property and contracts, with a narrow formalism indeed, yet with a pre-

1. It was not till the dictatorship of Sulla (80 B.C.) that standing criminal courts (*quaestiones perpetuae*) were systematically established. In the case of public crimes, where the penalty was capital or a fine exceeding a certain sum, the right of appeal to the people (*provocatio*) was allowed. Most crimes were treated as private wrongs, the state intervening only on the instance of the individual sufferer, and simulating in its procedure the methods of private redress.

2. The magistrate could not pronounce a judgement (*sententia*) in a disputed case; he could only refer the case to a *judex* and, in referring it, determine the nature of the claim. This constituted the hearing *in jure*. There followed the hearing of the facts *in judicio* before the *judex*, who gave his verdict. Only when the defendant admitted or acquiesced in the plaintiff's claim was reference to the *judex* dispensed with and the case decided straightway by the magistrate (*in jure cessio*).

cision and freedom from mysticism peculiar to Rome among all early societies known to history. Though all property was regarded as derived by implicit transference from the community and could therefore be held only by citizens, private ownership had long been an established fact, and the citizen, once secure in his title, was left in almost entire liberty of using it and disposing of it at will. The Roman law of inheritance was already far in advance of other early Indo-European codes, in that provision for intestacy was subordinated to the recognition of testamentary bequest, the Roman being at liberty to select his heir, to determine legacies, and to appoint guardians for his surviving children.[1] Within carefully defined limits the life and property of the citizen were protected by the law, which was as studious to provide a *tutor* for the infant and a *curator* for the lunatic as it was inexorable in its enforcement of the creditor's full claim against the person of the insolvent debtor.[2] The Twelve Tables penalized usury and fixed a legal rate of interest. They determined also the machinery of judicial procedure in a spirit that was straightforward and sternly practical; respect for legal forms went hand in hand with freedom from needless delay and cumber-

1. Before 450 intestate succession was the rule, and a testament required the assent of the people by a special law and was subject to control by the priestly college (the *pontifices*); after 450 this control becomes a mere form. Collective ownership doubtless once prevailed at Rome, private ownership being restricted to a small plot on which stood the citizen's house; but collective ownership had disappeared long before the Twelve Tables. The only restrictions on the citizen's liberty of using and disposing of his property were certain minor safeguards of the rights of neighbours and the interest of the community. Gibbon (c. 45) remarks that among the Romans 'the insolent prerogative of primogeniture was unknown.'

2. Women were allowed to hold property under the Twelve Tables. The law of debt was extremely rigorous. The only legal form of contract in early Rome was the *nexum* or loan (lit., binding tie). If the debtor failed to repay within thirty days of the time stated in the contract, the creditor could enforce his claim without further legal proceedings by arresting the debtor and haling him off to his private prison. The Twelve Tables provided that he must be detained there for a further period of sixty days; then, unless an agreement had been reached, he was brought thrice before the magistrate, and (unless a third party came forward as champion at his own risk) might be killed or sold into slavery by the creditor. At any prior moment, payment of the debt meant the debtor's liberation. The rigour of this law was gradually abated in the early centuries of the republic.

some ceremonial. Legal torture of citizens was unknown then and throughout the history of Roman law. The details of procedure rested as yet in the hands of the priestly colleges; the public might read the code, but were debarred from knowledge of its interpretation. It stands to reason that this first body of published law was characterized by a rigidity and narrowness expressive of the traditions of a small and simple community. The centuries that followed saw its progressive modification and expansion, till by the close of the republican epoch not a clause retained its original significance. But the Twelve Tables were never abrogated. While the Roman people held to their traditions as to a rock, their practical sagacity devised innumerable expedients for adjusting ancient law to the complex needs of a rapidly growing society, and for harmonizing radical changes of detail with a tenacious convervatism in regard to the legal inheritance of the past.[1]

§ 7. We know little or nothing of the men who thus fashioned the institutions and law of Rome. The work was wrought, not by individuals of exceptional genius, but by the people. The names that occur in the pages of early Roman history are those of average Romans, of citizen-soldiers whose lives are barely distinguishable one from the other, and form a monotonous sequence, save only when an Appius Claudius, decemvir or censor, appears upon the stage. Early Roman history is the record of laws and civic policy, the planting of colonies and the making of military roads. It is not Canuleius or Licinius that signify, but the measures that bear their names. Moreover, the character of these measures was determined not so much by deliberate forethought as by the pressure of present fact. The Romans never planned their constitution, which, like their law, grew up as occasion required, and presents in consequence a singularly unsystematic

---

1. The free use of legal fictions was a means of adjustment common both to Roman and English law. Adoption was an early and conspicuous instance. So was the tacit acceptance, to be noted later, of the modifications introduced into the law by the answers of jurisconsults, which claimed all the time to be strict interpretations of the traditional code. See Maine, *Ancient Law*, c. ii. A legal fiction is a natural device for combining conservatism and continuity in legal development with the requisite adaptation to new experience.

picture.[1] This absence of logical design is illustrated by the institution which formed the keystone of the structure. In the very heart of the republican government we find the absolute and indivisible *imperium* in the possession of two consuls, as equal and supreme executive officers. To the political theorist, such duplication of supreme authority would be a sure presage of disaster. Yet the device, inconceivable as it appears on paper, worked admirably in practice; for it was the outgrowth of experience and founded on the bedrock of fact. So overpowering was the burden of the magisterial *imperium* in the Roman commonwealth, that it was a more urgent need to impose limits on its abuse than to provide for its unfettered exercise. Dual control was the one expedient open for averting despotism. Inaugurated with the republic, it endured for five centuries; when in the event it proved powerless in the face of military autocrats, it was restored in altered form as the theory of the early empire.[2] In this, as in much else in the character of the Roman state, we are reminded of the temper and practice of our own people. The constitutional history of Rome and that of England present the same broad features of gradual development on a basis of racial tradition, of unbounded respect for form and precedent, of elasticity in practical application, and of restriction of theoretical powers by use and custom. Both endured for centuries with unbroken continuity, thanks to their adaptability to changing circumstances. Both form a tissue of illogical contrivances, quaint fictions, and effete survivals, the easy price paid for institutions that are not the work of a single lawgiver, but the congenial expression of national experience. The analogy holds good also of their conduct in war. War generally found the Romans unprepared, a sure sign that their policy was not militant but pacific. They almost invariably

1. Polybius (vi. 11) observes how the Romans shaped their constitution, 'not on a theory, but through frequent conflicts and practical crises', choosing the prudent course in each situation as it arose; and (vi. 43) contrasts the greatness of Rome with that of Athens, in that the former was chiefly due to the type of constitution, the latter to individual genius.

2. See Vol. i c. viii, § 7, on the dual control of *princeps* and senate in Augustus' scheme of reorganization.

suffered heavy reverses in the early stages of the struggle, but
always emerged victorious at the close. They learnt their
lesson in the midst of conflict, and never acquiesced in defeat.
We shall remark later on the similarity between the methods
by which Rome and Britain adjusted their maxims of government to meet the varying requirements of a vast empire.
The function of both has been to police the world within their
range of influence. Both were guided, alike in bestowing
privileges and in preserving peace, by motives of interest
rather than of imagination. But, despite these striking analogies, there remains one great difference in the constitutional
life of the two peoples. Whereas in England the centre of
political gravity lies in Parliament, that of Rome lay not in
the legislature but in the executive. 'The great contests for
freedom in this country', said Edmund Burke, 'were from the
earliest times chiefly upon the question of taxing. Most of
the contests in the ancient commonwealths turned primarily
on the right of election of magistrates or on the balance of the
several orders of the state. The question of money was not
with them so immediate.' [1] English political history is full of
such issues as the right of the Crown to levy ship-money, of
Parliament to tax America, of the House of Lords to reject
the Budget. In early Rome the question of taxation was non-
existent. There the whole struggle for liberty had for its goal
the limitation of the *imperium* of the chief magistrate.

III. THE EXPANSION OF ROME

§ 8. The process of the expansion of the Roman state
falls into three epochs: (*a*) the conquest of the Italian peninsula; (*b*) the struggle with Carthage for the sovereignty of
the western Mediterranean; and (*c*) the acquisition of a like
supremacy over the Hellenic East.

---

1. Speech on *Conciliation with America*. At Rome there was no direct, and
little indirect, taxation. Later, the provinces paid a fixed tribute (*stipendium*)
into the Roman exchequer; the quotas being either paid to the provincial
quaestors, or (as in Sicily and the East) being farmed out on a system that
brought much profit to Roman capitalists.

(a) The Expansion of Rome in Italy.[1]

The period (450–270) which saw the rise of Rome to be mistress of Italy coincided with the political conflicts which closed with the passing of the Hortensian law (287). For a century and a half after the expulsion of the kings she had fought uninterruptedly with her immediate neighbours; in the first fifty years of the struggle her very existence as an independent city-state was almost annually at stake. After 450 Rome began to forge ahead; by 350 she was supreme over southern Etruria and the plain of Latium. Even the victorious onset of the Gauls and their sack of the city in 390 only interrupted for a few years the even tenor of her advance. When once she was secure in Latium, the old Latin league ceased to exist, save in religious ceremonial. Rome was helped in these early days by the lack of any strong sentiment of unity among her Italian foes. We find little trace of a common Italian consciousness comparable to that which in early Greece found expression in leagues of cities and in the Olympic games. It arose doubtless at a later date, but only after Italy had been absorbed politically into the Roman state. The conquest of Latium brought Rome into direct relations with the Greek cities on the Campanian coast, and therewith into conflict with the powerful hill-tribes of central Italy. Rome stood forth already as the champion of order, commerce, and Hellenic culture against the marauders who found a happy hunting ground among the rich but unwarlike Greeks. There followed the long and arduous struggle with the Samnites (343–290), which left Rome the sole power northwards to the ridge of the Apennines and eastwards to the shores of the Adriatic. Finally, early in the third century, Pyrrhus, king of Epirus, the first captain of his age, brought his highland warriors and elephants across the sea, on the pretext of defending the Greeks of Tarentum against the southward

1. For the Romans of the republic Italy was bounded on the north, not by the Alps, but by the Apennines; the district between the Apennines and the Alps was called Cisalpine Gaul, i.e. Gaul on this side of the Alps. It was peopled by Celtic kinsmen of the tribes that inhabited Transalpine Gaul, i.e. Gaul on the farther side of the Alps, the modern France and Belgium.

advance of Rome. A professional soldier of the school of Alexander, he nourished wild dreams of achieving in the West triumphs like those of Alexander in the East; but he lacked Alexander's statesmanship; and Rome, a free and consolidated state, proved an antagonist of a quality far different from Persia. On Pyrrhus' failure the Greeks of the south fell an easy prey to the Roman legions, and Rome ruled unchallenged from the plain of Lombardy to the straits of Messina.

§ 9. That 'Rome was not built in a day' is true not only of the character and institutions of the sovereign city, but also of her world-empire; and these early struggles for supremacy in Italy covered a period twice as long as that which sufficed for her conquest of the whole Mediterranean area. We can trace in them the lines on which she afterwards mastered and ruled the world. We remark, first, the efficiency of her military organization. The legion, observed one of the Latin writers, was the inspiration of a god.[1] It combined the weight of the Macedonian phalanx with superior mobility, as was proved in the war against Pyrrhus. In armament and methods of warfare the Romans were always ready to learn from their enemies; defeat was the signal for reforms which enabled them to emerge from the war triumphant. Thus they borrowed the heavy javelin from the Samnites, as later they learnt the construction of large warships from the Carthaginians, and at the close of the second Punic war defeated Hannibal with the cavalry which had been the instrument of his early victories. Like the English, they 'muddled through' their wars, a slang phrase which signifies the triumph of racial persistence and the capacity of using defeat as a means to victory. They too were modest as to the reason of their successes; they ascribed them to the 'Fortune of the Roman people'. What is most impressive is their unflinching self-confidence; Rome never made peace while a single enemy remained on Roman soil. It is a profound error to suppose

1. Vegetius, quoted by Montesquieu, c. 2. In actual fact, it was modelled, but with improvements, on the military organization of the Greeks. On the organization of the legion and its superiority to the phalanx, see Polybius xviii. 11-15.

that the Romans were an aggressive people, bent on subduing, first Italy, and then the world. It is far truer to say that their wars came upon them inevitably, in the order of things. At each stage in their history they were faced with the alternative, to go forward or to go back. Rome never went back. Beset by turbulent neighbours, the task of policing her own borders involved her in constant war; and war meant in the long run extension of empire. She was compelled to intervene in order to allay the conflagration, and intervention entailed eventual occupation. There was cynicism in Rome's policy, and her diplomacy was always guided by the maxim of self-interest; but she never thirsted for conquest, and the story of her empire is that of the identification of self-interest with the cause of law, order, and civilization.

§ 10. The history of Rome's expansion over Italy illustrates, in a yet more striking manner, her native genius for administration. At each stage she riveted her conquests with the iron bolts of military roads and colonies. That 'all roads lead to Rome' is true, not only in metaphor of the highways of civilization, but literally of the great thoroughfares which radiated from Rome, first through Latium and southern Etruria, then over Italy, and finally over the countries of the Mediterranean area.[1] The Roman colony was not, like that of the Greeks, an independent city-state, but a military settlement of farmer-soldiers in the midst of conquered enemies. So long as these colonies remained faithful, the Roman legions might be beaten in the field, but the Roman state stood firm. In her treatment of the vanquished, the Roman maxim was 'divide and rule' (*divide et impera*). No bond of association, in early days not even the rights of trade and intermarriage, was

1. The earliest of these roads in Italy was the *Via Appia*, begun in 312 by Appius Claudius, the censor. It ran across Latium in a straight line to the coast, and was continued later through Samnium by Beneventum to Venusia (in Apulia) and Brundisium (the modern Brindisi). The *Via Latina* ran further inland from Rome to Capua; the *Via Flaminia* northwards across the Apennines to Ariminum (Rimini) on the Adriatic, and was extended in 187 to Placentia (Piacenza) on the Po under the name of the *Via Aemilia*. In the second century the *Via Domitia* was constructed along the *Golfe du Lion* to link Rome with Spain, and the *Via Egnatia* across the Balkan peninsula from Dyrrachium (Durazzo) to Thessalonica (Salonika) and the Hellespont.

tolerated among her subject-communities. The old local
federations were everywhere dissolved. Rome maintained
this cardinal principle unimpaired throughout her history.
The same mistrust of subordinate associations which led her
to abolish the Latin league, served under the empire as the
motive for her prohibition of a local fire brigade at Nico-
media, and for her persecution of the Christian church as an
unauthorized corporation.[1] On the other hand, all the Italian
communities alike were bound by links of varying stringency
to Rome. Italy formed henceforward a single state under
Roman suzerainty. War and peace, foreign relations and the
coinage, were the exclusive concern of the ruling city. For
the rest, a distinction was drawn between territory directly
administered by Rome and that of her Italian 'friends and
allies', analogous to that in the India of to-day between the
native states and the districts governed by the British Civil
Service. The former comprised about one-third of Italy,
including Rome, the colonies of full Roman citizens, and
other towns with full or partial citizen-privileges (*municipia*).
These colonies and *municipia* enjoyed a liberal measure of
self-government, though Rome retained the right of intervention, and prefects were annually sent from the capital to
administer justice. Among the Italian 'allies', on the other
hand, the 'Latin' colonies occupied a privileged position,
with full rights of trade and intermarriage with Roman
citizens. Up to the middle of the third century, the colonists
retained the right of recovering their Roman citizenship in
the event of their return to the capital. But the mass of the
'allies' had their status determined by special treaty. In the
case of Hellenic cities, the terms were generally liberal,
while other communities, in less civilized regions, were reduced to virtual bondage. All were liable to service with the
Roman army in the field.[2] No clearer example can be furnished

1. See Pliny's letters to the emperor Trajan (early second century A.D.).
Bk. x, letters 33, 34 (the fire brigade); 96, 97 (the Christians).
2. The division into citizens (full or partial) and allies dates from the fourth
century. Partial citizenship meant the possession of private without public
rights. The private rights in question were those of trade and intermarriage,
the public those of the franchise and eligibility to magisterial office. 'Latin'

of the elasticity of the Roman administrative system and its capacity for adjustment to varying local conditions than the picture presented by their rule in Italy in the period between the Gallic invasion (390) and the outbreak of the first Punic war (264)

(b) The Wars with Carthage

§ 11. The story is told how Pyrrhus, on leaving the Greek cities of southern Italy to their fate, exclaimed, 'What a battlefield we are bequeathing to the Romans and the Carthaginians!' For centuries the Sicilian Greeks had struggled against Carthage for their island; now only the narrow straits parted Sicily from Rome. The Carthaginian predominance in the western seas was yet unchallenged, though Rome had already begun to police the coast of Italy with her fleet. Since the sixth century she had carried on trade with Sicily, Sardinia, and Carthage, and had become thoroughly familiar with Hellenic and Phoenician custom. The conflict between the two great Western Powers was the most terrible in ancient history. It opened in 264, and lasted, with a twenty years' break for the combatants to recover strength (241–219), till the crowning victory of Scipio over Hannibal at Zama in 202. To dwell on its history lies beyond our scope. The first Punic (Phoenician) war (264–241) gave Rome her first provinces of Sicily and Sardinia and Corsica, and the sea power over the western Mediterranean. In the interval that followed, she subdued the Gauls between the northern Apennines and the Alps. The second war (219–201), ever memorable for the invasion of Italy by the great Hannibal, closed with the conquest of Spain and the reduction of Carthage to the position of a vassal-state. Never in her long history was the heroic patriotism of the Romans more conspicuous than in the dark hours when the relics of her shattered legions hung desperately round the invader. When the consul Varro drew near the city after the

rights were granted to communities outside Latium, both in Italy and (later) in the provinces; these are not to be confounded with the members of the old Latin league. The allies were autonomous as regards local government and lay outside the sphere of Roman legislation and executive government.

terrible disaster of Cannae (216), the senate – his political foes – went forth to meet him with their thanks that he had not despaired of the republic. A few years later, when Hannibal approached the gates of Rome, the land on which his camp was pitched was sold in the city at its full market-value in time of peace. The moral of the issue of this historic conflict is clear as day. A commercial oligarchy – like Venice at a later day, jealous of its greatest citizens and dependent on mercenary soldiers – could not prevail in arms against a free republic.[1] Nor could the genius of the greatest of military leaders avail to undermine the solid fabric of the Roman colonies. The issue once determined, Rome hunted her foe to death with merciless severity. She extorted, first the exile, and then the murder of Hannibal, the one individual she had ever deigned to fear. Finally, when half a century later Carthage rose from her death-agony in a supreme effort to regain her freedom, after a heroic resistance she was levelled with the ground (147).

(c) The Conquest of the East

§ 12. Rome emerged from this titanic conflict the unquestioned sovereign of the West. Henceforward the problem that confronted her in this quarter was that of consolidation and government. We shall return in the next chapter to the manner in which she discharged her mission as a civilizing agent in Spain, Africa, and southern Gaul. But before she could set her hand to this new task, she found herself perforce embroiled in the politics of the Hellenic East. It was no temper of *hubris* that impelled her to intervention, but the hard logic of facts. Exhausted by the Hannibalic war and staggering under the burden of her western provinces, she was in no mood for embarking on fresh adventures, the issues of which could not be foreseen. The militarist ambitions of the Greek kings of Macedon and Asia forced her hand. The dominant power in

1. Polybius (vi. 52) recognizes that the military superiority of the Romans to the Carthaginians was that of patriotic citizen-soldiers over mercenaries. He remarks also (iii. 118) that the Romans were saved after Cannae by 'the distinctive character of their polity and their excellence in counsel', and attributes the rapid expansion of their empire to the same causes.

Italy could not then, any more than now, view with indifference the course of events in the Balkan peninsula. As a great commercial Power, Rome had to keep the peace in the surrounding seas. Macedonian troops had fought for Hannibal, and the Seleucid Antiochus III (the 'Great') was menacing the independence of Rome's allies, Athens, Rhodes, and Pergamos. The issue was swift and overwhelming. Macedon was crushed in 197, Antiochus of Asia in 190. The Seleucid empire, dismembered by Rome in the West and by the rising power of Parthia in the East, sank, after the battle of Magnesia (192), into the petty principality of Syria. Thus almost in one day had the sovereignty of the eastern Mediterranean fallen into the hands of Rome. Montesquieu has observed that 'after the fall of the Carthaginians Rome fought only little wars and won great victories, whereas before she had won small victories and fought great wars'.[1] In the brilliant story of her eastern expansion we note three salient facts. First, Rome appears at every point as the champion of order, the one effective police amid the sorely troubled Hellenic world. Hence she was allied constantly with peaceful commercial states, such as Egypt, Rhodes, and Pergamos. Secondly, her policy was inspired by a sincere enthusiasm for Hellenism. We shall speak later of the pervasive influence of Greek culture in this age on the life and temper of the leading Roman citizens. Their idealism found expression in the dramatic scene that followed the victory over Macedon, when Flaminius proclaimed to the Greeks assembled at the isthmus of Corinth that they were henceforth free. A less ardent champion of Hellenism might have forecast the issue; anarchy raged throughout the peninsula for half a century, till Rome was driven to annexation. Thirdly, the reluctance of the

1. *Gr. et déc.*, c. 5. The swiftness with which Rome acquired world sovereignty deeply impressed contemporaries, e.g. the Greek historian Polybius, the aim of whose work was to show 'by what steps and under what type of constitution the whole world fell under the single rule of Rome within three and fifty years' (i. 1); i.e. between the outbreak of the second Punic war (219) and the partition of Macedonia (167). He further points out (i. 3) how in this half-century the detached currents of events in East and West met in a single stream in the Roman empire, the history of the Mediterranean area acquiring for the first time an organic unity.

Roman government to enlarge the bounds of their empire is most evident throughout this epoch. Their policy in Macedon will provide an illustration. After their first victory (197), they confirmed the vanquished sovereign as a dependent prince under Roman suzerainty; when his successor twenty years later provoked a second war, he was deposed, and his dominions were partitioned among four local authorities; only when this experiment failed was the country constituted a Roman province (146). In Asia, Rome took nothing for herself; the provinces wrested from Antiochus were entrusted to client-princes and to her Hellenic allies. We may compare the successive expedients devised by the British government in India to postpone time after time the annexation of the Punjâb.

§ 13. If our purpose had been to write a history of Rome, it would have been necessary to trace, point by point, the detailed incidents of these conflicts, and to mark, at each successive phase, their continuous influence upon the structure of her internal government. It was, for instance, the pressure of war at her gates that gave leverage to the plebeians, who formed the backbone of the army, in their struggle with the patrician aristocracy. So, again, the incorporation of the Italian and Mediterranean peoples within the sphere of Roman suzerainty had, as we shall see later, far-reaching issues upon her legal and administrative system. But our present interest in the story of the making of the Roman empire is not so much with the process as with the results.[1] These may be summed up in a word; by the middle of the second century Roman rule was established, in its broad essentials, over the Mediterranean world. In the west she ruled directly the provinces of Sicily, Sardinia, and Corsica, Gaul south of the Alps, Hither and Farther Spain, and Africa. In 121, the coastlands between the Alps and the Pyrenees were incorporated into the province of Narbonese Gaul, the 'Provence' of a

1. It is not the personality or the feats of Scipio Africanus that count in history, but the use that Rome made of his conquest of Spain. Hannibal overthrew Flaminius and his legions by the Trasimene lake, but the name of his victim still lives as the maker of the highway by which the Roman armies crossed the Apennines to the Po valley and the foothills of the Alps.

later day. In the East there were only two provinces, Macedonia with Achaia (Greece), and Asia – i.e. the western region of Asia Minor, bequeathed to the Roman state in 133 by the last Greek prince of Pergamos. Beyond the frontiers of these provinces lay a ring of principalities, such as Numidia in Africa, Egypt, Syria (the relic of the Seleucid monarchy) and innumerable minor states, ruled internally by their own governments, but controlled in respect of all foreign relations by Rome. The establishment of these client-states under Roman suzerainty was a cardinal feature of Roman policy under the later republic and the early empire. They served as buffer states between Rome and powers like Parthia, saved the burden of military occupation and government, and fostered the spread of civilization outside the bounds of the provinces. The succeeding century saw the rounding-off of this imperial system in the formation of new provinces and dependent states, the reform of internal administration, and the determination of the permanent frontiers of the empire. At the time we have reached, the function of Rome in world-history was already marked out. That function was twofold, in accordance with the difference of conditions confronting her in West and East. In the West, her mission was to implant law and civilization among barbaric or semi-barbaric peoples. In the East, on the other hand, she found in being a civilization far superior to her own. There her task was not to create, but to conserve; to save from anarchy and ruin the fabric of Hellenic culture, and to carry on the work of Alexander and his successors by leavening with that culture the peoples of the nearer and the Middle East.

IV. ROME IN THE SECOND CENTURY

A. Rome and Hellenism

§ 14. The ability of Rome to rise to the height of her responsibilities rested primarily on the character of her citizen-body. The influx of wealth and the spread of Hellenic culture during the period of the great wars had combined to effect a profound revolution in the moral and economic life of the

Roman community. Up to the time of the Punic wars Rome was comparatively poor, and a measure of real equality prevailed among the citizens. Now, almost suddenly, she found herself rich, the centre of Mediterranean commerce, with the markets of east and west at the feet of her merchants and financiers. The results were obvious in the rise of a plutocratic class whose wealth gave them influence at Rome and in the provinces; in the growth of luxury among the senatorial aristocracy which conservative magistrates like Cato the censor vainly strove to check; in the habit of financial speculation; in the appearance of huge landed estates; the decay of the yeoman-farmer; and the wholesale importation of slave labour from the East. Agriculture in Italy could not compete with imported corn from overseas. The moral and political results were of equal gravity. In the early days of Mediterranean expansion the Roman administrators and merchants astounded, by their simplicity of life and severe integrity, a world habituated to Punic and Hellenic corruption. But already in the first half of the second century Cato could complain that 'he who steals from a burgess ends his days in chains, but he who steals from the community ends them in gold and purple'.[1] The ancient code of morals yielded swiftly to the changed conditions; indolence and incapacity spread among the governing class; while the nobles lived in splendour on the spoils of the provinces, and the tax-farmers and contractors utilized their riches to found a new and rival power in politics, the impoverished masses, crowded in the capital, degenerated into an idle and pleasure-loving proletariat. These changes in social life and manners, consequent on Rome's swift rise to sovereign power, were fraught with

1. See Mommsen, Book III, c. ii. Cato (consul 195, censor 184), a veteran of the Hannibalic war and an able administrator of Spain, led the conservative opposition to the new influences. Polybius (vi. 56), himself a Greek patriot, contrasts the honesty of the Roman official in the first half of the second century with the corruptibility of the Greek: 'Those who handle public funds among the Hellenes, even though the sum be merely a talent, take ten account-checkers and ten seals and twice as many witnesses, yet cannot be faithful to their trust; while among the Romans, men who handle vast sums as magistrates or ambassadors, observe their obligations on the security of a simple oath.'

baneful issues, not only on her imperial policy, but on the internal stability of the state. Even more pervasive and far-reaching were the results of her assimilation of Hellenism.

§ 15. It was in Campania in the fourth century that Rome was first brought into constant relationship with Greek civilization. The fact that she started on her history as a city-state with institutions analogous to those of the city-states of Greece formed a link which Romans and Greeks alike were quick to recognize. When in 229 the Romans appeared for the first time on the eastern shores of the Adriatic, they were straightway admitted to membership in the Hellenic games. The Greeks never looked upon them as 'barbarians'. In return, the Roman government and individual Romans like Flaminius adopted eagerly a phil-Hellenic attitude in foreign policy. The fruits of this closer intimacy were seen during the third century in the impulse given by Greece to Latin literature. The native poetry of Rome, hymns, ballads and rustic comedy, was rude in form and matter. Poets were held in low esteem, and there is no sound basis for Macaulay's conjecture that the early political struggles inspired a rich ballad literature. Roman poetry had its beginnings in translations and imitations of Greek classics, and employed metrical forms of Greek origin, especially the epic hexameter.[1] But it would be an error to suppose that the Roman poets, in following Greek models, were slavish imitators of their masters. They infused into their works the spirit of Rome. Ennius, who was contemporary with the second Punic war and took that historic conflict for the theme of his epic, gave expression to the qualities of gravity and virile energy, of imperial pride and political sagacity, that were distinctive of Roman character. The same is true of the Latin comedy of manners in the second century; Greek models were adapted to reflect the interests and social life of Rome. One peculiar style of poetry was native to Roman literature, the 'satire' or medley (satura), first composed by Lucilius in the middle of the second century,

1. The earliest Roman verse was in the so-called 'Saturnian' metre, exemplified in the English line,

'The Queen was in her parlour | eating bread and honey.'

which portrayed in hexameter verse scenes of social life, interspersed with literary and political criticism, autobiography
and personal adventure, and the intercourse of friends. The
Roman writers displayed a peculiar felicity and charm in this
vein of poetry; in the words of a modern critic, 'Not Horace
only, nor all the satirists after Horace, but Montaigne and
Pepys also, belong to the school of Lucilius.' [1] Latin prose
literature had its birth in this same epoch; the practical
interests of the Romans led them early to break ground in the
fields of forensic oratory and history. Here again we feel their
ever-present sense of the greatness of Rome, her genius for
law and order, her imperial destiny. But there is yet another
characteristic distinguishing Latin literature from that of
Greece. The greatest Roman poets show a true understanding
and love of nature. The Greeks had written of nature in
imperishable verse; but with all their sense of her beauty and
grandeur, she remained to them an alien power, able indeed
to rouse their wonder, but one with which they never really
felt themselves at home. Nature to the Greek was always
something outside himself, something to be known about or
conquered, not something to be loved. [2] The Roman poets
loved nature as akin to themselves. The Greek lived in and for
the city, and, if he travelled abroad, it was to see the cities of
men; his estates were a source of revenue, not a chosen
retreat. The Roman gladly fled the city for the country; he was
the first to appreciate a country home and to create a resort for
time of leisure among the mountains or by the sea. So Catullus
quitted Rome for his villa on the lake of Garda, Horace for his
Sabine farm, Virgil for the bay of Naples. It was the same with
the man of business and the lawyer, when, as in Horace's
famous simile, he shook off the burden of public affairs and
retired to 'the fields of Venafrum or Lacedaemonian Tarentum'. [3] The Romans carried into their converse with nature
something of the warmth of intimacy that marked their

---

1. Mackail, *Latin Literature. Satura*, as the text implies, includes more
than the English term 'satire'; Quintilian (*Inst. Orat.* x. c. 1, § 93)
observes that it is purely Roman (*satura quidem tota nostra est*).

2. Hesiod and Alcman, however, must be excepted.

3. Horace, *Odes*, iii. 5, ll. 55–6.

personal relationships, and that draws the reader of their literature into sympathy with the poet's daily life. First of all races, they knew and expressed in their verse a sense of delight in natural beauty akin to that of Chaucer or of Shakespeare.

§ 16. With the spread of contemporary Hellenism of the Hellenistic, Alexandrian type, Roman society became at once more luxurious and more refined. Too often Greek culture meant but a thin veneer that hardly veiled the natural coarseness and brutality of Roman manners. On the mass of the people its influence was scarcely felt at all, except, perhaps, in the gradual effects on popular religion of the identification by the poets of Roman with Hellenic deities. The highly abstract gods of early Rome became somewhat more personal and concrete. The aristocracy, on the other hand, learnt from the Greeks to value literature and the arts.[1] The masterpieces of Greek sculpture were carried to Rome to adorn the houses of victorious generals. There is a saying of George Meredith to the effect that the one abstract idea which the military mind is able to grasp is that of booty, and doubtless the vulgar thirst for plunder had much to do with this spoliation of Hellenic treasures.[2] But when once the works of art were displayed in Rome, they exercised a subtle influence on the public taste. The Romans became interested not merely in preserving the monuments of the past, but in encouraging

1. The distinguished circle that gathered round Scipio Aemilianus (conqueror of Carthage in the third Punic war) included, besides noble Romans, the comic dramatist Terence, the satirist Lucilius, and the deported Greek statesman Polybius. Polybius (born c. 206, died c. 124) was restored to Greece from exile in 150; attended Scipio on campaigns in Africa and elsewhere, and acted as Roman commissioner in Greece from 145. His history comprised 40 Books, of which the first five only are extant in their entirety; extracts from the others have been preserved by Byzantine compilers. They cover the years between 219 and 145. Polybius' work is marked by impartiality of judgement and fidelity to ascertainable fact; the author, though consistently loyal to his native Greece, is inspired throughout by a sense of the invincible strength of the Roman power, and the nobility and greatness of Roman character and institutions. Chance largely rules human affairs (i. 4); but there was nothing fortuitous, in Polybius' eyes, in the acquisition of a world-empire by Rome (i. 63). The philosophical reflexions, which are obtrusively lavished on the reader, are, in general, somewhat banal and verbose.

2. Polybius (ix. 10) laments the Roman practice of robbing conquered cities of their art treasures, contrasting with it their earlier self-restraint and simplicity of life.

such new creations in art and literature as the Greek genius was still able to produce. Creative art implies a public, and this public was now furnished by Rome. The Romans never became artists; indeed, their patronage dealt Greek art its final blow. Greek philosophy, too, began to trickle into Rome during the second century, though the Romans had little capacity for disinterested speculation, and long resisted the intrusion. The doctrines of the Stoics and Epicureans, which centred round the problems of practical life, were the earliest to take root in Roman society. They helped to modify and eventually to undermine the old Roman standards of piety and virtue. Signs of sceptical thought are already present in the poems of Ennius. The elder statesmen of the second century, such as Cato, were suspicious of Greek influence; in the middle of that century the senate passed a decree that all philosophers should quit the city. But resistance to ideas was as impracticable as resistance to wealth and luxury; slowly, but surely, for good and for evil, the spirit of Greece, in Horace's phrase, 'took captive her rude conqueror'.[1]

B. *The Roman State in the Second Century*

§ 17. It was one thing to create an empire; another, and a far harder, to govern it. The problem that confronted Rome was not merely that of devising new machinery of administration for her provinces, but also that of readjusting the central government at home. The methods that sufficed for an Italian municipality were bound to prove inadequate for the metropolis of the Mediterranean world. Already in the epoch of the wars with Carthage the character of the Roman state had undergone radical transformation, not by deliberate design but under pressure from the facts. Power was concentrated not, as might have been expected after the Hortensian law of 287, in the hands of the citizen democracy, but in those of an exclusive ring of noble families, with the senate as their organ.[2] Recruited from magistrates and ex-magistrates, and

1. Horace, *Epp.* ii. 1, 156.
2. Polybius, writing of the Roman constitution at this epoch, describes it (vi. 10) as a blend of monarchy (the magistrates with *imperium*), aristocracy

comprising among its members tried soldiers and statesmen at a time when consuls and citizens were serving in the field, the senate was the only constitutional body qualified to direct affairs of state. The increase in the number of executive officers entailed by the enlargement of public responsibilities, until there were no less than twenty annual magistrates in possession of the authority to convene the people, and the fact that there were three popular assemblies competent to pass binding acts, called imperatively for the regulative control of a standing council.[1] Moreover, in days when the nation was fighting for life the senate proved itself worthy of power; it was, so Pyrrhus' envoy told his master, a council of kings. Thus it came about that the *imperium* of the magistrates and the legislative sovereignty of the people bowed before the moral authority of the senate. At the close of the third century, the senate, in addition to its historic power of giving advice to the magistrates, wielded almost exclusive control over foreign affairs, provincial organization, finance, religion, and all vital matters of public policy. A little later, it claimed the rights, foreign to constitutional tradition and disputed by the popular opposition, of suspending magistrates from their functions, and of endowing the consuls with virtually dictatorial powers by the decree 'that the magistrates should see that the state took no harm'.[2] We find in fact at Rome a

(the office-bearing families) and democracy (the *comitia*, or popular assembly). See also Mommsen, Book I, c. ii.

1. The magistrates possessed of *imperium* at the beginning of the second century were (i) the two consuls, (ii) six praetors, of whom two administered justice at Rome and four governed provinces, (iii) proconsuls and propraetors in increasing number, i.e. former consuls and praetors whose *imperium* was prolonged for military functions after the expiration of their year of office. In theory, the *imperium* knew no limits; but in practice distinctions were drawn between the 'greater' and 'less' *imperium* of the consuls and praetors respectively, and between the exercise of *imperium* in the civil area of Rome (*domi*) and in the military (*militiae*). The *imperium* of the pro-magistrate was restricted to the latter field. Except in the case of the dictator, whose *imperium* was *sine fine* (without limit), the *imperium* was restricted to a specific *provincia* (see n. 2 to p. 259). The watch-dog was thus provided with a leash.

2. In the first century B.C. the resolutions of the senate (*senatus consulta*) began to acquire legal force through a virtual usurpation of authority alien to the spirit of the constitution.

situation analogous to that which prevailed in eighteenth-century England, when the forms of parliamentary government were manipulated, in an era of commercial and imperial expansion, by a coterie of great Whig houses. At Rome also the senate and the higher magistracy became the monopoly of noble, i.e. office-bearing, families.[1] This growing exclusiveness, combined with the spread of wealth and luxury among the ruling aristocracy, issued inevitably in the outbreak of the disease chronic in the ancient city-state, i.e. party faction; from 134 onwards, civil conflict between senate and democracy raged with an intensity hitherto unknown in Roman history. A like narrowness was reflected in the dealings of the Roman government with the peoples of Italy. The line between Roman citizens and the non-citizen population became far more rigid. Those Italian communities which had joined Hannibal were reduced to practical serfdom. Even the loyal cities, e.g. those with Latin rights, found that they were left with burdens in lieu of privileges. When we consider that the Italians were akin in stock to the Romans, that in energy and character they were at least their equals, and that they were compelled to bear the brunt of military service in remote quarters of the empire, we can appreciate the ruinous issues that were bound to flow from this short-sighted and autocratic policy. In effect, all the symptoms that herald an epoch of internal disruption were rife in Rome and Italy before the close of the second century.

§ 18. The same period saw the foundation by Rome of her system of provincial government.[2] The organization of a new province was determined by a law, based on the report of a senatorial commission, which laid down the principles of

1. This new nobility was entirely unconnected with the old distinction of patricians and plebeians, which had ceased to have practical significance. Rank was now measured by the number of forefathers who had held the highest offices. It became increasingly difficult for a 'new man' to enter the ring of noble families.

2. The word *provincia* meant originally the special function of the magistrate. When in 241 the first extra-Italian territory, Sicily, was acquired, it was entrusted to a magistrate as his special sphere; and the like was done in the case of subsequent territorial extensions. The word thus came to mean a territorial region under the government of a magistrate with *imperium*.

administration and finance. As regards taxation, the practice was to maintain, as far as possible, the system previously in existence.[1] The law of Rome was introduced, save in the case of privileged cities, 'allied' and 'free', which had the right, if they chose, to their own law, and were exempt from interference by the governor. Even beyond these limits local law and custom were widely tolerated. Roman colonies and *municipia*, again, formed self-governing communities within the province. Hellenic cities, especially in Sicily and the East, enjoyed a large measure of autonomy; the Romans, with their keen eye for adjustment of methods to local requirements, realized from the first that civilized Greeks needed very different handling from the barbaric tribes of Africa or Spain. Yet even in these western provinces privileged urban communities were fostered as centres for the diffusion of Roman culture. In the provinces, as in Italy, old local confederations were everywhere broken up. Beyond the limits of the privileged towns, the authority of the governor was absolute, save only for the terms of the original constitution. Each province was assigned to a praetor, the number of these magistrates being increased to six after the second Punic war; or, later, to an ex-consul or ex-praetor, continued in power for the purpose during a second year. He was assisted by a quaestor as financial administrator, and by a military and civil staff. Since a governor held office only for a year, and brought out his staff with him from Rome, the difficulty of securing continuity in provincial administration was very great. It was met, partly by the standing constitution of the province, partly by the fact that each successive governor, like the praetors at Rome, published an edict on entering his office, normally inclusive of the contents of the edicts of his predecessors. While in office, he was sole commander of the forces, sole head of the executive, and supreme judge. In a province where military operations were not called for, the

1. So the old system of tithes was preserved in Sicily and in Asia. It led to the un-economic and oppressive practice of farming out the collection of the tithes in kind to *publicani*, who sold the produce and paid over a fixed sum to the state, keeping the profits on the sales.

judicial circuits constituted his chief duty.[1] As no Roman magistrate holding the *imperium* could be called to account during the tenure of his office, while charges lodged subsequently were heard at Rome and before a biassed tribunal, the temptations to rapacity were almost irresistible. In early days, governors prided themselves on their integrity; but, as Mommsen observes, 'It is not practicable for any length of time to be at once republican and king.'[2] The spread of luxury in the Roman aristocracy intensified the evils of provincial absolutism. Even a just governor found it increasingly difficult to control the host of tax-farmers and financial agents that swarmed over the more wealthy provinces. As time went on, just governors were few and far between. The system was doomed to eventual disaster for lack of effective control over the provincial autocrat. The central government was far away, and there was no trained bureaucracy to ensure permanent supervision on the spot. The signs of coming disruption that we have noted in Rome and Italy were evident also, and in an aggravated form, throughout the provincial empire.

§ 19. The transformation of a simple agricultural community into a populous and wealthy centre of world-commerce and world-dominion involved corresponding changes in the tenor and process of the law. The period between the legislation of the Twelve Tables and the close of the second century was a great constructive period in legal history, in which the rigidity of the early code was broken down, new machinery devised and a systematic body of jurisprudence brought into being by means of interpretation, revision, and enlargement. To the two recognized sources of (i) historic custom, which was constantly creative of new law, and (ii) positive statutes, in which this age was prolific, there had

1. The governor would judge cases normally by native law, which the Romans were careful to sanction. In criminal cases, a *consilium* of Romans, drawn from residents in the province and from the governor's staff, would be summoned for consultation. The two duties that no governor could neglect were war and judicial sessions. In other matters, a lax administrator might let a peaceful province govern itself, often with disastrous results. Cicero, when proconsul in Cilicia, inquired into the methods of the local magistrates and found that they had been plundering the local exchequer for years.

2. Mommsen, Book III, c. ii.

been added in the fourth century (iii) the praetorian edict.[1]
The higher magistrates had always possessed the right of
issuing, orally or in writing, notifications to the public (edicta);
and when in 367 the judicial functions of the consuls were
transferred to a special magistrate, the praetor of the city
(praetor urbanus), it became customary for him to affix in
court, for the information of litigants, tablets containing the
formulae of his procedure and the rules in accordance with
which he proposed to apply the law. This edict, called the
'standing edict' (edictum perpetuum), to distinguish it from
incidental orders relative to particular occasions, was in
theory valid only during the praetor's year of office; but it
became the practice for each successive praetor to embody in
his edict the main provisions of that of his predecessor, with
such modifications and additions as were deemed necessary.
Thus arose a body of judge-made law which soon took rank
beside the customary and statute law of Rome. The praetor, be
it noted, had no power to legislate or to adjudge a suit; he
could only grant or refuse an action at law by means of a
written 'formula' addressed to the judex, the private citizen
whom he appointed to decide the facts of the case. But this
restricted function was extended by the lex Aebutia (c. 150),
which empowered the praetor in giving instructions to the
judex to modify, or virtually to nullify, the literal provisions
of the civil law in the light of equity and reason.[2] A single

1. The praetorian edict was the source of most later Roman law. It represents the work, not of professed lawyers, but of generations of practical
administrators, who adjusted the civil law to the requirements of Italy and the
provinces. It is called in the Digest 'the living voice of the civil law'. The
ground of the development of praetorian equity lies in the practice of the
praetors of granting a 'formula' (i.e. a decree appointing a judex and instructing
him on the law of the case), whenever they considered that an action, even if
not covered by the narrow civil law, was reasonable and just. The edict indicated the sort of cases for which the praetor was prepared to grant a formula
(i.e. to allow an action) and the nature of the instructions which he would
issue to the judex.

2. The Aebutian law placed the praetorian formula on a level with actions
under the civil law. Since the procedure by formula was simpler and more
elastic, the older methods, though never abrogated, fell largely into disuse.
Moreover, the specific instructions on points of law embodied in the formulae
rendered the judex to whom the case was referred more dependent than here-
tofore on the praetor's ruling. Henceforward praetorian equity dominates
the history of Roman law.

example will make clear the nature of this development. By the strict terms of the law, an engagement entered into in due form was binding, even when secured by the fraud of one of the parties. The praetor, though bound to grant an action, would notify that in granting it he would instruct the *judex* to penalize the defendant only if he found that no fraud had been committed. Such procedure was capable of almost indefinite extension, and furnished an effective means for securing the victory of the spirit over the letter of the law. Moreover, this same period saw the birth of scientific jurisprudence. Up to the close of the fourth century, the principles of legal interpretation remained a closed secret in the hands of the priestly college. In 304 a freedman of Appius Claudius the censor published certain of the pontifical rules, and half a century later the first plebeian *pontifex maximus* started the practice of giving legal advice to the citizens in public. Henceforward a knowledge of the law was open to all Rome. As a natural consequence, a legal literature came into being. Practical law books were followed by methodical expositions of the principles of the civil law. In the last century of the republic, the foundations were laid of the system of legal science which was elaborated by the great jurists of the early empire.[1]

§ 20. By far the most important legal development in this epoch was that of the law of nations (*jus gentium*).[2] The civil law was confined to Roman citizens or to members of a non-

---

1. The answers to legal questions given by celebrated jurisconsults (the *responsa prudentium*) depended for their authority on the fame of the individual who gave them. Professedly interpretations of the Twelve Tables, they involved in fact modification, expansion, and reconstruction. Principles were developed which the framers of the early code had never dreamed of. Maine (*Ancient Law*, c. ii) points out that this kind of law was the work, not of the Bench (for at Rome there was nothing analogous to the Bench of judges in modern England), but of the Bar, though *prudentes* did not plead in court. Cicero was not a *prudens*. The opportunity thus afforded to the lawyer to consider hypothetical cases, as well as actual matters of fact, facilitated generalization and the formulation of broad principles. It must be remembered that almost every Roman who aspired to public office in republican times was trained to a knowledge of the law. It was the one serious profession, besides that of arms: and most of the governing class practised both.

2. On the *jus gentium*, see de Zulueta in *The Legacy of Rome*.

Roman community to whom legal capacity had been guaranteed by special treaty. When Rome became a great commercial power, there was obvious need for a law which should be applicable to foreigners, both in their dealings with citizens and among themselves. It was to meet this need that a second praetor was appointed in 242, with the special function of dispensing justice in suits where non-citizens were involved. His annual edict, embodying the necessary adjustments of the civil law to alien peoples, formed the basis of the law of nations.[1] It may be described as that part of the *jus civile*, which accorded with the local law of other peoples, modified to suit varying conditions, and enlarged by the assimilation of Hellenic and other foreign elements into a body of equitable principles suitable for application throughout the Roman world. This was no sudden creation; it grew by slow gradations in the course of centuries, and represented the accumulated experience of a race which possessed in a singular degree the power of adapting legal means to the ends of a political society. It reacted in turn on the civil law, chiefly through the equity law (*jus honorarium*) of the urban praetor.[2] Eventually, and by virtue of its inherent reasonableness, it replaced the narrow provisions of the *jus civile* as the law of Roman citizens. Thus it came to be regarded as a universal code, valid for all mankind and based on the sense of equity natural to man as man. From the court of the *praetor peregrinus* it spread to the provinces, where existing local law was supplemented by the law of nations and the edicts of the governors. The governors brought back to Rome their experience of foreign law, and helped to build on broad foundations the fabric of Roman jurisprudence. Thus, in the fullness of time, the local law of a single Italian city-state, enriched by accretions from

1. The second praetor was called the *praetor peregrinus*, because he adjudicated among non-citizens (*peregrini*). The origins of the *jus gentium* lay in a time prior to the institution of this office. It must be understood that *jus gentium* does not mean 'international law', but the law applicable to individuals belonging to non-Roman peoples. It was mainly concerned with contracts and was based on the custom prevalent among Mediterranean communities. See Maine, *Ancient Law*, c. iii.

2. The law of the praetorian edicts received this title, as issuing from the *imperium* of the magistrate (*honos* = magisterial office).

alien sources and transmuted by the adaptive genius of the Roman people, was fashioned into a juristic system for the whole Mediterranean world.[1]

V. CONCLUSION

§ 21. Before the world could reap the fruits of Roman jurisprudence, the republic was doomed to endure the throes of revolution. The second century had brought Rome face to face with the problem: Could a city-state with republican institutions rule an empire? Was it credible that, where Periclean Athens had failed, Rome, with her meagre experience of self-government, would succeed? Despite her ability to conquer and to police, she had never proved equal to the task of creating an organic public life. Her conception of authority remained to the end external and disciplinary. The Roman state rested upon force, and the weapon, as is its wont, recoiled upon the user. How deep-seated was the malady that preyed upon the social organism will be manifest if we recall the symptoms noted in the preceding pages. Economic stability was sapped by the wealth that flowed into the capital from all quarters of the Mediterranean, by the simultaneous rise of plutocracy and pauperism, by the decline of agriculture and the substitution of slave labourers for the free cultivators of the soil. Politically, power tended to be concentrated in the hands of a short-sighted and unimaginative oligarchy, enriched by the plunder of the provinces, who traded on the achievements of their forefathers and knew no public obligation save that of their own maintenance in office. Equally self-interested were the two centres of opposition to the senate, the order of knights (*equites*), comprising

1. The development of Roman law in the epoch between the Twelve Tables and the fall of the republic may be best studied in connexion with the history of contracts. See Maine, *Ancient Law*, c. ix: 'the positive duty resulting from one man's reliance on the word of another is among the slowest conquests of advancing civilization'. In early societies, where rights and duties are not voluntarily created by the individual, but are either (*a*) inherent in the station to which he is born, or (*b*) commands issued by the head of the family or tribe, there is no room for contract. The civilized world owes both contracts and wills to the legal genius of ancient Rome.

the rich bankers and merchants, and the indolent city proletariat, who thronged the assembly to barter the suffrages
of the sovereign people for a corn dole or for payment in
hard cash. The agricultural middle class that had saved Rome
from Hannibal either had vanished or lived too far from the
capital to play an effective part in public life. The cleavage
between the Roman and the Italian grew ever wider; the
grant of the franchise was denied, and the 'allies' of Rome,
who bore the brunt of her military service, were treated as
alien dependents. Morally, the old standards of piety and civic
virtue had fallen into decay; the rectitude and conscientious-
ness which were once the distinctive glory of the Roman,
were his no more. The Roman had learnt to rule by learning
to obey; now, even in the legions, a mutiny of citizen-
soldiers was frequent. Touched by the spirit of Greece, the
habit of solidarity and loyalty to the republic was yielding to
the claims of personal ambition. Was it possible that a community, torn by internal faction, who had alienated their
Italian kinsmen, should maintain control of a vast provincial
empire? The armies were massed upon the frontiers under the
command of proconsuls to whom, and not to the republic,
they had sworn allegiance.[1] Here was the point of danger for
the coming time. How long would a victorious general, with
unlimited authority over his soldiers and the resources of his
province, be content to exhibit the self-restraint and civic
loyalty that had been a second nature to the Roman of early
days? It was the conjunction of these conditions – the inherent
inability of a city to govern the world, the demoralization of
the Roman senate and people, and the new-born power of the
provincial governor – that led in the course of the succeeding
century to the fall of the republic and the creation of the
Roman Empire.

1. The *sacramentum* or oath of military allegiance was (probably) in early
days the oath sworn under penalty to the gods by both parties to a private
transaction, each asseverating that his assertion of claim was true. See Mommsen, Book I, c. ii. and *Encycl. Britannica*, art. *Roman Law* (11th edn.), vol. xxiii,
pp. 548 ff. The use of this word to signify the Christian 'sacraments' and the
Mithraic and Greek 'mysteries' is found in Tertullian. See Hastings' *Encyclop. of
Religion and Ethics*, art. *Sacraments* (*Christian Western*).

CHAPTER EIGHT

THE ROMAN EMPIRE

*

I. THE INSTITUTION OF THE EMPIRE

A. *The Fall of the Republic*

§ 1. THE story of the fall of the republic is of extraordinary interest, both for the sake of the events and personalities, and because we have so full a knowledge of the period. It opens with the tribunate of Tiberius Gracchus in 133, and closes with the definitive establishment of the empire by Augustus in 27 B.C. We saw in the last chapter how the seeds of revolution were germinating in the Roman state from the moment when it became the sovereign of the Mediterranean world. The problem confronting it was that which beset ancient civilization throughout its history, of uniting civic liberty with the expansion of empire. The Romans, with their capacity for adjusting principles of government to varying situations, might have discovered a solution, had they been able to realize the meaning of self-government within the bounds of their own civic community. The cause of their failure lay in the degeneration of public life. The Roman republic was divided against itself, and therefore could not stand. Of the three organs of the state, the magistracy, the senate, and the popular assembly, the last two were already evincing signs of atrophy. The *imperium* of the magistrate alone retained its force, and, when all checks had been removed, asserted itself in a new form and with overwhelming power. Victorious generals, seeing that the state lay at their mercy, seized the sovereignty thus placed within their grasp. Amid all the changes and chances of its destiny, the root-idea of the Roman commonwealth persisted in unbroken continuity. 'Arms and the man' was the watchword alike of the Rome of Aeneas and of the historic empire. The *imperium* was the bed-rock of the world-despotism that arose out of the ruins of the republic. It stood

forth, naked and unashamed, as the sole source of authority and
law. And in the shadow of the throne, where senate and
assembly once had stood, loomed ominously the dark pre-
sences of the legionary and the bureaucrat.

§ 2. We will summarize briefly the successive phases of the
crisis :

(i) The attack on the governing aristocracy was opened in
133, when Tiberius Gracchus, as leader of the democratic
opposition, carried a law to allot farms in Italy to free cultivators at the expense of rich occupiers of state lands. What is
significant is that he developed the latent powers of the
tribunate as a weapon against both the magistrates and the
senate, and that he found himself forced to use those powers
unconstitutionally. On his attempting to hold office for a
second year, he was murdered in a riot fomented by his
political enemies. Ten years later (123–122) his brother
Caius, also as tribune, took the field on wider ground, and,
securing the support of the financial order (the *equites*) by
granting them privileges as tax-farmers and as *judices* in the
courts, and that of the populace by a corn dole and the promise
of colonies overseas, challenged the senate's control of provincial administration and of finance. The senate retaliated
by open violence, and the party struggle was brought to the
verge of civil war.

(ii) Thus far the conflict was confined to the political
arena, though unconstitutional weapons had been employed
by both the contending parties. The tribunate had suddenly
been revealed as the most formidable power in the state. The
senate emerged from the conflict victorious but shaken, and
henceforward the reformers looked more and more to military support. They found their opportunity, when in the closing years of the second century Rome was roused by a menace
that threatened her very existence from without. Germanic
tribes had invaded Gaul, crushed the Roman armies in the
southern province, overrun Spain, and were about to move
on Italy. An able soldier, Caius Marius, summoned year after
year to the consulship by popular acclamation, remodelled
the army, and by two decisive victories (102, 101) saved the

state. His military reforms, the abolition of distinctions of rank and wealth in the legion, and the substitution of voluntary enlistment for the citizen-levy by creating a professional army, severed the tie that bound the soldier to the civil community. Henceforward the successful general was the arbiter of internal politics. Early in the first century the government was faced by a second crisis even nearer home. When Caius Gracchus had proposed in a spirit of true statesmanship to redress the grievances of the Italians by granting them the franchise, he had been deserted by the city democracy.[1] In 90 and 89 the Italians won the franchise by force of arms. This conflict passed without a break into a civil war (89, 88) between two rival generals, Marius, the champion of the popular party, and Lucius Cornelius Sulla, the champion of the senate. Sulla's triumph made him master of the state, and as dictator he used the power of the sword to restore the senate to almost uncontrolled supremacy (81). The Sullan restoration was itself a revolution, in that it was effected by arms. After a ruthless extermination of his political opponents, he reigned as an absolute sovereign; and though he acted in the interest of the old order and resigned his despotism when his work was done, it was inevitable that others should follow where he had shown the way, and use military power for less impersonal ends.[2]

§ 3. (iii) The twenty years that followed the Sullan restoration revealed the incapacity of the senate to maintain

1. The Italians represented the best stock of the Roman state; that they had to bear the heavier military burdens without corresponding privileges is the most serious proof of the incompetence of the government to handle problems of state. Many attempts were made, from 125 onwards, to redress their grievances, but in vain.

2. Mommsen's brilliant sketch of Sulla's work and personality (Book IV, c. 10) should be read, but with extreme caution. Sulla unquestionably possessed great ability, alike as soldier, diplomatist, and politician; he showed also considerable literary taste, introduced Aristotle's works at Rome, wrote his own memoirs, etc., and had a gift of ironical humour. An aristocrat to the backbone, his *hauteur* made him indifferent to personal power. He was entirely without moral scruple, and effected little that was constructive. His most enduring work was the organization of criminal law. Anyone who wished to argue that political expediency is a futile guide when divorced from ideal ends would find in the swift collapse of Sulla's restoration of the senate a striking confirmation of his case.

the position he had won for it. Foreign war, this time in the East against king Mithradates of Pontus in Asia Minor (88–64), brought to the front a new general in the person of Pompey (Cnaeus Pompeius). In 67 and 66 he was entrusted with extraordinary powers that clearly foreshadow the later autocracy of the emperors. By the Gabinian and Manilian laws he received the *imperium* with pre-eminence over all provincial governors in the East for three years, a staff of twenty-five *legati*, and unlimited resources of men, ships, and money. After carrying out the reorganization of the East, he returned to the capital in 61, the commanding personality in the Roman state.[1]

(iv) The history of the next twelve years (61–48) centres round three persons, of whom two owed their position to the support of the legions. On the one hand, Pompey, athirst for power yet too timid to clutch the prize within his grasp, drifted eventually into the role of a defender of the senate and the republic. On the other hand, the democratic leader, Caius Julius Caesar, the nephew of Marius, who in youth had narrowly escaped death at the hands of Sulla, secured, by a temporary coalition with Pompey and the rich financier Crassus, a military command in Gaul, analogous to that previously conferred on Pompey in the East.[2] During his nine

1. Mithradates was a most formidable antagonist. His death, after defeat, in 63, was followed by the reconstruction of western Asia by Pompey, referred to in the text. It occupied the best part of two years and was of permanent importance. To the old provinces of Asia and Cilicia were added three new provinces, Bithynia, Syria, and Crete. In Palestine, Pompey restricted the temporal power of the Jewish high priest, removing from his jurisdiction the Hellenic cities which had arisen in numbers under the Seleucids. Pompey showed great wisdom in recognizing vassal princes, free cities, tribal cantons, as instruments of government under Rome. He left western Asia in a position analogous to that of British India at the present day, part administered directly by Roman officials, part in the form of protected states. See Duckworth in Jackson and Lake's *Acts* (*Prolegomena*, vol. i, pp. 177 ff.), who compares the king of Cappadocia to the Nizam of Hyderabad, and the extra-Roman kingdom of Armenia to that of Afghanistan. Rome was studious to tolerate all varieties of religious belief and local custom. Vassal princedoms *within* the empire disappear in the first century A.D.

2. Caesar (born probably in 102) was late in rising to the front rank in Roman politics. Until his consulship in 59, he was a dark horse, though he had shown independence in opposition to Sulla in youth and conspicuous ability as a soldier and administrator when praetor in Spain in 61. On Roman Gaul, see below, § 15. It is impossible to judge to what extent Caesar planned his despotism in the years prior to 49.

years' tenure of this command (58–49) he not only forged the
weapon with which he dealt the death-blow to the republic,
but by his conquest of Gaul and the extension of the Roman
frontiers to the Rhine staved off for centuries to come the
tide of barbarian invasion. In this, as in so many incidents in
his career, Caesar displayed in an extraordinary degree the
distinctive capacity of so many great men in history, of
blending personal ambition with vital national interests.
Between these two rivals, eyeing one another with mutual
suspicion and sharpening their swords for the combat, stood
the figure of the great orator, Marcus Tullius Cicero, a liberal
conservative, who strove hard to save the republican constitution from falling a prey to military despotism. Like
Demosthenes at Athens in the fourth century, he filled the
role of the last champion of a free city-state. His policy was
one of twofold reform: to unite the senate and the financial
interest (the *equites*) in support of law and order against
anarchy, and to broaden the basis of the state by associating
the middle classes in the Italian municipalities with the
government of the Roman state.[1] But the narrow rigidity of
the senatorial nobility, who, having learnt nothing and for-
gotten nothing during the turmoil of over fifty years, still
clung desperately to the last shreds of their monopoly of power,
and the personal ambition of the two great military captains,
rendered futile all Cicero's efforts to combine senators and
equites, Romans and Italians, in defence of the historic principles of the constitution. Even he, born Whig though he was,
was driven at the close to advocate the institution of a single
'moderator of the republic', who, he vainly hoped, might
rule in loyal co-operation with the senate, by law and not by
the sword. Had the republic been capable of salvation, it
would have been saved by Cicero. It is equally true that if
Cicero had been capable of saving it, he would have recognized that the task was impossible. That in the event he died
rather than renounce the republican ideal goes far to explain

1. This twofold policy was summarized in the watchwords, *concordia
ordinum* ('harmony of the orders') and *consensus Italiae* ('the united opinion of
Italy').

the hold he won on the respect of after-times. For the rest, vanity and lack of courage blinded him to the realities of the situation he endeavoured to control.[1]

(v) We are thus brought to the final act of the drama, when in the spring of 49 Caesar at the head of his army crossed the Rubicon, the little stream that formed the boundary between his military command and Italy. To the amazement of all, who looked trembling for retaliation at his hand for Sulla's massacre of the democrats, his victorious advance was marked by a moderation and clemency that won him general support in Rome and Italy. The next year (48) saw Pompey crushed at Pharsalia. It was the triumph of genius over talent. The republicans held out in the west for three years longer; but in 46 Cato, the uncompromising idealist of the party, fell on his sword at Utica in Africa, and in 45 the crowning victory of Munda in Spain left Caesar the unchallenged sovereign of the Roman world.[2]

B. *Julius Caesar*

§ 4. Caesar invested his sovereignty with a show of legal sanction by concentrating in his person a number of republican offices, such as the consulship and the tribunate. It was definitely established in 45 by the bestowal of the dictatorship for life. This revival of an office which, save in Sulla's case,

1. Cicero's letters (a selection, translated admirably by Jeans, has been published by Macmillan) are an invaluable commentary on this period. See also the historical introductions in Tyrrell's edition of Cicero's correspondence. On Cicero as man of letters, see below, § 19.

2. Cato was a rigid Tory, who modelled his policy on that of his ancestor, the censor of the early second century; his uncompromising advocacy of a narrow senatorial policy, backed by his personal integrity, proved a serious hindrance to Cicero's liberal policy. Cato's high moral character, his republican idealism, and the fact of his self-inflicted death on realizing the hopelessness of further struggle, made him an object of reverence to after-time. So Lucan, under the early empire, wrote the famous line:

'*Victrix causa diis placuit, sed victa Catoni*' (i. 158).

('The victorious cause won the favour of the gods, but the vanquished that of Cato.')

Dante's selection of Cato, as the type of antique pagan virtue, to be the guardian of the shore beneath the mount of Purgatory (*Purg.*, canto i), was based on Virgil's picture of Cato dispensing justice to the virtuous dead (*Aen.*, viii, 670, '*his dantem jura Catonem*').

had long passed into desuetude, as well as his adoption of the style *Imperator*, shows how once again, as in the old days of the monarchy, the *imperium* was the sole fountain of authority in the state. Just as the monarchy had been transformed into a republic by the dual limitation of collegiality (two consular colleagues in place of a single king) and of time (election for one year), so now the abolition of these restrictions brought about the change from a republic to a monarchy. A real revolution had been effected, in true Roman fashion, without an absolute suppression of constitutional forms. In virtue of these and other powers, Caesar appointed magistrates and provincial governors, enlarged the number of executive offices, and gained exclusive control over questions of war and peace, foreign affairs, and the administration of the empire. Popular election became a mere form for ratifying the nominations of the dictator. The senate was increased in numbers to 900, of whom many were provincials; for Caesar initiated the imperial policy of levelling up the provincials to equality with Romans. High offices in communities overseas were thrown open to freedmen. In effect, the senate became an instrument for registering his edicts. In legislation he instituted a vast body of measures, many of them of far-reaching scope, including economic and agrarian reforms, the uniform regulation of municipal constitutions, the extension of the franchise, e.g. to Gades (Cadiz) in Spain, first of provincial cities to receive the grant, and the reorganization of the fiscal system.[1] Great public works were planned and carried out in Italy and the provinces; transmarine colonies were founded, e.g. at Corinth and on the site of Carthage. Caesar's reformed

---

1. A large part of the *lex Julia municipalis*, dealing with the Italian municipalities, and fragments of the *lex Rubria*, dealing with the urban organization of Cisalpine Gaul, are extant. These laws distinguish between the jurisdiction of the Roman praetor and that of the local magistracy, and regulate the form of municipal government by magistrates, senate, and assemblies, which had grown up in preceding times. Cisalpine Gaul was admitted to full citizenship by Caesar, and incorporated into Italy by Augustus (then Octavian) in 42. Caesar abolished the bad system of taxation by tithes in Sicily and Asia; and handled with great ability the economic situation caused by the civil wars. In Rome he restricted the corn doles and abolished the corrupt popular clubs. He intended, but did not carry out, a codification of the law.

calendar is still accepted, with slight modifications, by the
civilized world. The swiftness and energy with which he
designed and effected a great historic reconstruction were as
amazing as his movements in the field. Hegel justly discerned
in Caesar 'the paragon of the Roman adaptation of means to
ends'.[1] In the last five years of his life he spent but eighteen
months in Rome, and his achievements represent merely the
initial stages of a comprehensive scheme of imperial government. Nevertheless they determined the lines on which the
Roman world was governed for centuries – the personal rule
of a monarch through his personally appointed staff of officers,
the effective control of the legions and the provincial administration, the extension of citizen-privileges throughout the
empire, the maintenance of internal peace and equal law, the
delimitation of the frontiers and their defence against non-
civilized invaders. In all these respects, Augustus, his successor, built on the foundations laid so swiftly, yet with so sure
an insight, by Julius Caesar.

§ 5. The last mentioned problem, that of frontier defence,
had been perforce neglected during the epoch of civil revolution. We have spoken of the danger that threatened Italy at
the close of the second century through the westward movement of barbarian hordes from their homes in the north and
east across the Rhine and the Danube. Then Marius with his
reformed army had saved Rome. Half a century later Caesar's
conquest of Gaul permanently secured her northern frontier.[2]
In Africa, Cyrene (74) and Numidia (46) were added to the
roll of provinces. The immediately pressing danger was from
the East. Pompey (67–62) had reorganized the political

---

1. *Philos. of History*, Part III, Sect. II.
2. Caesar was only just in time. In his first campaign in Gaul (58) he had to
face two invasions, that of the Helvetii along the Rhone and that of the
Germans under Ariovistus through the Burgundy gap between the Vosges
and the Jura. Ariovistus was on the point of establishing a powerful Teutonic
state in Gaul. Had Caesar not been victorious, the Teutonic tribes must have
overwhelmed the empire and therewith the entire structure of Graeco-
Roman civilization. Caesar's conquest postponed the catastrophe until that
civilization, and, with it, the Christian faith, had taken root among the invad-
ing peoples. The new territory was at first attached to the old province of
Narbonese Gaul; Augustus established three new Gallic provinces.

system of western Asia at the close of the Mithradatic War.[1]
The Seleucid dynasty ceased to be; their western dominions
passed to Rome, while the new province of Syria marched
with the Parthian empire in the valley of the Euphrates. In 54
the Parthians annihilated a Roman army at Carrhae; honour
and safety alike called for the military action that had already
been too long delayed. Here, as in Gaul, the problem was
real and urgent. Caesar did not manufacture wars for war's
sake; in east, as in west, the existence of the Roman state was
in jeopardy. Caesar lost no time in grappling with the issue;
in the spring of 44 the eastern legions awaited their commander; but on the Ides of March (March 15), the eve of his
departure from Rome, he was attacked by conspirators in the
senate-house and perished at the foot of Pompey's statue.

§ 6. The murder of Caesar has been justly described as the
greatest blunder in history, for it accomplished nothing save
the removal from the scene of the greatest Roman; after
thirteen years of civil war – the death agony of the republic –
the empire was reconstituted by his adopted heir. The circumstances of the problem did not admit of any alternative.
In the view of after-ages, nurtured in the traditions of the
Roman empire, for whom that empire was sacred, not only
as the fount of law and civilization, but as the divinely pre-
destined instrument for the spread of the Christian faith, the
deed appeared as the blackest of crimes. In the lowest depths
of Dante's *Inferno* were placed the three arch-malefactors of
history, Judas Iscariot, the traitor to the founder of the
catholic church, Brutus and Cassius, the traitors to the founder
of the catholic empire. Crime it was not, but a blunder; for,
like the passionate resistance of Demosthenes to Philip of
Macedon, it was the outcome of an intelligible idealism.
We have observed again and again in these pages how profound
was the value to Greek and Roman civilization of the city-
state, with its atmosphere of free discussion and civic equality.
Small wonder if the descendants of the men who under the

1. See above, § 3. In addition to the provinces there mentioned, Crete was
attached by Augustus to the province of Africa; Cyprus (incorporated in 58) was
attached at first to Cilicia but constituted as a separate province by Augustus.

aegis of the city-state had fashioned the Roman empire, with its majestic structure of law and government, were jealous for the institutions that had made Rome and Romans great. No ties of personal gratitude, no experience of Caesar's clemency or admiration for his genius, could destroy that intense devotion for the republic to which he had dealt the death-blow.[1] We cannot expect the last republicans of Rome to have understood, what Cicero failed to understand, that the doom of the city-state was sealed. They avenged the blow by means which the moral code alike of Greece and Rome sanctioned as honourable, when employed against a despot, and slew Caesar, not for motives of personal vengeance or ambition, but for civic liberty and in the name of Rome.

C. Augustus

§ 7. In 31, by the victory of Actium over Antony, the young Octavian, Caesar's great-nephew and adopted heir, became, in Shakespeare's phrase, 'sole sir o' the world'.[2] It was Octavian, better known to history by his title of Augustus, who perfected in detail the imperial system under which the world was governed for well-nigh 300 years. The decree is still extant, inscribed on stone, which proclaimed the motive

---

1. Caesar's clemency to his fellow-countrymen was notorious; he refrained from proscriptions and confiscation, and in assigning lands to his veterans carefully respected the rights of existing owners. His answer to Cicero's expression of gratitude for his clemency towards the political adversaries who had fallen into his power at the surrender of Corfinium impressed Macaulay as 'the finest sentence ever written'. It is as follows: 'I triumph and rejoice that my action should have obtained your approval. Nor am I disturbed when I hear it said that those whom I have sent off alive and free will again bear arms against me; for there is nothing which I so much covet as that I should be like myself, and they like themselves' (see Trevelyan, *Life and Letters of Macaulay*, c. xvi). But Caesar's was not a lovable character and, as far as our knowledge goes, he made no real friends. Cicero, who disliked and distrusted him, testifies to the force of his personality. In both these respects, we are reminded of Marlborough and Napoleon rather than of Alexander.

2. *Antony and Cleopatra*, Act V, Scene 2. Octavian's father, Caius Octavius, was an Italian bourgeois who became governor of Macedonia and married the daughter of Caesar's sister. His son was born in 63, the year of Cicero's consulship, and was therefore nineteen at the time of Caesar's murder and thirty-one when he won the battle of Actium.

and character of this achievement.[1] It opens with a sentence that rings strangely in our ears when we think of the real nature of his work: 'I transferred the republic from my own authority to the control of the Roman senate and people.'

What was the intention of those words? They meant that Augustus, to quote a modern writer, had 'learnt his lession at the foot of Pompey's statue'. The haughty spirit of Julius – we may recall Dante's picture of him among the great of ancient days, 'Caesar with the falcon eyes' – would not brook to conciliate republican sentiment by a show of citizen equality. Augustus, the dispassionate master of statecraft, veiled an absolute autocracy under the guise of constitutionalism. A thorough child of Rome in his respect for outward forms and established precedent, he was resolved to preserve in being the cherished institutions of the past. Julius had been styled *dictator*, a term which offended republican sentiment by its association with military command, and *imperator*, the title by which soldiers hailed their victorious general; Augustus would be simply *princeps*, i.e. the first man among his fellow-senators.[2] In his bearing towards the Roman nobility, the dispossessed lords of the world, he acted the part superbly. His life was simple and severe, without a trace of the etiquette and ceremonial of a court. He saw to it that his powers were conferred in the old republican fashion by the vote of the senate or the assembly. His autocracy rested on the combination in his single person of two republican offices, the tribunate, the highest in rank, which formed the basis of his authority in Rome, and the consular *imperium*, with primacy over all other holders, which secured to him the control of the army and the provinces. These were precisely the two powers whose enlargement had brought about the dissolution of the republic in the preceding age. Henceforth the army took the oath of allegiance to the *princeps* alone. As chief pontiff, he

1. The Ancyran monument from Angora in Asia Minor. Copies were set up in various centres in the Roman world. Augustus defined his position as head of the state in 27, and again in 23. Both groups of measures are treated together in this section.

2. Until the time of Diocletian, *princeps* is the proper title of the emperor, and *principate* of the empire.

was master of the machinery of the state religion, which was still an important factor in law and politics. The same spirit of conservatism, which Augustus displayed in determining his personal status, was visible in his readjustment of the system of government. The city proletariat, it is true, was shorn of its legislative powers, and the assemblies of the people quickly degenerated into a farce.[1] On the other hand, the senate was treated with studied consideration. It conferred the *imperium* on the sovereign, voted from among his list of nominees for candidates for office, and passed decrees which had the force of law. The *princeps* and the senate ranked on an equality as supreme tribunals; each controlled a separate treasury, and the government of the empire was partitioned between the two authorities. But it was significant that the provinces entrusted to the senate were the peaceful districts of the interior; those on the frontiers, where the legions were concentrated, were kept by the emperor in his own hands. Egypt, in particular, because of its importance strategically and as the chief granary of Rome, was administered by him through a prefect of equestrian rank inferior in status to the governors of the regular imperial provinces. These last were styled *legates* or military lieutenants, while the senatorial governors retained the republican title of *proconsuls*.[2] It is obvious that this shadow of dual control was an artificial experiment designed to conciliate the old Roman aristocracy. For the time it served its purpose; but already under Augustus' successor the servility of the senate showed that, in spite of outward forms, the real power rested with the emperor and with him alone.[3]

1. There are only two recorded examples of popular legislation after Tiberius.
2. *Legates* held office for three years, and often for longer; *proconsuls*, who had no military command, for only one. Moreover, the emperor influenced the appointment of proconsuls through his control of consular elections and of admission to the senate.
3. Augustus saw this clearly, as is shown by his last recorded words: 'What think you of the comedy, my friends? Have I played my part well in it?' Through a reign of more than forty years his infinite patience, profound reserve, and keen insight into men and things never failed him. All his acts were the outcome of conscious forethought. The story goes that he never discussed affairs of state, even with the empress Livia, without making notes beforehand. He is perhaps the greatest of the *politiques* of history.

§ 8. Such, in principle, was the régime established by Augustus in Rome; if we look farther afield, there are three features of the work carried out by him during his long reign (31 B.C.–A.D. 14) that are deserving of special notice. First, as regards the administration of Italy and the provinces. Augustus strove earnestly to realize the hope that Cicero had vainly cherished of an incorporation of the Italians on equal terms in the fabric of the Roman state. They were encouraged to look upon the great past of Rome as their own and to join with patriotic pride in the task of imperial reconstruction. Among the burghers and country folk of Italy, Augustus found, not only the fresh blood which should reinvigorate the public service, but men of literary genius, Virgil, Horace, Livy, and Ovid, who could celebrate the glory of Rome and of Caesar in enduring monuments of verse and prose. He fostered the development of municipalities, agriculture, and public works throughout the peninsula. The first steps were taken in the process of breaking down the barriers that parted Rome from Italy, Italy from the provinces. A comprehensive survey, an imperial 'Domesday Inquest', was compiled for the whole empire; and the registers, stored in municipal archives, served as the basis for an equitable system of taxation. 'There went out a decree from Caesar Augustus that all the world should be enrolled.' [1] The provinces were for the first time administered as departments of a single state. The authority of the governors was controlled and oppression of the provincials checked by the withdrawal of the dangerous privilege of requisitioning supplies at will, by the appointment of an independent financial administrator personally accountable to the *princeps*, and by the provision of effective machinery for petition and appeal to Rome. Though taxation was lightened, the revenue was increased. Trade restrictions within the empire were everywhere abolished. Local government was

1. Luke ii. 1 (R.V.). Julius had already laid down the lines of the *census* and provincial survey. The whole undertaking took fifty years to complete. Its results were summarized in the 'Breviary of the empire', a register of the resources of the state and its budget, bequeathed by Augustus to Tiberius (see Tacitus, *Ann.*, i. 11). The work was carried on and kept up to date by the emperors of the second century and by Diocletian.

extended and reorganized on a uniform basis, and provincial councils were instituted with wide powers. When the populace of Ephesus broke into riot on the occasion of St Paul's visit, the town clerk bade them remember that there were *Asiarchs*, i.e. provincial councillors of Asia, to whom they might refer their grievances.[1] If Augustus was less generous than Julius in granting the citizenship, it was the desire to foster civic patriotism in Rome and Italy that made him chary of extending the franchise to provincials.[2] Further, he laid the foundations of a permanent imperial civil service, recruited at first from the order of knights (*equites*) and from the Italians, later in increasing measure from the ranks of freedmen (enfranchised slaves). The administration of the empire passed gradually from the hands of the Roman aristocracy into those, not merely of Italians, but of provincials of intelligence and education, especially men of Greek and Graeco-Oriental origin. Thus a career with brilliant prospects lay open to all, and the creation of an expert bureaucracy ensured continuity in provincial government. Secondly, Augustus endeavoured, by personal example and public legislation, to stem the tide of decay in Roman religion and morals. Poets were encouraged to uphold the ancient standards of austere simplicity and to celebrate the worthies whose piety and civic virtue had been the glory of the early republic. Temples were erected and historic rites restored. Stern penalties were imposed for moral offences, and laws were passed to discourage celibacy. The emperor's efforts proved futile; for morals cannot be reformed by law, and the degeneration of the wealthier classes and the spread of Hellenism precluded the return to the simple standards of a bygone age.[3] The one exception to the general failure of this policy was the worship of the emperor himself. Augustus had no illusions about the matter, and, while sanctioning the payment of divine honours to Julius, prohibited his own worship in Italy. But it spread like wild-

1. Acts xix. 18.
2. The number of Roman citizens in 70 B.C. was 450,000, in 28 B.C. (Augustus' first *census*) 4,000,000, in A.D. 13 (the second *census*) 5,000,000.
3. On Augustus' social and religious legislation, see Pelham, *Essays in Roman History*, 'The domestic policy of Augustus'.

fire in the provinces, and developed before long into the official religion of the world-state. There was nothing to outrage Roman feeling in the practice, for religion at Rome had always been largely political, and a statesman might be canonized without a violent breach of self-respect. As regards a living emperor, worship was addressed to his *genius* or guardian-deity; as applied after his death, it was but a natural expression of pious gratitude. The provincial councils, referred to above, were closely associated with this religious service of 'the *genius* of Rome and Augustus', which became in the course of the first century of our era the outward symbol of the political unity of the empire.[1] Lastly Augustus completed the work begun by Julius of fixing the boundaries of the empire. They had been marked out by nature; in the east, the Euphrates; in the west, the Atlantic; in the south, the deserts of Africa and Arabia; in the north, the Rhine and the Danube from the Channel to the Black Sea. War and diplomacy had combined to secure Syria against the Parthians, and the standards lost at Carrhae had returned to Rome in triumph. The gravest menace was on the northern frontier. Here the Teutonic tribes surged ceaselessly against the newly fortified entrenchments on the Danube and the Rhine. In campaign after campaign, Augustus' generals strove to master the Germans who dwelt between the last-named river and the Elbe. The defeat of Varus in A.D. 9 finally determined the emperor to renounce the forward policy. Along the natural frontiers were massed the legions, eight on the Rhine, eight on the Danube, eight in Syria, while the Roman navy policed the waters of the Mediterranean.[2] Thus was preserved the *pax Romana*, the Roman peace. It endured for four centuries, broken only now and again, when, on an emperor's death, the generals of the frontier armies moved Romewards and fought for the imperial throne.

1. The worship of the emperor implied no theological belief. Virgil and Horace readily accepted the deification of Julius. The emperors themselves were under no misconceptions; when the dying Vespasian was asked by his friends how he was, he replied, 'I fear I am becoming a god (*Vae, puto deus fio*).'

2. This represents the distribution under Tiberius. The total force was about 320,000, in twenty-five legions.

II. THE EMPIRE IN THE FIRST THREE CENTURIES [1]

§ 9. The Roman world was governed on the maxims of
Augustus until the accession of Diocletian in 284. For the
first and only time in history, civilized mankind was incorporated into a single state, and that state a military despotism.
It is not our task to trace the gradual disappearance of the
disguises in which its founder had shrouded the hard fact of
his autocracy; how first the popular assembly, then the civic
magistrates, and finally the senate either fell into disuse or,
where they survived, retained merely a local and honorific
value.[2] The state, for instance, was still officially known as the
'republic' till the close of the third century. Of the basis of
the emperor's power we have already spoken. The most disturbing factor in the system was the problem of the succession.
In practice, the reigning prince often designated a son or a
male kinsman as his successor by securing the conferment
upon him of the *imperium* and the tribunician power. Frequently, and above all in the second century, the Roman
usage of adoption was called into play. These precautions did
not avail to prevent periodic conflicts, as on Nero's death in
66, and with increasing frequency in the third century, when a
successful general, backed by one of the frontier armies or by
the praetorian bodyguard, claimed the vacant throne. The
empire, like the ancient kingship, was not hereditary, but
elective; and the theory that any Roman citizen was eligible
was preserved throughout its history. This explains why, as
will be seen in a later chapter, on its restoration in the West
in the ninth century, a Frankish chieftain could be regarded as
the legitimate successor of Augustus. Nor need we dwell, for
all their personal interest, on the lives of individual emperors.[3] For many readers, the story of the empire is that of its

  1. From this point onwards all dates refer to the Christian era, unless otherwise specified.
  2. The senate survived longest in effective being; of its powers, that of
appellate jurisdiction lasted until the third century.
  3. We may distinguish the following groups of emperors in chronological
sequence:

> (i) emperors of the Julio–Claudian line: Augustus (to 14), Tiberius
> (to 37), Caligula (to 41), Claudius (to 54), Nero (to 68).

rulers; while the system they controlled, affecting the destiny of millions, remains virtually unknown.[1] Even in the case of those princes whose ability is most conspicuous, the literary records are largely occupied with the trivial details of court-gossip. It is only by gathering up the tale told by inscriptions scattered over the provinces that we learn to gauge the imperial system in its true proportions. We then discover that the wild vagaries of a Caligula or a Nero, which loom so large in the pages of Tacitus and Suetonius, served only to rouse a transitory agitation in the capital. The huge machine performed its appointed revolutions, heedless of the caprices of its master. When St Paul appealed to the imperial tribunal, it was from Caesar, not from Nero, that he expected and received justice. How great, on the other hand, was the influence which a capable and energetic ruler could exert in the fields of military defence, internal administration, and law, will be manifest from a single illustration.

§ 10. If autocracy ever merits praise, the emperor Hadrian (117–138) might claim to be regarded as a heaven-sent autocrat. Born at Rome in 76 – his father, a native of Spain, but of Italian lineage, was Trajan's cousin – he was early trained to office; at fifteen he was serving in the army, at seventeen acting as judge in private suits; he held in succession commands in Britain, Moesia, and on the Rhine, and followed his great kinsman through his victorious campaigns in Dacia and in the East. Thus, when on Trajan's death he succeeded to the throne at the age of forty-one, his natural powers of judge-ment and imagination and his tireless ardour for work had been matured by wide experience both in peace and war. Hadrian was a statesman rather than a soldier, and used to

(ii) emperors of the Flavian line: Vespasian (to 79), Titus (to 81). Domitian (to 96).
(iii) Adoptive emperors: Nerva (to 98), Trajan (to 117), Hadrian (to 138), Antoninus Pius (to 161), Marcus Aurelius (to 180).
(iv) Barrack emperors (nominees of the army): from 192 to 284. The ablest of these were Septimius Severus (193–211), Aurelian (270–275), and Probus (275–282).

1. The Misses Maria and Julia Bertram, in Jane Austen's *Mansfield Park* (c. ii), aged 13 and 12 respectively, could repeat 'in chronological order, with the dates of their accession . . . the Roman emperors as low as Severus.'

boast that he had won more by the weapons of policy than by those of arms. In his reign of one and twenty years, he set his mark, in principle and in detail, on the entire structure of Roman administration and law. He organized the imperial council of state, the imperial secretariat, and the system of imperial postal communications.[1] Public works and charitable institutions sprang into being at his initiative; agriculture was fostered, universities were endowed, Roman citizenship and Latin rights liberally bestowed. 'He had as all-embracing a knowledge of the public finances,' wrote his biographer, 'as any careful householder of his private affairs'. No detail was too minute to engage his attention; a tablet discovered in S. Portugal shows him regulating the life of a mining village, laying down rules for the local shoemaker and barber, arranging for the monthly cleaning of the boilers in the public bath, and (merciful provision!) exempting schoolmasters from the payment of rates.[2] The emperor's labours were most evident and enduring in the fields of law and provincial government. He inaugurated the classic age of Roman jurisprudence. To his personal stimulus were due the practice of issuing imperial rescripts binding upon the courts, the compilation of the Perpetual Edict,[3] and the recognition of the opinions of the great jurists as possessing the force of law. The emperor now became the supreme judge of all criminal appeals. He mitigated the rigours of the *patria potestas*, granted to women the right of making wills, abolished human sacrifices, and severely restricted the torture of slaves. Humanity was the leading note of Hadrian's character and actions.[4] A favourite symbol on his coins was that of a weeping woman raised by the emperor from the ground. More than half his reign was spent in rapid progresses through the provinces. He is said to have marched

1. The average rate of travel in the postal service was five miles an hour: thirty to fifty miles was an ordinary day's journey, but 100 could be covered, if necessary.

2. See H. S. Jones in *The Legacy of Rome*.

3. On the Perpetual Edict, see below, § 17.

4. He refused to sanction charges of high treason (*majestas*), or to accept legacies save from personal friends, and from those only if they died childless; thus removing two of the worst abuses incidental to the empire.

20,000 miles, on foot and clad in full military accoutrements.[1] In 121–6 he visited every quarter of the empire, from Spain to Syria, from Britain to Africa, reforming the military administration, fortifying the frontiers, visiting sick soldiers in hospital, living when in camp on the rations of the legionaries, inspecting industries and, above all, instituting public works and rebuilding cities. After little more than a year in Rome, he set forth on a second journey, and passed six years (128–34) in the East, to whose compelling call his temper of mind was singularly responsive. What makes Hadrian so interesting is the insatiable curiosity and intellectual enthusiasm that cast a glamour of romance over his unwearied discharge of official duty. 'Restless in everything all his life' is the verdict of his biographer Spartianus. He was an inveterate sightseer, climbed mount Casius to see the sunrise and Etna to see the sunset, reinterred the bones of Ajax at Troy, visited the pot- ters' sheds in Britain, the tombs of Pompey in Egypt and of Epaminondas at Mantinea, was initiated into the mysteries of Eleusis, and carved his name on Memnon's statue. At Athens, where he rebuilt on a lavish scale, he presided as archon at the festival of the Great Dionysia. He was phil-Hellene to the core – as a lad he had been nicknamed *Graeculus* (the little Greek) – cultivated the society of men of letters, and prided himself not a little on a knowledge of music and the plastic arts, and on his own efforts in prose and verse.[2] His taste, like that of Hellas in its decline, was far from pure; he loved the exotic and extravagant, preferred Antimachus to Homer, Ennius to Virgil, and designed temples – one, in honour of Venus and Rome, was on the site of Golgotha – in which, as mocking critics remarked, the goddesses could not stand erect. His favourite, Antinous, an Asiatic Greek, set the type of sen- suous male beauty for the sculptors of the day. The second century was an age of religious revivals, and the stranger and more alien the worship, the stronger was its fascination for the

1. Hadrian was a great hunter as well as a great walker; he had extra- ordinary powers of physical endurance, led habitually a simple life, and was a stern disciplinarian.

2. He was on friendly terms with the Stoic slave Epictetus, and the Greek historian of Marseilles, Favorinus.

Roman world. Hadrian, too, was fond of consulting dreams
and oracles, forecast his life for each successive year, deified
Antinous and named a star in his honour after his death. The
tales recorded in the Talmud of his talks with the rabbis,
though legendary, are significant of the impression he left on
the Jewish mind. His endeavour to abolish the rite of circumcision, and to plant a Graeco-Roman colony (*Aelia
Capitolina*) on the ruined site of the holy city, provoked the
Jews to their last and most terrible revolt (134–6). To the
Christians the emperor displayed a scornful tolerance. In all
this he was the type of second-century culture, with its cosmopolitanism, its archaism, its preciosity, and its decadence.
'*L'Orient surtout l'attirait,*' writes Renan; '*il en voyait les
impostures, le charlatanisme, et s'en amusait.*' But Hadrian was
no mere dilettante; he remained at heart a son of pagan
Rome. 'He was most assiduous,' says Spartianus, 'in the
observance of Roman worships and despised those of other
lands.' He had no illusions; his caprices never disturbed the
even tenor of his judgement. In his person, the ideal civil
servant had donned the imperial purple; to illustrate by modern
analogies, Hadrian had more affinity with Lord Milner or Sir
Robert Morant than with Oscar Wilde. Fame, we are told, he
sought ardently, but by other paths than these. He knew well
that it was the Britannic and the Germanic *limes*,[1] the cities
he built and the laws he made, that gave him his claim to
rank as one of the greatest administrators that ever lived. His
last recorded acts, as he lay dying in Rome, reflect his many-
sided personality; the jibe at the court physicians, 'too many
doctors are death to a prince'; the lines addressed to his
departing soul, which mirror in Latin the lingering beauty of
the last age of Hellenism;[2] and, what concerned him more

1. On the *limes*, see below, § 13, *note* 2.
2.   *Animula, vagula, blandula,*
                Hospes comesque corporis;
                Quae nunc abibis in loca?
                Pallidula, rigida, nudula,
                Nec ut soles dabis iocos.

Rendered by Marcus S. Dimsdale (*Latin Literature*, p. 526):
                'Soul of me, vague, debonair,
                Guest of this body and friend,

than all the rest, the designation in the person of Antoninus
Pius of a worthy successor to the imperial throne.

§ 11. Turning from the emperor to the empire, we find
that the government of the world in the second century lies
in the hands of a vast bureaucracy. The heads of its departments at Rome were originally members of the emperor's
household, and were still regarded as his personal assistants,
analogous to the secretaries and estate managers of a private
noble. The chief of these were the four *procurators*, viz. the
controller of finance, the legal adviser, the receiver of petitions, and the imperial secretary.[1] In conformity with the
historic maxim that the magistrate should fortify himself by
advice, important business was habitually debated in the
imperial council of state. The administration of Rome and
Italy was entrusted to four prefects, of the city, of the praetorian guard, of the corn supply, and of the watch, all of whom
also discharged high judicial functions.[2] In the imperial courts,
which had gradually effaced the senatorial, appeals were
heard from all quarters of the Roman world. Of the provinces,
which had increased in the second century to over thirty, the
imperial were twice as numerous as the senatorial.[3] Firm and

> Say whither now thou wilt fare,
> Pallid and rigid and bare,
> Little soul,
> All thy jests at an end?'

1. Styled respectively, *a rationibus, a cognitionibus, a libellis, ab epistulis*.
From Hadrian's time onwards these offices were filled no longer by freedmen,
but by citizens of equestrian rank.

2. Styled respectively, *urbi, praetorio, annonae, vigilum*. The praetorian
prefect presided, from Hadrian's time, over the council of state and the
supreme criminal tribunal.

3. On the matter of this section, see W. T. Arnold, *Roman Provincial
Administration*, esp. cc. iv, vi, vii; a list of provinces is given, with explanatory
notes, in *Appendix* I. The following is the list under Augustus:

Sicily (senatorial), Sardinia and Corsica, Gaul (4: one senatorial), Spain
(3: one senatorial), Africa (senatorial), Cyrene and Crete (senatorial),
Syria, Galatia, Bithynia (senatorial), Pontus (senatorial), Asia (senatorial),
Macedonia (senatorial), Achaia (senatorial), Moesia, Noricum, Rhaetia,
Illyricum, the Alpine districts. Egypt was administered on special lines, by
a prefect of equestrian rank.

The following were added after Augustus' death:

Germany (2; in A.D. 17); Mauretania (2), Britain and Thrace (these

effective control was maintained by the central government; the provincial governors were selected for their integrity and talents, paid by the state, and assisted by independent financial officers and a permanent staff of trained administrators.[1] Under the Flavian and Antonine emperors, knights increasingly replace freedom in the impartial service. Free-born Romans were no longer unwilling to hold posts in 'Caesar's household'. Substantial justice was obtainable in the imperial courts throughout the empire. Taxation, if burdensome, was levied on an equitable and uniform basis, furnished by the census-registers which were periodically brought up to date. The chief source of direct revenue was the land tax, supplemented by a tax in kind for the maintenance of the army in certain provinces, an income-tax on special professions and trades, a five-per-cent legacy duty levied on the wealthier classes, and the income from state domains, mines, and the emperor's private lands (*patrimonium Caesaris*). Of indirect taxes, the chief were the customs duties which varied in different provinces. We shall see in a subsequent chapter how the burden of taxation increased during the third century until it became well-nigh intolerable, with ruinous results on the economic prosperity of the empire. But, before that date, the government displayed a singular liberality in the employment of the revenue. Relief was readily granted in cases of plague, famine, and other extraordinary calamity;

between 40 and 46); Arabia, Dacia, Armenia, Mesopotamia and Assyria (these between 105 and 141, under Trajan).

From time to time provinces were redistributed between the emperor and the senate. The senatorial provinces disappear at the close of the second century.

In addition, certain areas were administered by procurators under the supervision of a neighbouring provincial governor; when the process of Romanization had advanced, these were frequently constituted as provinces. Judaea was under a procurator, supervised by the imperial legate of Syria (see Luke ii. 1). Vitellius, the future emperor, when legate of Syria, secured the deposition of the procurator Pontius Pilate.

1. The tenth book of the letters of the younger Pliny (*tr.* in vol. ii of the Loeb edition) consists of the despatches that passed between Pliny and the emperor Trajan during the former's governorship of Bithynia in 111. Bithynia had been constituted an imperial province by Trajan. The correspondence furnishes an admirable illustration of provincial administration under the early empire.

restrictions on trade were everywhere abolished; public works, such as harbours, roads, bridges, irrigation, and the reclamation of waste lands, were vigorously carried out in all quarters of the empire. Especially noteworthy is the policy, initiated by Nerva and extended by his second-century successors, of establishing, in Italy and elsewhere, institutions for the relief of widows and orphans, professorships and other educational endowments, and land banks for the encouragement of agriculture, the profits from which were devoted to the maintenance and education of poor children.

§ 12. The city, as of old, was the chief instrument of civilization utilized by the imperial government for the maintenance of Hellenic culture in the East and the implanting of Roman culture in the North and West.[1] Under the early empire, the towns of a province comprised (i) the allied and the free cities, owing their independence in the one case to formal treaty, in the other to gift from Rome; (ii) Roman colonies and *municipia*, which differed rather in dignity than in privileges; and (iii) the mass of tributary unprivileged towns, which preserved their old local institutions under the control of the provincial governor. These last were in course of time converted for the most part into *municipia*, by the bestowal of citizen or Latin rights. From the third century, the allied and the free cities diminished in number and were restricted in their privileges. Pliny gives a list of 175 towns in the Spanish province of Baetica towards the close of the first century; there are three allied and six free towns, nine colonies, eight *municipia*, twenty-nine towns with Latin rights, and 120 tributary. Municipal government was almost everywhere aristocratic and modelled on the historic form of Rome; colonies and *municipia* were controlled by annual magistrates elected by the popular assembly from citizens possessed of a high property qualification, and by a senate consisting mainly of magistrates and ex-magistrates. In process of time, there

1. At first, the Roman policy was to make every possible use of the existing machinery; e.g. they recognized tribal chieftains and councils as instruments of local government. When this system proved inadequate, they established city communities, recruited from Italy, among the native population. Where they found cities in being, as was the case in the East, they utilized them.

was a marked tendency in the direction of interference by imperial officials; popular election fell into disuse, and it became increasingly difficult to induce candidates to face the heavy expenses attendant on the tenure of municipal office. The early centuries of our era saw the rise of a vast number of cities, many of which long survived the fall of the empire, and flourish even at the present day. The military stations of the frontier legions furnished the nucleus of new towns, and we can trace the fort growing into a village, the village into a town. The names of Leon in Spain, Caerleon upon Usk in . Britain, preserve the record of such an origin (*legionis*, *castra legionis*). Each municipality administered a considerable tract of surrounding country; sometimes a large city would control a number of dependent townships, giving rise to a municipal hierarchy. So in Gaul under Augustus, Lugdunum (*Lyon*) was the administrative centre for sixty-four communities, each of which had its own chief town (Amiens and Nantes were two of these), while Marseilles and Nîmes had authority over other towns in the vicinity. The provincial towns also elected deputies to attend the provincial councils, whose meetings, associated with the worship of the emperor, played an important part in local administration and furnished the closest approximation in antiquity to the institution of representative government.

§ 13. The most pressing responsibility, throughout the first three centuries, was the guardianship of the frontiers. Augustus' counsel, to keep within the bounds he had set, was faithfully observed by his successors. The chief exceptions were the inclusion of Britain under Claudius (41–54), and of Dacia (=Hungary prior to 1914–8), Armenia, and the Euphrates-Tigris provinces under Trajan (98–117). Trajan's victorious campaigns in the East crowned the energetic policy of the first-century emperors; Parthia ceased to be formidable, and the Euphrates frontier remained undisturbed till the rise of the Persian kingdom in the middle of the third century. In the North and West, on the other hand, the tide of barbarian migration swelled in ever-growing volume. The Teutonic tribes, a menace to Italy since the days of Marius, who had been thrust back from Gaul by Caesar, and had foiled the effort of Augustus to extend Roman sovereignty to the Elbe, now fought unceasingly against the fortress-barrier along the Rhine and the Danube.[1] The line had been strengthened by the stockade built by Hadrian from above Coblenz to near Regensburg on the Danube, enclosing the Black Forest within the empire.[2] It held out for two centuries; but fighting was incessant all along the frontier, and any laxity in the Roman grip brought instant retribution. Dissensions within the empire and movements of the tribes beyond its pale provoked periodic crisis of exceptional severity, followed by intervals of comparative calm. Thus, after the terrible wars waged by Marcus Aurelius against the Marcomanni and the Quadi on the upper Danube, quiet prevailed for two generations, till the storm-centre shifted to the lower reaches of the river, where Goths from the Euxine threatened the Balkan provinces in the middle of the third century (250–70). Their defeat by Claudius secured the line of the Danube for another 100 years. Coincidently with the Gothic war, the Rhine barrier was broken by the Alemanni and the Franks (c. 258).[3] After a desperate struggle, that lasted, with varying fortunes, from the reign of Gallienus to that of Diocletian, peace was once more restored in the north-west. In the course of these conflicts, the practice, inaugurated by Caesar, of granting lands to Teuton settlers within the empire, became part of the general policy of the government. The enemies of one generation furnished recruits

1. The original home of the Teutons was in the west-Baltic lands, i.e. southern Sweden, Jutland, and Pomerania. Thence, between 600 and 200 B.C., they moved west and south-west, expelling the Celtic tribes from the lands east of the Rhine. At the same time they absorbed much of the superior Celtic culture with which they were in contact. In the second century B.C., Teutons first crossed the Rhine and invaded Gaul.

2. Within the palisade ran the *limes* or military road. At a later date the palisade was partially replaced by a stone wall. Forts were erected at intervals of from two and a half to nine miles along the *limes*. The great bulwark stretched for several hundred miles.

3. The Alemanni, as their name (= all men) implies, were a confederation of tribes, as also were the Franks (= free men). The name of the former survives in the French *Allemagne*, that of the latter in *France* (also *Franconia*, *Franche-Comté*, *Frankfurt*). The Alemanni were in contact with Rome from 213, the Franks from 253.

for the defending legions of the next. The Roman armies were enlisted for long service, and almost wholly from the population of the provinces. Soldiers from Commagene in Asia Minor would be quartered in Germany or Britain, and established, on their discharge, with a bounty and a plot of land, in the countries where they had served. Many famous towns, such as Cologne (*Colonia Agrippinensis*) and Colchester (*Camulodunum*) owed their origin to these settlements of time-expired veterans. The cosmopolitanism of the army was but one symptom of the cosmopolitanism of the imperial system. The civil service also was recruited from provincials. The old lines of cleavage between Roman and Italian, Italian and provincial, had ceased to exist. When in 212, by the *Constitutio Antonina*, the emperor Caracalla bestowed Roman citizenship on all free-born citizens of the empire, his immediate motive may have been to increase the revenue, but the act was the logical completion of the policy of the two preceding centuries.[1] Thanks to the paternal government of the empire, the ideas and institutions for which Rome stands in history had taken firm root throughout the Mediterranean world.

§ 14. The significance of this fact and its bearings on the future will be made clear if we illustrate the manner in which Rome discharged her mission of government in the provinces of western Europe, Spain, Gaul, and Britain.

(1) *Spain* was one of the earliest of the Roman provinces. Conquered and organized in the third century B.C. by the great Carthaginian, Hamilcar Barca, it passed at the close of the second Punic war to Rome. To master the tribes of the interior was a long and difficult task that taxed to the full the energies of successive Roman governors, among whom Cato the censor and Tiberius Sempronius Gracchus, the father of the agrarian reformer, were conspicuous for their ability.

---

1. The immediate motive of Caracalla's edict was to extend the range of application of the five-per-cent tax on citizens' inheritances. The grant of citizenship was limited to the actual free inhabitants of the empire in 212; freedmen, persons with Latin rights, and those settled on lands within the empire, who acquired their position at a subsequent date, did not *ipso facto* become citizens. Justinian extended the citizenship to include these.

Natural conditions aided the guerilla warfare in which Spaniards have always excelled, and the labours of war and organization continued uninterruptedly through the second century. Cato developed the mines, which the Phoenicians had worked many centuries before, and cultivated the vine and the olive. Between 80 and 72 B.C. the democratic leader, Sertorius, finding in Spain a refuge from the Sullan restoration, trained the native tribes in the arts of war and peace and founded military colleges for the education of their noble youth. The policy of Romanization was actively fostered by Julius and Augustus. Fifty Spanish towns received the full citizenship; Gades and Tarraco were the centres respectively of commerce and of government; Saragossa and Astorga still preserve Augustus' name.[1] The great military and commercial highway that led from Italy round the Gulf of Lions was continued beyond the Pyrenees along the eastern coast of Spain, whence it struck through the interior to the Guadalquivir and the port of Gades (Cadiz). By the time of Augustus' death, Roman language, dress and customs prevailed over a great part of the peninsula. Spain was divided into three provinces; of the three legions stationed there by Augustus two could be safely withdrawn by the close of the first century. Pacification and Romanization went hand in hand. Julius Caesar's secretary and Augustus' librarian were native Spaniards. Already in the first century Spain had given to Roman literature the moralist Seneca, the republican poet Lucan, the geographer Mela, the agricultural writer Columella, Rome's best epigrammatist, Martial, and the greatest of her literary critics, Quintilian.[2] Early in the following century she gave Rome one of the noblest emperors in the person of Trajan. When at length the barbarian invasions broke upon the West, they found Spain so thoroughly Romanized that the continuity of her culture was not seriously imperilled. The Christian faith was securely

1. In 1861 fragments of the laws of Malaca (Malaga) and Salpensa, and in 1870 fragments of those of Osuna, were discovered, throwing much light on municipal government in Spain under the early empire.

2. On Seneca and Quintilian, see below, §§ 21, 22. It has been remarked as illustrating the civilizing work of Rome that Roman soldiers and officials taught foreigners like Seneca and Quintilian to write real Latin.

rooted in a country that had possibly been a scene of St Paul's later missionary labours, and had since played a prominent part in the life of the western church. Thirty-seven separate churches were represented at the council of Elvira in the third century. Hosius, bishop of Cordova, was the chosen counsellor of Constantine at the council of Nicaea. The Visigoths, unlike the Vandals, had taken kindly to Roman culture before they established their power in Spain. Isidore of Seville was one of the few scholars in the degenerate days of the seventh century who was able to pass on fragments of ancient learning and legal lore to the thinkers of the early middle age. Even the Saracen conquest of the eighth century did not avail to efface all traces of the past; Gothic chieftains kept the light of Roman and Christian tradition still flickering in the mountain fastnesses, and the stream of Roman influence can be traced unbroken from the days of Scipio to the rise of the modern kingdoms of Portugal and Spain.[1]

§ 15. (II) 'All *Gaul* is divided into three parts'; so run, as every schoolboy knows, the opening words of Caesar's *Commentaries*. Augustus, in apportioning the land into provinces, reorganized the three regions as *Belgica* (N.E.), *Lugdunensis* (N.W. and C.), *Aquitania* (W. and S.W.), names which survive as Belgium, Lyon, and Aquitaine. In the south along the Mediterranean coast lay the older province of Narbonese Gaul, through which ran the great road from Rome to Spain. Its centre in republican times was the ancient Greek colony of Massilia (Marseilles), an allied city of Rome, governed by an oligarchical constitution which excited the admiration of Cicero. After its fall before Caesar's army in the civil war,[2] it was outstripped by newer foundations such as Forum Julii (Fréjus, the station of the fleet, as is Toulon to-day) and Arelate (Arles) at the Rhone mouth, the great port for inland trade. This southern province, the 'Provence' of after times, was naturally Romanized long before the newly conquered interior;

1. In Africa the Saracens obliterated all traces of Roman influence. The Saracen emirs of Cordova, on the other hand, were enlightened rulers, who preserved many relics of the past.

2. Dante, *Purg.*, xviii. 102. 'Caesar, to subdue Ilerda, stabbed Marseilles and then raced to Spain.'

and the difference persisted at a later day, in the field of language, as that between the *Langue d'Oc* of Provence and the *Langue d'Oil* of the rest of France. The three new Augustan provinces were organized in tribal cantons under Celtic magistrates with a native militia. The chief seat of government and commerce was Lugdunum (Lyon), a colony founded in 43 and peopled by Roman citizens, at the point where the road up the Rhone valley diverged into branches leading to the various camps on the German frontier. There met the council of the Gallic provinces, which co-operated with the Roman government in taxation and in gathering the Celtic tribes around the worship of Rome and Augustus.[1] Urban life developed rapidly in the cantons; among the earliest towns to rise into importance were Rheims and Trier in the province of Belgica, the latter of which became the capital of Gaul and of the West at the opening of the third century. The east of Gaul was Romanized more quickly than the west. As urban communities arose, Roman rights were extended; Caesar had admitted Gauls into the senate, and a speech of Claudius has come down to us in which he granted the right of holding office to enfranchised Gauls.[2] 'Every community', wrote Caesar of this people, 'is split into two parties', and the Roman authorities made full use of these divisions to secure their rule against revolt. The Druidic religion was suppressed by law; it offered no long resistance, and had almost vanished when Christianity spread over the northern provinces. The country was rich in material resources; 'in Gaul', wrote Josephus, 'the sources of wealth have their home and flood the earth with their abundance'. Agriculture was the basis of its prosperity; while in the north-east sheep-breeding gave birth to the cloth industry which early brought to Arras and Tournai a foretaste of their mediaeval and modern fame. The Celts were great huntsmen and supplied large contingents to

1. The population of Gaul was not exclusively Celtic, but included Iberian and Germanic tribes. The Roman government settled conquered Germans on Gallic soil.

2. Tacitus, *Annals*, xi, cc. 23–5, summarizes the speech. Early in the sixteenth century portions of it were found at Lyon. See Arnold, pp. 145 ff. for details.

the cavalry of the Roman armies. They possessed a rare aptitude for learning; Autun (Augustodunum) and Bordeaux (Burdigala) were seats of famous universities and schools; the ready wit and gifts of speech of the Celts made them renowned as early as the first century for oratory and teaching.[1] Plastic art, especially of scenes from daily life, foreshadowing the reliefs that adorn the Gothic cathedrals of mediaeval France, developed round Trier; and in the fourth century Ausonius of Bordeaux, one of the most graceful of later Latin poets, sang in hexameter verse the praises of the charming scenery of the Moselle. The churches of Gaul, from the second century onwards, furnished many of the leaders of western Christendom. Bishops from Britain travelled to Arles to attend its councils. In a word, by the time that the Visigoths, Burgundians, and Franks poured over her plains and river-valleys, Gaul was fairly equipped for the task of Romanizing and Christianizing her conquerors. Later still, in the ninth century, her schools were the chosen home of mediaeval learning.[2]

§ 16. (III) *Britain* lay on the remote outskirts of the Roman world; its occupation under Claudius constituted the only permanent exception to the principle that the empire should not spread beyond the limits determined by Augustus. It was governed as part of the empire for almost four hundred years. Three legions (more than 15,000 soldiers), recruited largely from the Romanized natives, were continuously stationed in the island. The influence of Roman civilization was restricted, save for a brief interval, to the regions south of the wall that Severus built from Wallsend, east of Newcastle, to Carlisle, of which much is still standing.[3] Within this area Cornwall

1. The school at Autun for the noble youth of Gaul was already in existence under Tiberius.

2. It must be remembered that between the Gallic provinces and the frontier stretched the two German provinces (Upper and Lower), consisting of a narrow strip of country guarded by military outposts, with the great camps of the Rhine legions. Upper Germany was the broader of the two, since it comprised a large tract of debatable waste land, including the Black Forest. It was enclosed by Vespasian and settled with *coloni Caesaris*, cultivators tied to the soil. Roman culture spread here among the Germanic tribes to a greater extent than in Lower Germany above Coblenz.

3. Hadrian had already made a road (the *limes*) along this line. A ditch, earthwork, and road were erected farther north, from the Firth of Forth to

alone remained wholly untouched by Rome. In the north there were extensive military settlements massed chiefly along the wall, and in the town of York. But it was in the south, especially in Gloucestershire, the east of Somerset, Hampshire, and Northamptonshire, that there was, as is shown by the numerous remains of isolated Roman houses, a considerable population of Romanized civilians, and it was here mainly that Rome set her mark on the Celtic population. As in all parts of the empire, the rule of Rome meant colonies and military roads. Colchester, Lincoln, York, and Gloucester were Roman colonies; Verulamium (St Albans) enjoyed the dignity of a *municipium*. York was the scene of the coronation of the emperor Constantine and of the burial of the emperor Severus. Of the great roads, Watling Street ran north-west from London to Wroxeter; Ermine Street from Colchester by Huntingdon and Lincoln to York; the road from London by Staines forked at Silchester into branches towards Southampton, Salisbury and the south-west, and Gloucester; the Fosse Way ran diagonally from Lincoln by Leicester to Cirencester and Bath. Forest land was cleared for agriculture; Britain supplied corn to the Rhine legions; British builders were known over western Europe, British cloth was exported, Kentish oysters were in great request at Rome, and the south-eastern ports became thriving centres of trade. The influence of Rome was not always beneficial; on articles of common use, e.g. pots, fashions of stereotyped ornament destroyed the native Celtic freedom of design. The Roman language spread first among Celtic nobles, then among the main body of the native population in the south and east; Roman law and methods of government were potent instruments of civilization. Plutarch tells of his conversation with a Greek teacher returning from Britain to his home on the shores of the Levant. With the extension of Christianity, Britain came within the pale of the Church—the foundations of a Christian church have been disclosed at Silchester; and the new faith spread to Wales and beyond the bounds of the empire to Ireland. At the beginning of the fifth century, pressure on

the Firth of Clyde, by Antoninus Pius, and completed at the end of the second century by Severus.

the continental frontier of the empire led to the abandonment of Britain by the imperial government.[1] Upon the collapse of Roman rule the Celtic element in the province reasserted itself. Arthur, a Celtic leader who bore a Roman name, is the half-historical, half-legendary, impersonation of the Celtic resistance to the Saxons. With the Saxon occupation, most of the traces of Rome's influence perished: Anglo-Saxon law owed nothing of its contents to that of Rome; Christianity gave way to heathenism, save in Ireland and the unconquered fastnesses of Wales; and the Roman towns were laid waste by the invaders. So far as traces of the old provincial life survived in Saxon Britain, they were Celtic and not specifically Roman.[2] In London, the greatest of Roman towns, there is not a single existing street that can be proved to run along a Roman line.[3] A remnant of the Celtic population under Saxon masters can indeed be traced in Kent and Wessex; the clearings of cornland and the great roads preserved the record of Roman policy; and among the rich variety of designs which appear on the earliest Old English coins many can be traced back to Roman origins. More than thirty towns and villages still bear names derived from those (whether Celtic or Latin) in use during the Roman occupation.[4] But with these few exceptions Rome left no enduring mark on the life-history of Britain.[5]

III. LAW AND LITERATURE

A. Law

§ 17. The period from Augustus to Diocletian was the golden age of Roman jurisprudence, which was enriched and perfected

1. When the British appealed for protection to the emperor Honorius, he bade their cities defend themselves as best they could.
2. All over England the river names, which are *at latest* Celtic, were handed on unchanged to the Saxon conquerors.
3. E.g. the foundations of Roman buildings lie across the line of Cheapside. Many Roman roads come within a short distance of the city; e.g. Clapham High Street (Stane Street), Mile End Road (the London–Colchester road), Kingsland Road (Ermine Street), Oxford Street (the road to Silchester, with Watling Street branching off northwards at the Marble Arch).
4. E.g. Lichfield (*Lētocētum*), Manchester (*prob.* Mammium), Richborough (*Rutupiae*, *Repata Caestir*), Winchester (*Venta*) and the village of Mancetter in Warwickshire.
5. On Roman Britain, see Tacitus' life of his father-in-law Agricola, who

at the hands of illustrous jurists acting as the ministers of the sovereign *princeps*. The old civil law was shorn of formal excrescences and effete survivals; the *patria potestas*, for example, lost much of its traditional rigidity. The extension by Caracalla of Roman citizenship to all free provincials paved the way for the incorporation of the law of nations (*jus gentium*) into the civil law (*jus civile*) of Rome. The chief features of legal history in the three centuries under review were (i) the completion of praetorian law by the Perpetual Edict, (ii) the rise of imperial legislation, (iii) the development of a scientific jurisprudence.

(i) Praetorian activity in the field of law-making was at its height in the last century of the republic. Under the early emperors it became the practice for praetors to adopt the edict of their predecessors with scarcely any modification. This practice was recognized by Hadrian when he entrusted an eminent lawyer, Salvius Julianus, with the task of revising the edicts of the urban and peregrine praetors, and of issuing the codified result as a permanently binding edict (*edictum perpetuum*). Henceforward no additions or alterations could be introduced. The like was done also for the magisterial edicts in the provinces. The edict of Julianus thus completed and closed the body of praetorian equity, and thereby marked the final assertion of imperial sovereignty over the republican magistracy in the domain of law.

(ii) The legislative authority under the republic was the assembly (*comitia*) of the Roman people. Augustus still referred important measures, dealing with moral reforms, manumission of slaves, the status of freedmen, and judicial procedure, to the assembly for formal approval, but from Tiberius' reign onwards its legislative functions passed to the senate. Among the members of this body were many eminent lawyers, and its decrees (*senatus consulta*) play a large part in the legal development of the first two centuries. The emperors, while exercising an increasing control over the deliberations of the senate, hesitated as yet to legislate purely by their own

commanded in Britain under Titus and Domitian. In this section I have been specially indebted to the help of my former colleague, Professor F. N. Stenton.

authority. But already prior to the third century the imperial 'constitutions' obtained the force of law, and after that date became the sole instrument of legislation. They comprised (*a*) *edicts* or public ordinances, interpreting the law, which the emperor, by virtue of his *imperium*, posted up as the praetors had done in time past, (*b*) *rescripts* or written judgements on petitions addressed to him by private persons and by magistrates, (*c*) *decrees*, or rulings on judicial appeals, and (*d*) *mandates*, i.e. instructions, mostly of an administrative character, despatched to the governors of provinces.[1] A word must be added on the machinery of criminal law, which had been first effectively organized in the last age of the republic, when Sulla extended the system of standing commissions (*quaestiones perpetuae*) with praetorian presidents and equestrian *judices*. These disappear at the close of the second century, as does also the criminal jurisdiction of the senate, conferred upon that body by Augustus. Here, again, the emperor, acting through his delegates, especially the praetorian prefect, absorbed all judicial authority; so that both in civil and criminal causes his tribunal became the supreme court of appeal for the Roman world.

(iii) Roman law had been fashioned, not on a preconceived system, but inductively, on the basis of practical experience; and consisted of a huge aggregate of rules and practices, resting on ancient custom, or designed to meet particular requirements. Its principles were implicit in its structure rather than explicitly formulated. The first jurist who endeavoured to disengage these principles, and to arrange the vast body of private law in accordance with the nature of its contents, was Quintus Mucius Scaevola the younger, *pontifex maximus* about 100 B.C. Scaevola may fairly claim to be regarded as the founder of Roman jurisprudence. From his time onwards the scientific study of the law made rapid progress. Augustus granted official

---

1. Theoretically, the *edicts* lost their validity on the death of the *princeps*, though they were often renewed by his successor. *Rescripts* were binding instructions to the judge on the special matter of the case at issue, whereas *edicts* were rules of general import. *Mandates*, when concerned with points of law, had the force of *rescripts*; in many cases they dealt with matter of temporary policy. Strictly, they do not come under the head of *constitutions*.

recognition to the work of the jurists, by ordaining that certain of them, selected for their eminence, should possess the right of giving opinions with imperial authority (*jus respondendi ex auctoritate principis*). Their written answers to questions of law submitted to them, delivered to the court under seal, were henceforth binding on the magistrates and on the private citizens, often unlearned in the law, who served as *judices*. From Augustus' reign onwards the schools of jurisprudence, organized as corporate societies, wielded increasing influence on the development of jurisprudence.[1] They not only moulded the law into a system but leavened it with speculative ideas of an order undreamed of in republican times. The first-fruits of their labours were seen in the above-mentioned edict of Julianus and in systematic treatises composed by lawyers of the age of Hadrian and the Antonines, such as Celsus, Caecilius Africanus, and Gaius. These were followed between 170 and 230 by Quintus Cervidius Scaevola and his pupil Papinian, the greatest of all the Roman jurists. Both were of Hellenic race; it was characteristic of this age of cosmopolitanism that the mind of Greece impressed its stamp on Roman law. Under Severus Alexander (222–35) flourished Ulpian and Paul, the former of whom, a Tyrian by descent, furnished material for one-half of Justinian's *Digest*.[2] The line of great jurists closes in the middle of the third century with Ulpian's pupil, the Greek Herennius Modestinus. Not long afterwards imperial rescripts take the place of the *responsa prudentium*, and, in interpretation as in legislation, the emperor remains the sole fount of law.

§ 18. These great masters of jurisprudence infused a new spirit into the law of Rome. Their intellectual energy is manifest in the effort to trace the underlying intention of dealings between parties, and to formulate it as a regulative principle

1. In the first and early second century there were two great schools at Rome, founded respectively by Labeo and Atteius Capito, Augustan jurists, and called, after followers of the two founders, the Proculian and Sabinian schools. See Sohm, *Institutes of Roman Law*, § 15.

2. Scaevola was a member of Marcus Aurelius' council of state; Papinian was praetorian prefect under Severus, his old fellow-pupil, and was killed by order of Caracalla (212). Ulpian and Paul held the praetorian prefecture under Severus Alexander, an emperor of Hellenic race.

for all cases that might conceivably arise. In their treatment of the law of obligations, for example, they devoted much thought to contracts where the *bona fides* or unexpressed intention had to be taken into account. 'The law of obligations,' says a modern authority, 'and it alone, constitutes what is, in the truest and strictest sense, the imperishable portion of Roman law. It cannot be abolished. The intention of the purchaser and hirer, etc., is the same in all ages, and it is this intention that Roman law has made clear. . . . It is this wonderful discrimination, this clear-sightedness in the adjustment of conflicting principles, guided by a never-failing power of discerning the common elements; this unique faculty for giving outward expression to the law inherent in the concrete circumstances, which law, when found, supplies the rule – with many practical variations, of course – for all other circumstances of the same kind; these are the features to which the writings of the Roman jurists owe their incomparable charm, and the work they achieved its indestructible force.'[1] At the same time these thinkers inspired Roman jurisprudence with ideas derived from Greek philosophy, which were destined, in this new medium, to influence the ethical and juristic thought of later times. The most striking instance is the concept of law of nature (*jus naturale* or *naturae*). Its source lay in Stoicism, the one Hellenic system which evoked a wide response from the practical Roman mind, and still, in the second century, the foremost philosophical school of Greece. Ulpian was mainly responsible for incorporating this concept in the structure of Roman jurisprudence. It comprised the universal rules of conduct which flow from the nature of man as a rational being, irrespective of race or time; such as those enjoining recognition of the tie of kindred, respect for engagements, equitable apportionment of gain or loss, supremacy of the intention over the words in which it found imperfect expression. Thus a slave has, under the law of nature, rights denied to him by the civil law and the *jus gentium*. We shall return to this concept of *jus naturae* in a later chapter.[2]

1. Sohm, § 15, pp. 73–4.
2. See c. xi, §§ 15 ff. The dividing line between law of nature (*jus naturae*) and law of nations (*jus gentium*) was hard to draw. Ulpian solved the problem

It had a long and memorable history, and furnished a governing principle for the moral and political thought of western Europe through more than fifteen hundred years.

B. Literature

§ 19. The literature of the epoch stands in close relation to the changing public life of the Roman state.

(i) The last generation of the republic produced two great poets: Lucretius, who expressed in hexameter verse the philosophic doctrines of Epicurus, and Catullus, whose lyrics rival those of Burns or Heine, while his range and personality recall Byron.[1] Among prose writers two names stand pre-eminent. Caesar's genius in literature was second only to his genius in war and statesmanship. His speeches and letters were famous as masterpieces of style; his record of the Gallic war is incomparable as a great historical narrative, and the very self-suppression of the author conveys a unique impression of his magnificent achievement.[2] But the truest representative of the age was the orator and republican statesman Cicero, whose prose writings – speeches, letters, treatises on oratory and philosophy – were recognised as the supreme models of the

by defining the former as common to all animate beings, while the latter was common to all mankind. No other jurist of the epoch took this view, though it appears in Justinian's *Digest* and in mediaeval writings. Gaius, a pure Roman and of earlier date than the great Greek and Graeco-Oriental jurists, alone identifies *jus naturae* and *jus gentium*, defining the latter as 'the law which natural reason appoints for all mankind'. Justinian followed him in this. The case of the slave, referred to in the text, points the difference. War and slavery are both contrary to law of nature, under which all men are born free; they, and contracts, arise out of *jus gentium*: cf. *Institutes*, lib. i. Tit. iii. 2. *Servitus autem est constitutio juris gentium, qua quis domino alieno contra naturam subiicitur* ('Slavery is an institution of the law of nations, by which a man is made subject to a foreign lord contrary to nature'). *Jus gentium* included *jus inter gentes*, the nearest approach reached by antiquity to 'international' law. See *Encyc. Brit.*, 11th ed., art. *Roman Law*, pp. 561, 562.

1. On Lucretius' Epicureanism, see above, c. vi, § 18. He was little appreciated in antiquity, save by Virgil, whose thought and verse alike reveal his influence. Quintilian couples him with a third-rate Augustan poet, and writes him off as elegant in his own line but difficult to comprehend (*Inst. Orat.*, x, c. 1, § 87). It was left to the nineteenth century to recognize his poetic genius.

2. In Quintilian's judgement, had he possessed the leisure, Caesar's oratory would have equalled that of Cicero; it was marked by the energy, directness and fire that he showed in the conduct of war (*Inst. Orat.*, x. 1, § 114).

Latin language in his own and all after-time. Classical Latin means Latin as Cicero wrote it. Cicero used it to embody two great orders of ideas – the greatness of Rome and the ideal of humane culture. As to the one, we may quote the words of Newman: 'Cicero vividly realized the status of a Roman senator and statesman, and the "pride of place" of Rome, in all the grace and grandeur which attached to her; and he imbibed, and became, what he admired. As the exploits of Scipio or Pompey are the expression of this greatness in deed, so the language of Cicero is the expression of it in word. And, as the acts of the Roman ruler or soldier represent to us, in a manner special to themselves, the characteristic magnanimity of the lords of the earth, so do the speeches or treatises of her accomplished orator bring it home to our imagination as no other writing could do. Neither Livy, nor Tacitus, nor Terence, nor Seneca, nor Pliny, nor Quintilian, is an adequate spokesman for the Eternal City. They write Latin, Cicero writes Roman.'[1] Oratory had been from the first the art most respected and practised by the Romans; from Cicero's day onwards, it became the central subject of literature and of education. Poetry, history, philosophy, even science, were valued as instruments of rhetoric; to be an orator was the ambition of the able youth of Italy and the provinces, and all their studies, at school and at the universitiy, were organized as a discipline to this end. Cicero's influence, thus immediately operative on his own and the succeeding generations, continued uninterruptedly through mediaeval into modern times. While Cicero the republican was destined to inspire the French Revolution, Cicero the humanist deeply influenced the culture of the Renaissance. The matter of his philosophic writings may be lacking in originality and speculative power; but Cicero's fame as the greatest man of letters that ever lived rests rather on the union in his person of the thinker and the man of affairs, and, above all, on the fact that he embodied

1. *Idea of a University* (Lecture on *Literature*), pp. 281, 282. The last words mean, of course, not that Cicero's style was that of the typical Roman, but that it reflects supremely the pride and majesty of the imperial state. Some contemporaries accused him of being 'unduly turgid and Asiatic and redundant' (the *Orator* of Cicero, ed. Sandys, Introduction, p. lx).

and expressed the urbanity and humanism which mark the Graeco-Roman age of civilization. Thanks to the preservation of his letters, we know him better than any other historic figure of antiquity.

§ 20. (ii) As the war with Carthage furnished a theme to Ennius, and the conquest of Gaul to Caesar, so the consolidation of the civilized world under Augustus was the central fountain of inspiration to the writers of the Augustan age. Prolific in almost every field both of poetry and prose, it was, as the name suggests, an age of direct literary patronage on the part of the emperor and his ministers of state. We still speak, somewhat superficially, of periods such as those of Louis XIV or Anne as 'Augustan' ages in French and English literature. The favour of Augustus was free and generous, and doubtless served as a stimulus to men of letters to celebrate the empire and its ruler. But the chief source of inspiration was the empire itself – the golden age of law and peace, that seemed to embrace all civilized mankind, and to have closed for ever the disorder and tumult of the civil wars. Filled with a sense of this achievement, Livy compiled the history of Rome from its legendary beginnings to the crowning of the structure by Augustus; even the ex-republican Horace turned from the placid delights of his Sabine farm to glorify the work of the emperor and the duty of patriotism in a noble group of odes.[1] But the poem which stands for ever as the supreme embodiment of the splendour and majesty of Rome is the *Aeneid* of Virgil. Almost every line is inspired by a sense of the divine destiny of the imperial city, *nunc maxima rerum*, 'now sovereign of the world'. It was by decree of fate that Aeneas was driven a wanderer over land and sea after the fall of Troy, till the providence of heaven established him on Latin soil as the forefather of the founders of Rome.[2] Piety – filial loyalty to the gods – was the motive of all his actions; of his desertion of Dido, the foundress of Carthage,

1. The *Odes* referred to are Book III, *Odes* 1–6; *Odes* I, 12, 21, 35, 37; III, 14; IV, 2, 4–5, 14, 15, and the *Carmen Seculare*, bear on the same theme The reader unversed in the classics is advised not to burden himself with reading Livy, even in a translation. He is inferior as a historian both to the Greeks, and to Caesar and Tacitus among the Romans.

2. *Aen.*, i. 32 (*acti fatis*); cf. i. 208–10.

Rome's historic enemy; of his journey to the underworld,
where he beheld the forms of the great Romans that were to
be; of his alliance with a Latin prince, and his foundation of a
Latin city.[1] From first to last we are conscious of the poet's
purpose, to tell how great was the labour to found the race of
Rome.[2]

§ 21. The literature of the post-Augustan age is very different in tone. It was but for a moment that the stream of creative
imagination could find satisfaction in the fact of empire. It
could not permanently coalesce with what was after all a
military despotism. We see signs of the change already in Ovid,
the last poet of the Augustan era. A careless and irresponsible
man of pleasure, a lover of society and the gay world of the
capital, he possessed a marvellous skill in versification and
poetic craftsmanship, and, what is more significant, in
romantic narration. Ovid was not a poet of the highest rank,
but one of the best second-rate poets in literature.[3] He
deserves special mention in this place, because his best work,
the *Metamorphôses*, where the figures of Greek mythology are
reflected through a strange romantic atmosphere, exercised a
deep influence both on the Middle Ages and on the Renaissance.
Dante drew on it for his knowledge of Greek legend, and it
was the favourite classic of the great humanist, Montaigne.
Still more extensive is the debt of later ages to Seneca of Cordova, Nero's chief minister and victim, and the foremost
man of letters in his day. Seneca wrote voluminously, and in
the flamboyant style; his work on physics, though destitute of
scientific value, was received as authoritative by the Middle
Ages, and his tragedies, full of wearisome rhodomontade, were

1. *Aen.*, xii. 838–9. The pride of the Romans is as distinctive as their
piety (*Aen.*, vi. 781, 823). Virgil realized that the Roman temper was pacific
rather than militarist (*Aen.*, i. 286, *Romanos rerum dominos gentemque togatam*,
' the Romans, lords of the world, the race clad in the gown of peace').
2. *Aen.*, i. 37; cf. i. 1–300; vi. 679–end; vii. 1–285; viii. 608–end;
xii. 791–842; passages embodying the idea of imperial Rome. Virgil had been
moved to write his (earlier) *Georgics* primarily by his love of country life,
but also because of Augustus' express desire to commend the care of agriculture to the Roman aristocracy.
3. He was 'a poet utterly in love with poetry', to quote Professor Gilbert
Murray's appreciation of Ovid in his *Essays and Addresses*.

ranked by Ben Jonson with those of the Attic dramatists.[1] The ethical treatises, on the other hand, are more deserving, both in style and contents, of their former great reputation. They developed the tenets of Stoicism in an elegant and attractive form, and were marked by sincerity of conviction, insight into human nature, and a clear grasp of philosophical principles. To the humanists of the sixteenth century, and even to Descartes in the seventeenth, they appeared to be the last word in ethics. This is only one of many instances of the disproportionate value that attached, in the Middle Ages and in the Renaissance, to the post-Augustan writers who transmitted the noble inheritance of classical antiquity. In fact, Seneca was neither a great statesman nor a great thinker; his importance as a middleman of culture far outweighed his real merits.[2] In his sympathy for human weakness and sorrow, he struck a note which was alien to the traditions of orthodox Stoicism, and heralded the benevolent projects of the emperors of the second century. It was the presence of this new spirit in Seneca's writings that gave rise to the Christian legend of his personal friendship with St Paul. Nor must we ignore the part he played in the process by which the diction of classical Latin changed into that of the Middle Ages.[3] An analogous significance attaches to two others

1. Mackail, *Lat. Lit.* In the lines prefixed by Ben Jonson to the first folio Shakespeare, we read:
> 'And though thou hadst small Latin and less Greek,
> From thence to honour thee I would not seek
> For names; but call forth thund'ring Aeschylus,
> Euripides, and Sophocles to us,
> Pacuvius, Attius, *him of Cordova dead*,
> To life again, to hear thy buskin tread
> And shake a stage.'

2. Quintilian, who appreciated his merits, while deprecating the baneful effects of his faults on contemporary taste, concludes his *critique* with the words: 'He achieved the goal he set before him; yet his nature fitted him for higher aims' (*Inst. Orat.*, x. 1, § 131).

3. Seneca's dramas are stiff and pompous, but in his Dialogues and Letters he is really important as exhibiting Latin at a stage when it is acquiring the flexibility of the modern Romance languages. He shows a new freedom in using infinitives and adjectives as nouns, and in the enlarged use of prepositions which can carry in a concise way as much meaning as in French. He was an innovator in inventing words, or at any rate in introducing many of them to respectable writing. Such, for instance, are the Latin originals of the words 'inspector', 'favourable', 'vulnerable', and 'temporary'. How far the speech

of his contemporaries, both of whom shared his fate at Nero's
hands; Lucan, Seneca's nephew, who sang the civil wars in
epic verse and with republican sympathies; and Petronius
Arbiter, whose novel, descriptive of the adventures of a Greek
freedman in Italy, has preserved not only a brilliant picture of
social manners but the sole remnants of popular speech under
the early empire. [1]

§ 22. The period from Vespasian to Hadrian is known as the
silver age of Latin literature. Among a host of writers, three
stand in relief because of their hold on after-times, Statius and
Quintilian, who flourished under Domitian, and Tacitus, under
Nerva and Trajan. Statius is familiar to all readers of the *Divina
Commedia* as the poet whose spirit joined the pilgrims in Purgatory and, after Virgil's departure, mounted with Dante and
Beatrice into Paradise. He won this tribute partly as an epic
poet who followed, though at a far distance, in Virgil's foot-
steps, but chiefly for the strange legend that recorded his conversion to the Christian faith. Quintilian's writings were of
greater intrinsic merit and wielded an even more extensive
influence. Like Seneca of Spanish birth, he practised in Rome
as a teacher and an advocate, and sharing to the full the Roman
enthusiasm for oratory, published in 93 his chief work, the
Institutio Oratoria. Its rediscovery in the sixteenth century

of common or cultivated persons differed from the style of Latin imposed on
the world by the pre-eminence of Cicero it is difficult to estimate; but it is
clear that Seneca introduced many useful words hitherto regarded as colloquial
into good prose. The gain he shows in flexibility of language is remarkable, and,
though too anxious to make points, he writes at his best with a freedom and
naturalness which are quite modern. Quite modern, too, is his mastery of the
short sentence, his betrayal of his own little weaknesses, his confidential air
that the reader is interested in trifles concerning himself. The neglect of his
writings dates from the nineteenth century and is undeserved. Montaigne, the
father of the modern essay, learnt much from him. (For this note I am indebted to the kindness of Mr Vernon Rendall.)

1. The novel had come to stay. It originated among the Greeks of the
Hellenistic period, but the Roman *satura* contributed a new element. In the
middle of the second century, the chief Latin writer of prose romances was
Apuleius; the best-known of his works is the tale of *Cupid and Psyché* in
Books IV–VI of the *Metamorphóses* (or *the Golden Ass*). The tale has been trans-
lated by Walter Pater in *Marius the Epicurean*, in the Loeb translation of
Apuleius, in Andrew Lang's edition of Adlington's version, and by Robert
Graves in *Penguin Classics*. See Mackail, *Lat. Lit.*

marked an epoch in the history of humanism. In its twelve
books, along with much other matter relevant to the study of
rhetoric, were comprised a review of the entire field of Greek and
Latin literature, unequalled in antiquity for breadth of view and
appreciative judgement, and two discussions on the education of
young children and of those of riper years. It was these last
that specially stirred the minds of sixteenth-century scholars,
who devoted earnest thought to projects of educational reform. Treatises on education in all times have for the most
part borne the mark of mediocrity; but Quintilian's is an
honourable exception. In a style dignified, polished, and free
alike from verbosity and affectation, he sketched the training
proper to a Roman of the empire on principles that hold good
for every age.[1] Moreover, following closely the example of
Cicero, Quintilian fixed, for good or for evil, the conception
of rhetoric that loomed so large in later Roman and mediaeval

---

1. Quintilian has been translated in the Loeb series by Butler. The review of
classical literature is in Book X, c. 1, the treatment of education in Books I
and XII. Quintilian held that the moral vices of the age were due to defective
training, and insisted, among much else, on the value of literature in education,
on the necessity of studying in youth the best authors, on the harm done by
cramming and inferior text-books, on the need of the best teachers for begin-
ners, the injuriousness of corporal punishment and the value of eurhythmics
and physical exercises. On education under the early empire, see Hatch,
Hibbert Lectures (1888) on *The influence of Greek ideas and usages upon the Christian
Church*, lect. ii. There were grammar schools in the towns, and universities in
the chief cities throughout the Roman world. Professors were highly paid, by
state endowments and by grant of immunity from municipal burdens, a privilege of increasing value. University teachers were licensed, and selected either
by the Emperor (compare our Regius Professors), or by local councils, or by
special boards of electors; academic dress was worn by teachers and students;
the terms 'professor', 'faculty', date from this period. In fact, the Roman
system forms a stage in the development of the university, transitional between
the Platonic Academy and its Greek successors, on the one hand, and the
mediaeval (and modern) universities, on the other. The main branches of
education under the empire were (a) *Grammar*, i.e. the study of diction and
belles lettres, (b) *Rhetoric*, i.e. the study and practice of literary expression and
argument, including original composition, and also logic, which led on to (c)
Philosophy. Dio Chrysostom tells how he found, in a Greek colony north of the
Euxine, that nearly every resident knew the *Iliad* by heart. Public lecturing had
an enormous vogue, contributing (as also did state patronage) to the decline of
intellectual life by fostering a thirst for popular display in the lecturers and a
superficial curiosity in their audiences. That there was also a genuine desire
for knowledge is illustrated by Eunapius' tale of two college students, who
could afford only one gown between them, so that the one had to stay in bed
while the other attended lectures.

education. The third name that calls for mention, not so much for his unquestioned greatness as a writer, as for his influence on the judgement of posterity, is that of Tacitus. Amid the equable and halcyon atmosphere of the reign of Trajan, 'a time when men may think what they will, and say what they think', he looked back upon the days when Roman society trembled beneath the sinister suspicions of Tiberius and the wild caprice of Nero, and when the Roman world, on Nero's death, was devastated by the contending armies of the claimants to the throne. In the *Annals* and the *Histories* he stamped the rulers of the first century with the indelible brand of his irony and indignation. Tacitus, if not the greatest of Roman historians, was the greatest Roman writer of history; by the power of his style, his mastery of epigram and innuendo, and his subtlety in the analysis of motive, he determined for fifteen centuries the verdict of the civilized world upon the early empire. It is one of the triumphs of modern historical research to have reversed, or at least to have profoundly modified, that judgement. Neither Tacitus, nor the satires of Juvenal, his contemporary, suffice any longer to guide our estimate of imperial Rome; but their terrible indictment of the degradation of Roman life and morals, and their sense of bitter disillusionment, stand in dramatic contrast to the hopes with which, a century earlier, Virgil had hailed in the founder of the empire the herald of a golden age.

§ 23. Between Tacitus and Augustine there is no first-rank figure in Latin literature. A considerable body of writings have come down to us from the three intervening centuries, largely by Christian authors and of varying interest; the philologist, for example, can trace the change, referred to above, from classical towards mediaeval Latin. The beautiful *Pervigilium Veneris*, in its use of the stanza and the refrain, heralds the Provençal poetry of the early Middle Ages.[1] At the beginning of the fifth century, Jerome, in his cell in Palestine, composed the Vulgate, or Latin version of the Scriptures, which influenced the future language almost as deeply as Luther's translation influenced the German, or the Authorized Version of 1611

1. See Mackail, pp. 243–6. The authorship of the poem is unknown, and its date uncertain, though it indisputably belongs to this intervening period.

the English, tongue. Jerome's contemporary in the West, Augustine, was the last Latin author of original genius. Standing on the border-line between antiquity and the Middle Ages, he represents the fusion of Graeco-Roman culture, now in the throes of dissolution, and the victorious spirit of Christianity. Of his work as thinker and theologian, and his incalculable influence as an authority in western Christendom, we shall speak in a later chapter. We note here merely his reverence for Rome and Roman law, and the enthusiasm with which he absorbed the thought and literature of the past. Though he read the judgement of heaven in Alaric's sack of Rome, he vindicated the rightful claim of the empire to world dominion as the prize due to Roman virtue. The arguments of the second book of Dante's *de Monarchiâ* were drawn from Augustine's book *The City of God (Civitas Dei)*. The intimate association of Latin literature with the life of the imperial state was preserved in this last great utterance of ancient Rome. With Boethius, the minister of Theodoric the Ostrogoth in the sixth century, a writer noteworthy rather for his influence on mediaeval learning than for originality of mind, Latin literature reached its close.[1]

§ 24. Meanwhile, in the eastern provinces, the Greek language and literature held its own. The spread of Hellenism in the West had created for Greek works a wider public; every cultured Roman was able to read them in the original. Innumerable books on history, biography, the physical and mathematical sciences, literary criticism, and philosophy, were composed by Greek authors in the century before and after the birth of Christ. Galen's epoch-making work in medicine dates from the latter half of the second century. Of the course of philosophic thought and the rise of Christian theology we shall treat in the ensuing chapter. One name must be mentioned here, that of Plutarch of Chaeronea, who, both as a citizen and as a writer, revived something of the best spirit of the great days of Greece. He wrote much and on many subjects, including ethics and religion.[2] But his fame with

1. On Augustine, see below, c. ix, § 22; and on Boethius, c. x, § 8 and c. xi, § 8.
2. On Plutarch's philosophy of religion, see below, c. ix, § 7.

posterity rested chiefly on his incomparable biographies of the famous Greeks and Romans of the past. Plutarch was not a great historian, and wrote partly for edification, partly from an ardent sympathy with noble character and noble action. His *Lives* have probably influenced literature and history more widely than any other single work of classical antiquity. They furnished Shakespeare with material for his dramas; they went far to inspire the republican idealism of the French Revolutionary leaders. For young and old they still form the best introduction to Greek and Roman history. To all lovers of historic personalities they give as keen a delight to-day as eighteen hundred years ago.

IV. CONCLUSION

§ 25. The change from republic to empire was symptomatic of the deeper and more gradual change that was passing over the thought and life of the Graeco-Roman world. Hellenic civilization arose and flourished in intimate association with the city-state; its supersession by a world-despotism carried with it a revolution in men's intellectual and spiritual outlook. Ideals of life were henceforward dissevered from political activity. Men sought for consolation and support either in philosophic speculation or in supernatural religion. We saw, when speaking of the Hellenic world under the successors of Alexander, how both the dominant philosophical schools, the Stoic and the Epicurean, claimed to satisfy this demand of the individual soul, in detachment from the public life of the state. In religion, the conservative efforts of Augustus to restore the old national worships proved fruitless; they could not prevail against the new and strange faiths that spread in this age from the eastern world to Rome. The religions of Isis, Cybele, and Mithra found a multitude of adherents, in the imperial city and throughout the provinces, among those who had not the capacity or the inclination to pursue the austere paths of metaphysics. Those paths were for the wise and strong, and of such there were few; others, in equal need of spiritual satisfaction, turned elsewhere, and above all towards the East. The East, too, was turning towards them. Of the nature and issues of this contact we shall speak in the ensuing chapter; alike as a creative stimulus and as provocative of reaction, it proved the most momentous crisis in human history.

§ 26. Side by side with this demand for spiritual satisfaction on the part of the individual we remark a growing consciousness of the common humanity of mankind. We have seen its expression in the jurists' conception of a law of nature, in the reflexion within the sphere of law of Stoic cosmopolitanism, and in the measures of public philanthropy enacted by the paternal care of the great emperors of the second century, Trajan, Hadrian, and the two Antonines. Yet more striking is the presence of this sense of universal brotherhood in the epic poem of Virgil. We have spoken of the *Aeneid* as the noblest and most enduring monument of the majesty of the Roman empire. This is the thought to which Tennyson gave utterance in his lines on Virgil:

> Now thy Forum roars no longer,
> > fallen every purple Caesar's dome –
> Tho' thine ocean roll of rhythm
> > sound for ever of Imperial Rome.

Other Latin poets had voiced, if in less splendid verse, their sense of Rome's imperial greatness. But there is a further quality in Virgil's poetry that has no parallel in earlier literature. He looks out upon life with a breadth of sympathy, a deep and universal tenderness, that is in strange contrast with the pride of intellect and exclusiveness of culture which mark the literature and philosophy of his predecessors. In his catholicity of feeling Virgil is the herald of a new era in the spiritual history of mankind. Later generations, bred in the Christian faith, singled him out among pre-Christian writers as an *anima naturaliter Christiana*, a spirit by nature Christian – by nature, i.e. without the aid of revelation. Doubtless the famous fourth Eclogue, in which the poet foretold the return of the golden age in language strikingly suggestive of the Messianic prophecies of Isaiah, gave the stimulus to this reverence for Virgil of the uncritical spirit of the early Middle Ages.[1] Doubtless, too, the imperial poet shared in their eyes the peculiar sanctity which attached to the institution of the Roman empire. But the feeling sprang from something deeper than these more conscious motives. Virgil, alone among pre-Christian poets, was touched by the 'still sad music of humanity' to a breadth of human tenderness that heralds the democratic message of Christianity. In the sixth book of the *Aeneid*, the father of Rome beholds in the underworld the dead thronging the banks by 'the deep pools of Cocytus and the Stygian marsh'. 'Hither all crowded and rushed streaming to the bank, matrons and men and high-hearted heroes dead and done with life, boys and unwedded girls, and children laid young on the bier before their parents' eyes, multitudinous as leaves fall dropping in the forests at autumn's earliest frost, or birds swarm landward from the deep gulf, when the chill of the year routs them overseas and drives them to sunny lands. They stood pleading for the first passage across, and stretched forth passionate hands to the farther shore.'[2] We can trace in Virgil a desire for the life beyond the grave, which comes nearer to the spirit of Christian hope than any utterance of the Greek philosophers. It was no mere aesthetic devotion of poet to poet, nor a mere echo of popular tradition, that led Dante to seek Virgil's guidance through Hell and Purgatory to the threshold of the Christian Paradise.

§ 27. The Middle Ages, strong in the conviction of revealed truth, made bold to interpret the history of the Roman empire in the light of the divine plan of government for the world. They saw in the work of Julius and Augustus, as in the story of the chosen people of Israel, a *praeparatio evangelica*. Modern historians, on the other hand, have been content to limit their inquiry and their judgement to its actual effects upon the happiness and civilization of mankind. If in this spirit we ask what the establishment of the imperial system meant for the Roman world, we must rest our conclusions not so much on literary histories that express the natural hostility of republican

1. See above, p. 66, *note* 1. The sixth book of the *Aeneid* caused Virgil to be regarded also as an authority on the world beyond the grave.
2. *Aen.* vi. 305–14: *tr.* Mackail.

idealists, as on the evidence for the effects of the system on the silent millions, whose welfare was the chief concern of the imperial government. It is in the equitable adjustment of taxation, in the impartial administration of law, in the founding of cities and public works, in the unimpeded development of commerce, in the extension of citizen privileges and local self-government, which for the first time opened up wide prospects of advancement for all freemen, and, above all, in the effective defence of the frontiers and the maintenance of universal peace, that the true nature of the imperial system is disclosed. The two great historians who have interpreted Rome to the modern world manifest a striking agreement in their verdict. Gibbon, writing in the last half of the eighteenth century, summed up his survey of the state of the Roman world in the second century A.D. in these well-known words:

'If a man were called to fix the period in the history of the world during which the condition of the human race was most happy and prosperous, he would, without hesitation, name that which elapsed from the death of Domitian to the accession of Commodus.[1] The vast extent of the Roman empire was governed by absolute power, under the guidance of virtue and wisdom. The armies were restrained by the firm and gentle hand of four successive emperors, whose characters and authority commanded involuntary respect. The forms of the civil administration were carefully preserved by Nerva, Trajan, Hadrian, and the Antonines, who delighted in the image of liberty, and were pleased with considering themselves as the accountable ministers of the laws.'[2]

Gibbon's work was compiled in the main from literary records; since he wrote, the progress of historical inquiry has laid bare a vast and varied mass of contemporary inscriptions.[3] A century after the publication of the *Decline and Fall*, Theodor Mommsen embodied a comprehensive survey of this new material in his volume on the Roman provinces under the

---

1. A.D. 96–180.
2. *Decline and Fall*, c. 3.
3. Gibbon also made use of the records collected by the French *Académie des Inscriptions*.

empire. His judgement, if more cautious in expression, is to the same effect at that of Gibbon.

'Even now there are various regions of the East, as of the West, as regards which the imperial period marks a climax of good government, very modest in itself, but never withal attained before or since; and, if an angel of the Lord were to strike the balance whether the domain ruled by Severus Antoninus was governed with the greater intelligence and the greater humanity at that time or in the present day, whether civilization and national prosperity generally have since that time advanced or retrograded, it is very doubtful whether the decision would prove in favour of the present.'[1]

How far is this judgement true? The question must be faced, if we are to measure the value either of Rome's work in history, or of the new forces that broke in upon her sovereignty and possessed themselves of her inheritance. We must not suffer our vision to be blinded by the magnitude and the duration of her power, or forget that the verdict of history is always passed on the quality rather than on the quantity of the achievement. If we fix our minds on this, we shall hardly accept the statements of Gibbon and Mommsen without reserve. Their judgement is true, if by happiness we mean material comfort, and if we take economic welfare and the maintenance of social order as our standards of civilization. It is easy to understand how, after generations of public strife and private suffering, the advent of a world-peace under the aegis of the Caesars seemed to the poets of Augustan Rome like the dawn of a golden age.[2] The Roman empire realized the ideal of paternal government in a degree to which history affords no parallel, save in the rule of Britain over India and Egypt until recent times. And, if paternal government is the last word in civilization, the downfall of that empire in the centuries that followed was the most melancholy event in the annals of mankind. The poets dreamed that Rome would stand for ever, and even the stern reality of the decline and fall hardly availed to dispel the illusion. Yet already in the hour of its inauguration there was that within

1. *Provinces of the Roman Empire*, Introduction.
2. E.g. *Aen.*, i. 295, vi. 791-2.

the empire which foreshadowed its dissolution. A bureaucratic despotism, for all its integrity and its enlightenment, could evoke no living response from the subject-peoples who reaped its benefits. The spirit of man craves not comfort, but liberty, not economic stability or equitable administration, but the right, at the cost of infinite toil and tribulation, to work out its own salvation. Its desire in all ages is not for happiness, but for life. In the colossal structure of Roman government men were conscious only of the crushing burden, and awaited in dumb passivity the hour of their deliverance. They were pawns in the hand of the Fate, transcendent and inexorable, that brooded over the fortunes of the world.[1] Rome was impotent, for all her majesty of power, to reinvigorate the peoples beneath her sway. She offered them no 'causes' that could stir men's hearts to effort on their behalf with a good hope of triumphant realization, such as Christianity (or Communism) offers to the modern world.[2] The founts of life were elsewhere, in the wild hordes of Teutons that even now were beating against the frontiers, and in the new faith, born under Augustus' principate among a despised people of the East, and destined ere long to shake to its foundations the fabric of Graeco-Roman civilization.

1. Cf. Napoleon's saying: '*la politique est la fatalité*'. On the impossibility of an active sentiment of loyalty to the empire, see Davis, *Medieval Europe*, pp. 19, 20.

2. See Bevan, in *The Hellenistic Age* (pp. 98 ff.), on absence of 'causes' in his age, and how Christianity furnished a 'cause'.